Baxter's USARAIL PASS GUIDE

by
ROBERT BAXTER

illustrations by Alice Muller

Copyright © 1975, 1976 by Robert G. Baxter. All rights reserved. No part of this book may be reproduced or utilized in any form or by any means, electronic or mechanical, including photocopying, recording or by any information storage and retrieval system, without permission in writing from the Author, except by a reviewer who wishes to quote brief passages in connection with a review written for inclusion in a magazine, newspaper or broadcast.

Manufactured in the United States of America. Library of Congress Catalog Card No. 75-35438. International Standard Book Number 0-913384-21-6.

Published by
RAIL-EUROPE
P.O. Box 3255
Alexandria, Va. 22302

CONTENTS

GUIDE ORGANIZATION 8

ABOUT AMTRAK 9
   A Short History
   What is Amtrak?

TRAVELING BY TRAIN.................... 12
   Fares
   Bicentennial Fare
   Reservations
   Equipment
   Food Service
   Baggage
   Train Personnel
   Locomotive Whistles
   Amtrak To Bicentennial Destinations

THE STRUGGLE FOR INDEPENDENCE 29
   1775-1783

1776 DOCUMENT 36
   The Declaration of Independence
   Signers of The Declaration of Independence
   United States Constitution
   Historical Reproductions From Archives
   Presidents Of The United States
   Entrance of States Into Union
   The Change In America

THE EAST

BOSTON..................................... 46

PLYMOUTH................................. 52

CAPE COD 52

NEW YORK CITY 53

ROCHESTER 64

BUFFALO 65

NIAGARA FALLS 66

PHILADELPHIA.............................. 66

BALTIMORE 71

ANNAPOLIS.................................. 73

WASHINGTON 73

HARPERS FERRY 100

MOUNT VERNON 101

OLD TOWN ALEXANDRIA.................. 103
   Bicentennial Center
   Ramsay House
   Walking Tour
   Carlyle House
   Gadsby's Tavern
   Christ Church

THE SOUTH

FREDERICKSBURG 109

CHARLOTTESVILLE 109
   Monticello
   Ash Lawn
   Captain Jack Jouett

RICHMOND 110

WILLIAMSBURG............................ 113

JAMESTOWN................................ 117

YORKTOWN 117

ATLANTA 118

SAVANNAH 120

CHARLESTON 121

NASHVILLE 123

NEW ORLEANS 125

FLORIDA

ST. AUGUSTINE 130

DISNEY WORLD 132

MIAMI-MIAMI BEACH 133

THE MIDWEST

CHICAGO 137

MILWAUKEE 142

MINNEAPOLIS 143

ST. LOUIS 144

KANSAS CITY 145

ROCKY MOUNTAIN STATES

DENVER 148

CHEYENNE 149

SALT LAKE CITY 151

OGDEN 152

THE SOUTHWEST

DALLAS 153

HOUSTON.................................... 153

SAN ANTONIO 154

BY TRAIN TO MEXICO CITY 156

EL PASO 158

ALBUQUERQUE.............................. 160

LAS VEGAS 164

CALIFORNIA

LOS ANGELES 169

DISNEYLAND................................ 175

SAN DIEGO 178

SAN FRANCISCO 180

THE NORTHWEST

PORTLAND 186

SEATTLE 186

CANADA

MONTREAL.................................. 189

QUEBEC 192

VANCOUVER 193

U.S. NATIONAL PARKS...................... 196

GATEWAYS TO THE U.S.A. AND CANADA .. 205

USARAIL PASS INFORMATION.............. 217

ITINERARIES 222

TOURS 226

STATION INDEX 234

RESERVATION NUMBERS 240

FREEDOM TRAIN SCHEDULE 243

AMTRAK ROUTE DESCRIPTIONS 246

FLORIDA TRAINS........................... 257

THE SUNSET LIMITED...................... 273

THE SOUTHWEST LIMITED................. 281

THE NORTHCOAST HIAWATHA 287

THE SAN FRANCISCO ZEPHYR 296

ACCOMMODATIONS........................ 304

INTRODUCTION

GUIDE ORGANIZATION

This book is a guide to help you explore the U.S.A. and Canada by train. We first present you with a short history of rail travel, an explanation of how Amtrak was formed and how one of the departments in Amtrak is organized.

To further acquaint you with rail travel, we discuss the ins and outs of traveling by train. Included in this discussion are fares, including the special Bicentennial Fare, equipment, food service, baggage, and personnel aboard Amtrak trains. Furthermore, in the spirit of this guide, the appreciation of our country's beauty as well as its heritage, we have included a discussion about our struggle for independence 200 years ago. The complete text of the Declaration of Independence is also included in your guide.

The United States, to facilitate your travels, has been split up into various regions such as the East, the South, Florida, the Southwest and California. Similarly, Canada is divided into Eastern and Western Canada. In any case, each of these chapters will tell you what to see. A separate chapter is devoted to National Parks. And since many of our friends from abroad will visit us during our Bicentennial celebration, we have prepared a special chapter for them. Included in this chapter is an explanation of the new USARAIL PASS, available to visitors from abroad. Also three suggested rail itineraries, complete with departure and arrival times, is found in this section of the guide.

Toward the back of the book you will find a host of information which will make your travels by rail more convenient and enjoyable. This information includes available rail tours, a station index, description of popular rail routes, important telephone numbers, the schedule of the Freedom Train, hotel/motel accommodations and YMCA/YWCA accommodations. Look over the table of contents to find what page the information you are looking for is on. We have provided you with information on what to see, how to get there and where to stay in Bicentennial America. Have a nice rail trip!

A WORD OF THANKS

This Bicentennial Travel Guide has come about through the efforts and help of a great number of people and organizations. First of all, we want to thank the various State and Local Bicentennial Commissions, tourist information offices, the National Park Service, the Bicentennial Administration and Amtrak for their help. Then we want to thank the ticket agents and train crews who did not hesitate to share their rail travel experiences. We would like also to take this opportunity to thank James Bryant, and Edwin Edel, Barbara Graner and Carol Weber. A special note of thanks goes to Amtrak's Travel Editor, John McLeod and Eloise Holton, whose diligent efforts helped make this book a reality.

ABOUT AMTRAK

A SHORT HISTORY

With the introduction of the 'Tom Thumb' locomotive and its American built counterpart 'Best Friend of Charleston' in the early 1830's, passenger rail service came into being in the United States of America. The building of various railroad lines progressed at a fairly fast pace culminating in America's first transcontinental railroad in 1869. There was a great celebration at Promontory, Utah that year when the rail line from San Francisco by way of the high Sierra Nevada met the one from Nebraska. By 1883 Portland, Oregon was joined to the Mid-West and San Francisco was connected by rail to important New Orleans. By 1909 the last of the six main transcontinental rail routes in America was completed. Our neighbor to the north, Canada, has two transcontinental rail lines—completed in 1886 and 1914 respectively.

10 RAIL TRAVEL

In the development of rail traffic in this country, the comfort of the passenger was not overlooked. For instance in the 1860's the sleeping car came into service. Through the years the steam engine was replaced by the electric and the diesel locomotive. Air conditioning made rail travel even more relaxing and pleasant. Today you will find the Metroliner, one of the fastest trains in the world, race daily on a frequent schedule between New York and Washington, D.C. in 3 hours or less, with intermediate stops. The advanced Turbo train provides you with jet-age technology service between selected city pairs, including Boston—New York, Chicago—St. Louis and Chicago—Detroit. With the introduction of a nationwide passenger rail system, service standards and schedules have become part of a coordinated system.

It was still almost a hundred years ago that many rail tracks in the United States had different widths. It was not until the mid 1880's that the standard gauge of track became 4 feet 8-1/2 inches. Such standardization allows you today to not only travel coast to coast in the same sleeping car on the Amtrak network which came into being in 1971, but also enables you to reach exciting Canadian destinations such as Vancouver and Montreal. From coast to coast, America today has for the first time in its history one nationwide rail passenger system.

WHAT IS AMTRAK?

On October 30, 1970, the President of the United States signed the Rail Passenger Service Act. This enabled the newly formed National Railroad Passenger Corporation, now commonly known as Amtrak, to use innovative ideas to provide passenger rail service in the United States. Amtrak started on May 1, 1971. It is in part subsidized by the federal government.

With the increase in traffic congestion, short haul inter-city rail service between major cities has a place in a balanced transportation network. For long distance routes, rail travel provides an excellent comfortable way to explore many of the scenic areas in the United States. And now with our concern over ecology and the possibility of shortages in fuel and rising gasoline prices, it makes a lot of sense to travel by train.

Amtrak has merged services of 13 different passenger railroads to give America its first nationwide rail

RAIL TRAVEL 11

passenger system—from city to city and coast to coast. Today Amtrak operates more than 250 passenger trains every day over about 24,000 miles of track connecting about 450 cities throughout the United States and Canada. With such an extensive system and new attitudes toward selective rail travel, the goal 'to make the trains worth traveling again' is within grasp.

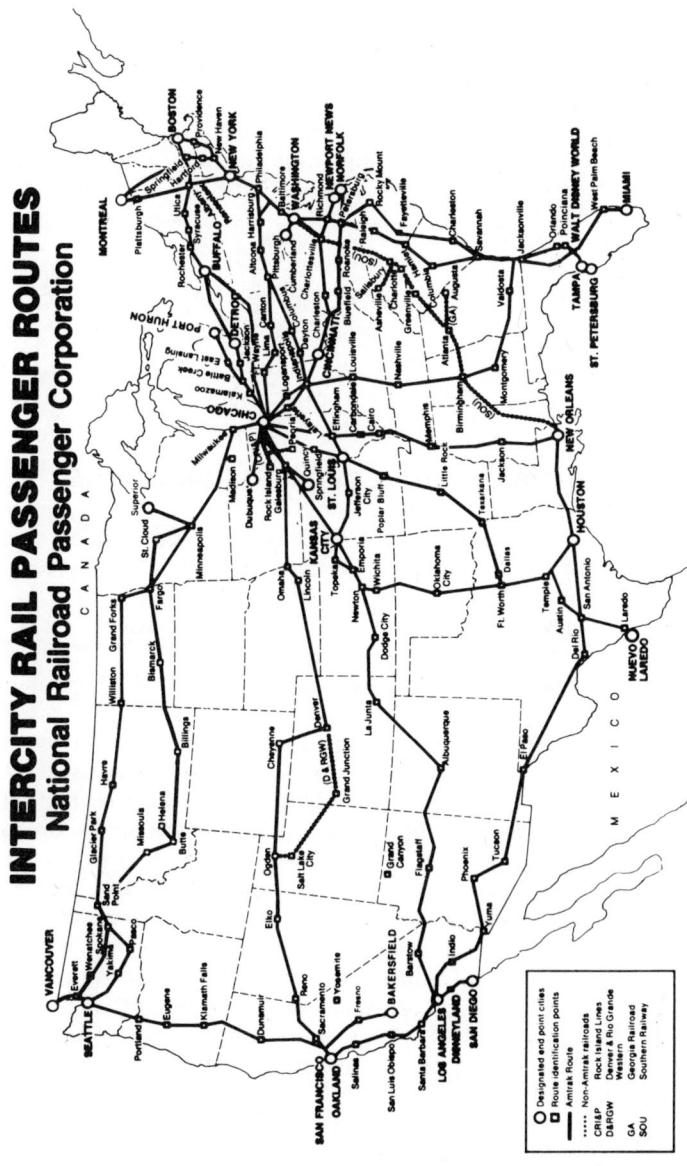

12 RAIL TRAVEL

TRAVELING BY TRAIN

FARES

USARAIL PASS

One of the greatest bargains in U.S. rail travel history is Amtrak's USARAIL PASS—the pass for unlimited rail travel on all of Amtrak's route system of 26,000 miles, as well as on the routes operated by Southern Railway. Whereas previously the pass was only available to visitors from abroad, a recent change in policy makes it available to all. Peak season prices in U.S. Dollars for the USARAIL PASS when bought in North America are as follows:

14 Days - $250
21 Days - $325
30 Days - $400

USARAIL PASS TERMS AND CONDITIONS

1. The USARAIL PASS itself is not good for passage. Valid for obtaining tickets only when signed by traveler. Not transferable.
2. Reservations for travel cannot be made prior to purchase of the USARAIL PASS. USARAIL PASS must be presented at ticket office for issuance of proper ticket(s).
3. Valid for transportation in regular (non-Metroliner) coaches only. Traveler may upgrade to Metroliner service or first class on a space available basis only, either on board the train or no more than 30 minutes prior to departure. Upgrade is made upon payment of the difference between regular coach class fare and fare of class of service desired. Appropriate full accommodation charges must also be paid.
4. Valid over all Amtrak and Southern Railway routes until end date shown on front of USARAIL PASS.
5. Use of USARAIL PASS must start within 15 days of date of sale shown on front of pass. USARAIL PASS and tickets issued on it expire at midnight of end date. Boarding for final leg of travel must be made before midnight of the end date shown on front of USARAIL PASS.

RAIL TRAVEL 13

6. Not refundable if start date of travel has been reached. All ticket(s) issued but not used must be surrendered with USARAIL PASS at time of refund application. Application for refund must be made within six months of date of sale. Not refundable if lost or stolen.

7. USARAIL PASS and ticket(s) must be presented on train. Signature matching that on USARAILPASS must be placed on ticket(s) in presence of conductor. Identification for signature verification must be presented as requested by conductor or trainman.

8. Any alteration invalidates the USARAIL PASS.

9. The USARAIL PASS is available to citizens of all countries.

On page 222 we present you 14, 21 and 30 day itineraries, complete with departure and arrival times, to help you plan your exploration of the U.S.A. with your USARAIL PASS.

AMTRAK'S SKI PASS

Amtrak's new reduced-rate SKI PASS will permit you unlimited travel during the ski season for 30, 45 or 60 days on a number of trains serving ski areas. Note that travel is not permitted on Fridays, Sundays and peak holiday travel dates. Some of the trains you can use include the 'Montrealer,' the 'Adirondack,' the 'San Francisco Zephyr,' and the 'Empire Builder.' We might note the pass can be combined with a variety of Amtrak ski week packages. For more information see your Amtrak Travel Agent.

SAMPLE FARES

Amtrak, besides the regular fares, has a number of excursion and money-saving fares available. First, let us give you a sample of the regular fares. For example, the one-way special Metroliner fare between Washington, D.C. and New York is $23. The fare on regular trains between the two cities is $17. From New York to Boston the fare in coach is $16.50. If your want to travel in coach from New York to Miami, the one-way fare is $72. From Chicago to Miami, the one-way coach fare is $74. For a longer trip, the one-way coach fare from Chicago to Seattle is $104.

AMTRAK'S FAMILY PLAN

Amtrak's Family Plan provides substantial discounts, both for coach and first-class travel, good any day but Fri-

14 RAIL TRAVEL

day and Sunday. When one member of a family pays full fare, a spouse and accompanying children 12 through 21 get a 25 per cent reduction; children 2 through 11, 62.5 per cent, with children under 2 generally riding free. The Family Plan is applicable when the one-way regular fare is $20 or more.

BICENTENNIAL FARE

Amtrak's Bicentennial Colonial Corridor Excursion Ticket offers a saving of some 30 percent from the current Washington-Boston round-trip coach fares. The Colonial Corridor circle ticket allows a complete round trip from Boston to Washington, originating at any Amtrak stop on the route. It allows visits to New York and Philadelphia—

plus any one stop between each of the major four cities. A simple punch-type excursion ticket is issued for the entire circle. Fare is $40 for adults, $20 for children under 12. The trip must be completed within one month from the date of first use. In addition, the ticket is not valid for travel originating between 1 p.m. and 8 p.m. on Fridays and Sundays. The ticket is not transferable, is good for travel on conventional coaches only, is not good for travel on Metroliner or premium fare trains and is not good for travel on non-Amtrak trains. The ticket is available through 1976. A one-way Colonial Corridor ticket between Washington, D.C. and Boston is also available for $25, children under 12 paying half-fare.

SERVICE TO WILLIAMSBURG

Direct train service now links the metropolitan areas of the Northeast with historic Williamsburg. Amtrak will use its modern Amfleet equipment on the new route with both coach and first-class seating. Southbond schedule: noon departure from New York's Penn Station, 4:08 p.m. from Washington, 6:45 p.m. Richmond, 8:30 p.m. Williamsburg, arriving 9:10 p.m. at Newport News. Northbound: departing Newport News at 2:50 p.m., Williamsburg 3:25 p.m., Richmond 5:20 p.m., Washington 8:05 p.m., arriving New York 11:59 p.m.

WEEKEND SERVICE BETWEEN LOS ANGELES AND LAS VEGAS

The Las Vegas Limited now provides weekend service between Los Angeles and Las Vegas—a special 3-day round trip discount ticket costs $36. The new train leaves Los Angeles every Friday at 1:30 p.m. and arrives at Las Vegas at 8:55 p.m. The Sunday train departs Las Vegas at 2 p.m., arriving in Los Angeles at 9 p.m.

EXCURSION FARES

Amtrak has a number of excursion fares available whether they be for weekend trips or longer distances. For example, Amtrak's special Saturday and Sunday round-trip excursion fare from Washington, D.C. to Harpers Ferry is only $4.90. And during special periods of the year

16 RAIL TRAVEL

Amtrak has an excursion fare from either Chicago or New York to Florida points which costs only $99 round-trip! For details and conditions, as well as other excursion fares, consult your Amtrak Travel Agent or Ticket Agent.

CREDIT CARDS

Amtrak accepts American Express BankAmericard, C&S, Carte Blanche, Diners Club, Eurocard and Master Charge for the purchase of tickets at all Amtrak ticket offices. Amtrak tours, which we discuss at the back of the book, can also be charged on these credit cards.

MAKING YOUR AMTRAK RESERVATION

There are several ways to make your train reservations. Keep in mind that you must have a seat reservation on many inter-city services in the United States. One way to make your Amtrak reservation is to visit your Travel Agent—there are over 5000 Amtrak appointed Travel Agents in the country. Or you can personally visit your local Amtrak Ticket Office. Another way to make your reservation is to use the toll-free telephone number that feeds directly into an Amtrak Reservation Center. In the back of this guide you will find an index of passenger stations, and addresses, as well as reservations and information numbers and data about city ticket offices. You might note that there is no charge to make your reservations.

As we have pointed out earlier, you can use various credit cards to pay for your ticket, as well as check, money order or cash. In order to make the concept of train travel more convenient to you, Amtrak gives you the option to obtain your tickets through the mail when you make your reservations telephonically. This saves you a trip to the ticket office or the train station. However, keep in mind several time limits. When payment is made by credit card, the mailout request must be made at least seven days before the intended departure date. When payment is made by check or money order, the mailout request must be made at least twenty-one days prior to departure.

BENSALEM RESERVATION CENTER

To give you a little bit of understanding of how your reservation is made, we will provide you with some background information on one of the largest reservation centers in the United States—one located in Cornwells Heights in Bensalem Township, 17 miles to the northeast of Philadelphia, Pennsylvania. In fact, if you travel on the high speed inter-city rail route Washington, D.C.-Philadelphia-New York—you will see from your train the modern one-story building where the reservations are handled.

The Bensalem center serves an area from Maine to North Carolina to northern Ohio, except for New York City. In the two years the reservation center has been in operation, the center has received over 13 million calls! On a busy day 30,000 calls come in, although the average is between 18,000-22,000 daily calls. To take care of these calls, there are up to 200 Reservations and Information Agents on duty daily. These personnel, which go through a thorough training period as well as recurrent training sessions, can answer all your questions about rail travel as well as make your train reservations.

EQUIPMENT

TRAVELING BY METROLINER

Many travelers are surprised to find that America's first nationwide passenger rail system operates one of the world's fastest trains—the Metroliner. Besides the high speed of electrically powered Metroliners, the traveler will find that over a dozen departures of this fast train take place daily between Washington, D.C. and New York City. Intermediate stops are made in Baltimore, Maryland, Wilmington, Delaware, Philadelphia, Pennsylvania, and Trenton, New Jersey. Stops are also made at two suburban train stations to serve the traveler from the suburbs. These modern and convenient stations with ample parking spaces are the Capital Beltway Station, just outside Washington, D.C., and Metropark at Iselin, New Jersey, between Trenton and New York City.

The Metroliner train is usually made up of four sleek cars consisting of two metrocoaches, and metroclub and a metro snack-bar coach car. The metroclub car is for those who want to travel first class. A spacious rotating chair allows you to view the passing countryside in great comfort. Individual dining and beverage service is available at your chair. For those traveling in the metrocoach, snack and beverage service is available in the snack-bar coach car.

18 RAIL TRAVEL

Here are some additional thoughts about your travel by Metroliner. Keep in mind that you must make a seat reservation. A good way to reserve your seat is to make your reservation by phone (or let your travel agent do it for you) as much in advance as possible. When you make your reservation by phone you have up to 30 minutes prior to your departure to pick up the tickets at the station.

Just as you board the Metroliner, your image of uncomfortable and slow rail travel is destroyed. You will find carpeting on the floor, wide windows, comfortable reclining chairs and individual reading lights. You hardly notice as the Metroliner quickly accelerates out of the station (another advantage of an electrified rail line). Soon an announcement is made welcoming you aboard the Metroliner and you will be informed where the snack bar and the club car are found, the location of the smoking and non-smoking car (thank goodness that non-smokers finally have a place of their own) and the location of the public telephone on the Metroliner—it works just fine. Each stop on the Metroliner route is announced about 3-4 minutes before your arrival.

After you have pulled out of the station, the conductor will come along to collect your ticket. Above each seat he will place a colored stub which indicates to the conductor where you will be getting off. This seat check is also proof that you have a ticket. When you go to the snack bar, take your seat check with you. And while you are in the snack bar you will find that you can purchase hot and cold sandwiches, little snacks, soft drinks, beer and other alcoholic drinks.

One thing we would like to emphasize is that you must make reservations for Metroliner travel. You cannot buy your ticket on board. Those passengers traveling in Metroclub (first class) will get a seat assigned when making reservations. Passengers making reservations for coach travel will not get a particular seat assignment. Thus when you board the train, you have a choice of where to sit—including the option of sitting in a non-smoking car.

THE NEW AMFLEET

One of the newest developments in equipment for rail passengers is the introduction by Amtrak of modern equipment, just in time for the Bicentennial celebrations. These 492 Metroliner-type of coaches are replacing passenger equipment with an average age of 24 years in the Northeast. This new 'Amfleet' consists of a number of different coaches—the 'Amcoach' for economy travel seating up to 84 passengers; the 'Amclub' car for first class accommodations; the 'Amcafe' for snack cars and the 'Ampub' for lounges.

For your information, we now include some of the characteristics of the Amcoaches. They are over 85 feet long and over 10 feet high, capable of speeds up to 120 miles per hour, locomotive-hauled. There is overall fluorescent lighting plus individual seat reading lights. There are luggage racks above the seats for the entire length of the car. A luggage-valet closet is located at one end of the car. The seating configuration consists of 2 seats, fully reclinable, on either side of the aisle. Fold-down tables are in the seat ahead and center arm rests are available between seats. The seats are track-mounted to alter seat density. For example, for corridor travel the seating may consist of a total of 84 seats, while for long haul overnight trips the seating configuration can be reduced to only 52 seats. Restroom facilities are available in each car. For your added comfort, electric dual air conditioning and heating systems are employed in the modern coaches.

WHAT IS A ROOMETTE?

A roomette is a private compartment for one person. It consists of a comfortable adjustable seat for daytime travel which converts into a bed for night travel. There are a host of features in the roomette which allow you to view the passing countryside in privacy and great comfort. When you look into a roomette, you at first might not be impressed by all the features that make up this type of accommodation. Besides containing toilet facilities, there is a wash basin (with hot and cold running water), a little cabinet with towels, soap, glasses, drinking water, and a mirror. A closet will allow you to hang up your coat and there is a small compartment to store your shoes. Switches allow you to control heat and air conditioning and there is even a fan to help you circulate the air in your roomette. If you wish to call the porter, there is a 'call' button. A light switch allows you to control the illumination in your private compartment. A safety lock permits you to lock the roomette door from the inside.

Because of its compactness, the entire floor area of your roomette will generally be taken up by the bed which you pull down from the wall. Therefore, if you plan to

20 RAIL TRAVEL

pull down the bed, simply zip up the curtain which you will find next to your roomette, and open the door completely. This will give you enough room to stand on the floor and retain privacy while you are pulling the bed

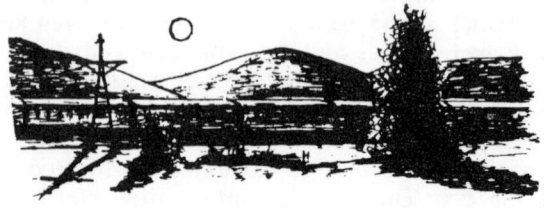

down. Once you are in bed, you can simply close the roomette door for complete privacy. Of course, the reverse procedure is applicable when you prepare your roomette for day travel. With the curtains zipped up and the door open, you can push the bed up against the wall while you are standing next to the curtain. Now you are ready to enjoy the passing countryside from your comfortable chair.

WHAT IS A LOUNGE CAR?

Besides the dining car, sleeping accommodations cars, regular coach cars and dome cars, there is usually a lounge car included in the equipment make-up of a long distance train. A lounge car is a great place to stretch, relax, perhaps have a snack or even a drink, or just carry on an interesting conversation with your fellow travelers. In the lounge car you will find comfortable lounge chairs and tables. From your seat you usually have an unobstructed view of the passing countryside on either side. If you can't strike up a conversation at first, you will find the latest issue of some of the leading magazines available for your reading enjoyment. Sometimes the conductor or porter will even arrange to pickup for passengers, at no charge, the latest edition of the local newspaper at certain stations.

A LOUNGE CAR DESCRIPTION

One of our favorite lounge cars in the entire Amtrak system is the "Lewis and Clark Traveler's Rest" usually found on the route between Chicago and Seattle. Have a look at the walls of this well-decorated car. On one wall you will see depicted the dress of various Indian tribes—such as the Shoshone or the Blackfeet. On the other wall you will see the animals which have become synonymous

RAIL TRAVEL 21

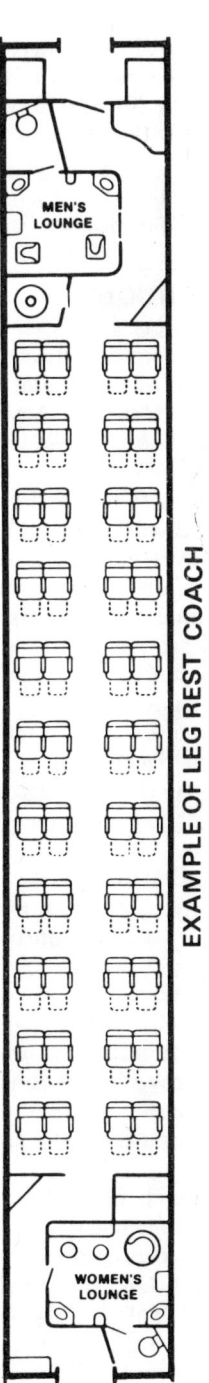

EXAMPLE OF LEG REST COACH

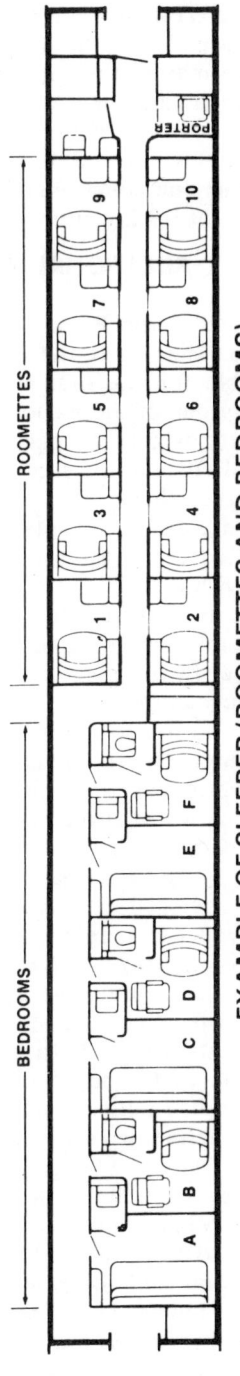

EXAMPLE OF SLEEPER (ROOMETTES AND BEDROOMS)

22 RAIL TRAVEL

with the West—such as the buffalo. Portraits of Lewis and Clark are also in the lounge car. One section of the wall shows a map of the route these famous explorers took to chart the unknown Northwest between 1804-1806. Such a map represents practically a living history lesson, for your train might very well pass through regions these 33 gallant men and one courageous woman explored at the beginning of the 19th century.

ADDITIONAL ACCOMMODATIONS

Besides the Roomette type of accommodations we have just described, there are additional accommodations available for the first class traveler. Here are Amtrak descriptions of the various accommodations, besides the roomette, which you can choose from.

A Bedroom is a comfortable room with two beds, one above the other, floor space, toilet and washbasin. These rooms are designed for two persons travelling together. In some Bedrooms, the toilet is enclosed in a separate small room within the bedroom, called an annex. Bedrooms are sometimes referred to as Single Bedrooms or Double Bedrooms, according to whether they have been engaged by one or by two persons. The two terms do not signify any difference in the room itself, except in a few cars in which there is no upper bed in the Bedrooms. In these cars, the term Single Bedroom is always used. By day, a Bedroom is converted by the attendant into seating accommodations for two or three persons.

A Compartment is similar to a Bedroom but with slightly more floor space. The toilet in a Compartment is always enclosed in a separate annex. By day, a Compartment seats two persons.

For day travel, the first class traveler will be in comfortable surroundings. Generally, parlor cars (called Metroclub cars on the Metroliners) contain large comfortable seats which both recline and revolve, arranged singly on each side of a center aisle. Some parlors cars however, are arranged as lounge salons; in these the seats do not recline or revolve.

For those passengers traveling coach class, here is brief discussion about the coach seat. Coach seats are arranged in pairs, two on each side of a center aisle. The seats usually recline and have foot-rests. On all long-distance trains and some shorter-distance trains, the coach seats also have leg rests, which pull out to support the calf. Pillows are provided on overnight trains. Restroom facilities are at the ends of each car.

RAIL TRAVEL 23

FOOD SERVICE ON TRAINS

One of the greatest misconceptions about traveling on the nationwide Amtrak rail network is the price of food on trains. You will be pleasantly surprised that food and beverages on trains are served at moderate prices.

MEAL PRICES

All long distance trains usually have a dining car. A dining car is a great place to relax, have your meal and watch the passing countryside. Regular hot meals are served. You can also have a choice of a number of different kinds of sandwiches. There is a special children's menu. Once you have entered the dining car, the steward will show you to your seat. You will then receive a menu and a pencil/order form to write down your order.

On-board food services provided by Amtrak can be divided into three basic groups—long haul diners offering full course meals, snack/lounge cars offering mainly sandwich service (hot and cold), and club car services offering limited hot and cold meal selections. Some of the reasonable breakfast prices on long-haul diners include 90 cents for Continental style to Club Breakfast selections for about $1.75-$2.10. At lunch you can get anywhere from a grilled cheese sandwich to hot braised ribs of beef. Dinner prices range from a baked half spring chicken for $3.50 to a 12 ounce charcoal broiled steak for about $6.75 or fillet of beef/lobster tail for $7.75. Keep in mind that, for example, the dinner prices include salad, dessert and a beverage. Moreover, some of the trains serve regional specialties such as fried chicken, peanut soup and hominy grits on Florida trains or charcoal broiled salmon filet on the 'The Coast-Starlight.' To give you a better idea, we have included a sample of one of the many types of menus available on Amtrak trains.

DINING CAR HOURS

The diners on most of the long-haul routes are open for breakfast, lunch and dinner. For breakfast the diner is open generally between 6 and 10 in the morning. Luncheon is served between 11:30 a.m. and 2:30 p.m., while normal dinner hours are from 6-10 p.m. On some of the longer routes as well as on the Florida trains, you have the opportunity to have an early bird dinner, served from 4 p.m. until 6 p.m. The entree is usually either London Broil or Baked Half Chicken; the cost is less than three dollars—a real bargain!

24 RAIL TRAVEL

PAYMENT FOR ON-BOARD SERVICES

Besides cash, you can pay for your meals and beverages on all long-haul diners and lounge cars with the following credit cards: American Express, BankAmericard, Carte Blanche, Master Charge, and Diner's Club. Personal checks are also accepted for purchase of food and beverages on long-haul diners. Have two unexpired personal identifications available, such as a drivers license, national or local credit cards.

BAGGAGE

CHECKING AND CLAIMING BAGGAGE

Amtrak provides free checked baggage service at most locations. Each ticketed passenger may check up to three pieces of baggage, not exceeding a total weight of 150 pounds. Baggage will be accepted for checking up to 30 minutes before departure time and at destination will be ready for claiming within 30 minutes after train arrival. All baggage must be locked or securely tied. Each piece must have the passenger's name and permanent address in the baggage. Amtrak's liability shall not exceed $500 per ticketed passenger, without payment of additional charges. Consult Baggage Agent for charges on excess weight pieces and additional valuation.

SPECIAL ITEMS

The following items may be accepted as baggage in lieu of an allowable piece of baggage upon payment of the following handling charges: $3 up to 500 miles and $5 over 500 miles. Bicycles (without articles attached), golf bags (with carts attached), golf carts (empty—not motorized), surf boards (ropes securely tied to surf board), trunks (not exceeding 150 pounds. Accepted in lieu of three pieces of baggage), musical instruments (in suitable container). Also note that there is no charge for transporting skis!

PROHIBITED ARTICLES

The checking of the following items are prohibited. Amtrak will not accept liability for loss or damage to such items when checked separately or included in other checked baggage: cartons (exceeding 50 pounds), china, glassware or silverware, clocks, watches, cameras, small firearms and ammunition, food stuffs—all types, hairdryers, household goods, inflammable articles, jewelry (genuine or costume), liquids (except in separate nonbreakable container), money, perishable articles, radios, record players, records, radioactive materials (other than medical isotopes, properly packed and labeled), television sets, tape recorder, tapes, calculators and other electronic equipment, typewriters, sewing machines, valuable papers (stocks, bonds, etc.), internal combustion engines (gasoline or propane), weight—any piece of baggage exceeding 300 pounds.

CARRY-ON BAGGAGE LIMITATIONS

In the interest of your comfort, convenience and safety—and when checked baggage service is available—only baggage needed enroute and not more than two pieces of baggage per passenger may be carried into an Amtrak coach. Sleeping car passengers may carry on the baggage which can be safely accommodated within their room. Baggage checking facilities are available at most stations to handle baggage and there is no service charge. Baggage not needed enroute and all bulky items should be checked to destination.

TRAVELING WITH PETS

There are several things to remember if you want your pet to travel on Amtrak trains. Be sure the train you are taking has a baggage car (Metroliners, Amfleet and some short haul trains do not have baggage cars) and that both your departure and arrival stations accept checked baggage. Remember with the single exception of seeing-eye dogs, no pets may travel in coaches, sleeping cars, parlor cars, or any other type of Amtrak passenger car.

Be sure to provide a kennel that meets Amtrak's minimum standards for safety and security; fully enclosed, well ventilated, constructed of any rigid and substantial material. You may supply your own or purchase an Amtrak Rail Kennel at 36 major Amtrak stations. Rail kennels can also be picked up at smaller Amtrak stations, if advance notice is given.

No excess baggage charge is made for First Class passengers whose pets are traveling in the baggage car. Coach passengers are charged an excess baggage charge based on the total weight of pet and kennel. For additional information such as kennel costs, care and feeding enroute, pets traveling alone and health documents, see your Amtrak station agent or baggage clerk.

RAIL TRAVEL

TRAIN PERSONNEL

It takes quite a number of people to run a train. There are engineers who operate the train, porters, conductors, attendants, waiters, cooks and trainmen. Some trains also have Amtrak Passenger Representatives; these helpful young men and women answer questions you might have about rail travel. They make your trip throughout the U.S.A. even more enjoyable.

The Conductor is the boss of the train. His responsibility includes the entire train-passengers and crew as well as tickets. As you can imagine he is quite a busy man. However, despite the fact that he has so many things to do, we seldom have met a conductor who would not spend a little time with us during the course of a trip and talk about railroading.

The Trainmen are the Conductor's assistants. They take care of tickets, seat and room assignments as well as directing passengers on and off trains. When trains are especially long, Flagmen/Brakemen are also part of the crew.

Attendants take care of you in the snack car and the Porter is at your service when you take a sleeping car. He will prepare your bed and will awaken you in plenty of time to have breakfast in the diner before you reach your destination.

There are a host of other people who make your dining experience on the train enjoyable. The moment you step into the restaurant on wheels you will be met by the steward. The waiter brings your food which has been prepared by the "behind the scenes" personnel—the chef and his cooks.

LOCOMOTIVE WHISTLES

If you are like us, you often wonder what the various whistles mean that come from the locomotive. Quite significantly, the different signals that you hear have a definite meaning. In order that you may enjoy your journey by train a little more, we are including a short listing of signals and what they mean. The small "o" means a short sound; whistle "-" indicates a somewhat longer sound.

Sound	Indication
o	Apply brakes. Stop.
oo	Engineer's answer to any signal not otherwise provided for.
ooo	When standing back.
oooo	Call for signals.
Succession of short sounds	Alarm for persons or livestock on the track.
One long sound	Approaching stations, junctions and railroad crossings.
-oo	A second section is following.
-ooo	Flagman protect rear of train.
- -	Release brakes. Proceed.
- -o-	Approaching highway crossings at grade.
- - - -	Flagman may return from west or south.
- - - - -	Flagman may return from east or north.

AMTRAK TO BICENTENNIAL DESTINATIONS

We have pointed out at the beginning of this book that your travel guide has been organized on a regional basis to better allow you to discover the beauty and heritage of the U.S.A. and Canada. However, we might note here, in the spirit of the Bicentennial period, seven park installations nominated by Amtrak especially interesting to visit because of their Bicentennial significance. All can be reached by Amtrak and other public transportation.

Minute Man National Historical Park—The area between Concord and Lexington, Mass., where the embattled farmers fired "the shot heard around the World." Amtrak offers a dozen trains daily to Boston, like the Minute Man, Bunker Hill and Flying Yankee. Commuter trains from Boston's North Station provide the links to suburban Concord and Lexington.

Independence National Historical Park—Here are Independence Hall, where the Declaration of Independence was signed, and the original Libery Bell. A sound and light show tells the story. Speedy Metroliners and many other Amtrak trains offer frequent service to Philadelphia, and a subway links the historic area and the 30th Street Amtrak station.

Saratoga National Historical Park—The first big victory for the Revolutionaries—where Gen. Burgoyne surrendered. Guides in period costume tell the story of the era as well as the battle. Nearby Saratoga Springs, a famous spa and racing center, is served by Amtrak's Adirondack, the scenic daylight New York-Montreal service through New York State.

Wolf Trap Farm Park for the Performing Arts—If you come to Washington, D.C., you will, of course, visit National Capitol Parks' prime responsibilities, like the Washington Monument and Lincoln Memorial. An entirely different kind of park attraction is found in the Virginia suburbs. Here the Bicentennial will be celebrated in music and dance. Take a Metroliner or one of dozens of other trains to Washington and a Metro bus on to Wolf Trap.

The Colonial National Historical Park—This embraces 7,000 acres in the historic Virginia triangle of Williamsburg, the colonial capital; Jamestown, the first permanent English Settlement, and Yorktown where the Revolutionary War ended. Amtrak serves Williamsburg and nearby Newport News via a leg of its James Whitcomb Riley from Chicago and Cincinnati.

Harpers Ferry National Historical Park—George Washington undoubtedly slept here while surveying this part of the huge estate of Lord Fairfax, but major historic associations of this West Virginia park have to do with John Brown's raid and Civil War battles. It's only 65 minutes and $3.50 from Washington, D.C., on Amtrak's scenic Blue Ridge, which continues on to Cumberland, Md.

Golden Gate National Recreation Area—One of the very newest of the national parks is in a city which will celebrate its very own Bicentennial in 1976. The Presidio is where the city began and is the center of the new park area. San Francisco is served by Amtrak's San Francisco Zephyr (from Chicago and Denver) and the Coast Starlight (with terminals in Seattle and Los Angeles). A 25-cent Muni bus takes you to the park area.

REVOLUTION 29

THE STRUGGLE FOR INDEPENDENCE

One of the main purposes of this guide is to help you discover the places that played such a focal point in the birth of our Nation. America, it must be remembered, obtained its independence from Britain through military action. The belief in a strong defense force has continued throughout our 200 year history. In saluting the Army on its 200th birthday on June 14, 1975, at Fort Benning, Georgia, President Ford stated: "There are times when principles must be defended with force of arms." It is that spirit which guided us toward independence from Britain 200 years ago.

In our discussion we will try to put Lexington and Yorktown in perspective. Thus when you visit these and other historic areas on your discovery of America, it will be easier for you to trace the development of America 200 years ago. The discussion is by necessity an outline since the author is not a historian. His interest in the military struggle for independence is an outgrowth of his service as a paratrooper officer in the U.S. Army.

The contest for control of colonial North America between France and Britain resulted in several wars in Europe as well as in North America. Britain asserted its influence along the eastern seaboard, from what is now Maine to Georgia, while France concentrated on extending its control over what is now eastern Canada as well as the Mississippi Valley to Louisiana.

In the struggle against the French, colonists from the various colonies founded by the British joined forces with regular British soldiers. Each colony had its own Militia, members of which had to appear for training and be prepared to serve extended periods during an emergency or for a specific military campaign. One such expedition by the Virginia Militia, under Lt. Col. George Washington, failed in 1754 to capture the strategic Fort Duquesne held by the French (present day Pittsburgh, Pennsylvania area). In July 1755, a British contingent led by General Braddock, with Washington as an aide, again failed to take the important fort. The tide however turned when the British in 1759 defeated the French on the Plains of Abraham in Quebec. Britain gained control of Canada.

KING ASSERTS CONTROL

Ever since the founding of the English Colony of Jamestown, Virginia in 1607, the colonists developed politically and economically separate from Britain. There was relatively little interference from Britain in this development. However, in the 1760's George III of Britain, asserted his influence on colonial trade as well as implementing means to tax the colonists. Thus in March of 1765, the British Parliament passed the Stamp Act. This meant that the colonists had to pay for revenue stamps affixed to newspapers and legal documents, among other articles. In October of that year colonists protested against "taxation without representation." A successful boycott of goods requiring a revenue stamp caused Parliament to repeal the 1765 Stamp Act in 1766.

The Townshend Act of 1767, the payment of import duties on tea, paper and glass, however, was another attempt by Parliament to collect money from the colonists. Again the colonists resisted. In May of 1769, the Virginia House of Burgesses (as the legislature was called) at Williamsburg, issued resolutions rejecting the right of Parliament to tax the colonies. Although the House of Burgesses was dissolved by the crown, members of the Virginia House met as private citizens to plan for the boycott of goods taxed under the Townshend Act. We might note that the House of Burgesses' opposition to the tax is vividly portrayed in the orientation film at the visitors center in Williamsburg.

By April 1770, the act was repealed, except for the tax on tea. However, in the spring of 1773 the Tea Act was enacted by Parliament which in effect, through the reimbursement of duty paid, subsidized the East India Company in selling tea in the colonies. As a result, the East India Company was able to sell tea at lower prices than the American tea sellers. On December 16, 1773, Bostonians dressed as Indians, threw more than 300 chests of tea overboard from British ships. The British government, as a result, imposed restrictions on the colonists. For example, public gatherings could not take place unless the British Governor gave his approval. On September 5, 1774, the colonists met in Philadelphia to declare their rights to "life, liberty and property." This gathering was the First Continental Congress.

1775

The fever of resentment against British rule hit a high pitch in 1775. Early in the year, Patrick Henry declared in Richmond, "Give me liberty or give me death." In April the "shot heard around the world" was fired as the British

REVOLUTION 31

were on their way to seize the colonists' collection of arms and ammunition at Concord, outside of Boston. In May, the Americans had a victory against the British at Ft. Ticonderoga, gateway to British ruled Canada. The Second Continental Congress met.

18-19 April, 1775	— Lexington and Concord
May, 1775	— Fort Ticonderoga attack
14 June, 1775	— Second Continental Congress forms Army
15 June, 1775	— George Washington chosen as Commander-in-Chief
17 June, 1775	— Breed's Hill confrontation near Bunker Hill
30-31 December, 1775	— Attack on Quebec

1776

The year began with the British burning of Norfolk and ended with Washington's surprise attack on Trenton. Thomas Paine wrote 'Common Sense'—calling for independence from Britain. The British attempted to control the southern colonies with a doomed attack on Charleston, South Carolina. As a result of this failure, the battlefield was mainly in the northern colonies for the next several years. On June 10, Congress appointed a committee to draft the Declaration of Independence. Thomas Jefferson was its chief author. On June 12, the Virginia Bill of Rights, authored principally by George Mason, was adopted as part of the Virginia constitution. By June 23, Jefferson submitted the draft of the Declaration of Independence to Congress. Members of Congress, after making several changes in the document, voted for independence on July 2. On July 4, 1776, John Hancock, President of the Congress, signed the document. Today, the original Declaration of Independence can be viewed at the National Archives in Washington, D.C.

The thrust of Jefferson's Declaration of Independence is that if government (as Parliament had done in the eyes of the colonists) seriously threatens the interests of society, the people (those living in the colonies) have the right "to alter or to abolish" that government. The document then lists over twenty indictments against the British King which gave cause for the colonies to declare themselves independent of Britain.

32 REVOLUTION

17 March, 1776 — British withdraw from Boston
28 June, 1776 — British attack on Charleston, S.C. fails
4 July, 1776 — Declaration of Independence signed
27 August 1776 — Battle of Long Island
26 December, 1776 — Surprise Attack on Trenton

1777

After Trenton in the last few days of 1776, the former colonists continued their pressure against the British early in 1777. At Princeton, the American Army inflicted losses on the British troops about to join Cornwallis, the British commander. After the battle, Washington quartered his troops near Morristown, New Jersey, and the British took up quarters in New York. For the next six months there was little military action between the two sides.

Later in the year, military engagements took place in upstate New York and in Pennsylvania. The New York campaign led to the British surrender at Saratoga, while the Pennsylvania battles led to the British capture of Philadelphia. Washington and his troops spent the winter at Valley Forge. During 1777, military supplies started to arrive from France to help the American cause.

3 January, 1777 — Battle of Princeton
September, 1777 — Battle of Brandywine
26 September, 1777 — British occupy Philadelphia
4 October, 1777 — Battle of Germantown
17 October, 1777 — Part of British Army surrenders at Saratoga.
Winter 1777-78 — Washington at Valley Force

1778

In 1778, France formally joined the war against Britain. This gave America the ability to counteract the strong British naval force. Thus Clinton, the British general, evacuated his army from Philadelphia to New York by land. Washington pursued and there was military action between the two sides at Monmouth. By the end of the year, Washington held his position outside of New York at West Point. For the next three years, there was a stalemate in the North. However, the British took the initiative in the South since Tory (supporters of the British) strength was greater in the southern states.

27 June, 1778 — Battle of Monmouth
late 1778 — Renewed British efforts in the South
Winter 1778-79 — Georgia overrun by British

1779

One decisive action in the North was the American attack on the British at Stony Point. In the South, the British regained control of Savannah. The French fleet had given the Americans temporary control of the sea, but Admiral D'Estaing withdrew his fleet. As a result, the Americans returned to Charleston, South Carolina.

16 July 1779 — Attack on Stony Point (N.Y.)
9 October 1779 — Attack on Savannah

1780

The withdrawal of the French fleet enabled Clinton to move his troops from the North and consequently capture Charleston. It was one of the worst defeats of the war for America. Clinton returned with part of his force to New York, and Cornwallis started to establish British control along the coastal areas in the South. Guerilla warfare erupted in the South, led by officers such as Lt. Col. Francis Marion. However, at Camden, S.C., the Americans were again defeated. But on October 7, at Kings Mountain, North Carolina, where American patriot fought American tory, the cause for independence from Britain was immensely advanced with a victory.

12 May, 1780 — American surrender Charleston, S.C.
16 August, 1780 — Battle of Camden, S.C.
7 October, 1780 — Battle of Kings Mountain, S.C..

1781

This is the year America was finally able to coordinate its army with the powerful French fleet for a decisive blow against the British. Cornwallis, early in the year, embarked upon a plan to gain greater British control of the South by attempting to invade North Carolina and Virginia. At Cowpens, N.C., the British suffered a great defeat on their way to Virginia. While Cornwallis was attempting to move north to Virginia, Clinton in New York, wanted to establish a base of operation on Chesapeake

34 REVOLUTION

Bay from which he could disrupt American efforts in Virginia.

As a result of Clinton's orders, Cornwallis began to establish a base at Yorktown, a small tobacco port where the York River flows into the Chesapeake Bay. On hearing that the powerful French fleet from the West Indies under de Grasse could be used against the British, Washington's American Army and Rochambeau's French Army moved from the north toward Yorktown, hoping to defeat Cornwallis before Clinton could come from New York.

The battle of the Virginia Capes between the French fleet under de Grasse and the British fleet under Rodney, gave control of the bay to the French while the British sailed back to New York, leaving Cornwallis. The combined American-French Army arrived near Yorktown on September, 26. With Washington holding control of the ground around Yorktown and de Grasse controlling the bay, the siege of Yorktown began. Clinton from New York came too late to help Cornwallis and on 19 October the 6,000 man British Army at Yorktown laid down its arms to the tune of "The World Turned Upside Down." The political effect of Cornwallis' defeat was the overthrow of the British Cabinet. The new government in Britain was convinced that the war against the United States had been lost.

17 January, 1781	— British defeat at Cowpens, N.C.
15 March, 1781	— American defeat at Guilford Court House, N.C.
6 July, 1781	— Lafayette and Cornwallis meet at Green Spring near Williamsburg
July-October, 1781	— Cornwallis establishes base at Yorktown
26 September, 1781	— Washington's army arrives in Yorktown area
6 October, 1781	— Siege of Yorktown Starts
16 October, 1781	— Cornwallis attempts to escape
17 October, 1781	— Fighting ceases at Yorktown
19 October, 1781	— British Army surrenders
30 November, 1782	— Armistice agreed upon
January, 1783	— Britain and France sign preliminary articles of peace
11 April, 1783	— U.S. Congress officially proclaims Armistice
3 September, 1783	— Peace treaty finally signed
3 November, 1783	— Washington directs army to turn in arms

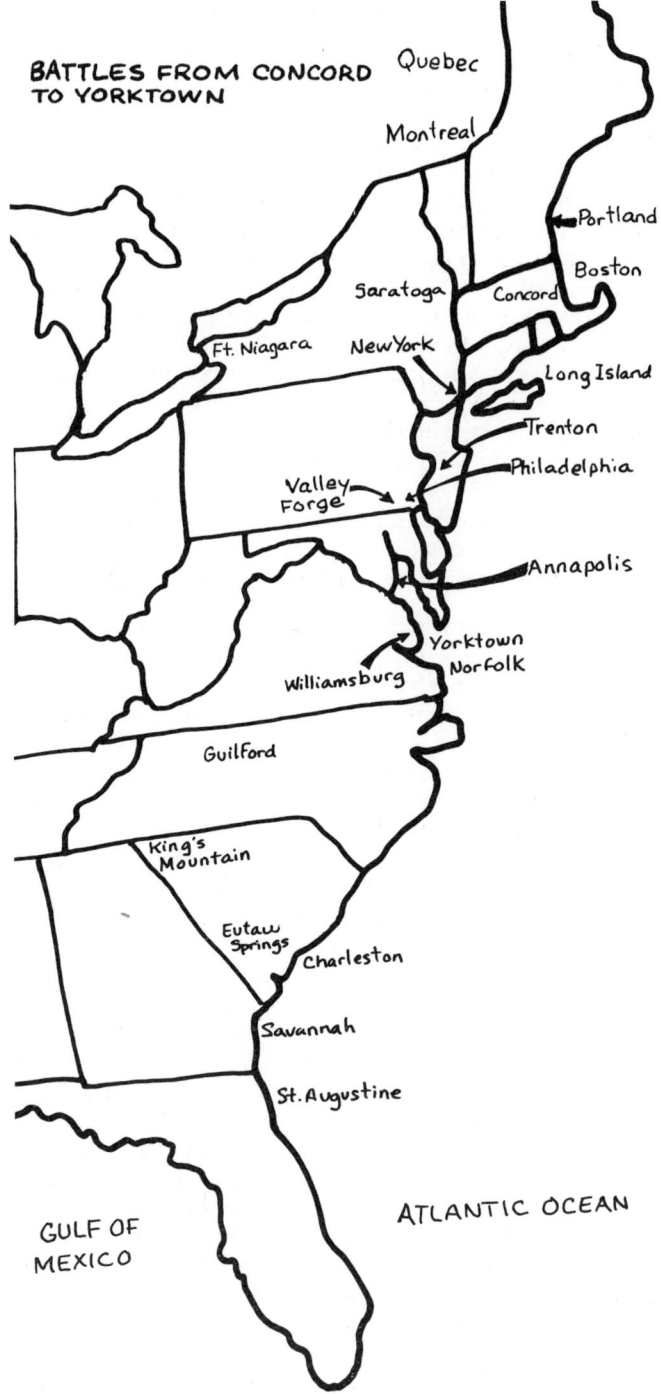

1776 DOCUMENT

The most important document that came out of America's struggle for independence 200 years ago is the Declaration of Independence. Thomas Jefferson, a Secretary of State, second Vice-President and third President of the United States, wanted to be remembered as the author of the Declaration of Indpendence. It was chiefly through his efforts that the document was ready to be approved and then signed by Congress President John Hancock on July 4, 1776. As we have noted in our chronological presentation of America's struggle 200 years ago, the original copy of the Declaration of Indpendence can be viewed at the National Archives, in Washington, D.C.

Since many of us might not be familiar with the entire document, we are including the text in your guide. In fact, a recent survey of over 2000 public servants showed that almost half (47 percent) did not recognize the document and 68 percent would not sign it. Even in todays environment, John Hancock would have been a courageous man!

THE DECLARATION OF INDEPENDENCE

When, in the course of human events, it becomes necessary for one people to dissolve the political bands which have connected them with another, and to assume, among the powers of the earth, the separate and equal station to which the laws of nature and of nature's God entitle them, a decent respect to the opinions of mankind requires that they should declare the causes which impel them to the separation.

We hold these truths to be self-evident, that all Men are created equal; that they are endowed by their Creator with certain inalienable Rights—That among these, are Life, Liberty, and the Pursuit of Happiness. That, to secure these rights, governments are instituted among men, deriving their just powers from the consent of the governed; that, whenever any form of government becomes destructive of these ends, it is the right of the people to alter or to abolish it, and to institute a new government, laying its Foundation on such principles, and organizing its powers in such form, as to them shall seem most likely to effect their safety and happiness. Prudence, indeed will dictate that governments long established, should not be changed for light and transient causes; and, accordingly, all experience hath shown, that mankind are more disposed to suffer, while evils are sufferable, than to right themselves by abolishing the forms to which they are accustomed. But, when a long train of abuses and usurpations, pursuing invariably the same object, evinces a design to reduce them under absolute despotism, it is their right, it is their duty, to throw off such government and to provide new guards for their future security. Such has been the patient sufference of these colonies, and such is now the necessity which constrains them to alter their former systems of government. The history of the present King of Great Britain is a history of repeated injuries and unsurpations, all having, in direct object, the establishment of an absolute tyranny over these States. To prove this, let facts be submitted to a candid world:

He has refused his assent to laws the most wholesome and necessary for the public good.

He has forbidden his governors to pass laws of immediate and pressing importance, unless suspended in their operation till his assent should be obtained; and, when so suspended, he has utterly neglected to attend to them.

He has refused to pass other laws for the accommodation of large districts of people, unless those people would relinquish the right of representation in the legislature: a right inestimable to them, and formidable to tyrants only.

He has called together legislative bodies at places unusual, uncomfortable, and distant from the depository of their public records, for the sole purpose of fatiguing them into compliance with his measures.

He has dissolved representative houses repeatedly for opposing, with manly firmness, his invasions on the rights of the people.

He has refused, for a long time after such dissolutions, to cause others to be elected; whereby the legislative powers, incapable of annihilation, have returned to the people at large for their exercise; the state remaining, in the meantime, exposed to all the danger of invasion from without, and convulsions within.

He has endeavored to prevent the population of these States; for that purpose, obstructing the laws for naturalization of foreigners, refusing to pass others to encourage their migration hither, and raising the conditions of new appropriations of lands.

He has obstructed the administration of justice, by refusing his assent to laws for establishing judiciary powers.

He has made judges dependent on his will alone, for the tenure of their offices, and the amount and payment of their salaries.

He has erected a multitude of new offices, and sent hither swarms of officers, to harass our people, and eat out their substance.

He has kept among us, in time of peace, standing armies, without the consent of our legislatures.

He has affected to render the military independent of,

and superior to, the civil power.

He has combined, with others, to subject us to a jurisdiction foreign to our Constitution, and unacknowledged by our laws; giving his assent to their acts of pretended legislation:

For quartering large bodies of armed troops among us:

For protecting them by a mock trial, from punishment, for any murders which they should commit on the inhabitants of these States:

For cutting off our trade with all parts of the world:

For imposing taxes on us without our consent:

For depriving us, in many cases, of the benefit of trial by jury:

For transporting us beyond seas to be tried for pretended offenses:

For abolishing the free system of English laws in a neighboring province, establishing therein an arbitrary government, and enlarging its boundaries, so as to render it at once an example and fit instrument for introducing the same absolute rule into these colonies:

For taking away our charters, abolishing our most valuable laws, and altering, fundamentally, the powers of our governments:

For suspending our own legislatures, and declaring themselves invested with power to legislate for us in all cases whatsoever.

He has abdicated government here, by declaring us out of his protection, and waging war against us.

He has plundered our seas, ravaged our coasts, burnt our towns, and destroyed the lives of our people.

He is, at this time, transporting large armies of foreign mercenaries to complete the works of death, desolation, and tyranny, already begun, with circumstances of cruelty and perfidy scarcely paralleled in the most barbarous ages, and totally unworthy the head of a civilized nation.

He has constrained our fellows citizens, taken captive on the high seas, to bear arms against their country, to become the executioners of their friends, and brethren, or to fall themselves by their hands.

He has excited domestic insurrections amongst us, and has endeavored to bring on the inhabitants of our frontiers, the merciless Indian savages, whose known rule of warfare is an undistinguished destruction of all ages, sexes, and conditions.

In every stage of these oppressions, we have petitioned for redress, in the most humble terms; our repeated petitions have been answered only by repeated injury. A prince, whose character is thus marked by every act which may define a tyrant, is unfit to be the ruler of a free people.

Nor have we been wanting in attention to our British brethren. We have warned them, from time to time, of attempts made by their legislature to extend an unwarrantable jurisdiction over us. We have reminded them of the circumstances of our emigration and settlement here. We have appealed to their native justice and magnanimity, and we have conjured them, by the ties of our common kindred, to disavow these usurpations, which would inevitably interrupt our connections and correspondence. They, too, have been deaf to the voice of justice and consanguinity. We must, therefore, acquiesce in the necessity which denounces our separation, and hold them, as we hold the rest of mankind, enemies in war, in peace, friends.

We, therefore, the representatives of the United States of America, in general Congress assembled, appealing to the Supreme Judge of the world for the rectitude of our intentions, do, in the name, and by the authority of the good people of these colonies, solemnly publish and declare, that the united colonies are, and of right ought to be, free and independent states; that they are absolved from all allegiance to the British Crown, and that all political connection between them and the state of Great Britain is, and ought to be, totally dissolved; and that, as free and independent states, they have full power to levy war, conclude peace, contract alliances, establish commerce, and to do all other acts and things which indepedent states may of right do. And, for the support of this declaration, with a firm reliance on the protection of Divine Providence, we mutually pledge to each other our lives, our fortunes, and our sacred honor.

SIGNERS OF THE DECLARATION OF INDEPENDENCE

According to the authenticated list printed by order of Congress on January 18, 1777 the following signed the Declaration of Independence. We might note that Matthrew Thornton's name was signed on the engrossed copy following the Connecticut Members, but was transferred in the printed copy to its proper place with the other New Hampshire Members. Thomas McKean's name was not

40 DOCUMENTS

included in the list of signers printed by order of Congress on January 18, 1777, as he did not sign the engrossed copy until some time thereafter, probably in 1781. Of course, keep in mind that John Hancock, as President of the Congress also put his signature to the document.

New Hampshire
Josiah Bartlett
William Whipple
Matthew Thornton

Massachusetts-Bay
Samuel Adams
John Adams
Robert Treat Paine
Elbridge Gerry

**Rhode Island
and Providence, etc.**
Stephen Hopkins
William Ellery

Connecticut
Roger Sherman
Samuel Huntington
William Williams
Oliver Wolcott

New York
William Floyd
Phillip Livingston
Francis Lewis
Lewis Morris

New Jersey
Richard Stockton
John Witherspoon
Franics Hopkinson
John Hart
Abraham Clark

Pennsylvania
Robert Morris
Benjamin Rush
Benjamin Franklin
John Morton
George Clymer
James Smith
George Taylor
James Wilson
George Ross

Delaware
Caesar Rodney
George Read
Thomas McKean

Maryland
Samuel Chase
William Paca
Thomas Stone
Charles Carroll

Virginia
George Wythe
Richard Henry Lee
Thomas Jefferson
Benjamin Harrison
Thomas Nelson, Jr.
Francis Lightfoot Lee
Carter Braxton

North Carolina
William Hooper
Joseph Hewes
John Penn

South Carolina
Edward Rutledge
Thomas Heyward, Jr.
Thomas Lynch, Jr.
Arthur Middleton

Georgia
Button Gwinnett
Lyman Hall
George Walton

THE CONSTITUTION OF THE UNITED STATES

The U.S. Constitution was completed on September 17, 1787 and became effective on March 4, 1789. It too can be viewed at the National Archives. After it was completed, Benjamin Franklin stated "I agree to this Constitution with all its faults..." Another delegate stated sometime after "While some have boasted it as a work from Heaven, others have given it a less righteous origin. I have many reasons to believe that it is the work of plain, honest men, and such, I think, it will appear." The Constitution begins:

> We the people of the United States, in order to form a more perfect union, establish justice, insure domestic tranquility, provide for the common defense, promote the general welfare, and secure the blessings of liberty to ourselves and our posterity, do ordain and establish this Constitution for the United States of America.

William Gladstone, the 19th century British Prime Minister, stated: "As the British Constitution is the most subtle organism which has proceeded from the womb and long gestation of progressive history, so the American Constitution is, so far as I can see, the most wonderful work ever struck off at a given time by the brain and purpose of man."

HISTORICAL REPRODUCTIONS FROM ARCHIVES

To help you in the planning of your Bicentennial activities we note that the National Archives has assembled a selection of reproductions of historical documents, maps and prints for the Bicentennial. The reproduction available, which include the Declaration of Independence, the Constitution and the Bill of Rights, as well as poster-sized reproductions of these charters, are listed in a 24-page booklet that can be ordered free by anyone who writes for a copy of "Documents from America's Past," Consumer Information, Pueblo, CO 81009. Some items are available for $.25 while some cost $3.50.

42 PRESIDENTS

PRESIDENTS OF THE UNITED STATES

NO.	NAME	TERM IN OFFICE
1	George Washington (1732-1799)	1789-1797
2	John Adams (1735-1826)	1797-1801
3	Thomas Jefferson (1743-1826)	1801-1809
4	James Madison (1751-1836)	1809-1817
5	James Monroe (1758-1831)	1817-1825
6	John Quincy Adams (1767-1848)	1825-1829
7	Andrew Jackson (1767-1845)	1829-1837
8	Martin Van Buren (1782-1862)	1837-1841
9	William Henry Harrison (1773-1841)	1841
10	John Tyler (1790-1862)	1841-1845
11	James Knox Polk (1795-1849)	1845-1849
12	Zachary Taylor (1784-1850)	1849-1850
13	Millard Fillmore (1800-1874)	1850-1853
14	Franklin Pierce (1804-1869)	1853-1857
15	James Buchanan (1791-1868)	1857-1861
16	Abraham Lincoln (1809-1865)	1861-1865
17	Andrew Johnson (1808-1875)	1865-1869
18	Ulysses S. Grant (1822-1885)	1869-1877
19	Rutherford B. Hayes (1822-1893)	1877-1881
20	James A. Garfield (1831-1881)	1881
21	Chester A. Arthur (1830-1886)	1881-1885
22	Grover Cleveland (1837-1908)	1885-1889
23	Benjamin Harrison (1833-1901)	1889-1893
24	Grover Cleveland (1837-1908)	1893-1897
25	William McKinley (1843-1901)	1897-1901
26	Theodore Roosevelt (1858-1919)	1901-1909
27	William H. Taft (1857-1930)	1909-1913
28	Woodrow Wilson (1856-1924)	1913-1921
29	Warren G. Harding (1865-1923)	1921-1923
30	Calvin Coolidge (1872-1935)	1923-1929
31	Herbert C. Hoover (1874-1964)	1929-1933
32	Franklin D. Roosevelt (1882-1945)	1933-1945
33	Harry S. Truman (1884-1972)	1945-1953
34	Dwight D. Eisenhower (1890-1969)	1953-1961
35	John F. Kennedy (1917-1963)	1961-1963
36	Lyndon B. Johnson (1908-1973)	1963-1969
37	Richard M. Nixon (1913-)	1969-1974
38	Gerald R. Ford (1913-)	1974-

STATES 43

ENTRANCE OF STATES INTO UNION

ORIGINAL 13 STATES

STATE	CAPITAL	ENTERED UNION
Connecticut	Hartford	1788
Delaware	Dover	1787
Georgia	Atlanta	1788
Maryland	Annapolis	1788
Massachusetts	Boston	1788
New Hampshire	Concord	1788
New Jersey	Trenton	1787
New York	Albany	1788
North Carolina	Raleigh	1789
Pennsylvania	Harrisburg	1787
Rhode Island	Providence	1790
South Carolina	Columbia	1788
Virginia	Richmond	1788
Alabama	Montgomery	1819
Alaska	Juneau	1958
Arizona	Phoenix	1912
Arkansas	Little Rock	1836
California	Sacramento	1850
Colorado	Denver	1876
Florida	Tallahassee	1845
Hawaii	Honolulu	1959
Idaho	Boise	1890
Illinois	Springfield	1818
Indiana	Indianapolis	1816
Iowa	Des Moines	1846
Kansas	Topeka	1861
Kentucky	Frankfort	1792
Louisiana	Baton Rouge	1812
Maine	Augusta	1820
Michigan	Lansing	1837
Minnesota	St. Paul	1858
Mississippi	Jackson	1817
Missouri	Jefferson City	1821
Montana	Helena	1889
Nebraska	Lincoln	1867
Nevada	Carson City	1864
New Mexico	Santa Fe	1912
North Dakota	Bismarck	1889
Ohio	Columbus	1803
Oklahoma	Oklahoma City	1907

44 THE CHANGE

Oregon	Salem	1859
South Dakota	Pierre	1889
Tennessee	Nashville	1796
Texas	Austin	1845
Utah	Salt Lake City	1896
Vermont	Montpelier	1791
Washington	Olympia	1889
West Virginia	Charleston	1863
Wisconsin	Madison	1848
Wyoming	Cheyenne	1890

THE CHANGE IN AMERICA

There have been a lot of changes from the time of the 13 colonies to the present 50 states. Not all the colonists wanted to be independent from Britain 200 years ago. Some historians have estimated that only one-third of the population was for independence, one-third was in favor of keeping ties with Britain while the remaining one-third was undecided and awaited the outcome of the struggle.

Whereas in 1775 the 13 colonies were along the Atlantic Seaboard, by 1783 the country had grown to the Mississippi. Thomas Jefferson engineered the Louisiana Purchase in 1803, then Florida and then the Oregon Country from Great Britain in 1846 became U.S. territories. When the Republic of Texas became part of the United States in 1845, it did so under the condition that Texas could be divided into five smaller states. In 1848 and 1853 more of the Southwest and the West became part of the country. Alaska was purchased from Russia in 1867 and in 1898 Hawaii was made a part of U.S. territory. In 1917, the Virgin Islands were bought from Denmark; in 1925, Swains Island was annexed to American Samoa. In June 1975, the people of the Northern Mariana Islands in the Pacific voted to become citizens of the United States. Several steps must be followed through, including United Nations approval, before the 14 islands achieve commonwealth status.

Just as there have been territorial changes, increasing our size by a factor of four in our 200 years, the population has increased by a factor of about 86 to around 213 million. Our lifestyle has changed considerably over this period. Most of the population lived on farms 200 years ago—today less than 4% of the population is on farms. And according to the latest figures from the Census Bureau, 96% of American families now own television sets and 82% own cars.

THE EAST

COLONIAL CORRIDOR TRAIN TRAVEL

The cities that stretch along the Atlantic Ocean from Boston to Washington, D.C. make up what is commonly known as the Colonial Corridor. The train service in this Northeast Corridor is one of the best in the world. For instance, besides regular train service between Boston-New York-Philadelphia-Washington, D.C., two technologically advanced Turbo trains speed daily between New York and Boston in either direction. Moreover, over a dozen superfast Metroliners shuttle back and forth in either direction between New York and Washington, D.C.

Traveling by train in this densely populated corridor is practically a lesson in the development of our country. From your train window you can see the Old Swedes Church just outside the Wilmington, Delaware Station. It was built before the end of the 17th century. In Providence, Rhode Island you can see the State Capitol, whereas in Washington D.C. the U.S. Capitol itself is just a short way from the station. Traveling south from Springfield, Mass., your route follows alongside the scenic Connecticut River. The rail route takes on a different pitch as your train flashes through industrialized areas of Southeastern Pennsylvania and northern New Jersey where you will see the names of companies whose trademarks have become household words. The New York skyline with the Empire State building and the twin towers of the World Trade Center towering over Manhattan Island are part of the panoramic picture you get as you approach America's largest metropolitan area. The hustle and bustle here is a dramatic change from the rustic scenery you witness from your train as you travel through New England.

Travel by train in the Northeast is not only an experience in speed and scenery, but also a real convenience. Traveling by car or public transportation to the train terminals here in the Northeast Corridor is a simple matter. Subways feed directly into the train stations in Boston, New York and Philadelphia. Convenient bus service is available at the Washington train station to take you to all points in the city. In the near future, the Washington, D.C. station will be part of America's truly first multimodal terminal. Besides the inter-city train service, there will be commuter trains, buses, subways, and inter-city bus companies which will use the terminal. Besides that, the Visitors Center on the site of the old terminal will host millions of visitors when they come to our Nation's capital during the Bicentennial celebrations.

BOSTON, MASSACHUSETTS

Ever since the beginning of American history, Boston has played a significant role in the development of America. Here the 'Boston Tea Party' took place in 1773 and on April 19, 1775 the Revolutionary War started in nearby Lexington and Concord. Today Boston is a great center of education with a multitude of universities in and around the city. Also keep in mind that Boston is an important transportation center. Public transportation makes it easy to get around between the various transportation terminals. Boston is not only your gateway city to nearby important American cities such as New York, Philadelphia and Washington, but also to the Canadian Maritime Provinces as well as Quebec and Montreal.

One of the first places you should visit after your arrival in Boston is the Visitor Information Center next to the Boston Common on Boylston Street. (This is also where the marked Freedom Trail starts.) You get a great deal of information here and the staff is extremely pleasant and helpful. If you run into a problem getting around on the MBTA system (Massachusetts Bay Transportation Authority) call 722-5000.

BOSTON 47

48 BOSTON

Besides taking walks in nearby Cambridge (do not miss it—there is excellent public transportation to Cambridge) with our friends from Harvard and Northeastern Universities, we like to go up the Prudential Center in Boston to get a great view of the city. Also, if you want to splurge, may we suggest you have dinner herein the restaurant which is practically on the top floor. It is quite an experience. Another huge concrete development we might add is the new Government Center.

THE ADAMS FAMILY

As you learn about America's early heritage when you walk along the "Freedom Trail," keep in mind that Boston is the home of one of the most important families in America—the Adams family. President John F. Kennedy once stated that the Adams family "runs like a scarlet thread of moral courage and strength of character through the whole fabric of American history." The family gave the United States its second and sixth Presidents; its first Vice President; a delegate to two Continental Congresses; its first ambassador to Britain, among others and members of the House of Representatives.

THE FREEDOM TRAIL

There is no better way to experience America's early heritage in Boston than a stroll along the Freedom Trail. For the Bicentennial, two loops have been made of the trail. The one in the North End contains points 5—8, the remainder are downtown. The entire Freedom Trail is marked in red along the various pavements.

The points of Freedom Trail include, in addition to # 8A, the U.S.S. Constitution and # 12A, The Boston Tea Party Ship and Museum, the following points: 1. Boston Common; 2. State House; 3. King's Chapel; 4. King's Chapel Burying Ground; 4A. City Hall Hospitality Center with its information booth, child care facilities, seating, storage lockers, food server and restrooms; 5. Paul Revere House; 6. Paul Revere Mall; 7. Old North Church; 8. Copp's Hill Burying Ground (with its view of the U.S.S. Constitution and the Bunker Hill Monument); 9. Faneuil Hall; 10. Quincy Market; 11. Boston Massacre Site; 12. Old State House; 13. Site of Benjamin Franklin Birthplace; 14. Old Meeting House; 15. Old Corner Book

BOSTON 49

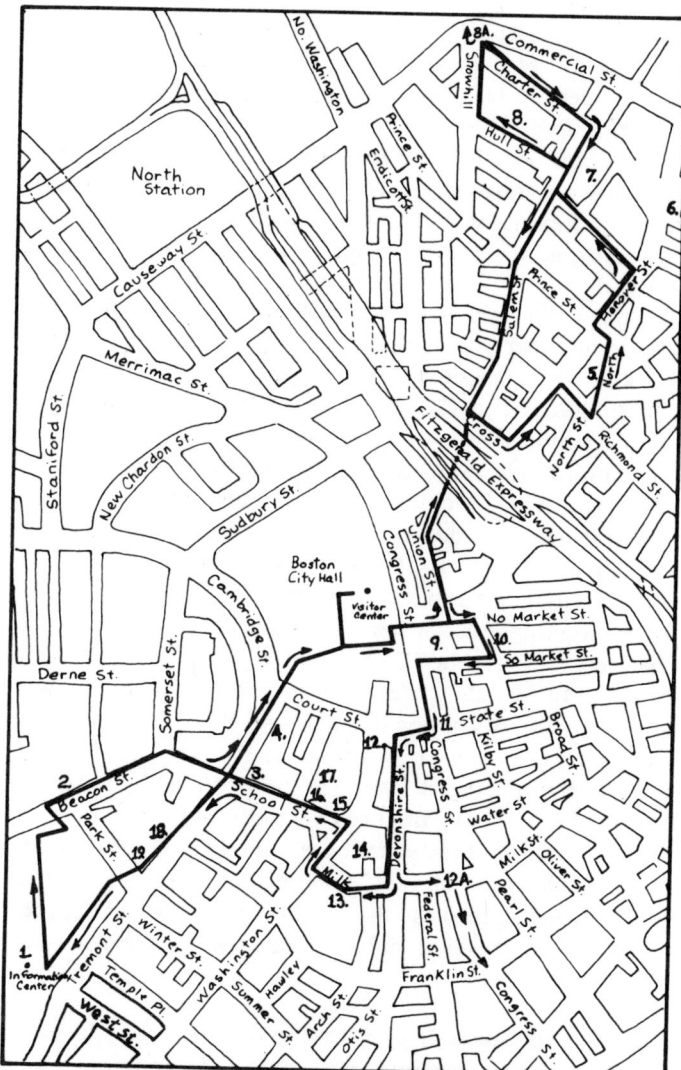

Store; 16. Benjamin Franklin Statue; 17. Site of First Public School; 18. Granary Burying Ground; 19. Park Street Church.

FREEDOM TRAIL ATTRACTIONS

The Boston Common, the start of your Freedom Trail tour was bought by the city in 1634 as a training field and as a grazing area for cattle. Point 2 is the State House built in 1795. Open Weekdays 10—5, Weekends 10—4. Guided tours. Point 4, contains the William Dawes grave.

Point 5 is the Paul Revere House, built in 1677, the oldest home in Boston. Paul Revere lived here from 1770 to 1800. Open daily 10—6. Admission $.50. Point 6 is the beautiful Paul Revere Mall. Point 7 is the Old North Church built in 1723. On the night of April 18, 1775 two lantern were hung in its steeple to signal the British advance on Lexington and Concord. Open daily 10—6. Sunday services at 11 a.m. Point 8 is Copp's Hill Burying Ground.

Point 9, Faneuil Hall, was called by John Adams "The Cradle of Liberty." Open daily 10—6. Point 10 is Quincy Market, next to Faneuil Hall. Open daily 10—8, adults $1.50, children to 12, half price. Point 11, marked by a ring of cobblestones, is the Boston Massacre, March 5, 1770. Point 12 is the Old State House, where according to John Adams "The child Independence was born.". The Declaration of Independence was read from the east balcony in July 18, 1776. Open daily 10—6. Point 13 — Site of Benjamin Franklin Birthplace. Point 14 is the Old South Meetinghouse, where the signal was given for the Boston Tea Party in 1773. Point 15 is the Old Corner Book Store. which served as a meeting place of famous American authors. Open daily 10—6. Point 16 is a Statue of Benjamin Franklin. Point 17 is the site of the First Public School erected in 1635. Point 18 is the Granary Burying Ground, the final resting place of three signers of the Declaration of Independence—John Hancock, Robert Treat Paine and Samuel Adams. Paul Revere is also buried here. Open daily 8—4. Point 19 is the Park Street Church were the first public singing of "America"took place in 1831.

During the summer months, the Gray Line, Inc., operates three shuttle bus tours. One covers the Freedom Trail sites, including transportation to the U.S.S. Constitution and Bunker Hill. Service is available daily 9:30 a.m. to 4:30 p.m.; last bus departs at 2:30. Fare—$2 adults; $1 children. Tickets are sold at the Visitor Information Center on the Boston Common, at the City Hall Hospitality Center, and at The Boston 200 Faneuil Hall shop.

We might note that opening—closing hours are subject to change, especially after Labor Day. Check the Visitor Information Center for new hours.

BOSTON 51

BARGAIN TICKET IN BOSTON

For $4 you can obtain a ticket which will save you several dollars off the normal price of admission to three expositions—"Where's Boston," (Prudential Center), "Victorian Boston" (105 Arlington Street) and "The Revolution" (near Faneuil Hall, a stop on the Freedom Trail). Moreover, you get a 25 cent discount on Boston's Bicentennial Shuttle Bus, (reg. price is $2), as well as the Skywalk atop the Prudential Center (reg. $1), and the "Official Boston 200" Guidebook (reg. $1.50). You can purchase your $4 ticket at the "Boston 200" information center at City Hall, the Boston Common or Faneuil Hall.

BOSTON TRAIN STATIONS

Boston, your gateway to New England, has two rail stations. One is the Back Bay Station, located near a number of hotels, and the other is South Station, the terminal rail station in Boston. The larger South Station is located directly next to one of Boston's subway stations. Therefore, if you want to reach other parts of Boston by public transportation, such as the Freedom Trail, the South Station is your best bet. We might add that the old Essex Hotel is located right across the street from the South Station.

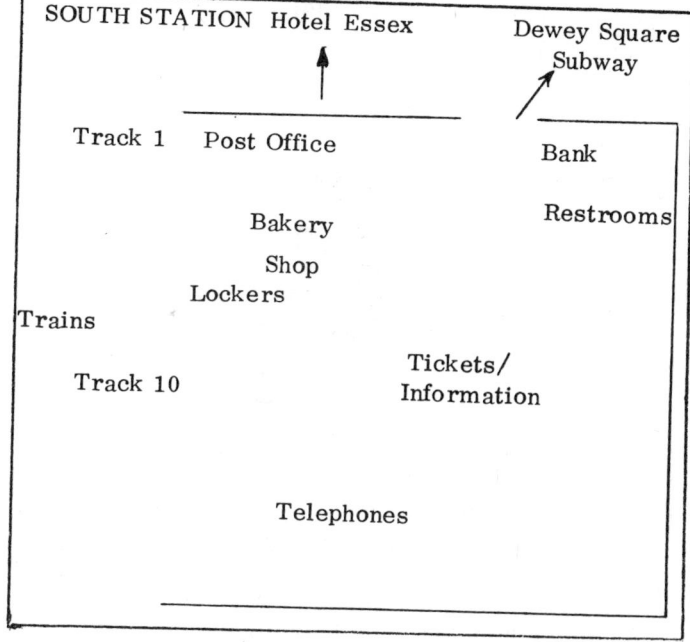

52 PLYMOUTH

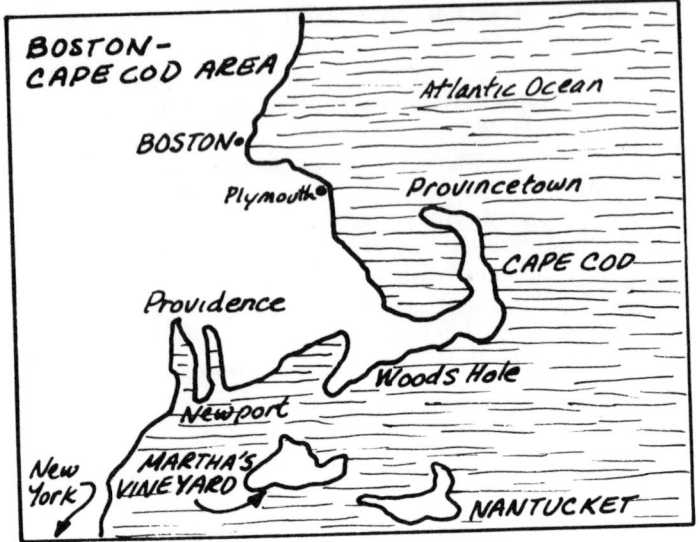

PLYMOUTH, MASS.

Plymouth, where the Pilgrims landed in 1620, is less than an hour by bus from Boston. Here you can view the Plymouth Rock where the Pilgrims came ashore to establish the first permanent settlement north of Jamestown (1607). Visit the Mayflower II, an exact replica of the original ship that brought the 102 settlers to the New World.

CAPE COD

A delightful bus excursion from Boston is the visit to Cape Cod and the islands of Martha's Vineyard and Nantucket. By looking at our map you will see that Hyannis is the focal transportation point of Cape Cod. It is your connecting point for travel to the furthermost town on the Cape, quaint Provincetown. It takes only about 1-1/2 hours to reach Hyannis from Boston.

Woods Hole, about one hour and 45 minutes from Boston, is your gateway to Martha's Vineyard or Nantucket Island. Because of the popularity of these resort destinations, you will find buses crowded. However, there are frequent departures (hourly during the peak periods). We suggest that you try to visit these coastal areas during the week. On Fridays, all of Boston seems to be heading to the islands or Cape Cod.

For your information, the boat trip between Woods Hole and Martha's Vineyard takes about 45 minutes and the one way cost is about $3. A one-day excursion rate will save you a little bit. The boat trip from Woods Hole to Nantucket takes about 2-1/2 hours and the one way fare is about $5. There is a sizeable discount on the one day excursion fare. Keep in mind that there is also direct bus service from New York and Providence to Woods Hole and Hyannis.

We believe that an excursion to the islands off Massachusetts will be an enjoyable experience. The sand beaches, the cozy little harbors and the breezes provide an ideal background for relaxing or swimming or a host of other activities. We suggest you may want to rent a bicycle—it is a great way to discover all kinds of new places. And if you want to shop, you will find a great number of antique shops, art galleries (artists' colonies can be found here) and specialty shops.

NEW YORK

NEW YORK ORIENTATION

We hope our map will allow you to gain a general perspective of what is where in New York. You will notice that Manhattan is an island—it is here that you will find your departure terminal for transportation to major cities, including Washington, D.C., only several hours away. On Manhattan you will also find the Empire State Building, the New World Trade Center (taller than the Empire State Building), Fifth Avenue, Rockefeller Center, Times Square, and the United Nations Building, the many fine New York museums, Central Park and Federal Hall in the Wall Street area where George Washington was inaugurated as President of the United States on April 30, 1789 and where Congress met from April 1789 to August 1790 before it moved to Philadelphia.

54 NEW YORK

New York City has another very historical attraction—Fraunces Tavern, a historic four story brick building built in 1719 and now surrounded by skyscrapers. In 1762 it was bought by a Black merchant from the West Indies who gave it its present name. George Washington said farewell here to the officers of the Continental Army.

NEW YORK'S PENNSYLVANIA STATION

Most Amtrak trains leave from the Pennsylvania Station. Trains bound for Albany, Rochester, Chicago (via Buffalo), and Montreal (via the Hudson Valley), leave from the Grand Central Station.

NEW YORK 55

As you can imagine that with practically all inter-city train arrivals/departures taking place at the Pennsylvania Station, the station is a busy place. To add to the crowds is the fact that a multitude of commuter trains use this station. Moreover, right above the station is the new Madison Square Garden Center. Not only do sports events like basketball take place here, but you will find a theater and art gallery among other attractions. Weekdays you can take a tour of the center at 11 a.m. or 2:30 p.m. Cost is $2 and $1.50 for students.

Another reason the Pennsylvania Station seems so busy is that it is also a very important subway stop. In fact,

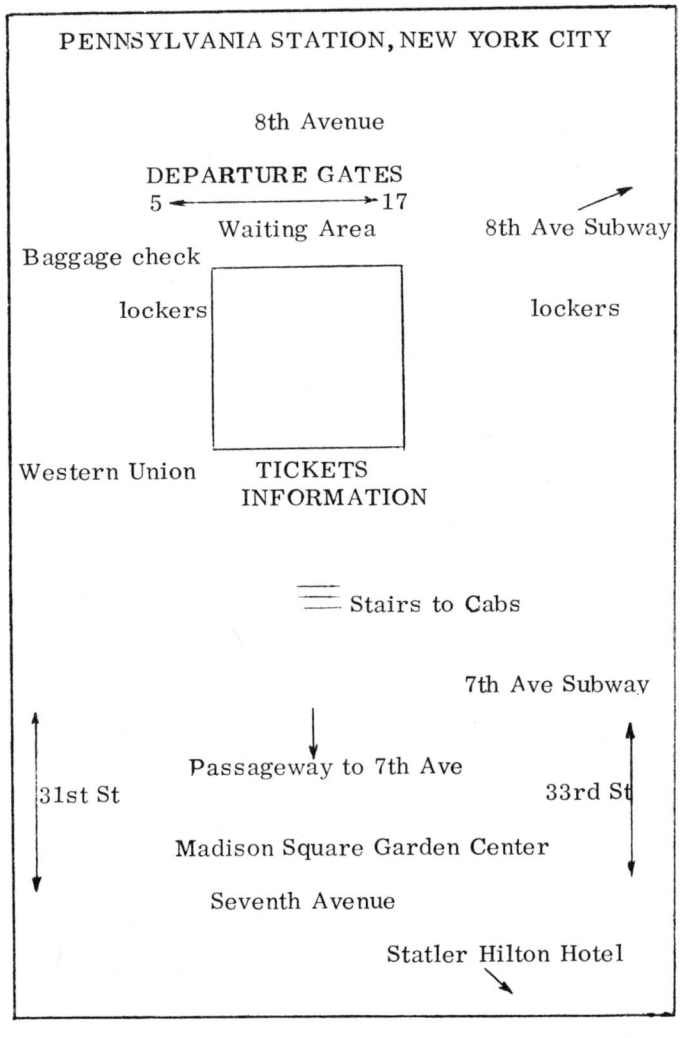

56 NEW YORK

you can reach practically any part of New York City by subway from here.

In order that you might get a general picture of the train station let us first emphasize that this huge structure is a multi-level affair. The lowest level is the level at which your trains arrive or depart. The level above that is your subway level. Also on this level you will find lockers, restrooms, and the Amtrak Lounge between gates 16 and 17. Free coffee while you are awaiting your train! The next level up is the level on which you will find the ticket and information counter, the waiting area and shops. Subways can also be reached from this level. The next level is street level and the Madison Square Garden complex. You might want to keep in mind that the modern Pennsylvania Station is located between 7th and 8th Avenues and 31st and 33rd Streets. You are right across the street from the Statler Hilton, Macy's, and Gimble's department stores and just two blocks away from the Empire State Building. An excellent location from which to start exploring New York City. However, if you want to start walking down Fifth Avenue, you can easily reach Fifth Avenue and 42nd Street from the station by subway. Just follow the signs to the 7th Avenue Subway line; take the subway one stop 'uptown.' When you get off at the Times Square Station, walk one level down and follow the 'Queens' sign. From here it is one stop to Fifth Avenue and two stops to Grand Central Station. Getting back to Pennsylvania Station from anywhere along this area of Fifth Avenue is quite easy. Besides the subway, bus #4 will take you from Fifth Avenue directly back to the Pennsylvania Station. You might keep in mind that subway tokens now cost 50 cents.

NEW YORK CITY BICENTENNIAL SLIDE SHOW

One of the newest attractions in New York City is the sight and sound show at the Museum of the City of New York at 103rd Street and Fifth Avenue. Here you can see a slide show, through 1976, which takes you back to the day General Washington had the Declaration of Independence read to his troops at what is now City Hall Park. On that same day, July 9, 1776, a patriotic crowd toppled the statue of King George III from a pedestal at Bowling Green. There is no admission charge to see the 18 minute show.

GETTING AROUND IN NEW YORK

You can visit many of New York's tourist attractions by public transportation. The New York subway will get you to many places for only 50¢ — and if you cannot get there by subway, chances are a bus will take you there. Anyway, here are some thoughts about traveling around by subway.

At practically all subway stations you can obtain a free copy of 'New York Subway Guide', a large folded sheet with a map of all the subway routes. It will greatly help you to get oriented.

From Times Square, an important subway transfer point, you can reach South Ferry (for the Statue of Liberty and the Staten Island Ferry) with a #1 subway. This is the Broadway Local of the IRT line. You will understand this designation a little bit better when you look at your New York Subway Guide. Keep in mind that each route of the New York City subway system is identified by a number or letter and a color on the subway map. At the end of each line on the map you will see the particular subway number. Next to the subway number or letter designation on the map you will see three letters such as IRT, IND or BMT. These identify the former subway routes/companies.

In our example you will see next to the #1, the letters IRT. Thus if you are walking along Times Square (corner of 7th Avenue and 42nd Street) you will see the letters IRT at the entrance to the subway. These three letter designations are very important because at the corner of 7th Avenue and 42nd Street you will not see a sign that says "#1 Subway stops here," but rather you will only see the letters IRT. Once you are below ground in the subway station, you will see frequent reference made to "downtown" or "uptown" trains. In Manhattan, uptown is north and downtown is south. Thus to get to South Ferry from Times Square, you would take the "Downtown" subway of the IRT Broadway Local line. To save time, take the Downtown "Express," which stops only at Pennsylvania Station (the main New York train station) and Chambers Street, before reaching South Ferry. The Downtown Local subway can make up to 12 stops before you reach your destination. While you are on the platform, you can also take the opportunity to look at the number of the subway as it comes into the station. Thus when you want to go to South Ferry, look for the number 1. Also on the side of the various subways, you will see signs listing destinations; the one that is lit up will also tell you the destination of that train. Thus if you see 'South Ferry' lit up, you know this is your subway. And while we are discussing Times Square as a departure point, also be alerted to the fact that there is a subway that very frequently shuttles back and forth between Times Square and Grand Central Station. Across the street from the Grand Central Station you will find the New York City Visitors Information Center.

UPTOWN MANHATTAN

One of the dominant features of Uptown Manhattan is Central Park which extends from 59th to 110th Streets between 5th Avenue and Central Park West. Besides containing walkways, wooded and landscaped grounds, it has a zoo and the Delacorte Theater where you can watch Shakesperian plays during the summer free.

The Lincoln Center for the Performing Arts is at Broadway and 64th Streets. In this complex you will find the Metropolitan Opera House, the New York State Theater and Philharmonic Hall, among others. Guided tours of the whole center are given between 10 a.m. and 4p.m. daily ($1.85, students ($1.25). Number 1 subway (take Uptown direction) will speed you to the 66th Street station from Times Square.

If you want to visit five museums located close together, take the #1 subway to 157th Street. The Washington Heights Museum Group at Broadway and 155th Street houses the excellent Museum of the American Indian—which contains just about the largest collection of Indian art and examples of Indian culture in North, Central and South America. The admission is free. Hours are Tuesday-Sunday 1-5p.m. The musuem is closed on legal holidays and also during August. Other museums here include those of the American Numismatic Society (coins), American Geographical Society (maps), Hispanic Society of America (arts from Spain and Portugal) and the American Academy of Arts and Letters.

One of our favorite museums includes the American Museum of Natural History at 79th Street and Central Park West. Is is open Monday-Saturday 10 a.m.-5 p.m., Sunday and holidays 1-5 p.m. It is closed Thanksgiving and Christmas. Take the #1 subway to the 79th Street Station (take the local Uptown subway from Times Square.)

The Metropolitan Museum of Art (82nd Street and Fifth Avenue) is open Tuesday 10 a.m.-9 p.m., Wednesday-Saturday 10 a.m.-5 p.m., Sunday and holidays 11 a.m.-5 p.m. Take the #6 subway (IRT) to 86th Street. The Guggenheim Museum at Fifth Avenue and 89th Street (modern painting and sculpture) is open Wednesday-Saturday 10 a.m.-6 p.m., Tuesday 10 a.m.-9 p.m., Sunday and holidays noon-6 p.m. The museum is closed July 4th and Christmas, as well as Mondays. ($1.00, students 50¢) Use the same subway stop as the Metropolitan Museum of Modern Art. The Museum of the City of New York at Fifth Avenue and 104th Street shows the development of New York City, from its founding to the present. This museum is open Tuesday-Saturday 10 a.m.-5 p.m. and Sundays and holidays 1-5 p.m. (Free admission) Take the #6 subway to 103rd Street.

LOWER MANHATTAN

Since Manhattan contains many of the New York attractions, let us point out a few things you can visit in the lower part of Manhattan (the southern section) or Downtown Manhattan, as it is commonly called.

We have already discussed how to reach the Statue of Liberty and the Staten Island Ferry — two sights you should not miss. Remember you have to take the subway to the South Ferry station.

After you get off the subway at the South Ferry station, you have a choice of following the arrow to the Staten Island Ferry or the departure point for the short boat trip to the Statue of Liberty. First you will find the ferry terminal a place with several snack bars. You have to pay 25¢ to board the ferry to Staten Island.

60 NEW YORK

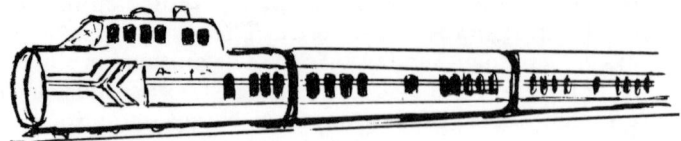

Besides taking the Staten Island Ferry you can visit the Statue of Libery, presented to the United States of America by France in 1886. At the Statue's base is the new American Musuem of Immigration. You get to the Statue of Liberty by boat ($1.25), just a little distance from the South Ferry subway station.

Another place you might visit is the World Trade Center, its 110 floors making it slightly taller than the Empire State Building. Fulton Street is your World Trade Center subway stop. Also on the #1 subway you have the opportunity to visit the Stock Exchanges — your subway stop is Rector Street. Both the New York Stock Exchange and the American Stock Exchange offer free tours on business days.

Another place you will just have the visit in Downtown Manhattan is Greenwich Village. You will find wonderful boutiques, coffeehouses and restaurants, art shows and night clubs here. Also one of the oldest theaters in New York, the Cherry Lane Theatre, gives you 'off-Broadway' productions. And if you are looking for untried ideas in theater works and want to listen to the latest sounds, visit the East Village. Your subway stop on the #1 subway for the Greenwich Village area is Christopher Street.

In Chinatown, just west of Chatham Square, you will have the opportunity to taste excellent Chinese food at reasonable prices. It's a great place to stroll around. From Times Square you have a number of subways which go close to Chinatown. For example subway N, BMT designation, quickly will take you to Canal Street, your stop. Remember you are still going in the 'Downtown Manhattan' direction from Times Square.

MIDTOWN MANHATTAN

Here in Midtown Manhattan you will find all your transportation terminals—the East Side Airlines Terminal (New York airport bus departures/arrivals), Pennsylvania Station and Grand Central Terminal, rail stations catering not only to inter-city travelers but also to the thousands of commuters who daily venture into the city from the far away surburbs. The Port Authority Bus Terminal, with its three floors, also caters to the inter-city travelers and to the hundreds of buses which link New York to nearby communities such as Newark, New Jersey, or Stamford, Connecticut.

The United Nations Headquarters, Fifth Avenue, the Empire State Building, Rockefeller Center, the Museum of Modern Art, Times Square, Broadway, and Carnegie Hall, among other attractions are in this area. However, perhaps of immediate importance to the traveler is that you will find the Information Center of the New York Convention and Visitors Bureau located at 90 East 42nd Street, just across the street from the Grand Central Terminal. (Buses from the airport stop here before reaching the East Side Airlines Terminal). Hours at the Information Center are 9 a.m. to 6 p.m. daily. Another excellent source of information and maps is the Times Square Information Center at 43rd Street (at Times Square). Hours here are Monday-Friday 10 a.m.-8 p.m., and 10 a.m.-6 p.m. on Saturdays and Sundays. We must point out to you that at both places you can obtain discount tickets for many off-Broadway and Broadway shows. The tickets which you pick up here allow you to purchase two regular tickets for the price of one. You will find on the special tickets the name of the show, the regular price for the show and how much it will cost with the special ticket and the box office hours for turning in the special ticket for two regular ones. Keep in mind that for some shows you cannot get these special tickets and that they might not be available during peak evenings, such as Friday nights. Anyway, look the selection of tickets over and take the ones that interest you.

The Empire State Building, built in 1931, is located at Fifth Avenue and 34th Street. #6 subway takes you there. Get off at 33rd Street. It is open 9:30 a.m. to midnight except the 24th of December. Cost is $1.66. For a magnificent view, go up at night (check the weather first).

The United Nations Building area is from First Avenue to the East River and from 42nd Street to 48th Street. The Grand Central Terminal is as close as you will get by subway. Buses along 42nd Street will get you within a block or so of the beautiful Secretariat Building. The visitors' entrance is at First Avenue and 45th Street. One hour guided tours are given between 9:15 a.m. and 4:45 p.m. ($2.00, 75¢ for students).

62 NEW YORK

Queensboro Bridge
EAST RIVER
Queens-Midtown Tunnel

1st Ave
2nd Ave
E. 59th St.
E. 57th St.
3rd Ave.
26.
E. 34th St.
Lexington Ave.
Park Ave.
12.
Madison Ave.
6,7
5th Ave. 13.
18.
14.
24. 23. 5.
10. 25.
9.
21.
1.
3. CENTRAL PARK
(6th Ave.)
Ave. of the Americas
Broadway
7th Ave
2.
19. 9.
4.
27.
8,15
8th Ave
17.
22.
11.
W. 66 St.
16.
W. 59th St.
W. 57th St.
9th Ave.
10th Ave.
W. 42nd St.
W. 34th St.
11th Ave.

MAIN ATTRACTIONS
HUDSON RIVER
Lincoln Tunnel

SOME NEW YORK CITY SIGHTS

Our map of Midtown Manhattan is keyed to a number of attractions. Empire State Building 1, Times Square 2, Central Park 3, Madison Square Garden 4 and the Museum of Modern Art 5. Number 6, Metropolitan Museum of Art, 7 Guggenheim Museum, 8 American Museum of Natural History and 15 Hayden Planetarium, are just off the map, as is number 11, Greenwich Village. Number 9 Rockfeller Center, 10 Radio City Music Hall, 12 New York Convention and Visitor's Bureau, where you can get information about the city. Number 13 is St. Patrick's Cathedral, 14 Central Park Zoo, 16 Lincoln Center, 17 Coliseum, 18 Fifth Avenue Shopping Area, 19 Theatre District, 20 United Nations Building, 21 New York Public Library, 22 Gallery of Modern Art, 23 Whitney Museum of American Art, 24 C.B.S. Center, 25 N.B.C. TV Studios, 26 East Side Terminal (bus from Kennedy Airport) and 27, Pennsylvania Station.

Y ACCOMMODATIONS IN NEW YORK CITY

William Sloane House YMCA—Men and Women; 356 West 34th St.; (212) 695-5000; Single $8; telephone reservations accepted;

Vanderbilt YMCA—Men only (Women upon special arrangement); 224 E. 47th St. (212) 755-2410; Single $9; Bus #27.

West Side YMCA—Men as well as Women who are full time New York students; 5 West 63rd Street; (212) 787-4400; Single $9.75; 5 minutes by 8th Ave. subway or bus #104 from 41st Street terminal.

McBurney YMCA—Men only; 215 West 23rd Street; (212) 243-1982; Single $6.75; 6th, 7th, 8th Ave. Bus.

Flushing YMCA—Men only; 138-46 Northern Blvd., Flushing, N.Y. 11354; (212) 354-7100; Single $10.25; Flushing Line Subway.

Central Queens YMCA—Men only; 89-25 Parsons Blvd., Jamaica, N.Y. 11432; (212) 739-6600; Single $7.50; Subway 20 minutes.

Yonkers YWCA—Women only; 87 So. Broadway, Yonkers, N.Y. 10701; (914) 963-0640; Single $8; Broadway subway to last stop then Bus #1 or #2.

Greenpoint YMCA—Men only; 99 Meserole Ave., Brooklyn, N.Y. 11222; (212) 389-3700; Single $6.50; One block from Independent Subway line.

Prospect Park/Bay Bridge YMCA—Men only; 357

Ninth Street, Brooklyn, N.Y. 11215; (212) 508-7100; Single $7; IND or BMT subway.

YWCA, The Residence, Women only, 135 East 52nd St., New York, N.Y. 10022, (212)753-4700; single rooms from $8 and double rooms from $14.

GRAY LINE TOURS

Gray Line operates a great number of tours to help you discover New York City. These include the "Lower New York and Chinatown," "Upper New York and Harlem," and the "Hyde Park, West Point, Vanderbilt Mansion and Bear Mountain" tours. There are also "Evening in New York" and "Night Club" tours. For further information call 765-1600.

ROCHESTER, NEW YORK

Rochester is a thriving city in upstate New York, close to Lake Ontario. It is an ideal place from which to visit Niagara Falls, since Rochester is only about 80 miles away. On the other hand, Rochester is over 300 miles from New York City, to the south.

The first place you should try to visit is the Rochester Convention Bureau, War Memorial, in the heart of the city. Telephone 546-3070. By all means try to take a guided tour of the Eastman Kodak Company manufacturing facilities. They are conducted daily except weekend and holidays. Tours are available at the Kodak Park Division, which at 200 Ridge Road West manufactures films paper and chemicals. Tours at 9:30 a.m. and at 1:30 p.m. Bus #1 will get you there.

Bus #17 takes you to the International Museum of Photography at 900 East Avenue. Former home of George Eastman, dedicated as a Museum in 1949. Now an outstanding museum devoted to the art and technology of photography and cinematography. Frequently changed exhibits, old and new cameras and photographs. Open daily, 10 a.m.-5 p.m., except Mondays and Christmas day. For last minute film schedules call 271-4090.

The Memorial Art Gallery is at 490 University Avenue near Goodman St. Contains extensive collection of all important periods of art—old masters and contemporary paintings, sculptures, prints, and decorative arts. Presents an active program of loan exhibitions, lectures, films, day and evening classes for children and adults.

Admission 50c for adults. Open Sunday 1-5 p.m., Tuesday 10 a.m.-9 p.m., Wednesday-Saturday 10 a.m.-5 p.m. Bus 4. The Susan B. Anthony House is at 17 Madison Street. Residence of the famous suffrage leader from 1866 to 1906. Open Wednesday thru Saturday 11 a.m.-4 p.m. Other times by appointment. (235-0816). Buses 2, 4, 8, 12.

BUFFALO—Niagara Falls Gateway

Buffalo, where the Niagara River flows into Lake Erie, itself is a very large city. With over one million inhabitants it is New York State's second largest city. You might want to visit the Albright-Knox Art Gallery at 1285 Elmwood—open 10 a.m.-5 p.m. Tuesday through Saturday and 12-5 Sundays. 'Main Place,' a mall in the heart of Buffalo is a good place for shopping. Then there is the Buffalo and Erie County Historical Museum as well as the Wilcox Mansion, where Theodore Roosevelt was inaugurated in 1901 as the 26th President of the United States following the assassination of President McKinley. For information about city buses call 884-6800.

Buffalo, in the western part of New York State, is about 436 miles away from New York City. Buffalo is an ideal gateway to the nearby fabulous Niagara Falls as well as Canada. The train station here is located several miles from the city center. However, once you walk up to the concourse from the tracks you will find that taxi service as well as bus service is available to the city from directly outside the station. The bus fare to town is forty cents. On the other hand, to get to the train station from downtown Buffalo take bus #17 from the corner of Main and Court Streets.

If you want to continue your trip to Canada by rail, Canadian Pacific has a connection from Buffalo at 5:25 p.m. to Fort Erie, Ontario, Welland, Hamilton, and arriving in Toronto at 8:35 p.m. Remember that this late afternoon Buffalo departure connects with a 8:30 a.m. New York City departure which arrives in Buffalo at 5 p.m. The equipment utilized for the Buffalo to Toronto trip is a comfortable and air conditioned Rail Diesel Car.

NIAGARA FALLS

One of the first places you might want to visit in Niagara Falls is the Niagara Falls Area Chamber of Commerce at 45 Falls Street. The personnel here can give you additional information about the area. Prospect Point is an ideal place to view the American Falls. The Niagara Viewmobile (a "train" on rubber wheels) is an easy way to get around the Niagara Reservation, including Prospect Park and Goat Island.

Probably one of the most exciting experiences you will have on your discovery of the U.S.A. and Canada is a half hour tour on the 'Maid of the Mist' boat below the falls. Boats usually operate from mid-May to mid-October. During July and August and up to Labor Day, tours run from 9:15 a.m. until 8 p.m.. Other days boat tours start, from either side of the falls, at 10 a.m. and continue until 5 on weekdays and 6 on weekends. For further information, call 284-4233 in Niagara Falls, New York or 358-5412 in Niagara Falls, Ontario. And if you are interested in ceramics, visit the Carborundum Museum of Ceramics at Third and Niagara Streets, just four blocks from the falls. Open Tuesday-Saturday 10-5, Wednesday evening 6-9, Sunday 1-8. The museum is closed on Mondays.

Just 20 minutes from Niagara Falls is Old Fort Niagara, the only "French Castle" in America. In 1796, after both the French and the British had control of the fort, the American flag was first raised here. During the War of 1812, America lost control of the fort for a time. With almost 300 years of history under three flags, Fort Niagara provides an excellent opportunity to learn about America's heritage.

PHILADELPHIA, PENNSYLVANIA

Philadelphia, the metropolitan city between the Delaware and Schuylkill Rivers, played a major role in the development of the United States. On July 4, 1776 the Declaration of Independence was signed here. The Con-

PHILADELPHIA 67

stitution was also drafted here in 1787. It is no wonder that Philadelphia became the capital of the early United States of America. Therefore Philadelphia has a lot to offer from an historical as well as a contemporary point of view.

The first place you should visit after your arrival in Philadelphia is the Tourist Center at 16th and Kennedy Blvd. You will easily recognize the round building of the Tourist Center, which is in the area of City Hall and the modern Penn Center complex (William Penn was the founder of the city back in the 17th century). At the tourist center you will be able to get a variety of information including programs of cultural events and city maps. We suggest while you are here you pick up three brochures—all free. They are a 'Visitors Guide Map of Central Philadelphia,' 'Cultural Loop Bus' and 'The Liberty Walk through Historic Old Philadelphia.' If you are here on

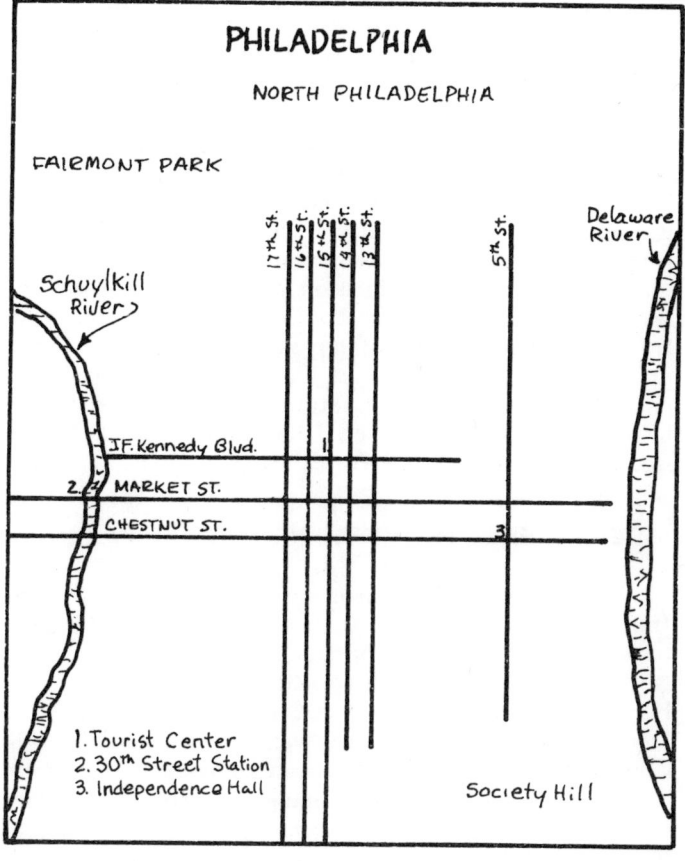

68 PHILADELPHIA

Sundays you might pick up 'The Philadelphia Flea Market.' And if you plan to spend a lot of time riding buses, subways or the elevated train, pick up the SEPTA Street and Transit Map of Philadelphia for 25¢. For transit information call 329-4800. For tourist information call Tourist Center at 561-1200, from 9-5, except Christmas.

CULTURAL LOOP BUS

One of the best ways to see the historic sights as well as the cultural attractions of Philadelphia at your own pace is to take the Cultural Loop Bus. This bus operated by SEPTA (the Southeastern Pennsylvania Transportation Authority) travels back and forth every 20 minutes between 10 attractions in Philadelphia on a daily basis between 9:30 a.m. and 5:30 p.m. from the end of April to October, on weekends during the rest of the year. The cost is only 50¢ and you can re-board the bus as many times as you want to. Here are some of the places the Cultural Loop Bus enables you to visit: Independence Hall (and the Liberty Bell), City Hall, the Pennsylvania Academy of Fine Arts, the Tourist Center, the Free Library of Philadelphia, the Academy of Natural Sciences, the Franklin Institute and Fels Planetarium (Science and Technology), the Rodin Museum (The 'Thinker'), the Philadelphia Zoo. Also, if you show your Culture Loop Bus ticket at the various attractions you receive a substantial reduction on the admission price. Thus whereas the regular admission to the Rodin Museum is 50¢, your Loop Bus discount admission price is only 35¢. Of course, places such as Independence Hall are free to everyone. Also keep in mind that 'A Nation is Born,' a presentation in sound and lights, is given Tuesday-Saturday at 9 p.m. free at the Independence Hall during summer.

INDEPENDENCE NATIONAL HISTORICAL PARK

Although the Cultural Loop Bus makes a stop in the Independence National Historical Park, it is used mainly to explore the attraction outside the area.

The center of the historical park is Independence Hall where, as we have previously mentioned, the Declaration of Independence was adopted and the U.S. Constitution was written. You can almost hear Benjamin Franklin saying "We must all hang together, or surely we shall all hang separately." Located at 5th and Chestnut Streets, it is open daily 9-5 and in July and August 8-8;

Carpenters' Hall was the meeting place of the First Continental Congress in 1774. You can still view the original chairs at this 320 Chestnut Street address. Open daily 10-4. At 6th and Chestnut Streets you can visit Congress Hall, where Congress met between 1790-1800. This is where President Washington delivered his last message before retiring. Open daily, April-October from 9 a.m.-8 p.m. From November to March open 9-5.

Christ Church, built between 1727 and 1744, where Benjamin Franklin and other leaders worshipped, is at 2nd and Market Streets. Franklin is buried at 5th and Arch Streets. And while you are in the area, you might want to stop off at the Todd House, built in 1775, home of the future Dolley Madison. The house is at 4th and Walnut—open daily from 11 a.m.-noon and 1 p.m.-3 p.m. At 239 Arch Street you will find the Betsy Ross House where Betsy Ross lived and where she made the first United States Flag. Open daily from 9:30 a.m. to 5:15 p.m. The Atwater Kent Museum gives you information about Philadelphia history. It is located at 15 S. 7th Street, open daily from 8:30 a.m. to 4:30 p.m. Adjacent to Independence Park is the 18th century residential section known as Society Hill. The area has been extensively renovated. Stroll through the streets and enjoy the architecture and the atmosphere. And if you want to see the rooming house where Jefferson drafted the Declaration of Independence, visit the restored Graff House.

PHILADELPHIA TRAIN STATION

The main Amtrak station in Philadelphia is at 30th and Market Streets, next to the Schuylkill River, in the western section of the downtown area. This 30th Street station is your inter-city train departure point for travel along the East Coast. Trains to and from Chicago leave/arrive at the North Philadelphia station, several miles to the north of the 30th Street Station.

The 30th Street Station is a huge place. Probably a good way to orient yourself is to look at the track number posted in the main hall of the station. Around track 1 you will be on the Schuylkill River side of the station while the exit around track 10 leads to cabs and 30th Street. A train information office is located in the middle of the hall.

We will now point out some of the important facilities you will find in the 30th Street Station. Near track 1 you will find the helpful Travelers Aid Office. Hours are M-F 8:45 a.m.-9 p.m. and on Saturdays 10 a.m. to 6 p.m. In this area you will also find the baggage office which is

70 PHILADELPHIA

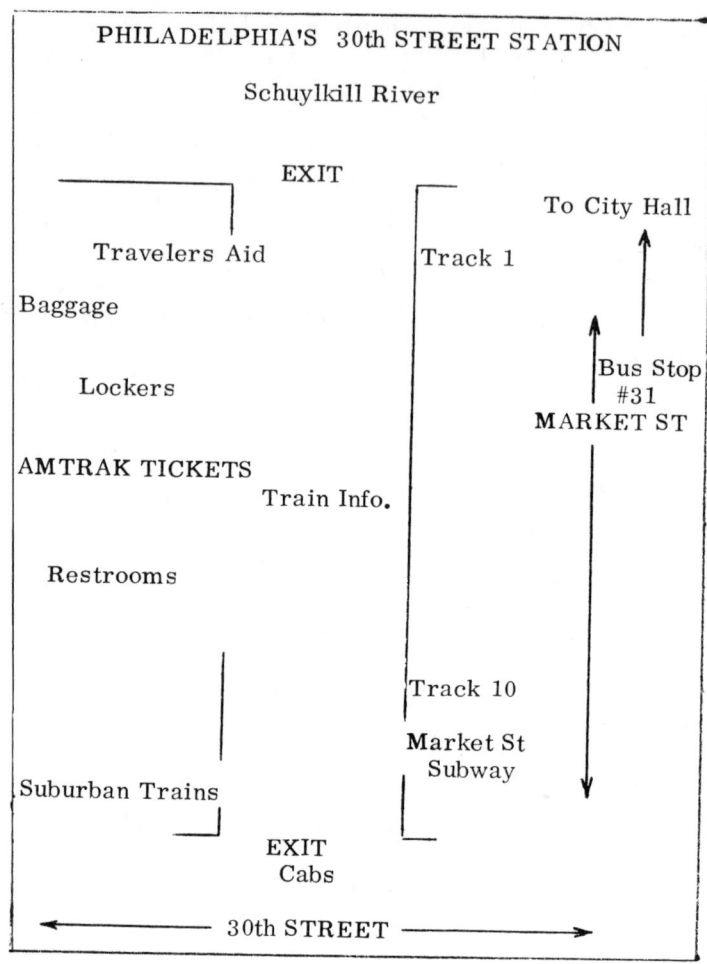

open 7:30 a.m. to 9 p.m., and a number of coin operated lockers. The Amtrak Ticket Counter as well as several rental car company counters are located near the center of the arrival/departure hall. Further along near track 10 is the hall that leads to the suburban train departure points. You might note that on the opposite side of the main hall is the entrance to the Market Street Subway. Because it is quite a walk to reach the subway, we suggest that if you have a lot of bags you take bus # 31 to City Hall or the Tourist Center at 16th and Kennedy Blvd. Bus or subway costs 35¢—have the exact change. Bus number 42 on Chestnut Street, (one block south of Market Street) takes you directly to the Independence National Historical Park, including Independence Hall and the famous Liberty Bell.

Y ACCOMMODATIONS IN PHILADELPHIA

The Central Branch of the YMCA at 1421 Arch Street, just one block from the Tourist Information Office, accepts both men and women. To make your reservation for the low cost accommodations call (215) 569-1400 and ask for extension 261. The Y is centrally located to all the sights since the Cultural Loop Bus stops nearby.

The West Branch YMCA, men only, at 5151 Sansom Street, can be reached by the Market Street Subway. Telephone (215) 476-2700, $18 per week.

GRAY LINE TOURS

Gray Line provides tours of the city and perhaps more significant to historic areas outside of Philadelphia. You can visit Valley Forge, the Pennsylvania Dutch Country or Hershey, "Chocolatetown U.S.A." For example, the tour to Valley Forge takes 3-1/2 hours and costs $10. For further information call 569-3666.

BALTIMORE, MARYLAND

Between Philadelphia and Washington, D.C., is Baltimore, the country's seventh largest city. Located in the "Free State," the state in which a civil regime for the first time legislated freedom of religion.

There are a great number of sights in Baltimore. The Maryland Historical Society at 201 W. Monument Street includes a number of historical displays, including the original transcript of the 'Star-Spangled Banner.' The Baltimore and Ohio Railroad has an interesting Transportation Museum, which includes the 'Tom Thumb.' It is located at the Nation's first railroad station, the Mount Clare Station on Pratt Street. The U.S. Frigate Constellation, the country's oldest warship, launched in 1797, is also docked in Baltimore. At Mt. Vernon Place is one of the oldest monuments to George Washington, completed half a century before the Washington Monument in Washington, D.C.

Ft. McHenry, the fort which resisted bombardment by the British for over a day and a night, guards the Baltimore harbor, as it did during the War of 1812. Francis Scott Key, a lawyer from Georgetown (later United States attorney for the District of Columbia) witnessed the barrage. When in the early hours of September 14, 1814

72 NATIONAL ANTHEM

he saw the American flag still fluttering in the wind, the sight inspired him to write the words of the Star-Spangled Banner—adopted in 1931 as our National Anthem. We include the words for your reference.

THE STAR-SPANGLED BANNER

O say! can you see, by the dawn's early light,
What so proudly we hail'd at the twilight's last gleaming,
Whose broad stripes and bright stars, thro' the perilous fight,
O'er the ramparts we watch'd were so gallantly streaming?
And the rockets' red glare, the bombs bursting in air,
Gave proof thro' the night that our flag was still there.
O, say, does that Star-Spangled Banner yet wave
O'er the land of the free and the home of the brave?

On the shore, dimly seen thro' the mists of the deep,
Where the foe's haughty host in dread silence reposes,
What is that which the breeze, o'er the towering steep,
As it fitfully blows, half conceals, half discloses?
Now it catches the gleam of the morning's first beam,
In full glory reflected now shines on the stream;
'Tis the Star-Spangled Banner, O long may it wave
O'er the land of the free and the home of the brave.

O thus be it ever when free man shall stand
Between their loved homes and the war's desolation!
Blest with vict'ry and peace, may the heav'n-rescued land
Praise the Pow'r that hath made and preserved us a nation.
Then conquer we must, for our cause it is just,
And this be our motto: "In God is our trust."
And the Star-Spangled Banner in triumph shall wave
O'er the land of the free and the home of the brave.

THE BICENTENNIAL IS USHERED IN

On July 4, 1975, our 199th Birthday, about 75,000 people arrived at Ft. McHenry at dawn to witness the re-enactment of the bombardment in 1814. Later in the day, the President spoke at the historic site and said "our third century should be an era of freedom." Furthermore he stated, "Let us resolve that this shall be an era of hope rather than despair. Let us resolve that it shall be an era of achievement rather than apathy. Let us resolve that it shall be a time of promise rather than regret."

ANNAPOLIS, MARYLAND

To the east of Washington, D.C., just 50 minutes away by Greyhound bus, is Annapolis, the capital of Maryland. For a 10-month period, Annapolis served as the capital of the United States. The "Old Towne" area contains many historic homes.

The Maryland State Capitol, completed in 1779, is the oldest capitol building still in use in the country. In fact, it is the only state capitol in which the U.S. Congress was ever convened. In 1783, General George Washington resigned his commission as Commander-in-Chief of the Continental Army before Congress in the Old Senate Chamber. On January 14, 1784, The American Revolution officially ended when Congress ratified the Treaty of Paris. The United States of America became a sovereign Nation.

WASHINGTON, D.C.

When our Nation was born in 1776, Washington, D.C. as we know it today, did not exist. Georgetown and Alexandria were the dominant towns at that time. George Washington chose the site of the city as well as the location of the Capitol and the White House in 1790. The location of the city was chosen since it was midway between North and South. Maryland donated 69.25 square miles and Virginia 30.75 for the District of Columbia, or "D.C." In 1848, Washington, D.C. returned Virginia's land, then largely undeveloped. Today this area is made up of Arlington County and the City of Alexandria. Washington, D.C. became the capital of the United States in 1800.

Washington D.C. is divided into 4 sections, Northwest, Northeast, Southeast and Southwest. The streets that run north and south are numbered (such as 17th Street) and the east-west streets are named after letters, such as K Street. Therefore you will find us stating the Douglass House is at 14th and W Streets S.E., (Southeast). Many other attractions are in the Northwest section of the city, the largest.

The Bicentennial period will be an exciting time for the city. The National Visitor Center, within a few minutes of the Capitol, serves in 1976 as a central location to get an introduction to the city. For example, you will see a 28 minute color film "City Out of Wilderness: Washington." At the Capitol, when the British Parliament approves, you will see the Magna Carta, the charter of English liberties granted by King John at Runnymede on the Thames in 1215. The Declaration of Independence draws on the philosophy put forth in the Magna Carta. The new home of the National Air and Space Museum, next to the new Hirshhorn Museum, will be open. The 'Sound and Light' shows at various national shrines will add to the drama of visiting places of historical significance. Of course, on July 4, the biggest fireworks ever will take place on the Mall—the green area that stretches between the Capitol and the Lincoln Memorial. And starting in June of 1976 a 12-minute Kodak-produced film will be shown on George Washington and the city continuously in a 300-seat auditorium near the Washington Monument. These and other events and presentations will make your Bicentennial visit to the Nation's Capital even more rewarding. Many of the tours are free. For example, at the Capitol you can take a free guided tour daily at frequent intervals between 9 a.m. and 3:45 p.m. Keep in mind that the President does not have an office here. Rather, the Capitol is the home of the Legislative Branch of government. The Supreme Court, the Judicial Branch, is located practically across the street from the Capitol. The third branch of government, the Executive Branch, is of course headed by the President who lives at 1600 Pennsylvania Avenue, N.W., the White House.

FINDING OUT ABOUT EVENTS

Because there are so many things usually going on in Washington D.C., you might want to look in the two daily newspapers before you plan your activities or check on latest changes. The morning newspaper, 'The Washington Post,' has a weekday column in the front section of the paper entitled, 'Activities in Congress Today.' Besides giving you the subject of various committee meetings, it also lists the times and whether or not the hearings are open to the public. The Friday edition has a section called 'Style Calendar'—a calendar of events in the week ahead. The afternoon 'Washington Star' has a column in the back section of the paper called 'Tomorrow in Washington.' This information can help you plan some of your activities the next day since it lists a variety of events taking place.

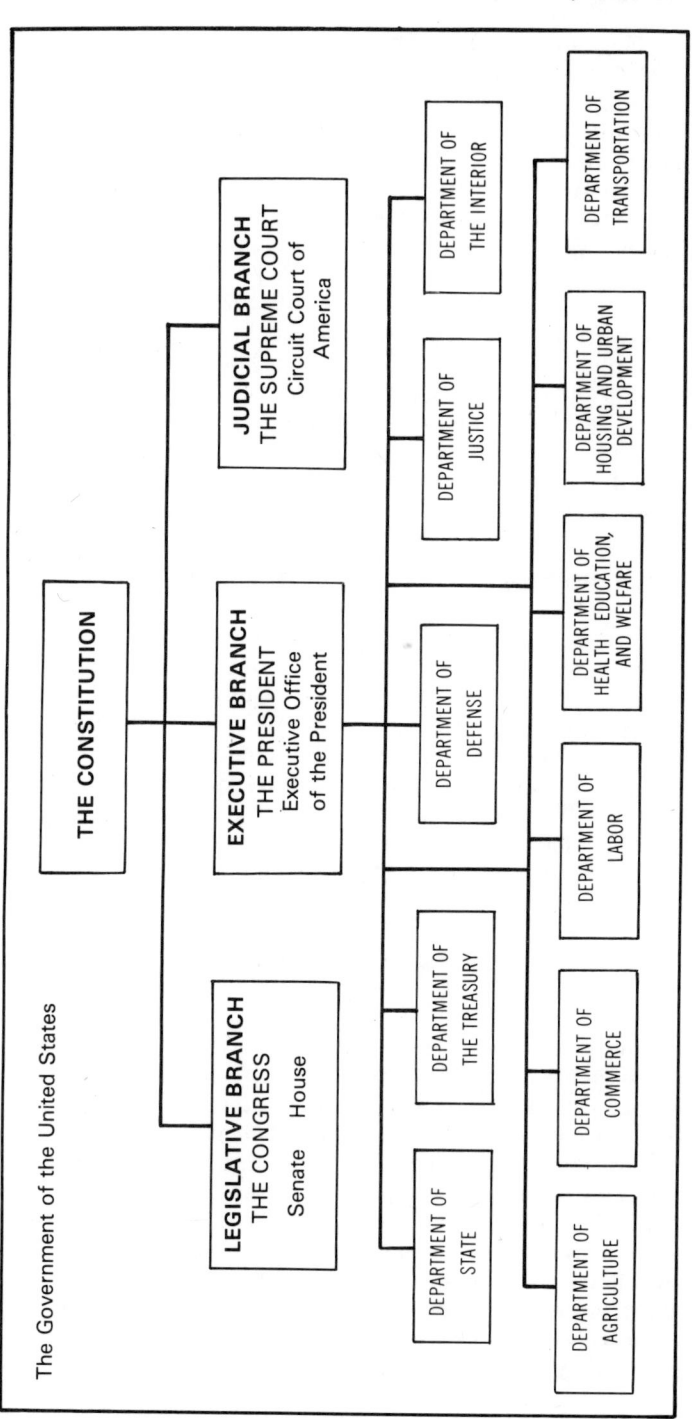

WASHINGTON, D.C.

Here are some telephone numbers which you might keep in mind while in Washington D.C. For emergencies dial 911. For daily events in Washington, D.C. dial 737-8866. Information of special events at the Smithsonian, dial 737-8811. The Box Office number of the John F. Kennedy Center for the Performing Arts is 254-3600.

An extremely worthwhile place to visit for information is the Washington Area Convention and Visitors Bureau at 1129 20th Street N.W. (659-6400), second floor. This friendly and helpful place is open Monday-Friday from 9-5. They have a great deal of literature available. Here are some of the ones, among many others, you can obtain free of charge. 'Where to Stay', 'Do You Know' (a handy calendar of events put out by the D.C. Department of Recreation), 'This Week', and a map of the city. Metrobus #L-4 takes you there. And, of course, the National Visitor Center, near the Capitol, is a prime orientation place for the Bicentennial period.

THE J. EDGAR HOOVER BUILDING

On September 30, 1975, the FBI's new headquarters building was dedicated by the President. The building is located very close to Washington's Union Station at 10th Street and Pennsylvania Ave., N.W. The one hour and forty-five minute guided tour of the complex will acquaint you with the history of the FBI and its fight against crime. You will be amazed at the advanced technology being utilized. The tour also includes a visit to the firearms range where you watch FBI agents practice their shooting skills.

THE TOURMOBILE

There are a number of ways to see the sights in Washington. However, if you are interested in seeing the monuments between the Capitol and the Lincoln Memorial, as well as visiting Arlington Cemetery across the Potomac River in Virginia, then we highly recommend that you take the Tourmobile, a motorized train. The Tourmobile follows a defined route, stopping at most of the important buildings and tourist attractions. You can get off whenever you want and reboard when you have completed your sightseeing in a particular area. It is a great way to be independent, save a lot of walking, and get a guided tour of the city. Every tourmobile has a narrator who tells you all about the many points of interest as you pass them.

WASHINGTON, D.C. 77

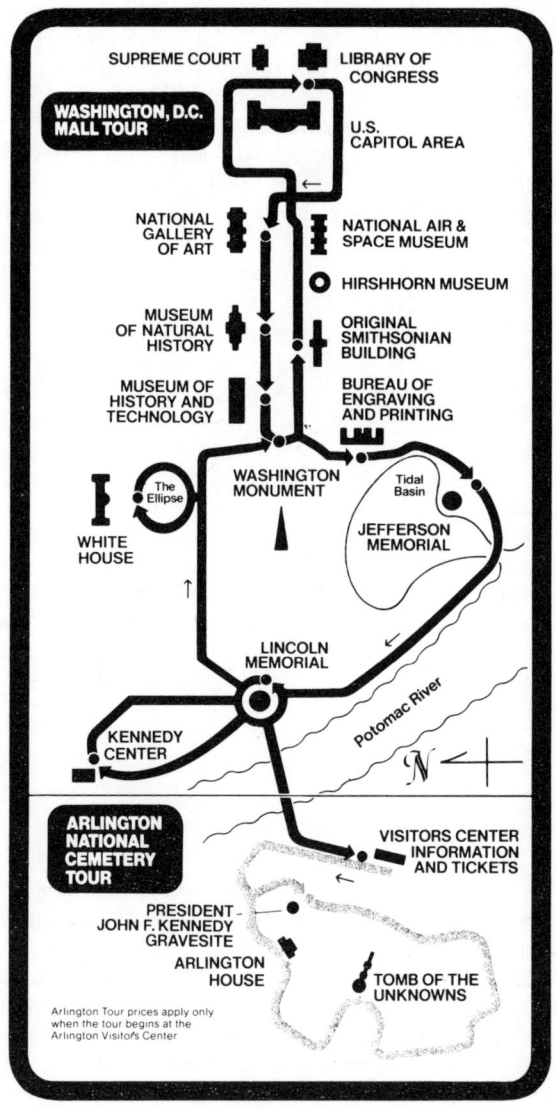

The Tourmobile stops at the Capitol, only a short walk away from a free guided tour of both Houses of Congress, Library of Congress and the Supreme Court. Other stops include the National Gallery of Art, the Museum of Natural History, the Museum of History and Technology, the Bureau of Engraving and Printing (where all the money is printed), the Jefferson Memorial, the Lincoln Memorial, the White House, Kennedy Center, the National Visitor Center (in 1976), the Washington Monu-

78 WASHINGTON, D.C.

ment, the Smithsonian Institution Building, and the Arlington National Cemetery Visitors' Center. Here you can transfer to another Tourmobile (an additional charge) which takes you from the Visitors' Center to President Kennedy's Gravesite, the Tomb of the Unknown Soldier, and the Custis-Lee Mansion (do not forget to visit the mansion—it is well preserved inside and from the outside you have a beautiful panoramic view of Washington, D.C.).

The Washington, D.C. Tourmobile operates daily except Christmas from 9:00 a.m.-6:30 p.m. between June 15th and the 1st of September and 9:30 a.m.-4:30 p.m. the remainder of the year. The last complete tour starts one hour prior to closing. The Arlington National Cemetery Tour, on the other hand, operates every day 8:00 a.m.-7:00 p.m. (April-October) or 8:00 a.m.-5:00 p.m. (November-March). Keep in mind that there are two distinct Tourmobile routes—the Washington, D.C. one and the Arlington Cemetery one. The Washington, D.C. Mall tour costs $2.50 while the Arlington Cemetery one costs $1.25. The combination Tourmobile ticket, including both the Washington, D.C. and the Arlington Cemetery tours costs $3.50. The Tourmobile Route map is reproduced with permission of Landmark Services who run the sightseeing service.

THE WASHINGTON MONUMENT

On July 4, 1848, the cornerstone of the Washington Monument was laid. For almost 25 years the monument to the Nation's first President stood incomplete at a height of about 150 feet. You can still see the different shades on the sides of the monument. The completed monument was opened to the public on October 9, 1888. To reach the top, and get an excellent panoramic view of the city, you take an elevator. During the summer, the monument is open at night.

Here are some statistics on the monument: Total cost: $1,187,710; Height of monument above floor: 555 feet 5-1/8 inches; Width at base of shaft: 55 feet 1-1/2 inches; Width at top of shaft: 34 feet 5-1/2 inches; Thickness of walls at base of shaft: 15 feet; Thickness of walls at top of shaft: 18 inches; Depth of foundation: 36 feet 10 inches; Weight of monument: 90,854 tons; Sway of monument in 30-mile-per-hour wind: 0.125 of an inch.

THE WHITE HOUSE

The White House on Pennsylvania Avenue is the home of the President of the United States. The President heads the Executive Branch of Government. The Legislative Branch is centered at the Capitol while the home of the Judicial Branch is at the Supreme Court.

The cornerstone of the White House was laid October 13, 1792, on a site selected by President George Washington. Washington never occupied the White House. Rather, John Adams, the second President of the United States, moved in November, 1800. It was Thomas Jefferson, the third President of the U.S. who started the practice of opening the White House each morning to all visitors—a tradition still carried on today and unrivaled anywhere.

On August 12, 1814, British forces captured Washington, D.C. and burned the White House in retaliation for the destruction by American troops of some public buildings in Canada. President James Monroe moved into the restored White House in September, 1817. Major renovation took place between 1948 and 1952. There are about 132 rooms, approximately half of which are used as living quarters.

THE LINCOLN MEMORIAL

The memorial, located near the Potomac River, the Kennedy Center, Watergate and the State Department, honors Abraham Lincoln, the 16th President of the United States. By all means take the opportunity to visit the Lincoln Memorial (closes at midnight). If you have an opportunity to visit the Memorial during evening hours, the view of the Capitol, the Washington Monument, the Custis-Lee Mansion and the Eternal Flame in Arlington Cemetery are even more striking. And if you are wondering about the great amount of noise from passing airplanes, keep in mind that the Potomac River is used as an approach path for landing at nearby National Airport.

80 WASHINGTON, D.C.

As you walk up the steps of the Lincoln Memorial you will see a seated President Lincoln, 19 feet tall from head to foot (if he were standing he would be 28 feet tall). To the left of the statue (on the south wall) see the famous Gettysburg Address. The writing on the north wall is President Lincoln's Second Inaugural Address. After many false starts, the Memorial was dedicated in 1922— its 36 columns represent the 36 states that made up the Union at the time of his untimely death in 1865.

THE JEFFERSON MEMORIAL

One of the most picturesque areas in the Nation's capital is the location of the Jefferson Memorial, next to the Tidal Basin. It is this part of the city which is the focal point for the visitor during the first week in April when the 650 cherry trees, a gift of the city of Tokyo in 1912, are in full bloom.

The cornerstone of the Jefferson Memorial was laid on November 15, 1939 and it was dedicated on April 13, 1943. Throughout this guide, you will find references to Thomas Jefferson. The location of the memorial site for this famous American dovetails with the plans envisioned by L'Enfant. On one axis is the Lincoln Memorial, the Washington Monument, and the Capitol. On the north-south axis intersecting at the Washington Monument, is the location of the White House and the Jefferson Memorial. When you visit the White House, take the opportunity to look out across the South Lawn and you will see the silhouette of Jefferson.

One of the first things you will see when you walk up the imposing memorial is the sculpture, by the sculptor Adolph A. Weirman, of Jefferson, 33 at the time, standing before the committee appointed by the Continental Congress to draft the Declaration of Independence. On the left you will see Benjamin Franklin, 70, and John Adams, 40, seated to the right are Roger Sherman of Connecticut, 55, and Robert R. Livingston of New York, 29. The significance of Jefferson's work has been echoed throughout the history of the country. Perhaps at no time was the praise more dramatic, than on July 4, 1826, the fiftieth anniversary of the signing of the Declaration of Independence. On that date, John Adams, the first Vice-President of the United States, and the Nation's second President uttered his last words "Jefferson still lives."

The inscription engraved on the interior walls of the memorial room are Jefferson's words from the Declaration of Independence, thoughts on religious freedom, his belief in education (he founded the University of Virginia), and his perception of the evolving state of government. The Jefferson Memorial is open daily to the public until midnight. There is no admission charge.

ARLINGTON NATIONAL CEMETERY

Arlington Cemetery, on the Virginia side of the Potomac River, right across from the Lincoln Memorial, is the final resting place of many who have served the Nation. That period of service stretches from the Revolutionary War, War of 1812, Mexican War, Civil War, the Indian Campaigns, Spanish-American War, Philippine Insurrection, World Wars I and II, the Korean War to Vietnam. The graves of two Presidents of the United States, William Howard Taft and John Fitzgerald Kennedy, are also located here. In front of the Custis-Lee Mansion, you will find the final resting place of Major Pierre Charles L'Enfant, the man who laid out the plans for our Nation's Capital. The flag in front of the Custis-Lee Mansion is flown at half-mast.

The land for the Arlington National Cemetery was purchased in 1778 by John Parke Custis, son of Martha Danridge Custis Washington by her first marriage. John Parke Custis joined the Continental Army and served as an aide to General Washington. After his death during the siege of Yorktown in 1781, two of his four children, George Washington Parke Custis and Eleanor, were adopted by George Washington. They lived in Mt. Vernon.

Tombs of the Unknown Soldier of World War I, the Unknown American Serviceman of World War II and the American Serviceman of the Korean War are located in the plaza of the Arlington Memorial Amphitheater.

CUSTIS-LEE MANSION

Many people rate the view from the Custis-Lee Mansion (Arlington House, the Robert E. Lee Memorial, as it is also known) in Arlington Cemetery as the most scenic in all of America. The mansion ties together some of the most important families in American History. Its builder, George Washington Parke Custis, was the adopted son of George Washington, first President of the United States.

82 WASHINGTON, D.C.

Later, Custis became the father-in-law of Robert E. Lee, who was the South's leading general during the Civil War, 1861-1865.

If you want to find out what life was like in the Nation's early years, by all means visit this wonderful home. There is no admission charge. Guided and self-guiding tours are available at no cost. The entrance is through the "Greenhouse."

THE NATIONAL ARCHIVES

One of the most interesting and important buildings in Washington, D.C. is the National Archives Building on Constitution Avenue. Here you will find the original copies of the Declaration of Independence and the Constitution. However, it was not until 1952 that those documents were transferred from the Library of Congress to the Archives. Now, each night, the documents are lowered 20 feet below the surface into a 50 ton safe.

The Archives, however, is much more than those important documents. It contains 5 million still pictures, 1.5 million maps and close to a 100,000 reels of motion picture film. Moreover, there are about 2.5 billion pieces of paper! As you can imagine, not all of these are readily available to the visitor. If you want to explore more apply for a "research card" valid for one year.

SMITHSONIAN INSTITUTION

James Smithson, a wealthy English scientist, willed over half a million dollars in 1829 to the United States "to found at Washington, under the name of the Smithsonian Institution, an establishment for the increase and diffusion of knowledge among men." Today the Smithsonian Institution is a great complex of museums and art galleries. The red castle-like building close to Independence Avenue was the original building. Most of the interesting displays, however, are located in other buildings. Your first stop should be The National Museum of History and Technology, on the corner of 14th Street and Constitution Avenue, Northwest, close to the Washington Monument.

MUSEUM OF HISTORY AND TECHNOLOGY

The modern building on Constitution Avenue contains many things to bring alive the history of the United,

WASHINGTON, D.C. 83

States. Facilities to make your visit more enjoyable are also in the building. A cafeteria, snack bar and restrooms are located on the basement level. A post office, museum shops, and a bookstore are in the museum. When you enter the building, stop by at the Information Desks, located near both the Mall and Constitution Avenue entrances.

Although there are so many things to see in the Museum of History and Technology, and we suggest you buy an excellent guide book for $1.75 at the Museum of the various displays, we do want to alert you to some of our favorite things to see. For example, have a look at the Focault Pendulum which demonstrates the rotation of the earth. Other exhibits more in line with the focus of this guide, include the display of the original flag which inspired Francis Scott Key to write our National Anthem. In the East Wing you can view No. 1401, the huge Southern Railway engine. The dress of the various First Ladies can be seen in the West Wing. Another interesting display is the one about campaigning in the U.S.A. The exhibit does an excellent job to inform you about this facet of politics in the country. You might also note that you can see George Washington's field headquarters tent in this building.

One of the special exhibitions in the Smithsonian Institution's National Museum of History and Technology is "We the People," financed by a special congressional appropriation. This Bicentennial exhibition, includes 6,000 objects, and is divided into three sections: "Of the People," "By the People," and "For the People." By all means take the opportunity to experience over 200 years of American history. It will be on display through 1976.

OTHER MUSEUMS/GALLERIES

Next door to the National Museum of History and Technology is the National Museum of Natural History. Further down Constituion Avenue, toward the Capitol, around 6th and 7th Streets, is the National Gallery of Art. Free tours are conducted daily at the Gallery. Sunday evenings are free concerts. The cafeteria in the building is open 10-4 weekdays and 1-7 p.m. on Sundays.

On Independence Avenue, near the original Smithsonian Building, you will find the Freer Gallery of Art, the Arts and Industries Building and the Air and Space Building. Further toward the Capitol, you will find the new

84 WASHINGTON, D.C.

Hirshhorn Museum and Sculpture Garden. Modern paintings by European and American masters are highlighted. In this area you will find starting in 1976 the new home of the National Air and Space Museum.

JOSEPH H. HIRSHHORN MUSEUM AND SCULPTURE GARDEN

The Hirshhorn Museum on 8th Street S.W., between Independence Avenue and the Mall, was created by Public Law 89-788 passed on November 7, 1966. The ground for the new museum was broken on January 8, 1969. It opened in the fall of 1974. The museum contains over 4,000 paintings and 2,000 sculptures, all given to the United States by Joseph H. Hirshhorn, born on August 11, 1899. The sculpture collection includes 19 Rodin Bronzes, 55 Henry Moores, 11 Calders, 24 Giacomettis, 24 Matisse bronzes, 25 David Smiths and many works by Nadelman, Lachaise, Picasso, Degas, Ducham-Villon, Manzu and Daumier. The painting collection, includes works by Eakins, de Kooning, Gorky and other Americans, covers the period from the late 19th century to the present.

The "donut shaped" or cylindrical structure is 231 feet in diameter. It is 82 feet tall and the open circular court is 115 feet in diameter. The plaza and the garden cover 4.4 acres.

THE KENNEDY CENTER FOR THE PERFORMING ARTS

This cultural center housing the 1,100 seat Eisenhower Theater, the 2,200 seat Opera House, the 2,750 seat Concert Hall and the American Film Institute, was created in 1958 by Congress and designated as the John F. Kennedy Center for the Performing Arts in 1964 as a memorial to the 35th President of the United States. The Kennedy Center was officially opened on September 8, 1971. The Tourmobile makes a stop here. There are three restaurants on the top floor of the building. And while you are on the top floor, walk around on the outside. You get a wonderful panoramic view of the city—Lincoln Memorial, the Watergate complex, Arlington Cemetery and Roosevelt Island.

Outside of the Kennedy Center you will find a two-part frieze, one of the gifts from foreign countries presented to the Center. If you don't like the gift, you are not alone. One writer has called it "a sardonic slap at the country it is meant to honor." We agree.

MUSEUM OF AFRICAN ART

Another fine and interesting museum in Washington, D.C. is the Museum of African Art. It is located behind the Supreme Court Building on Capitol Hill at 316-318 "A" Street, Northeast, telephone 547-7424. It contains traditional African sculpture, textiles and musical instruments and shows the influence of African sculpture on modern Western art. There is a Frederick Douglass Memorial Room. Open Mon-Fri. 11-5, Sat-Sun. and holidays 12:30-5. Public tours Wednesdays and Saturdays at 3:30 p.m.

GEORGETOWN

Georgetown, in the western part of Washington, D.C., existed about 40 years before George Washington chose the site for the Nation's Capital. Today Georgetown is as busy as it was 200 years ago—only in a different way. Then, it was a busy port shipping the flour, tobacco and lumber from surrounding plantations to the other colonies and abroad. Today it is busy with shoppers, for there are a host of little shops and boutiques. At night the area comes alive with the sounds of music from nightclubs and bars until the early morning hours.

The focal point in Georgetown is the corner of M Street and Wisconsin Avenue. Bus #36 from the downtown area will get you here. Just a few steps from these bustling streets you will find quiet streets with enchanting houses—the homes of diplomats, congressional leaders and other prominent families. In fact, the family of Martha Custis, granddaughter of Martha Washington, built a home here. Descendants of the family still live in Tudor Place at 1644 31st Street. At 3307 N Street you will find the house purchased by John F. Kennedy in 1957. From here the family moved to the White House. As you stroll through the quiet streets, make your way to Dunbarton Oaks at 1703 32nd Street. This wonderful mansion, the Center for Byzantine Studies, and the adjoining impressive gardens are open daily from 2 p.m. to 5 p.m. except holidays. Try not to miss this attraction.

86 WASHINGTON, D.C.

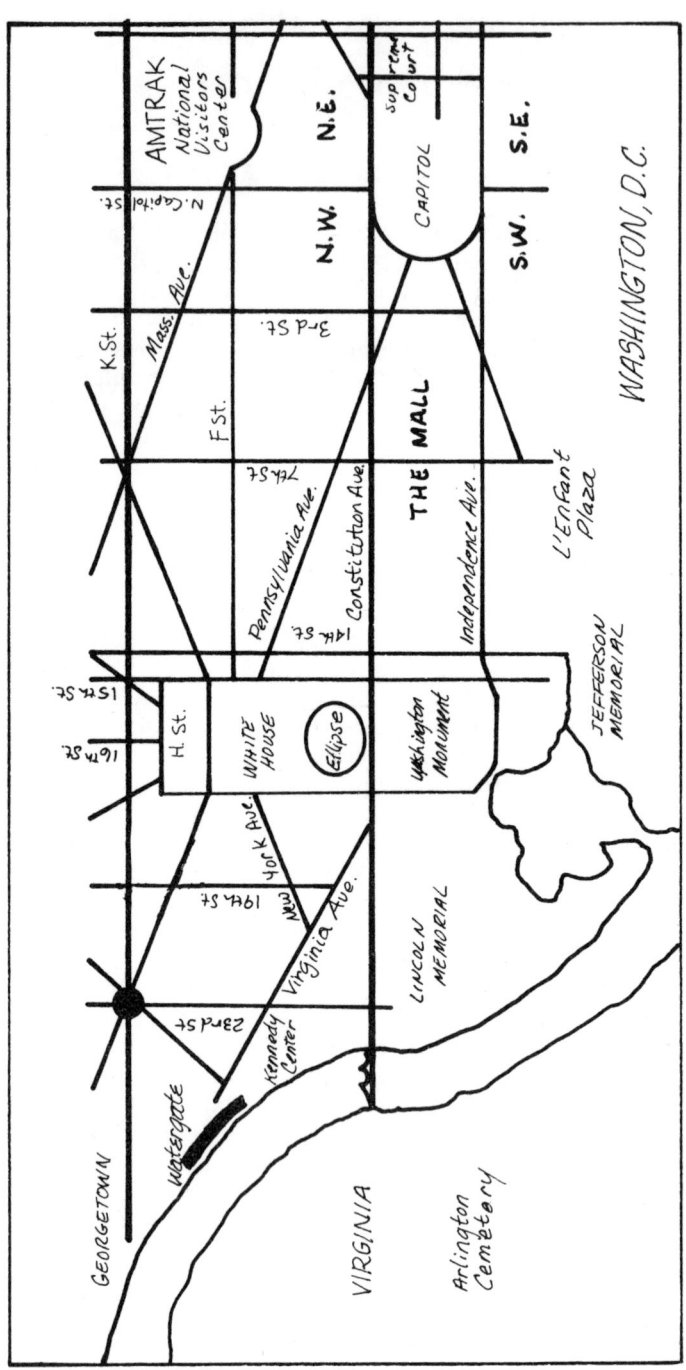

THE NATIONAL ZOO AND PANDA BEARS

One of the most interesting sights in Washington is the National Zoo. It is located between Rock Creek Park and Connecticut Avenue, in the Northwest part of the city. Bus #L-4 will let you off at the Connecticut Avenue entrance to the zoo.

Probably one of the most popular things to see at the zoo are the two Panda Bears—a gift from the People's Republic of China to the people of the United States. Since very few of these species exist outside of China, you might want to see Hsing-Hsing and Ling-Ling, the two Pandas. They are housed in a special building close to the Connecticut Street Entrance. Visiting hours are daily from 0900-1630. From the Panda House the zoo slopes down to the Rock Creek Park.

CRUISE ON THE POTOMAC RIVER

Just recently, the visitor to Washington has been given another way to see the beauty of the city. Glass-roofed boats leave hourly from a special dock near the Lincoln Memorial. Washington attractions such as Georgetown, the Kennedy Center, Watergate, Roosevelt Island, the Pentagon, the Tidal Basin with the Jefferson Memorial, National Airport, among others, take on an exciting perspective from the water. Fares for the one hour trip are $2.50 for adults and $1.75 for children. For further information call Potomac Boat Tours at 548-5210.

WASHINGTON, D.C.

KEY TO ABBREVIATIONS

Visitors to the Nation's Capital are sometimes confused over the abbreviations that are used to describe government agencies in the city as well as other organizations. To help you understand better we now list a number organizations as well as the initials that are commonly applied to them. Keep in mind the main business in Washington, D.C. is government.

AID Agency for International Development; BLS Bureau of Labor Statistics; CAB Civil Aeronautics Board; CIA Central Intelligence Agency; DAR Daughters of the American Revolution; DCA Washington National Airport; DOD Department of Defense; DOT Department of Transportation; DNC Democratic National Committee; EEOC Equal Employment Opportunity Commission; EPA Environmental Protection Agency; FAA Federal Aviation Administration; FBI Federal Bureau of Investigation; FCC Federal Communications Commission; FDIC Federal Deposit Insurance Corp.; FPC Federal Power Commission; FTC Federal Trade Commission; FDA Food and Drug Administration; GAO General Accounting Office; GSA General Services Administration; GW The George Washington University; HEW Health, Education and Welfare; HUD Housing and Urban Development; IAD Dulles International Airport; IRS Internal Revenue Service; ICC Interstate Commerce Commission; IMF International Monetary Fund; NIH National Institutes of Health; NLRB National Labor Relations Board; OAS Organization of American States; PBS Public Broadcasting System; RNC Republican National Committee; SALT Strategic Arms Limitation Talks; SEC Securities and Exchange Commission; SBA Small Business Administration; USIA United States Information Agency; VA Veterans Administration.

ADDITIONAL BICENTENNIAL INFORMATION

During the Bicentennial Period, the Nation's Capital is one of the showcases of the country, offering a comprehensive spectrum of the Nation's history. Culture, art, music, monuments, exhibits and displays are the main fare. The National Visitors Center, housed in the shell of the turn-of-the century constructed Union Station, will give the visitor an interesting and stimulating overview of

WASHINGTON, D.C.

the city during the Bicentennial Celebration and after. Constitution Gardens, with a lake, dominate the area to the side of the Mall between the Lincoln Memorial and the Washington Monument. "America on Stage" at the Kennedy Center, traces the history of theater, music, dance and other entertainment from our early beginning to the present. In addition, stage productions reflect the history of cultural America.

The French government, which made possible America's struggle for independence 200 years ago, has offered America a 'sound and light' show, dramatizing historic events at night. George Washington's Mount Vernon will be the scene of this unique entertainment. The U.S. Capitol is also a possibility for the application of this interesting approach to making history and events come alive.

PUBLIC CITIZEN VISITORS CENTER

One of the newest places in Washington, D.C. where to obtain information is at the Ralph Nader's organized Public Citizen Vistors Center, 1200 15th Street, N.W., telephone (202) 659-9053. It is located on the corner of 15th and M Streets, just down the street from the Lee Pick House. Right across the street is the plush Madison Hotel and the National Housing Center.

The Public Citizen Visitors Center was established in 1974, in response to a demand by citizens interested in learning more about how their government functions and how they can experience the workings of the federal establishment. In addition to providing the useful brochure "Inside the Capitol" with a calendar of events in Congress, the PCVC serves as an information source for questions about Washington and the federal government, presents lectures, discussions and films about vital public interest topics, acts as a consumer reference service, compiles tours of seldom-visited places in Washington, arranges seminars for high school and college groups, and prints pamphlets about consumer issues. PCVC depends entirely on public contributions. The Publication Visitors Center is open Mon-Fri. 9-5, Saturday 9-1.

SEEING WASHINGTON, D.C. BY METROBUS

The Washington Metropolitan Area Transit Authority operates the city buses, Metrobuses, which serve Washington, D.C. and neighboring Maryland and

WASHINGTON, D.C.

Virginia. In addition, the 98 mile subway system is being completed in stages. In the fall of 1975, a route of several miles in the downtown area became operational. For additional information about the everincreasing subway service, as well as Metrobus service, call 637-2437.

Keep in mind that when you board a Metrobus you must have the exact change. So keep several quarters, dimes and nickels handy. Also you can get "transfers" when you board your first bus which will enable you to continue your trip with other buses if you need to. Although the Tourmobile gets you to many of the important places of interest, you might have to use the bus to reach other places. Here are a few destinations, and some of the Metrobuses which serve them: Anacostia Neighborhood Museum, A2, A4, A8, 94; Frederick Douglass Home B2; Dulles Airport 3X, 3S; Ford's Theater, D2, D4, 40, 42; National Zoo, L2, L4, L6; RFK Stadium, B2, 40, 42; National Shrine of the Immaculate Conception, H2, T4, 80, 81; Union Station and the National Visitor Center, D2, D4, 2, 7, 40, 42.

The head office of Metro is at 600 Fifth Street, N.W.. Be sure to pick up your free 'getting about on Metrobus' pamphlet.

BICYCLE RENTALS IN THE WASHINGTON, D.C. AREA

There are a number of places you can rent bicycles to explore the splendor of the Capital Region. Principal routes include the C and O Canal Towpath (which starts in Georgetown), Rock Creek and along the Potomac to Mt. Vernon. Big Wheel Bikes, 337-0254, at 1034 33rd Street, N.W., charges $1.50 per hour, $7 per day. A $10 deposit required. Fletcher's Boat House, 244-0461, 4940 Canal Rd., N.W., charges $1 per hour and $3.50 per day. Thomson's Bicycle Rental, 331-4861, at Rock Creek Parkway and Virginia Ave., N.W. (near Kennedy Center), charges $1.50 per hour and $3 per day.

If you want to explore the Virginia area of the Capital Region by bike, may we suggest you rent your bikes at the Bicycle Rack, 594-4900, 1114 South Washington Street in Alexandria; $2 for 1-1/2 hours, $6.50 per day. The place is ideally located on the exclusive bicycle path along the Potomac River to Mt. Vernon. You'll love it here.

UNION STATION

The cavernous Union Station now houses not only Amtrak trains but also the National Visitors Center. From here it is easy to explore the beauty and splendor of the

WASHINGTON, D.C. 91

Nation's Capital. Close to the terminal you will also find a number of hotels, including the Quality Inn and in 1976, the new Hyatt Regency Hotel. Bus service to practically all parts of the city is available. Westbound #40 takes you to Dupont Circle and the Hilton Hotel. Eastbound the bus takes you to nearby Capitol Hill and RFK Stadium. Bus #2-T takes you to Pennsylvania Avenue, the White House, Georgetown and Rosslyn, across the Potomac River in Virginia, where quite a number of motels are located at.

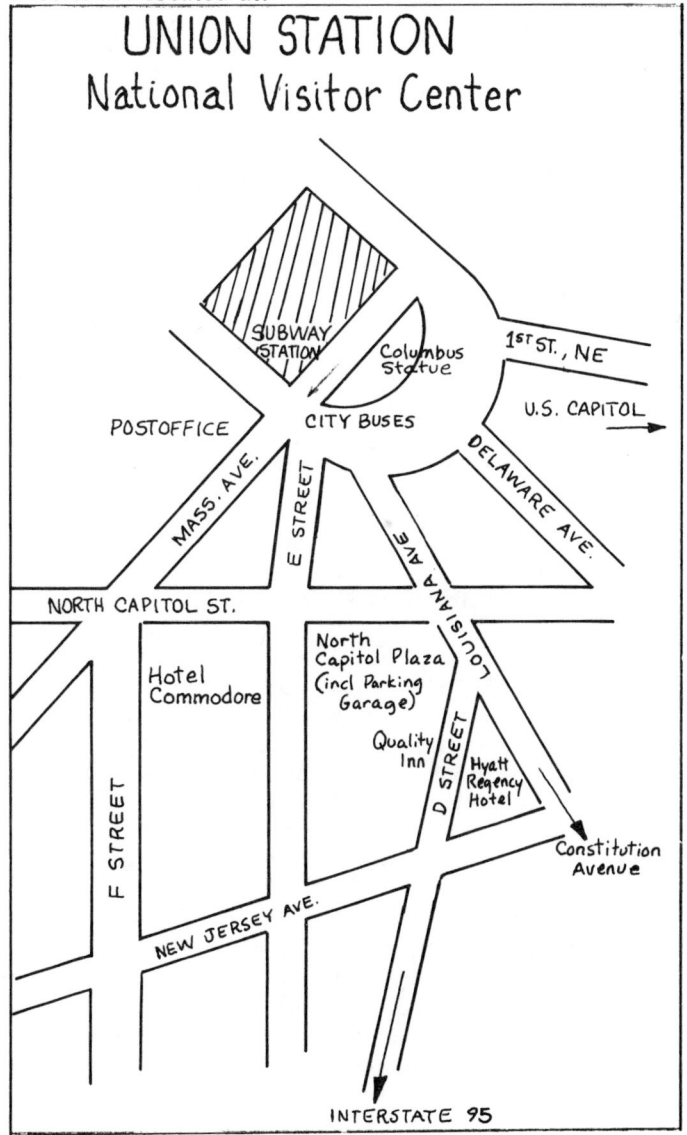

INTERNATIONAL VISITORS ARE WELCOME

IVIS (the International Visitors Service Council) at 801 19th St. NW, corner of 19th St. and Pennsylvania Ave., provides free multilingual assistance and information to international visitors in the Washington, D.C. area.

Telephone or visit IVIS to obtain the following free services:

- Information about restaurants, lodging, sightseeing and shopping in the Washington area.
- Informal visits in the homes of citizens of the Washington area.
- Multilingual escorts to assist non-English speaking visitors in touring the city, shopping, going to medical appointments, etc. (Requests for visits with Washington citizens and multilingual escorts must be made in person in the IVIS office at least 48 hours in advance.)
- Appointments with individuals or organizations sharing the visitor's professional or special interests.

IVIS office hours: 9 a.m. - 5 p.m., Monday-Friday. Bus #2T, 30, 32, 34, 36 will get you there.

EMERGENCY ASSISTANCE is available by telephone 24 hours a day. 872-8747.

WASHINGTON, D.C. HOTELS

Since most travelers will want to visit Washington, D.C., we have included a listing of a number of hotels in the Nation's Capital. We have included a wide variety of hotels. Remember that just because the hotels are listed here does not necessarily mean we recommend them. However, the list is sufficiently broad enough to help you find the accommodations you may want in your price range. "S" stands for a single room and "D" for a double room.

The telephone area code for Washington is 202. Thus when you attempt to call from other parts of the country to make advance reservations (we strongly recommend that you do), just dial '202' plus the number we have listed. To save time you might just ask for "Front Desk" when the hotel operator answers. Also keep in mind that the hotels we have listed are in the Northwest section.

WASHINGTON, D.C. 93

You will find a number (1-27) before each Washington, D.C. hotel. This number refers to the number you will find on the map. This hotel location map will make it easier to find your way around and help decide where you might want to stay. Note that #4 and #20 hotels are no longer in business. The YMCA/YWCA accommodations and other low priced accommodations follow this list.

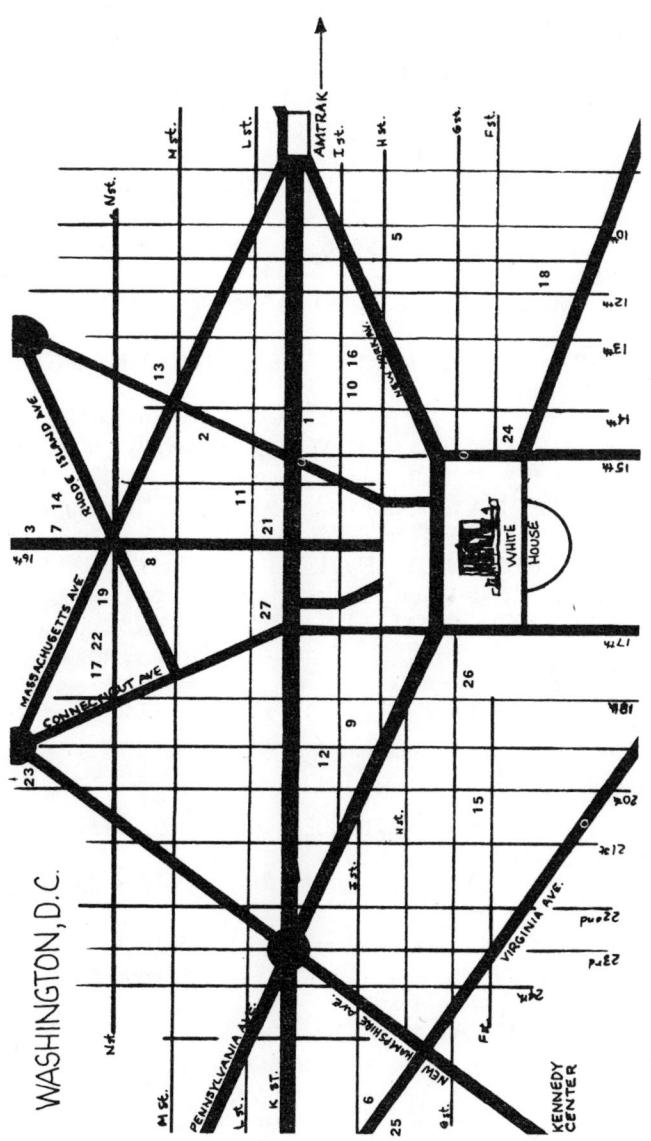

94 WASHINGTON, D.C.

1—AMBASSADOR HOTEL; 628-8510. 14th & K Streets; S-$19; D-$27.
2—BURLINGTON HOTEL; 785-2222. 1120 Vermont Ave.; S-$19.50; D-$22.
3—CHRISTIAN INN; 483-6116. 1509 16th St.; S-$11.60; D-$15.90.
5—EBBITT HOTEL; 628-5034. 1000 H Street; S-$16.86; D-$21.26; reduced rates if you stay at least three days.
6—HOWARD JOHNSON'S; 965-2700. 2601 Virginia Ave.; S-$27; D-$32. "Across from Watergate complex and Kennedy Center".
7—INTERNATIONAL YOUTH HOSTEL; 387-3169. 1501 16th Street; check in 4:30-7 p.m., and at 8 p.m. and at 9 p.m.; $3.18/bed. "Must be a member."
8—JEFFERSON HOTEL; 347-4704. 16th and M Streets; S-$32; D-$37.
9—NATIONAL; 628-5566. 1808 I(Eye) St.; S-$13; D-$17.
10—PARKSIDE; 347-3230. 1336 I(Eye) St.; S-$14; D-$16.
11—PICK LEE HOUSE; 347-4800. 1100 15th St.l S-$22; D-$28.

12—PRESIDENTIAL HOTEL; 331-9020. 900 19th Street; S-$15; D-$18.
13—INTERNATIONAL INN; 783-4600. Massachusetts Ave. and Thomas Circle; S-$28; D-$36.
14—EXECUTIVE HOUSE MOTOR HOTEL; 232-7000. 1515 Rhode Island Ave.; S-$26; D-$34.
15—FRANCIS SCOTT KEY HOTEL; 628-5425. 600 20th St.; S-$15-19; D-$3 more. "Near The George Washington University."
16—FRANKLIN PARK; 347-3125. 1332 I (Eye) St.; S-$10; D-$14.
17—THE GRALYN; 785-1515. 1745 N Street; S-$20; D-$24.
18—HARRINGTON HOTEL; 628-8140. 11th and E Streets; S-$14-$17; D-$18-$20.
19—HOLIDAY INN; 296-2100. 1615 Rhode Island Ave.; S-$25; D-$31.
21—STATLER HILTON HOTEL; 393-1000. 16th and K Streets; S-from $32; D-from $44. "Arrival-departure point for airport buses."
22—HOTEL TABARD INN; 785-1277. 1739 N Street; S-$18; D-$24.
23—WASHINGTON HILTON; 483-3000. 1919 Connecticut Ave.; S-from $32; D-from $44.

WASHINGTON, D.C.

24—WASHINGTON HOTEL; 638-5900. 15th and Pennsylvania Ave.; S-from $30; D-from $34.
25—WATERGATE HOTEL; 965-2300. 2650 Virginia Ave.; S-from $38; D-from $48.
26—YMCA.
27—YWCA.

YMCA AND YWCA ACCOMMODATIONS

Both the YMCA and YWCA in Washington, D.C. are located close to the White House. The YMCA at 1736 G Street, N.W., 628-8250, charges $7.40 for a single, plus a $2 key deposit. The YWCA at 1011 17th St., N.W., (corner of 17th and K Streets), 638-2100, charges $9 per night. Has weekly and monthly rates.

LOW COST ACCOMMODATIONS IN WASHINGTON, D.C.

Besides the various hotel and "Y" accommodations we have mentioned, there are a number of places you might try to stay at. Especially in summer, some of the colleges will open their doors to visitors. In any case, we present you with the address and telephone numbers and approximate prices of the various places. Always call to find out if accommodations are available and what it costs to stay there.

Hartnett Hall—21st & P Streets, N.W., 293-1111; about $40 a week-2 meals a day-5 days a week.
Immaculata College—4300 Nebraska-Corner of Wisconsin Ave., 966-0040. $3 a night for 3 in a room. Women only.
Mt. Vernon College—2100 Foxhall Road, N.W., 331-3540. $6 dorm. per night, share bath, 2 in a room, $5 key deposit. Women only.
Trinity College—Michigan & Franklin N.E., 269-2339. Spacious dorms, clean, available school vacations only. $8 per day per person in a double.
Hotel John Kilpin—2310 Ashmead Pl., 462-4336. $7 a night.
Marifex Hotel—corner of 20th & P Streets, 1523 22nd St., N.W., 293-1885. Singles daily-$8.00.
National 4-H Foundation—7100 Conn. Ave., Washington, D.C. 20015, (301)-656-9000. $10 a night-single. $6 per person, 4 in a room. Groups only.
Argyle Guest House—232-6606, 2201 Mass. Ave. N.W. on Florida Ave., $45 a week.

WASHINGTON, D.C.

Evangeline Residence—638-1222, 1000 14th St., N.W., (for stay of 3 weeks or over). $37.50 per week plus 2 meals a day.
Guest House—1754 N St., N.W., 2005 Mass. Ave., N.W., 638-0149. $75 a month.
International Guest House—1441 Kennedy St., N.W., 20011, 726-5808, (off 16th St. near Carter Baron amphitheater). $5 a night-single, $8 a night-married couples, $1.50-$2.50 children (will take non-foreign students if not filled up).
International Student House—1825 R St., N.W., 232-4007. Single-$165-$190 a month, meals included.
Hotel 1440—1440 Rhode Is. Ave., N.W., 232-7800. $9.54, small room with sink, share bath.
Manchester Inn—1426 M St., N.W., 785-2770. $20 daily furnished apt.; $10 single room, share bath; $12 single, private bath (plus tax).

There is a new service available to families who are visiting the Nation's Capital. Holiday Hosts will try to find 'bed and breakfast' accommodations with a family living in the area. Call (301) 434-4336 or write P.O. Box 1108, Langley Park, Md. 20787, and state how many there are in your party and how long you wish to stay.

TOURS IN WASHINGTON, D.C.

There are many tours available for the visitor to Washington, D.C., including a tour coach-boat combination to Mount Vernon and Alexandria, Virginia. There is also a "Historic Alexandria Tour and Shopping Expedition" tour, a "See Washington at Night" tour, and a "Happy Time Tour" to the new Kings Dominion Amusement Park between Washington, D.C. and Richmond. For further information call Gray Line at 347-0600. Diamond Tours also operate tours throughout the area. For example they conduct a tour to Annapolis. For information call Diamond Tours at 546-9800.

WASHINGTON, D.C. FROM A-Z

AMTRAK TERMINAL (Union Station)
50 Massachusetts Ave., N.E.
AQUARIUM—Basement of Dept. of Commerce, 14th and Constitution Ave., N.W. 967-2825. Daily 9 a.m.-5 p.m.

ARLINGTON HOUSE—Arlington Cemetery. 557-3153. Daily, October through March, 9:30 a.m.-4:30 p.m.; April through September, 9:30 a.m.-6 p.m.

ARLINGTON NATIONAL CEMETERY—692-9875. Daily, November through March, 8 a.m.-5 p.m. April through October 8 a.m.-7 p.m.

BUREAU OF ENGRAVING AND PRINTING—14th and C Sts., S.W. 964-7611. Monday through Friday only, 8 a.m.-2:30 p.m. Closed holidays. Tours available.

CAPITOL—Capitol Hill, 224-3121. Daily 9 a.m.-4:30. Tours 9-3:45. Closed Christmas, New Year's and Thanksgiving. Free.

CORCORAN GALLERY OF ART—17th and New York Ave., N.W. 638-3211. Tuesday through Sunday, 11:00 a.m. to 5 p.m. Entrance free on Tuesday and Wednesday. Admission charge $1.00 Thursday through Sunday.

FEDERAL BUREAU OF INVESTIGATION—9th and Pennsylvania Ave., N.W. 324-3447. Open Monday through Friday, 9:15-4:15 p.m. Closed Saturday, Sunday and Holidays. Hour tours every 15 minutes.

FORD'S THEATER AND LINCOLN MUSEUM—511 10th St., N.W. Daily 9 a.m.-5 p.m. Free except for theater performances. Box office 426-6924.

FREDERICK DOUGLASS HOUSE—1411 W St., S.E. Restored home of noted educator-diplomat open 9 to 4 p.m. Monday through Friday, Saturday and Sunday 10 a.m.-5 p.m.; closed Christmas Day. A-2 bus.

GREYHOUND TERMINAL—11th and New York Avenues, N.W. Open 24 hours.

JEFFERSON MEMORIAL—South bank of Tidal Basin. 426-6821. Open daily until midnight.

JOHN F. KENNEDY CENTER FOR THE PERFORMING ARTS—Box office, 254-3600. Building open 10 a.m. for tourists, group tours 10 and 1:15 Monday through Saturday.

LIBRARY OF CONGRESS—1st and Independence Ave., S.E. 426-5000. Monday through Friday 8:30 a.m.-9:30 p.m.; Saturday 8:30 a.m.-6:00 p.m. and Sunday 11:00 a.m.-6:00 p.m. Tours available 9-4 daily, on the hour, Monday through Friday.

LINCOLN MEMORIAL—West Potomac Park, foot of 23rd St., N.W. Open daily 8 a.m. to midnight. Free.

NATIONAL ARCHIVES—7th and Constitution Ave., N.W. 963-6404. Declaration of Independence, Constitution. Monday through Saturday, 9 a.m.-10 p.m.; Sunday 1 p.m.-10 p.m. Call 962-2000 for recorded informa-

WASHINGTON, D.C.

tion on exhibits. During the winter months closes at 6 p.m.
NATIONAL GALLERY OF ART—6th and Constitution Ave., N.W. 737-4215. Daily, 10 a.m.-5 p.m.; Sunday, noon to 9 p.m. April through Labor Day; daily 10 a.m.-9 p.m. Sunday noon-9 p.m.
NATIONAL VISITOR CENTER—(Union Station) Open in 1976.
MOUNT VERNON—Mount Vernon, Va., 780-2000. Daily, March 1 to October 1, 9 a.m.-5 p.m.; October 1 to March 1, 9 a.m.-4 p.m.
OCTAGON HOUSE—18th and New York Ave., N.W. Served as James Madison's White House following destruction of real White House by British in 1814. Treaty of Ghent signed here, ending War of 1812. Open Tuesday through Saturday, 10 a.m.-4 p.m.; Sunday 1-4 p.m.
ORGANIZATION OF AMERICAN STATES—17th and Constitution Ave., N.W. 331-1010. Formerly Pan American Union, features tropical courtyard garden, Hall of Americas, Gallery of Heroes. Open Monday through Saturday, 8:30 a.m.-4 p.m.
PETERSEN HOUSE (WHERE LINCOLN DIED)— 516 10th St., N.W. 426-6830. Daily 9 a.m.-5 p.m.
SMITHSONIAN INSTITUTION GROUP—628-4422.
    AIR AND SPACE MUSEUM—Independence Ave., between 4th and 7th Streets S.W. (1976).
    ARTS AND INDUSTRIES BLDG.—9th and Jefferson Dr., S.W.
    FREER GALLERY OF ART—12th and Jefferson Dr., S.W.
    HIRSHHORN MUSEUM AND SCULPTURE GARDEN—Independence Avenue at 8th Street, S.W.
    MUSEUM OF HISTORY AND TECHNOLOGY— 12th and Constitution Ave., N.W.
    MUSEUM OF NATURAL HISTORY—10th and Constitution Ave., N.W.
    NATIONAL COLLECTION OF FINE ARTS— 8th and G Sts., N.W. 381-5180. American art.
    NATIONAL PORTRAIT GALLERY—8th and F Sts., N.W. 628-1810.
    RENWICK GALLERY—17th and Pennsylvania Ave., N.W. American culture. (near White House).
    SMITHSONIAN BLDG.—10th and Jefferson Dr., S.W. Administration.
All above are open daily, 10 a.m.-5:30 p.m. Information on special events recorded daily. 737-8811. The Air and Space Museum, Arts and Industries Building, Hirshhorn Museum, Museum of History and

WASHINGTON, D.C. 99

Technology and Museum of Natural History are open until 9 p.m. during summer months.

SUPREME COURT—1st and Maryland Ave., N.E. 393-1640. Open Monday through Friday, 9 a.m.-4:30 p.m. Closed Saturday, Sunday and holidays. Tours 9:30 a.m. to 4 p.m. every half hour except when court is in session. Last tour weekdays at 4 p.m. Court usually not in session July-September.

THE PHILLIPS COLLECTION—1600-1612 21st St., N.W. World-famed art collection. Tuesday through Saturday 10-5, Sunday 2-7. Closed Mondays. Free.

TREASURY DEPARTMENT—15th and Pennsylvania Ave., N.W. Displays of money, both real and counterfeit; also sales of uncirculated coins. Open Tuesday through Friday 9:30 a.m.-3:00 p.m., Saturday 10:00 a.m.-2:00 p.m. and closed on Sundays and Mondays. 393-6400.

VOICE OF AMERICA—330 Independence Ave., S.W. 755-4744. Tours Monday through Friday 9 a.m.-4 p.m.

WASHINGTON MONUMENT—On the Mall at 15th St., N.W. 426-6839. Open daily March 15 through Labor Day, 8 a.m.-12 midnight; day after Labor Day through March 14, 9 a.m.-5 p.m. Elevator fee 10¢ for adults.

WHITE HOUSE—1600 Pennsylvania Ave., N.W. 456-1414. Open Tuesday through Saturday, 10 a.m.-noon, and Saturdays, June thru August, 10 a.m.-2 p.m. Closed some holidays. No passes required. Free.

ZOOLOGICAL PARK—3001 Connecticut Ave., N.W. 628-4422. Grounds open daily 6 a.m.-dark, gates close one hour after buildings. Panda Bears!

HARPERS FERRY

For a delightful rail excursion from Washington, D.C. we suggest you take the hour long train trip to Harpers Ferry. Harpers Ferry, where the Shenandoah and Potomac Rivers meet, played an important part in our nations history when in 1859 John Brown made his raid on the Federal Armory here.

You might keep in mind that on weekends the train leaves Washington D.C. at 11:00 a.m. and arrives in Harpers Ferry just after noon. A return trip leaves at 6:22 p.m. This gives you about six hours in this historic town. Or you might want to spend the night. A hotel in Harpers Ferry which is known for its good homecooking is the Hilltop House Hotel. For reservations call (304) 535-6321. It was in 1747 that Robert Harper settled this area and started the ferry business. George Washington also visited this scenic area which Thomas Jefferson called so magnificent that it was well worthwhile to cross an ocean to see the view overlooking the Shenandoah/Potomac Rivers. As soon as you leave the train station you will spot the Toy Train Museum. Walking down to the left on Potomac Street you will pass nearby historical markers which give an indication of what used to stand here including the now famous U.S. Armory. Keep walking straight and you will reach the Point (where the Shenandoah and Potomac Rivers meet), or turn to your right and walk along Shenandoah Street. You will spot the West Virginia Information Center. Several buildings further along the street is the Visitor Center. Here you can learn about the history of Harpers Ferry and also watch a brief slide presentation. Restrooms are also located in this building.

High Street is the main shopping street—with a host of antique, gift, and arts and crafts shops. The stone steps from High Street lead up to the church built in the 1830's as well as Jefferson Rock where you will see a wonderful scenic view.

We might note that the train actually runs from Washington D.C. to Cumberland. On weekdays the train caters mainly to commuters. Therefore, these days there is a morning arrival in Washington D.C. from Cumberland and Harpers Ferry and an afternoon departure from the Nation's Capital to these historic towns. For your information, the one way fare to Harpers Ferry, West Virginia from Washington D.C. is $3.50.

MOUNT VERNON 101

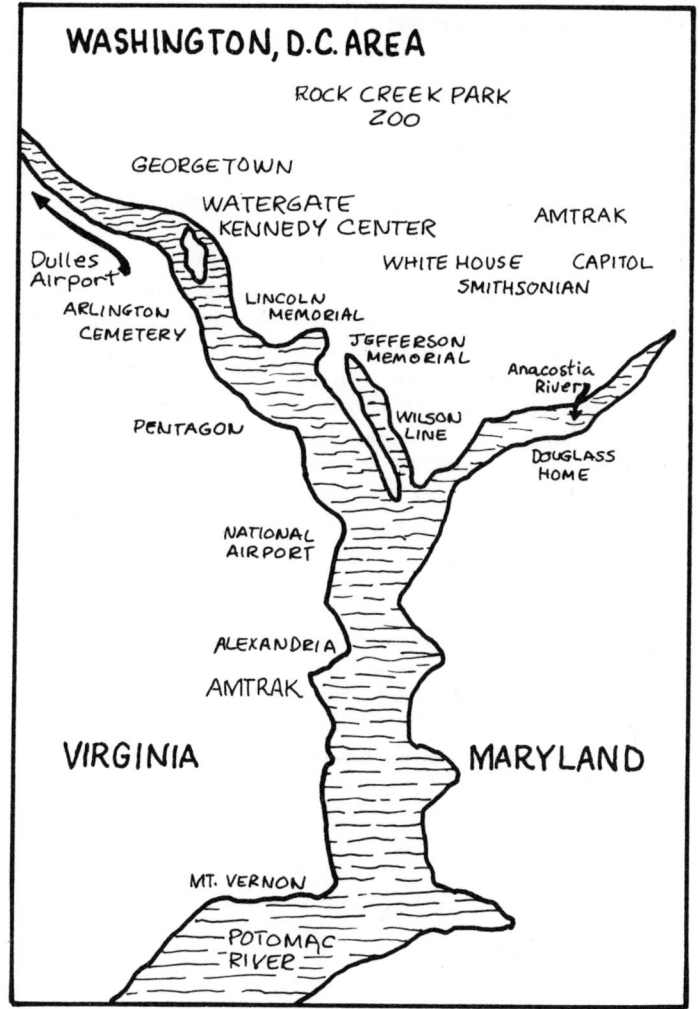

MOUNT VERNON — GEORGE WASHINGTON'S HOME

Mount Vernon, the beautifully preserved home of America's first President, is located just to the south of Washington, D.C. and Alexandria, Virginia, on the Potomac River. You can reach this estate, George Washington's home between 1754 and 1799, by taking a tour, by city bus, or by taking the Wilson Line (a boat company) excursion boat to Mount Vernon.

102 MOUNT VERNON

MT. VERNON BY BOAT

Since Mount Vernon is practically on the river, taking a boat is a convenient way to reach the beautiful gardens and the buildings which make up Washington's estate. Once you dock at Mount Vernon, you have a splendid walk up to the main part of the estate. Also Washington's tomb is fairly close to the river. Boat departures during the peak season from Washington, D.C. take place at 9:30 a.m., 10:30 a.m., 2 p.m. and 3 p.m. The trip to Mt. Vernon takes 70 minutes. Departures from Mt. Vernon, back to Washington, D.C., take place at 12:15, 1:15, 5, and 5:15 p.m. For further information call 393-8300. To get to the Wilson Line Dock by Metrobus you can leave from 7th and Pennsylvania with the Fort McNair bus. Get off at 6th and M. The docks are practically across the street. The $5.50 charge for the boat trip includes the price of admission at Mt. Vernon.

MT. VERNON BY BUS

If you want to go out to Mount Vernon by city bus, take #11A from 10th and Pennsylvania to the beautiful home. On your way back, the same bus will take you through Alexandria. Read our chapter on Old Town. Mount Vernon itself is open daily 9-5 (March-September) and from 9 a.m.-4 p.m. for the remainder of the year. Admission is $1.50. If you are looking for a place to eat, there is a restaurant right outside the estate, as well as a post office, snack bar, souvenir shop and restrooms.

SOME DATES

Mount Vernon was restored and is now maintained by The Mount Vernon Ladies' Association, founded in 1858. In retracing the development of the estate, it must be noted that title to the land dates from 1674, when John Washington, great-grandfather of George, was granted 5,000 acres. In 1743, Lawrence Washington renamed the plantation "Mount Vernon" in honor of Admiral Vernon under whom he had served in the Caribbean. In 1752 Lawrence died, and the title passed to George. In 1759, George Washington married Martha Custis, widow of Daniel Parke Custis. From 1775, when Washington became commander-in-chief of the Continental Army, until 1783, Washington only briefly stayed at Mount Vernon. That year he resigned from the Army, returned to his home, but in 1789 was elected as the first President of the United States. In 1797 he returned and died December, 1799. Martha Washington died in 1802.

OLD TOWN ALEXANDRIA

One of our favorite places anywhere (that is why we live here) is Alexandria, Virginia, just to the south of Washington D.C. Any #11 Metrobus from the corner of 10th and Pennsylvania Avenue N.W. in Washington D.C. will take you to Alexandria. By getting off at Washington and King Streets in Alexandria (in front of Penney's Store) you are only a few blocks away from the historic section of this thriving city of about 110,000 and about one block from the Nation's first Bicentennial Center. Even in the early part of our nation's history, Alexandria was an important commercial center and seaport. George Washington had a home here. Robert E. Lee grew up in the city and General Lafayette paid a visit in 1824.

GEORGE WASHINGTON BICENTENNIAL CENTER

The Bicentennial Center at 201 S. Washington Street is open daily except Christmas and New Year's Day between 9 and 5. Telephone number 750-6677. Here you will find various interesting exhibits, including a pictorial presentation 'Legacy of Freedom.' There is no better place in America to find out about freedom than in Northern Virginia for the area produced many of the leaders which led us to independence—both on the battlefield and in the minds of man.

ALEXANDRIA

In the late 18th Century, among the Founding Fathers of our country, Virginia was represented by such men as Washington, Jefferson, Madison, Monroe, Patrick Henry, the Lees, the Randolphs, and George Mason. Mason, sometimes called the "Pen of the Revolution," was the author of the Fairfax Resolves, of the first Constitution of Virginia, and of the Virginia "Declaration of Rights." This document, adopted by the House of Burgesses at Williamsburg on June 12, 1776, was to become the chief basis of the Federal Bill of Rights. It was also to be the basis in 1789 of the French Declaration of the Rights of Man; and, since then, of almost every written constitution of the countries which gained their freedom in the 19th and 20th centuries, and of the Charter of the United Nations. By all means try to visit George Mason's home, Gunston Hall, which is just below George Washington's home, Mt. Vernon. Various tours we have listed under the the Washington, D.C. section visit Gunston Hall.

In addition to the exhibits and presentations at the Bicentennial Center, you will find a Museum Shop open Mon.-Sat. from 10 a.m. to 4:30 p.m. and Sundays 1 p.m.-4:30 p.m. There is also a full service Virginia Travel Information Desk here and the personnel will gladly make your accommodations reservations for you. Stop by at this Greek Revival building. It is well worth a visit.

RAMSAY HOUSE

After you have visited the Bicentennial Center, head down King Street, crossing Washington Street, to a most interesting part of the city with unique shops, historic homes and great places to eat. Within two blocks you will see the new Tavern Square Shopping Center, and in the next block the sparkling fountain in Market Square in front of City Hall on Royal St., across from the Alexandria National Bank. Right at the corner of Fairfax and King Streets you will spot Ramsay House (built in 1724)—which is the home of the Alexandria Tourist Council. Here you can get all kinds of additional tourist information about Alexandria. Open daily 10 a.m. to 4:30 p.m., except for Thanksgiving, Christmas and New Year's Day. Telephone 549-0205. You can view a film here about historic Alexandria. Reservations for entertainment, dining and overnight accommodations are also made here. Walking tours maps are available and for our friends from abroad, foreign language brochures are available.

A WALKING TOUR

After your visit to the Ramsay House keep on walking down King Street. As soon as you leave the Ramsay House, you will see a great number of interesting stores. For a snack on a weekday stop at the 'Snack Bar'—good sandwiches and delicious homemade soup. For an evening meal you can stop off at the Wharf or the Seaport Inn, both on lower King Street. If you are looking for a place to relax in the evening, we suggest you stop off at the bar which is above the Wharf restaurant. It's one of our favorite places. Further down is the Torpedo Factory,

OLD TOWN ALEXANDRIA

Washington D.C.
National Airport

LEE'S BOYHOOD HOME

Potomac River →

Queen St.

Cameron St.

• CHRIST CHURCH | GADSBY'S TAVERN | MARKET SQUARE | CARLYLE HOUSE | OLD PORT SECTION
King St. | | | • RAMSAY HOUSE |

← AMTRAK | Holiday Inn

Prince St.

• GEORGE WASHINGTON BICENTENNIAL CENTER | | | | • CAPTAIN'S ROW

Duke St.

OLD CLUB RESTAURANT

Washington St. | St. Asaph St. | Pitt St. | Royal St. | Fairfax St. | Lee St. | Union St.

Mt. Vernon and Bicycle Path along Potomac ↓

• POINTS OF INTEREST

106 ALEXANDRIA

where you can watch artists at work. Open until 5 p.m.

Apart from these places you will also see Dockside (closes at 9 p.m.) where you can buy assorted goods imported from all over the world. When you reach Union Street, turn right one block up Prince Street. You will recognize 'Captain's Row' by the enchanting homes and the cobblestone street. Walk up to Fairfax Street, turn right for two blocks (crossing King Street) until you come to Cameron Street. Just before you reach Cameron Street, you will see to your right at 121 N. Fairfax Street the John Carlyle House, property of the Northern Virginia Regional Park Authority.

CARLYLE HOUSE

Scottish merchant John Carlyle built this stately mansion in 1752 for his bride, Sara Fairfax of Belvoir. For 30 years it was a social and political center of Alexandria, visited by many of the great men of the time, including George Washington. It was here that five royal governors were summoned by the British General Edward Braddock in April, 1755, to find a way to induce the colonists to pay for his campaign against the French and Indians. The Stamp Act which followed, eventually provoked the American Revolution. A public-spirited citizen, Carlyle played a leading role in defying the crown's oppression, and his only son was to die in the cause of American freedom. The fine stone mansion is a rare survivor of the mid-Georgian plantation style. The design is based on Craigiehall in West Lothian, near Edinburgh, Scotland, where the author attended school for several years. The stone cornice across the front is a unique feature in Virginia, and the mansion's council room where the governors met is justifiably famous for its superb paneling.

GADSBY'S TAVERN

Once you reach Cameron Street, turn left, walk past the city hall, and George Washington's restored townhouse at #508. At 128 North Royal Street, you will find the famous Gadsby's Tavern—one of the best remaining examples of Georgian architecture. Here George Washington was a frequent visitor, as a young man, as President and in his short life in retirement. Here George and Martha Washington danced—danced where it is said George Washington recruited for his first military command in the early 1750's. February 22 is always an exciting time here.

CHRIST CHURCH—LEE HOUSE

A couple of blocks further down Cameron and you will be at the intersection of Cameron and Washington Streets. You will see here Christ Church (built between 1767-1773) where George Washington had a pew. Several blocks down Washington Street (in the direction of Washington, D.C.) at the corner of Oronoco Street you will note several interesting homes. At 607 Oronoco Street is the home of Robert E. Lee—the house is open daily 9-5.

PLACES TO EAT

The above historic sights are by no means the only attractions in Alexandria. If you look to the west, you will see a huge monument. It is the George Washington National Masonic Memorial, built in 1922-32. If you are looking for a fine place to dine, we suggest you consider two ideas. One restaurant is as old as the city and the other is as new and contemporary as this book. First—the Old Club Restaurant where George Washington met with his friends. It is a nice place with a fine colonial atmosphere. It is located several blocks past the Bicentennial Center at 555 S. Washington St., closed on Mondays. Telephone 549-4555 for further information. The other restaurant is a floating restaurant on the Potomac River aboard the cruiseship 'Dandy.' The boat leaves from the foot of Prince Street (near Captain's Row) at noon, Tuesdays-Saturdays for a 2 hour luncheon cruise (luncheon cost is $6.50). A three hour dinner cruise leaves at 7:30 p.m. (Tuesday-Sunday) and the cost is $11.50. For further information and reservations call (202) 333-7500.

108 ALEXANDRIA

WHERE TO STAY IN ALEXANDRIA

There are several hotels/motels on the fringe of the historic area in Alexandria. The Ramada Inn, near the Potomac, on 901 N. Fairfax, 683-6000 charges from $20 for a single and $24 for a double. The next three motels are on the National Airport side of Alexandria. Metrobus service directly to the door. The Old Colony Motor Lodge on N. Washington and 1st Streets, 548-6300, charges $18 for singles and $20.76 for doubles. The Virginia Motel at 808 N. Washington, KI 8-3500, charges $18 for a single. The Virginia Motel at 700 N. Washington, TE 6-5100, charges $12.72 for a single.

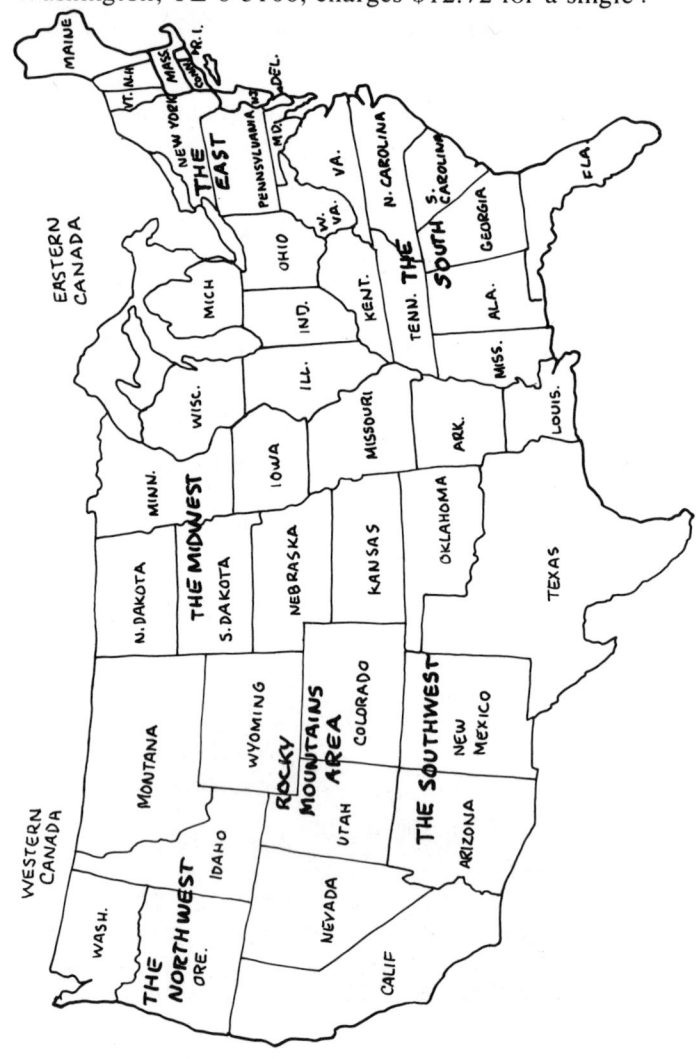

THE SOUTH

FREDERICKSBURG, VIRGINIA

Between Washington, D.C. and Richmond, Virginia, on the banks of the Rappahannock River, is Fredericksburg which some have called "America's most historic city." Amtrak serves the town.

A walking tour of the historic area of the town will enable you to visit the Mary Washington House, bought by George Washington for his mother in 1772. Then there is the James Monroe Museum and Memorial Library where you will find the desk on which President James Monroe signed the Monroe Doctrine. The Hugh Mercer Apothecary Shop allows you to see many relics of medicine and pharmacy. The Historic Stoner's House contains merchandise popular during earlier days. Betty Washington, only sister of George, lived in the Kenmore Mansion from 1752 with her husband Colonel Fielding Lewis. It is a beautiful house. All of these historic places, among others, you will be able to visit in Fredericksburg.

Fredericksburg not only played a significant part in our development during the struggle for independence, but it also was a key objective during the Civil War. Near here, the Battles of Fredericksburg, Chancellorsville, the Wilderness and Spotsylvania Court House took place during 1861-1865.

CHARLOTTESVILLE, VIRGINIA

The Charlottesville area, about 2 hours to the southwest of Washington, D.C. and less than 2 hours west of Richmond, contains the beautiful homes of two giants in American history—Thomas Jefferson, the third President of the United States, and James Monroe, the fifth President of the United States. Both homes are outside the town but limousine service is available.

MONTICELLO

Monticello, Jefferson's home, a classic example of American architecture, is a three story building with 35 rooms. Admission charge is $2. The beautiful gardens were restored in 1939 according to Jefferson's plans. And while you are inside and outside his house, reflect upon

Jefferson's genius and his contribution to the United States. He died at Monticello on July 4, 1826, the fiftieth anniversary of the signing of the Declaration of Independence.

ASH LAWN

Ash Lawn, Monroe's home, was designed and built by his neighbor and friend, Thomas Jefferson in 1798. Visit the completely furnished house and the lovely boxwood garden. Have a look at the old oak tree, already a hundred years old when America was born. Ash Lawn, where the admission charge is $1, is open daily from 7 a.m. to 7 p.m.. Monticello, on the other hand, is open every day from 8 a.m. to 5 p.m. except November 1 through February 28, when the hours are 9 a.m. to 4:30 p.m.

CAPTAIN JACK JOUETT

While you are visiting Charlottesville, you might for a minute reflect upon the heroic deed of Jack Jouett, a captain in the Virginia Militia. On June 3, 1781, (just months before Yorktown) when Thomas Jefferson was Governor of Virginia and the Virginia legislature had been forced to move from Richmond and meet in Charlottesville, a British force under Col. Tarleton was on its way to the new meeting place of the legislature. Jouett, who noticed the British while sitting in a tavern, rode 40 miles across the rolling countryside, while Tarleton took the highway.

It was about 4:30 in the morning that Jouett arrived at Monticello and warned Jefferson of the danger. Other leaders, including Patrick Henry and Richard Henry Lee were also warned, and most escaped before Tarleton and his mounted soldiers arrived.

RICHMOND, VIRGINIA

Richmond, the capital of Virginia is many times overlooked as a treasure of American heritage. However, it has so much to offer the visitor, we strongly recommend you give yourself at least a day in this thriving city. Its ideal location as a transportation center for travel to nearby Charlottesville and Williamsburg, in addition to being on the main New York/Washington, D.C.-Florida route, makes the city even more convenient for sightseeing.

CENTRAL RICHMOND WALKING TOUR

There are three areas in Richmond where you can concentrate your sightseeing activities. For more information, we suggest you visit the Greater Richmond Chamber of Commerce at 616 East Franklin Street (649-0373). In any case, we now present you an outline of three separate walking tours you can take in the city. Six points of interest on the 1 1/2 mile "Central Richmond Walking Tour" include The Lee House, house of Robert E. Lee, at 707 E. Franklin Street. Open daily 10-4, St. Paul's Church, at 9th and Franklin Streets and the nearby Capitol Building are next on the tour.

Richmond is the third city which has served as the capital of the state. Jamestown was the capital of the colony until 1699 and then Williamsburg until 1779 when Richmond became the seat of government. The General Assembly held its first session in the State Capitol in 1778, in a building modeled after a Roman Temple in Nimes, France. The Capitol of Virginia is the meeting place of the oldest legislature in the Western Hemisphere. It is open weekdays 8:15 a.m.-5 p.m., Saturdays and holidays 9-5, and Sundays 1-5. Closed Christmas.

The building has been the scene of many historic events. In 1807, Aaron Burr was tried for treason here, with John Marshall, Chief Justice of the Supreme Court of the United States, presiding. On April 23, 1861, Robert E. Lee, accepted in this building command of the Confederate forces in Virginia. You might note that Richmond was the capital of the South during the Civil War of 1861-1865. Ironically, Lee, the military genius of the South, was the son-in-law of George Washington Parke Custis, son of George Washington. It was Washington who tried to reconcile the differences of the northern states and the southern states by locating the Nation's capital halfway between the two.

Inside the Virginia Capitol are Houdon's statue of Washington and an original portrait of the Virgin Queen, Elizabeth I, for whom the state was named. Outside you will find an 1858 equestrian statue of Washington with statues of Thomas Jefferson, Patrick Henry, George Mason, John Marshall, Thomas Nelson and Andrew Lewis—all famous Virginians.

The next point of the tour, reached by walking down 12th Street from the Capitol of Virginia at 1201 E. Clay Street, is the Museum of the Confederacy which served once as the Confederate White House. Open daily 10-5; Sundays 2-5.

112 RICHMOND

Central Richmond Walking Tour

1. LEE HOUSE
2. ST. JOHN'S EPISCOPAL CHURCH
3. CAPITOL SQUARE
4. CONFEDERATE WHITE HOUSE
5. VALENTINE MUSEUM
6. JOHN MARSHALL HOUSE
7. COLISEUM

AMTRAK STATION AT 7519 STAPLES MILL RD.

WILLIAMSBURG 113

The Valentine Museum at 1009 15 E. Clay Street specializes in local history. Open Tues.-Sat. 10 to 4:45; Sun. 1:30-5; closed Mondays. At 402 N. 9th Street is the John Marshall House, home of the Chief Justice of the United States from 1801-1835. Open Mon.-Sat. 10 to 4:30 and Sundays 2-5.

EAST RICHMOND TOUR

From the downtown area you can take a city bus along Broad Street to 24th Street, the oldest section of Richmond to St. John's Church where Patrick Henry delivered his stirring "Give me Liberty or give me Death." From there you can continue to Carrington Square, historic homes along East Grace Street and East Franklin Street to Libby Hill Park at 27th and Franklin Streets. This walking tour is about 1-1/4 miles long. In addition, at 1914 E. Main Street you will find the Edgar Allan Poe Museum. Open Tues.-Sat. 10 to 4:30 and Sunday-Monday 1:30-4:30. Admission one dollar.

WEST RICHMOND TOUR

From the downtown area take the city bus to Grove Avenue and Boulevard to the Virginia Museum of Fine Arts. It is open Tues.-Sat. 11-5; Saturday evening 8-10; Sunday 2-5 and closed on Mondays. Within easy walking distance is the Confederate Memorial Chapel and Battle Abbey, home of the Virginia Historical Society and a collection depicting Virginia history. Open Mon.-Fri. 9 to 5, Saturdays and Sundays 2 to 5.

WILLIAMSBURG

One of the most beloved places to visit in all America is the historical town of Williamsburg, Virginia. This former capital of Virginia and one of the most important towns of early America, is only about three hours to the south of Washington, D.C. or about an hour east of Richmond, the present capital of Virginia. You will find Williamsburg, with its restored houses from the 18th century and beautifully kept gardens, one of the most enjoyable places to visit in your tour of the U.S.A. Besides that, you get an excellent lesson in history here. About 88 of the buildings you will see here are practically the original ones as they existed over 200 years ago. Other buildings

114 WILLIAMSBURG

have been located and built exactly as they were in those historical times. Today the people who live here follow the trades which were found here previously. You will be able to watch a bookbinder, a printer, a silversmith, a basketmaker and many other people at work in the dress of the 18th century.

The Amtrak train station in Williamsburg is about a 10-15 minute walk away from the Information Center, the place where you start discovering Williamsburg. Here is where you purchase your General Admission ticket for $5. This allows you to visit eight of the buildings as well as give you unlimited bus travel in the historic area for one day. Because the historic area is quite large, you will find the bus service very convenient. In any case, before you start on your tour, you might want to see the 35 minute film at the Information Center about early Williamsburg. Besides showing scenes of the various buildings you will see, the film discusses the important role Williamsburg played in the struggle for independence. You will hear names like Patrick Henry, George Washington and Thomas Jefferson—they all knew Williamsburg in those early historic days.

At the same time you buy your General Admission ticket, you might pick up a guidebook available for 50 cents. It tells all about the buildings and includes a large map. Downstairs in the Information Center Building you take the bus to the historic area only about 5 minutes away. Remember that this bus takes you to all the places you might want to visit. It makes about 15 stops in the historic area. You just get on and off the bus whenever you want to. You might note that when you come back to the Information Center from the historic area, there is also a Virginia Travel Desk. Here you can obtain additional information about the State of Virginia.

We might draw your attention to the fact that you can also rent bicycles at the Motor House Office, right across the street from the Information Center. For us, this is one of the best ways to see Williamsburg. Since only buses and bicycles are allowed to travel the streets of old Williamsburg during the day, traveling by bicycle is easy and fun. In fact every time we have been here, we have rented a bicycle for at least part of the day. You must have a General Admission ticket (unless you are staying at the plush Williamsburg Inn or the Motor House) in order to rent a bicycle. It costs 70 cents an hour to rent a bicycle. It is an interesting way to see an early part of the U.S.A. Of course, besides the bicycle rental office, there are also restaurants, souvenir shops and restrooms in this area.

Note also that there are German, Spanish, and French pamphlets about Williamsburg available at the Information Center. The 35 minute film which serves as an introduction to the role Williamsburg played in the early development of the U.S.A. can also be seen in German, French and Spanish. For further information ask at the information desk in the Center.

FROM TERMINAL TO HISTORIC AREA/CHAMBER OF COMMERCE

To get from the Williamsburg terminal to the Information Center, walk up Boundary Street take a left on Lafayette Street, then take another left on Henry Street, cross the tracks and bear to your right with the road. You will soon see the parking lot and the information center.

To reach the Chamber of Commerce just walk up Boundary Street past the College of William and Mary until you come to Francis Street. Right across from the post office, in the middle of the block, you will find the Chamber of Commerce. Here you can get additional information about accommodations. Quite a number of private homes accept overnight guests. The cost is reasonable.

TICKET PRICES

You purchase your ticket at the Information Center. The 1976 ticket prices leave various options open to you. An "8 Building Ticket" good for one day costs $6 ($3 for children). The "14 Building Ticket" costs $7.50 ($3.50 for children). The "25 Building Ticket" costs $10 ($5 for children). The validity period for the 14 and 25 Building Tickets is one year. Thus you can use these tickets on a later visit or allow somebody else to use the remainder of the ticket. A hole is punched in your ticket when you enter a place of exhibition. In each case, admission to the Governor's Palace is $2 extra.

WHERE TO EAT

The cafeteria across from the Information Center is open continuously from 7 A.M. to 8 P.M. daily. The Cascades (behind the cafeteria) serves breakfast 7:30 to 10 A.M.; luncheon, 12 to 5; dinner 6 to 9:30 P.M. Sunday Brunch, 8:30 A.M. to 3 P.M.; dinner, 6 to 9 P.M. Dancing Friday and Saturday. 9 P.M. to Midnight. Cocktail Lounge open Sunday through Thursday, 5 to 10 P.M., Friday and Saturday, 5 to Midnight. Williamsburg Inn serves breakfast 7:30 to 10 A.M.; luncheon, 12 to 2; din-

WILLIAMSBURG

ner, 6:30 to 9:30 P.M. with entertainment during the dinner hours. Dancing Friday and Saturday, 9 to 11:30 P.M. Regency Cocktail Lounge, 11:30 A.M. to 11 P.M. daily. Entertainment in the Lounge 5 P.M. to 11 P.M. nightly. Williamsburg Lodge serves breakfast 7:30 to 10 A.M.; luncheon, 12 to 2; dinner, 5:30 to 8:15 P.M. featuring Family Virginia Dinner nightly. Coffee Shop daily 7 A.M. to 10 P.M. Garden Lounge for cocktails and refreshments, 11 A.M. to Midnight, entertainment nightly, 9 to 11:30 P.M.

Three taverns in the historical area serve meals enjoyed by such American patriots as George Washington, Patrick Henry and Thomas Jefferson. Chowning's Tavern serves luncheon and cocktails 11:30 to 4:30. Dinner from 5:30, cocktails from 5:00 with entertainment by costumed musicians. King's Arms Tavern serves luncheon, 12 to 2:30; dinner from 5:30. Campbell's Tavern serves luncheon, 12 to 2:30; dinner from 5:30. Strolling musicians during lunch on weekdays.

With the exception of the cafeteria, dinner reservations are advisable and usually required. Call 229-2141 between 9 A.M. and 9 P.M. At the Information Center there is a special telephone you can use. Also, menues are listed there.

ACCOMMODATIONS IN WILLIAMSBURG

There are many hotels in the Williamsburg area but keep in mind that there are also many visitors who come here. When you visit the Chamber of Commerce pickup a "Directory of Hotels and Motels in Historic Williamsburg." It lists the accommodations available from the high priced to the medium priced. There are two major clusters of accommodations—along the Richmond Toad to the west of the historic area and the other along Capitol Landing Road, to the east.

RICHMOND ROAD AREA

Some hotels in this area include: Commonwealth Inn 229-6922; Holiday Inn West 229-5060; Superior Motel 229-1532; Tioga Motor-Court 229-4531.

CAPITOL LANDING ROAD

Some hotels in this area include: Capitol Motel 229-5215; Greenbrier Lodge 229-2374; King William Inn 229-4933; Rochambeau Motel 229-2851.

WILLIAMSBURG 117

PRIVATE GUEST HOMES

Private guest homes provide accommodations at considerably lower prices than the hotels/motels. Usually the number of rooms available in a particular home is limited to two or three—but you might call to find out if there is a vacancy. Here is a partial list of individuals who allow visitors to stay at their homes—Mrs. Roy Buchanan 229-2990; Mrs. C. Casey 229-2944; Mrs. Raymond Foltz 229-2234; Mrs. Charles Ragland 229-3591; Mrs. W. Thompson 229-3455. The area code for the Williamsburg area is 804.

JAMESTOWN—JAMESTOWN FESTIVAL PARK

Just a few miles south of Williamsburg is Jamestown, site of America's first permanent English settlement in 1607. This historic part of America, along the James River, is divided into two general areas—Jamestown and Jamestown Festival Park. Tours from Williamsburg, your nearest terminal, are available to the Jamestown settlement and park. Ask downstairs at the Visitor Information Center in Williamsburg. The Jamestown Tour leaves daily at 10:15 a.m. and the cost is $6. Jamestown Festival Park is maintained by the Commonwealth of Virginia to help you understand what life was like and how the settlers lived upon their arrival in 1607.

CARTER'S GROVE PLANTATION

The beautiful plantation house overlooking the James River was begun in 1750. Here George Washington, Thomas Jefferson, and other American patriots were guests. Today the plantation is owned and operated by the Colonial Williamsburg Foundation. The plantation is open daily March through November. Tours leave the Colonial Williamsburg Information Center at 10:15. Cost is $1.50. House admission is extra ($2).

YORKTOWN

To the east of Williamsburg, on the York River is Yorktown. The American struggle for independence culminated in the battle fought here in 1781. Today you can walk over these historic fields and fortifications. The visitors center, especially built for the Bicentennial, includes a showing of an exciting pictorial presentation of

YORKTOWN

the events which shaped our destiny.

You can take a tour, March-October to Yorktown from Williamsburg, Tues., Thurs., and Sat. at 2:30 p.m. Cost $4. For the latest price information and tour departure times to Jamestown, Carter's Grove Plantation, Yorktown and the new exciting Busch Gardens (Old Europe), call Colonial Virginia Tours at (804) 229-4716.

Busch Gardens is open during the peak summer period from 10 a.m.-10 p.m.; at other times it closes earlier. The $6.50 admission price for adults ($5.50 for children 4-11) includes all rides and attractions.

And if you are looking for a souvenir or a gift from this historic area of America, you might think of a Smithfield Ham. The town of Smithfield is across the James River from Jamestown. Legend has it that friendly Indians gave hams to the starving settlers at Jamestown. Thus Jamestown survived as a settlement.

ATLANTA

Atlanta is not only the capital of Georgia, but it is also becoming the capital of the South with its modern buildings, attractions for industry and financial institutions and its importance as a transportation center. Today, the Atlanta metropolitan area includes over 1 1/2 million people, a far cry from the town of the aftermath of the destruction of 1864 after the struggle between the North and South.

Peachtree Street is the main street in Atlanta. It is on this street that you will find the Peachtree Center, including stores, an information center and a hotel with a glass elevator. This is the hub of the commercial district. However, when it comes to entertainment and eating you must visit Underground Atlanta, south on Peachtree Street and close to the state capitol.

Underground Atlanta, which actually is only a few years old, came about because of the many trains which daily passed through here. Because the trains interfered with other vehicular activity, the street level was simply raised, thus leaving the tracks and stores below isolated. You'll recognize the entrance to revitalized Underground

Atlanta by the old street car located there. (You can also get information here.) Once "underground" you can select from a variety of restaurants, musical entertainment and bars. Whatever you do on your visit here, do not forget to visit the Musical Museum, with its many kinds of instruments. You will not forget "Mighty Mortier," the antique Belgian Dance Organ.

One of the first places you should go after you arrival in Atlanta is the Visitor's Information Center located on Peachtree Street, in the area of the Peach Tree Center, a modern complex of buildings. Amtrak does not serve Atlanta, but Southern Railway provides service to the city on its New Orleans to Washington, D.C. route. The Terminal is at 1688 Peachtree St., N.W.

TOURS IN ATLANTA

Gray Line offers a host of tours including the "Atlanta Grand Circle" tour and the "King Tomb, Ebenezer Church and the Atlanta University Complex" tour. There is also at "Night Life Party" tour. Call 524-6086 for further information. American Sightseeing also offers a number of tours including those visiting the Dr. Martin Luther King Memorial and Stone Mountain Park. Call 524-2492 for further information.

SIX FLAGS OVER GEORGIA—ON YOUR OWN

Some of the tours include Six Flags over Georgia, a popular amusement park outside of the city. However, the Atlanta Transit System provides bus service (#78) to the park as well as other destinations. For further information call 524-2492. Six Flags over Georgia is open daily from 10—10 and the $7 admission charge includes all rides and attractions.

SAVANNAH—GEORGIA'S COLONIAL CAPITAL

James Oglethorpe and his followers settled Savannah, Georgia in 1733. Savannah was one of the earliest cities that had a definite plan to it. Today's parks and squares are a testament to the early planning. The 24 town squares are present at two block intervals.

The city once was a thriving cotton trading center, its population doubling between 1840 and 1860. The Civil War and Sherman's march from Atlanta proved to be the start of Savannah's downward trend in importance. Today, however, Savannah is again becoming a pleasant place.

When you arrive in Savannah, you will find the historic downtown area restored. Stop by at the Chamber of Commerce and pick up "Touring historic Savannah." This pamphlet is a guide to four scenic walking tours.

Note that the Savannah Visitor Center is now located in the former Central of Georgia Railroad Station, at 301 West Broad Street, tel. (912) 233-3067. Open daily until 5 p.m. Two steam locomotives are housed under the shed. A shuttle "train" ($2) leaves from here to take you through Savannah's historic district. You can also rent a bike at the Desoto Hilton.

CHARLESTON, SOUTH CAROLINA

One of the most historic and beautiful cities in all of North America is Charleston, S.C. The city, with over 300 years of history, can be easily reached since it is on the main route along the east coast of the country. The city is in a state which has been called "The Battleground of Freedom." More than 150 battles were fought here. Although for over three years South Carolina saw little military action in the fight for freedom, the state bore a heavy burden during the last years of the struggle. During March, April and May 1780, the British Army under Clinton laid siege to Charleston, with the Americans finally giving up the city. At the Battle of Eutaw Springs, Sept. 8, 1781, just a month before Yorktown, one of the hardest battles of the war was fought between the British and the Americans with more casualties than at Yorktown. It was not until 1782, that the British evacuated Charleston. Charleston, back on June 28, 1776, had been the site of one of the first complete American victories of the Revolution when American forces under the command of Col. William Moultrie repelled the invading British forces commanded by Clinton.

SIGHTSEEING IN CHARLESTON

One of the first places you should visit in Charleston is the Information Center in the Arch Building at 85 Calhoun Street. Open daily from 8:30 a.m. to 5:30 p.m. Here you can obtain a map to take a do-it-yourself walking tour of historic Charleston. Also ask about renting a bicycle to explore historic Charleston. Call 722-8338 for further information.

Some of the historic homes you can visit include the Joseph Manigault House (1803), at 350 Meeting Street. Adam-style mansion. Adults, $1.25. Open 10-5 Monday-Saturday and 2-5 on Sunday. The Nathaniel Russell House, 51 Meeting Street. Built before 1809 at an estimated cost of $80,000, it is Charleston's finest example of Adam architecture. Spacious garden. Admission $1.25. Open Monday-Saturday, 10-1, 2-5; Sunday, 2-5. The Heyward-Washington House, 87 Church Street. Built in 1770, this was the home of Thomas Heyward, Jr., a signer of the Declaration of Independence. George Washington resided here on his Southern tour in 1791. Adults, $1.25. Open Monday-Saturday, 10-5, and 2-5 on Sunday.

122 ASHEVILLE

Some of the other places you might visit include the Charleston Museum on Rutledge Avenue, between Bennett and Calhoun Streets. Open 10-5 and Sundays 2-5. The Confederate Museum at 188 Meeting Street is open March 15-Labor Day. Closed Sundays and Mondays. Hampton Park, entrance on Cleveland Street at Rutledge Avenue, is a public park with beautiful gardens. The Old Slave Mart at 6 Chalmer Street is open Mon.-Sat. 10 to 5 and Sundays between 2 and 5.

To explore some of the other sights in the city as well as absorb the atmosphere, you might want to splurge and take a horse drawn carriage tour. Call 722-3269 for further information. Gray Line offers tours of the city and the harbor (historic Ft. Sumter).

LOCAL BUS SERVICE

The South Carolina Electric and Gas Company provides daily bus service to most sections of the metropolitan area including the City, North Charleston, West of the Ashley, Mt. Pleasant, Sullivan's Island, and the Isle of Palms. For schedule information, contact: Transportation Department of the South Carolina Electric and Gas Company, 722-2226. Bee Line operates a bus to the wonderful Folly Beach, call 556-1862 for further information.

ASHEVILLE, NORTH CAROLINA

Asheville is located in the western part of North Carolina. Southern Railway has discontinued regular service to the city from Salisbury, but it is expected excursions trains will be operated during the peak season.

The area around Asheville offers a lot to see. The best and most convenient way to enjoy the mountain beauty of western North Carolina is with Gray Line. One tour covers part of the Great Smokies and the Indian Village of Cherokee. For an afternoon tour you might take the "Mount Mitchell" tour—Mt. Mitchell being the highest peak east of the Rockies. Finally, Gray Line offers a tour of the Biltmore Estate—the famous castle with its beautiful gardens. The tour leaves daily at 1 p.m. from Asheville motels or the bus terminal. For further information call Gray Line in Asheville at 252-8450. For convenient accommodations you might try the 'Downtowner Motel,' close to the bus station.

Asheville not only is your gateway to the beautiful scenery surrounding the city, but it is also the home of Thomas Wolfe (1900-1938), author of "Look Homeward Angel." Wolfe's house, the 'Old Kentucky Home,' is located just a few blocks from the heart of Asheville's business district. It is open mid-May to mid-October.

NASHVILLE, TENNESSEE

Whereas Atlanta is called the capital of the South, Nashville, Tennessee is truly the capital of country music. Of the 50 country music singles records released in the country during an average week, 35 come from Nashville. There are over 50 recording studios in the area as well as over one thousand music publishers. Nashville then is the obvious place to enjoy and learn about our musical heritage from which developed a unique style of music—country and western music. Amtrak's 'Floridian' between Chicago and Florida serves the city.

CITY SIGHTS

One of the first things you will see after you arrive is the splendid Capitol Building in Nashville, for the city is the capital of the State of Tennessee. The city also contains the Parthenon, an exact replica of the Greek Temple of 438 B.C. The area is also the location of the Hermitage, the mansion built by Andrew Jackson in 1819. And if you are interested in the history of Country Music, visit Ryman Auditorium, at 116 Fifth Ave., North. It was the home of the Grand Ole Opry from 1941 until 1974. Admission is $1 and guided tours are available daily from 8:30 a.m. to 4:30 p.m. The Country Music Hall of Fame and Museum at 700 16th Ave., South, is dedicated to entertainers, composers and leaders of the country music industry. Open June-August: Sunday-Tuesday 8:30 a.m.-5 p.m.; Wednesday-Saturday 8:30 a.m.-8 p.m.

OPRYLAND U.S.A.

Opryland U.S.A: is a $28 million family entertainment complex in a beautiful 110-acre park setting. Five musical theme areas tell history of American music with continual live performances. Specialty restaurants, exciting rides, animal exhibits and craft shows. Open March 29-May 18: Saturday 10 am-8 pm; Sunday 10 am-6 pm. May 24-June 15: Sunday-Friday 10 am-6 pm; Saturday 10 am-8 pm. June 16-September 1: Daily 10 am-10 pm. September 6-October 26: Saturday 10 am-7 pm; Sunday 10 am-6 pm. All inclusive park ticket: Adult $6.50.

GRAND OLE OPPRY

The Grand Ole Opry, located at Opryland U.S.A. is the place for Country Music. Opry shows Friday and Saturday nights as well as matinee performances Friday, Saturday and Sunday during peak summer season. Getting tickets to the shows is quite a task. You might consider ordering tickets by mail, in addition to purchasing tickets at the box office. On Friday evenings there is an 8 p.m. show and on Saturday evenings there are shows at 6:30 p.m. and at 9:30 p.m. Indicate on your ticket request the time of the show you want tickets to, how many tickets and the date. Reserved tickets are $5 each. Make checks payable to "Grand Ole Opry" and send to Grand Ole Opry Ticket Office, 2800 Opryland Drive, Nashville, Tennessee 37214. Good luck! For further information call (615)889-3060. Keep in mind that there is no public bus service out to Opryland although some hotels have limousine service.

NEW ORLEANS

New Orleans, where the Mississippi River meets the Gulf of Mexico, is many things to many people. But one thing we, and all our friends who helped write this book, will say is that New Orleans is an absolutely enchanting place. Not only will you find the city an exciting place to visit, but New Orleans is truly accessible because practically every mode of transportation serves this city. Some people have called New Orleans the "Paris of America" or the "Birthplace of Jazz." Both of these names of course describe the city. However, the city is more frequently known as the "Crescent City." This name has come about because of its location in the bend of the mighty Mississippi River. In fact, the river has played an important part in the development of New Orleans.

Although Bienville founded the present city in 1718 and named it in honor of the Duke of Orleans, Regent of France, it was not until January 10, 1812, when the steamer "New Orleans" arrived, that the city really began to grow. The "New Orleans" was the first steam boat to successfully navigate the Ohio and Mississippi Rivers. This fact contributed significantly to the importance of the city. In fact, the port of New Orleans still provides the city with its largest income, although tourism now ranks second as an industry.

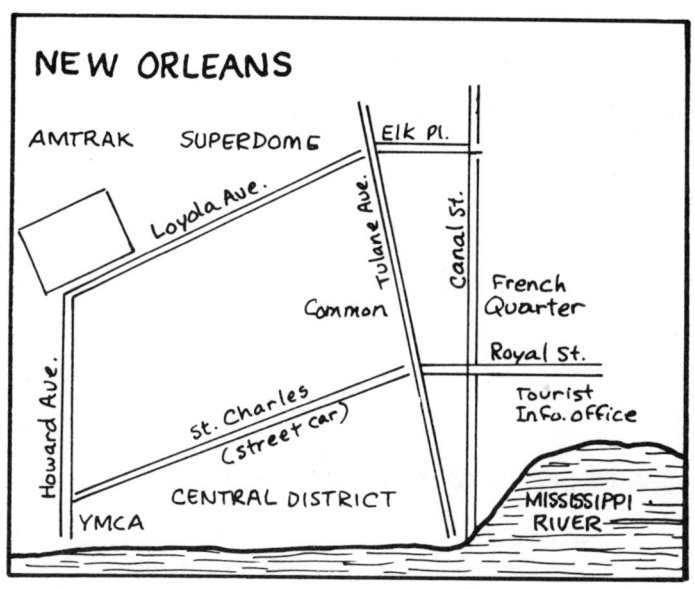

As you can imagine, a river as mighty as the Mississippi can create very difficult flooding problems in the spring. Through an ingenious number of flood prevention programs, the city has been saved by the opening of a number of "spillways" which in effect diverts water from the swollen Mississippi to nearby Lake Pontchartrain and the Gulf of Mexico. No matter how you arrive in New Orleans, you do become aware of the great role that water plays in the location of the city. New Orleans is located on a relatively narrow strip of land, with water on all three sides. This enabled the city to escape disaster by allowing the water to be diverted.

However, the threat of national disaster, whether it be floods or hurricanes, has played only a part in the history of the city. Political forces have also in great part played a role in shaping the New Orleans of today. In fact, it has been the various cultures that dominated New Orleans in its development which give it the exciting atmosphere today. It became a French crown colony in 1731, was under Spanish rule from 1776-1803, returned to France in 1803. The same year the United States of America obtained the city as part of the Louisiana Purchase.

With this kind of history, it is easy to see that the VIEUX CARRE, or the French Quarter, the site of the original settlement, is a mixture of Old and New World charms. The old buildings with their large iron balconies, world famous restaurants, the many interesting antique shops and the sound of jazz, make the French Quarter a most worthwhile place to visit.

AMTRAK TERMINAL LOCATION

The Amtrak rail station is located in the modern transportation center, practically next door to the new Superdome. At the terminal you will find a host of facilities, including showers for 50¢. The excellent YMCA which accepts both men and women is about 4 blocks down Howard Ave. If you want to reach the French Quarter you can take a city bus or just walk down Loyola Ave. until you reach Canal Street. There turn right and you soon will come to the familiar Bourbon and Royal Streets on your left.

NEW ORLEANS TOURIST INFORMATION OFFICE

As soon as you have arrived in New Orleans, we recommend the first place you visit is the Greater New

Orleans Visitor Information Center located at 334 Royal Street, in the heart of the wonderful French Quarter. Our map shows you the location of this excellent Information Center. The Center is actually a 147 year old bank building, and as you view it from the outside with its columns, it will be very easy to recall the splendor of past years. As you walk in, you are pleasantly surprised by the furniture and style which reinforces your image of yesterday. However, there is nothing antiquated about the service and the wealth of information you can obtain here. One of the great aids here is the descriptive folders which are displayed under a glass cover. Since each folder has a number, just note the ones that appeal to you, go to the main desk in the center of the large room and call out your choices to the attendant. Also a useful city map is available. If you have any specific questions, the young ladies will answer them.

Now that you have a number of brochures (also available in Portuguese, German, French and Spanish), you might sit down in one of the soft chairs and plan your exploration of New Orleans. Note that in one corner of the room you will find that coffee is available - free! As you are sitting back, have a look at the walls of the room. On these walls you will see the faces and names of men and women who have played a prominent part in the history of New Orleans—from Andrew Jackson (the Battle of New Orleans 1812) to Louis Armstrong (Jazz).

Here are a couple of other things you might note about the Center. It is open every day (except Christmas) from 8:30 a.m. to about 5:00 p.m. Also note there are restrooms, telephones and an auditorium featuring films about the city.

BOURBON STREET

One street that you absolutely must visit, although it has degenerated in the last years, is Bourbon Street. The street really comes alive at night. And if you are like us, you will be delighted with the many places where you can listen to jazz. Not only is jazz important here but dining is also. One of the greatest restaurants is Galatoire's. It is located near the corner of Bourbon and Iberville. Men are required to wear coat and tie after 5 and all day on Sunday. The line outside this restaurant seems always to be long. You might try to come early or a little bit later in the evening to avoid the crowd. However, if you cannot get in and you must have something to eat, Toney's Pizza across the street will fill you.

In any case, if you did manage to get something to eat somewhere, let us now talk about jazz. Just a couple of doors down from Galatoire's is the Blue Angel—here you hear authentic Dixieland Jazz. The Economy Nite Club (at the corner of Bourbon and Conti) is another good place to listen to jazz. The place has pictures of famous jazz performers. Remember you have to walk downstairs to listen to the jazz. Further down Bourbon Street at St. Peter is Maison Bourbon—dedicated to the preservation of jazz. You can actually watch and listen from the outside. At 726, turn right onto St. Peter, is Preservation Hall—the place for good jazz. And if you still want more jazz, try 628 Dauphine (one street over from Bourbon) near Toulouse. Jazz is usually played in the courtyard here. The Wax Museum (with its life-size figures) is on Conti, near Dauphine. We might note that the 'Al Hirt' is at the corner of St. Louis and Bourbon.

ROYAL STREET/FRENCH MARKET

Another important street in the French Quarter of New Orleans is Royal Street. We have mentioned that your first stop in New Orleans should be the Visitor Information Center at 334 Royal Street. Almost next door at 400 Royal is the Louisiana Wild Life Museum, open until 4:45 p.m. Monday-Friday. Besides all the fascinating shops, sounds and architectural styles you will experience here, we will mention a couple of practical things you might find useful. Walgreen (a drug store with reasonable food prices) is located at Royal and Iberville. An A & P foodstore is at the corner of Royal and St. Peter. A self-service laundry (open from 7:00 in the morning to 11:00 in the evening) is also nearby. Also here you will find less expensive hotels than other places on Royal Street. For instance, a single room at tne Holiday Inn at 124 Royal Street is about 28 dollars. Further down the street at the Nine O Five Hotel, Cornstalk Fence Hotel and the Andrew Jackson Hotel, the prices are considerably lower. For "Great Creole Cooking" try the Le Patio Royale Restaurant, at 621 Rue Royale. When you walk down Dumaine, past Chartres, you will be at the famous French Market. Here you can really watch people since practically everyone sooner or later comes to this area. Also you can catch bus #91 from here to Pontchartrain Beach. At St. Ann and Decatur you can also watch people from the outside cafe "Cafe du Monde." Now you are in the famous Jackson Square, the historic

NEW ORLEANS

center of the old city. Have a look at beautiful St. Louis Cathedral, completed in 1794, after having been destroyed by the fire of 1788. While you are here in the square, walk up the platform which gives you a panoramic view of Jackson Square, the Mississippi River and New Orleans harbor. At Royal and St. Louis you can catch the Vieux·Carre Bus'—it takes you through the French Quarter. Antoine's Restaurant is on St. Louis, between Royal and Bourbon. And if you are looking for a shoe repair place—there is one at 112 Royal.

TOURS IN NEW ORLEANS

Gray Line offers at least six tours of the city and its surroundings. They range from a 1 1/2 hour of "Old Homes, Parks and Gardens" to a "Night Tour" lasting four hours. Call 525-0138 for further information. Southern Tours at 288-7696 also offers several tours. Ask about the Southern Plantation Tours.

One of the things we recommend you do is a boat trip on the Mississippi to the Bayou. The 'Voyageur' leaves the dock at 10 a.m. and returns about 3 p.m. Cost is $6—call 523-5555 for further information. The 'Mark Twain' leaves the Canal Street docks at 11 a.m. and returns at 4 p.m. Cost is $6—call 525-6545 for further information.

CAJUNS AND CREOLES

Much of South Louisiana was settled by Acadians from Nova Scotia. The Acadians, because they were loyal to France, were expelled by the British when the two powers fought for control of North America, several decades before the struggle for independence. These Acadians, or Cajuns, as they are now called, have kept much to themselves and have retained their customs. Whereas the Cajuns are primarily French Canadians, the Creoles of the area are of French or Spanish background or a mixture of the two. As you can imagine, the food that you can get in New Orleans has been influenced a great deal by these groups. Spicy and delicious.

ST. AUGUSTINE
FLORIDA

ST. AUGUSTINE, FLORIDA

St. Augustine, the first permanent settlement in the United States, can be easily reached by a 45 minute bus trip from Jacksonville, the important Amtrak rail center just to the north. St. Augustine, settled by the Spaniards, celebrated its 400th anniversary in 1965! Considering that we are only celebrating our nation's 200th anniversary in 1976, St. Augustine's older sections offer a long history. St. George Street, the restored historic street with shops and old Spanish style houses, is a wonderful area to explore on foot. In fact, the historical area is only about a 10 minute walk away from the Greyhound Terminal (148 Malaga). Also while you are in St. Augustine, you will be able to view the Castillo de San Marcos National Monument. The well preserved fort with its 16-foot thick walls, was started in 1672.

One of the first places to stop is the Information Center (829-5681), near the historic area, at 10 Castillo Drive. Open daily from 8-5:30 p.m. You can get a map here as well as see a short film about St. Augustine. The sightseeing train allows you to get around the historic area for $2.50. The ticket, valid for 24 hours, allows you to get on and off at the many points of interest. Then there is a free bus tour with a lecture. It leaves from the Old Jail Parking Lot but note that you cannot get off at will.

A WALK DOWN HISTORIC GEORGE STREET

From the Information Center you have the opportunity to walk down historic George Street, Calle Real.

ST AUGUSTINE 131

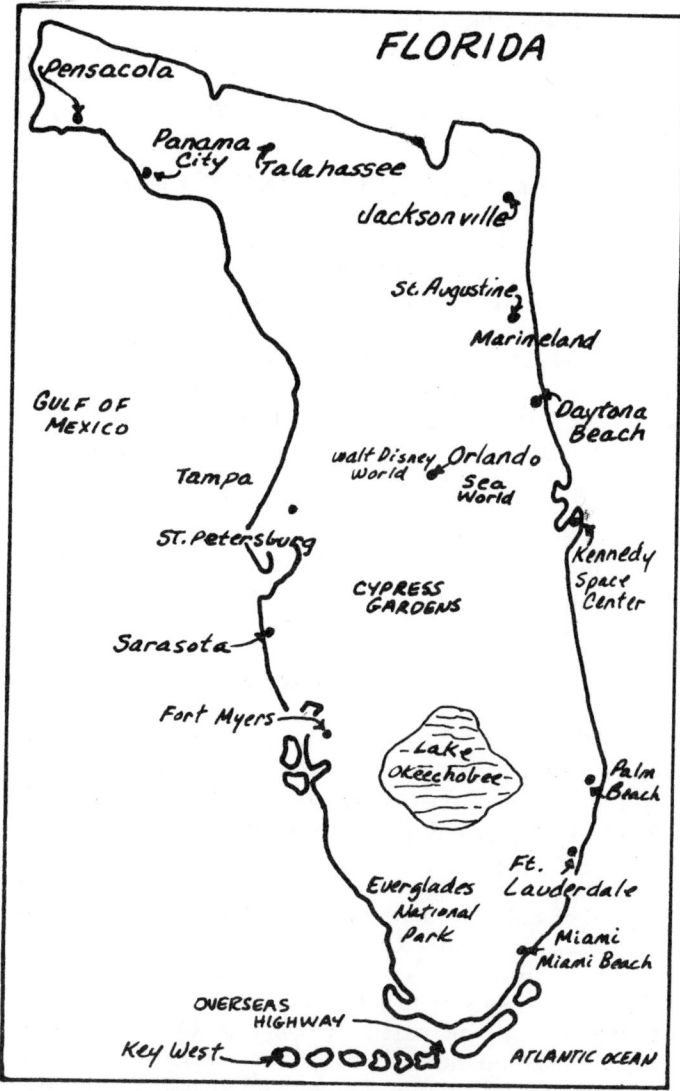

This whole area has been restored. At #14, you will find the "Oldest Wooden School House," built of cedar and cypress. The Ribera House is an example of a Spanish home during the early Spanish period. At #46 you will find the Arrivas House where domestic crafts such as weaving and candle dipping as well as baking are demonstrated. The Posado is an old Spanish Inn re-created in an original Spanish Colonial house. At the Oliveros House, #59, you can watch hand made cigars being made. Across from the Oliveros House you will find

132 DISNEY WORLD

a wood working shop. The Benet Store at #62 is a country store. Really interesting to see all the various articles on display. These attractions are only a few of the things you will be able to see and visit on the historic street.

ORLANDO, FLORIDA TRAIN STATION

Orlando of course is your gateway to fabulous Disney World. The white-washed Spanish structure which makes up the Orlando train station is a little bit out of town. When you arrive here in the morning, for instance, you have the whole day to explore wonderful Disney World. You have several ways to reach Disney World. You can rent a car at the station (make your reservation well in advance and check with your travel agent to see if your party qualifies for Amtrak's "Week of Wheels" plan). You can also take a taxi out to Disney World—but that can be fairly expensive, especially if you are traveling by yourself. Our choice was to take a taxi (about $2) to the Greyhound Terminal. From there take one of the frequent low cost bus departures out to Disney World.

DISNEY WORLD

After about a 20-30 minute bus trip from Orlando, you approach the wonderful area of Walt Disney World. In the distance you can see the Magic Kingdom Castle. Your bus lets you off just a few yards from the entrance to Disney World.

Once you have actually arrived at the Walt Disney World complex, you have a great number of choices about what to do and what kind of tickets to buy. First, Disney World is open from 9 a.m. to 1 a.m. daily in the summer. During the remainder of the year hours of operation are changed, with an earlier closing in the evening. The General Admission Ticket costs $3.75 and includes transportation for one day and admission to the Magic Kingdom Theme Park. You also have a choice of buying the Eight Ride Ticket Book ($6.50—eight attractions) and the Twelve Ride Ticket Book ($7.50—twelve attractions).

The Theme Park has over 35 major attractions within the following lands: Adventure land; Main Street, U.S.A.; Frontierland; Liberty Square; Fantasyland; Tomorrowland. Here are some of the major attractions including Cinderella's Castle, Jungle Cruise, Swiss Family Island Tree House, Sunshine Pavillion, Riverboat and Keel

Boats on Rivers of America, Haunted Mansion, Hall of Presidents, Diamond Horseshoe Review, Country Bear Band Jamboree, 20,000 Leagues Under the Sea, Golden Carousel, Mickey Mouse Revue, It's a Small World, Mr. Toad's Wild Ride, Peter Pan's Flight, Grand Prix Raceway, Circle-Vision Theater, Flight to the Moon, Snow White Adventures, Dumbo the Flying Elephant, The Mad Tea Party and Skyway.

JOHN F. KENNEDY SPACE CENTER

The east coast of Florida has been the scene of many dramatic events in America's history. To the north of Cape Canaveral is St. Augustine, the Nation's oldest city, while at the "Cape", the first rocket, a V-2, was launched on July 24, 1950. By 1960, NASA, The National Aeronautics and Space Administration charged with the conduct of space exploration for peaceful purposes, acquired the launch facilities. On May 5, 1961, NASA launched Freedom 7, flown by Alan Shepard for 115 miles in space. On February 20, 1962, John Glenn became the first American to orbit the Earth. On July 20, 1969, Neil Armstrong and Edwin Aldrin became the first ever to step on the moon—launched from an area so close to where Columbus first sighted the Western Hemisphere.

However, it will be on July 4, 1976, the 200th anniversary of the signing of the Declaration of Independence, that the most ambitious, expensive and far reaching event of the American Bicentennial is scheduled to occur. On that date, a Viking spacecraft will be in the final stages of landing on Mars and hopefully transmit pictures back to Earth upon its landing. You can visit the exhibits which led to the miraculous scientific achievements the past 15 years, in the Space Age Museum at the Visitor Information Center. Daily NASA tours of the spaceport facilties are available at the Kennedy Space Center. The two hour bus tours leaving from the Visitor Information Center cost $2.50.

MIAMI—MIAMI BEACH

There are really two distinct areas in this southeastern part of Florida—the sprawling city of Miami and the smaller Miami Beach with its luxury hotels. Miami has a population of about 350,000 while that of Miami Beach is about 90,000. Biscayne Bay separates Miami from Miami Beach but buses run over causeways which connect the two cities.

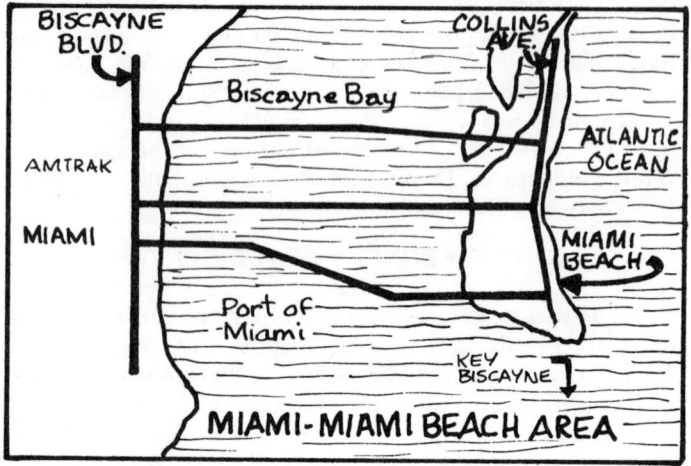

Although you arrive in Miami, the object of your visit is probably Miami Beach. The main street in Miami Beach is Collins Avenue. Take a bus trip up and down this street to get a good perspective of the many big hotels here. Just watching all the people come and go is entertaining in itself. Although most of the beach area seems to be taken up by the big hotels, there are a number of public beaches available at 21st, 46th, and 64th Streets, among others!

VIZCAYA

One of the most interesting sights in Miami on Biscayne Bay is the Italian Palace-like Vizcaya, the former home of James Deering. The building of the stately 70 room estate began in 1914 and completed in 1916; with its reflecting pools, fountains, shaded walks and gardens the estate is a worthwhile visit. It is located at 3251 South Miami, south of the Rickenbacker causeway, and can be reached by city bus. Open daily except Christmas from 9:30-5:30.

SIGHTSEEING TOURS IN MIAMI

Gray Line has a number of tours available including a Greater Miami City tour, Everglades National Park tour, a one day Walt Disney World and a two day Disney World and Kennedy Space Center tour. For other tours and further information call 945-6513. American Sightseeing Tours also offer a number of tours including a Miccosukee Indian Village tour, the Magic City (Greater

Miami) tour and a Key West and the Florida Keys tour. For other tours and further information call 448-1711.

NIGHT CLUB TOUR

If you want to have excellent entertainment at reasonable prices, you might want to take a night club tour. For example, a night club tour, with complete dinner, one drink and two shows costs about $24. For further information call Leblang's Night Club Tours at 865-0341.

"Y" ACCOMMODATIONS IN MIAMI

One of the nicest Y's that we have visited is the practically brand new YWCA of Greater Miami, at 100 S.E. 4th Street, Miami, Florida, 33131. Both men and women can stay here—single rooms are $9 and doubles $12. Your best bet is to make reservations as soon as your plans are firm—either send one night's deposit to the above address, make checks payable to 'YWCA of Greater Miami' or telephone (305) 377-8161. This residence is really super fantastic! Lounge and laundry areas on each floor; an outdoor pool, roof top tennis court and a sauna are yours to enjoy.

MIAMI—KEY WEST

The trip from Miami to Key West is quite interesting as you seem to travel from one island to another on connecting bridges. Sometimes the strip of land is so narrow that there is barely room for the road. Always beside you is the glimmering water. The pipe you see now and then alongside the road still is the main way fresh water is transported from the mainland to Key West.

Besides the wonderful climate, Key West has a number of other attractions. Ernest Hemingway lived here off and on for 30 years. His former home is open to the public. And while you are visiting this island, try some of the local food including conch chowder and key lime pie. For further sightseeing take the Key West Conch Tour Train. For $1.25 you get a 14 mile tour of the city's sights as well as the Navy Base. Departures take place during the summer every half hour from the depot at 303 Front Street.

136 TAMPA

TAMPA-ST. PETERSBURG

If you are like us, you sometimes wonder about the exact locations of these cities. Tampa is the larger of the two, being a commercial and industrial city, while St. Petersburg is a residential city across the bay. Tampa is not only large, but it also has plenty of attractions. The University of South Florida and the University of Tampa are located here. Busch Gardens with its landscaped gardens, African animals and Monorail is also here.

TAMPA

However, if you are looking for a Latin flavor may we suggest you stop off at Ybor City, between East Broadway, Columbus Drive, 22nd Street and Nebraska Avenue. The city was founded by a cigar manufacturer just before the turn of the century. Here in Ybor City you will find some excellent restaurants such as the Columbia. The narrow streets with stores and the lively atmosphere everywhere makes a visit to this part of Tampa worthwhile. Before you leave Ybor City promise yourself to have at least one cup of the delicious coffee at one of the many coffeehouses. You might also keep in mind while you are in Tampa that you are only about 1 1/2 hours away from Disney World.

ST. PETERSBURG

St. Petersburg is the tourist center on the Florida west coast. Its sunshine draws thousands of visitors here every year. Many tourists decide to stay. And if you are interested in plants and trees, we suggest you visit Florida's Sunken Gardens, conveniently located near the downtown area for the traveler (cost is $2.50). At the St. Petersburg dock (at the foot of Second Avenue N.E.) you will find the "Bounty"—built for the movie "Mutiny on the Bounty."

THE MIDWEST

CHICAGO

Louis Joliet and Father Jacques Marquette explored the area around Lake Michigan in 1673. Almost 200 years later, in 1871, Mrs. O'Leary's cow is said to have kicked over the lantern that set the city in flames, leaving over 100,000 homeless. However, the city survived and grew even more important as a great trading and transportation center. The city is rich in museums and stores. Along the famous State Street you can buy almost anything.

THE CHICAGO SKYLINE

When you arrive in Chicago, look up at the towering skyline. It is dominated by three of the tallest buildings in the world. The 110 story Sears Tower, at 1,454 feet, is the world's tallest building. The fourth tallest is the 1,136 foot Standard Oil Building and the fifth tallest, also in the 'Windy City,' is the 1,127 foot John Hancock Center. New York City, on the other hand, has the 1,350 foot World Trade Center, the world's second tallest building and the third tallest building in the world, the 1,250 foot Empire State Building.

THE SEARS TOWER

Besides being the world's tallest building, the Sears Tower, owned by the huge Sears, Roebuck and Company,

138 CHICAGO

is also the world's largest private office building with its 4.5 million square feet of space. Only the Pentagon in Virginia, across the Potomac River from Washington, D.C., is larger. The Sears Tower faces Wacker Drive bounded by Adams, Jackson and Franklin Streets practically next to Chicago's Union Station—the Amtrak Terminal.

The observation level is on the 103rd floor, 1,353 feet high, and is served by two non-stop elevators. Over 16,500 people work in the building completed in 1974. More than 76,000 tons of structural steel were used in the building's construction. There are 80 miles of elevator cables and more than 16,000 bronze-treated windows—most 5 feet by 8 feet in size. In addition, there are 1,500 miles of electric wiring and 25 miles of plumbing pipe.

TOWER ARCHITECTURE

The style of architecture of the building is quite interesting. The Sears Tower reaches its 1,454 foot level by employing a number of "setbacks." Nine 75 by 75 foot square columns make up the base. If you look at the building, you will be able to make out the three columns on the sides of the building. At the 50th floor, two columns end, creating the first setback. Additional setbacks occur at the 66th floor and the 90th floor. The Sears Tower is open daily from 9 a.m. to Midnight. Cost to the "Skydeck" (observation deck) is $1.50.

CHICAGO—RAIL CENTER OF THE NATION

Chicago's Union Station, with its improved baggage facilities and enlarged lounge area, is an important transfer point for Amtrak passengers. The terminal acts as a link for rail travel between East and West. For example, during the summer months about 100 passengers from the eastbound Southwest Limited, the Los Angeles to Chicago train, transfer to such trains as the Broadway Limited (Chicago to New York) and the Chicago to Detroit trains.

ARRIVING AT CHICAGO'S UNION STATION

All Amtrak inter-city trains arrive/leave from Union Station. You therefore do not have to transfer from one station to another. For instance, if you are coming from the East, you have direct connections to the West and vice versa. To get yourself properly oriented with our station diagram, remember that on one side of the terminal are

CHICAGO 139

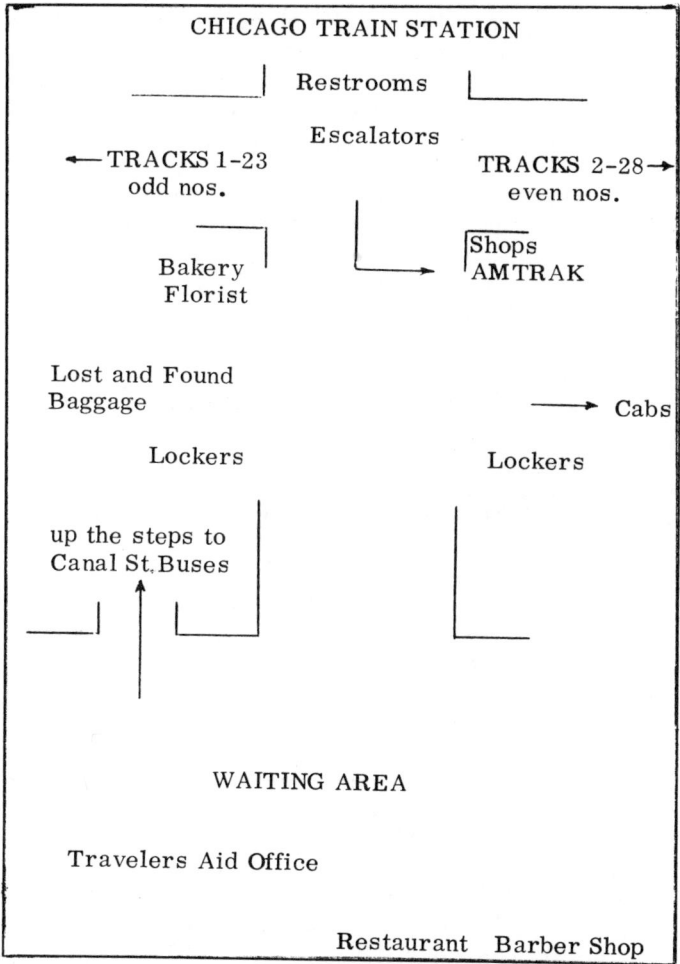

the even numbered tracks like 2,4,6... and on the other side you will have the odd numbered tracks such as 1,3,5. In any case, no matter what direction you come from, you will soon see a number of shops and restaurants. To reach the main part of the station do not take the escalators but continue down the hall. We might note that around the escalators you will find the restrooms. As you walk down the hall you will spot a bakery shop on your right and a florist. Right across from these, on the left side of the hall, you will see the spacious Amtrak Information Center—for information, tickets and reservations. Right around the corner from the Information Center you will find the place where you catch cabs. On the opposite side is the improved baggage claim area as well as automatic lockers (25¢ for small ones and 50¢ for the larger ones).

Once you enter the old part of the station, you will be in the waiting area. Here are plenty of benches for relaxing or reflecting on what to do next. In this large area of the station you will find the stairs that lead up to Canal Street where you catch buses to the Loop (main shopping district in Chicago). The waiting area is also the location of the Traveler's Aid Society Office, and a barber shop. From this waiting area you just walk up the stairs to catch the CTA (Chicago Transit Authority) buses. Bus no. 151 will take you for 35¢ (correct change!) to the downtown area. The CTA number for information is 664-7220.

NEW PASSENGER LOUNGE

Amtrak opened a new $1.5 million passenger lounge and baggage facility in 1975 inside Chicago Union Station. Located opposite the Amtrak ticket counters, the lounge offers waiting passengers the comfort of upholstered seats, restful surroundings and refreshments in a 5,000-square-foot fully carpeted enclosure.

The lounge has 314 seats in the waiting area and seating for another 34 in the refreshment section. All Amtrak train announcements are made inside the lounge over a modern sound system.

Immediately adjacent is a new baggage carousel—similar to those found at major airports—capable of handling the luggage of 200 detraining passengers every 10 minutes. Baggage is unloaded from the train, placed on a mechanized chute and automatically unloaded onto the revolving carousel. Taxicab stands for departing passengers are just a few steps away.

Amtrak has undertaken other modernizations at Union Station. In the station's huge main waiting room the plastered walls have been cleaned and repaired, and the vaulted ceiling around the massive skylight has been restored to its original cream color.

Chicago's Union Station handles 52 Amtrak trains a day and is the first Amtrak passenger station in the country to get modern, automatic baggage handling facilities. About 2 million Amtrak passengers use the station annually.

CHICAGO 141

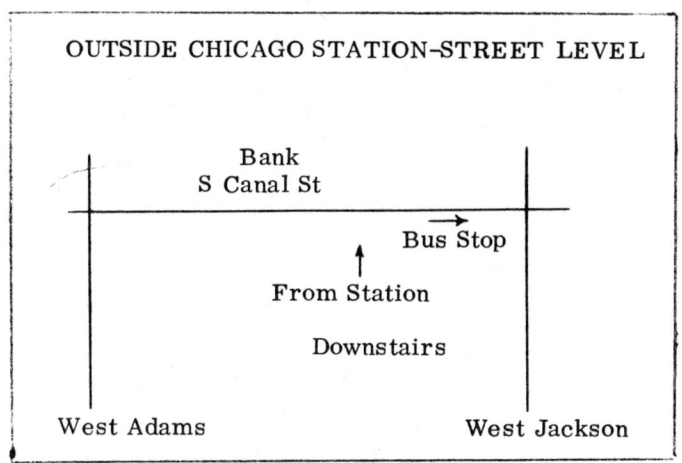

CHICAGO MUSEUMS

Chicago has a great number of museums—something of interest for practically everyone. The Adler Planetarium at 1300 S. Lake Shore Dr. (294-4620) is devoted to astronomy and related sciences. Open 9:30 a.m. Sept. 1 through June 15—closed 4:30 p.m. Monday, Wednesday, Thursday; 5 p.m. Saturday, Sunday and holidays; 9:30 p.m. Tuesday and Friday; June 16 through Aug. 1—9:30 a.m. to 9:30 p.m. Closed Thanksgiving, Christmas and New Year's Day.

The Field Museum of Natural History, founded in 1893 and located in Grant Park at Roosevelt Rd. and Lake Shore Drive (922-9410) charges $1 for adults and 35 cents for students and Senior Citizens. Fridays free! Open 9 a.m. Nov. through Feb. to 4 p.m. (5 p.m. weekends); March, April, Sept., Oct.—5 p.m.; May to mid-June—6 p.m.; mid-June through Labor Day—6 p.m. Monday, Tuesday, Thursday; 9 p.m. Wednesday, Saturday and Sunday. 9 p.m. Friday year-round. Closed Christmas and New Year's Day.

The John G. Shedd Aquarium, the worlds largest, is also located in Grant Park at 1200 S. Lake Shore Dr., (939-2426). Admission is $1 for adults, 35 cents for students and Senior Citizens. Friday is also a free day here. Open May, June, July, Aug.—9 a.m. to 5 p.m.; Sept., Oct., Mar., Apr.—10 a.m. to 5 p.m.; Nov., Dec., Jan., Feb.—10 a.m. to 4 p.m. 9 p.m. Friday year-round. Closed Christmas and New Year's Day.

The Art Institute of Chicago (236-7080) is located at Michigan Avenue and Adams Street. Thursday are free.

142 MILWAUKEE

Open 10 a.m. to 5 p.m. Monday, Tuesday, Wednesday, Friday, Saturday; 10 a.m. to 8:30 p.m. Thursday; 1 to 6 p.m. Sunday and holidays. Closed Christmas.

The Chicago Academy of Sciences (549-0606) founded in 1857 is located at 2001 N. Clark Street. It houses geological and ecological exhibits. Free nature field trips are provided on Saturday mornings. There is no admission charge. Open from 10 to 5 p.m. every day. Closed Christmas.

The Museum of Science and Industry in Jackson Park at 57th Street and S. Lake Shore Drive, (tel. 684-1414) has about 2000 displays that explain the principles of science and how they are applied to industry. No admission charge. Open during Daylight Saving Time—9:30 a.m. to 5:30 p.m. weekdays and Saturday; open during Central Standard Time—9:30 a.m. to 4 p.m.; 10 a.m. to 6 p.m. Sunday and holidays.

The Chicago Historical Society (642-4600) is well known for its collection of Chicago and Midwestern history, the American Civil War, and Abraham Lincoln. Sunday afternoons films are shown. Admission is 50 cents and 25 cents for students and Senior Citizens. Mondays are free. Open 9:30 a.m. to 4:30 p.m. Monday through Saturday; 12:30 p.m. to 5:30 p.m. Sunday and holidays. Closed Thanksgiving, Christmas and New Year's Day.

The Lincoln Park Zoo, near Lake Michigan in Lincoln Park, has a collection of more than 2,600 mammals, birds and reptiles from almost every part of the world. Telephone 294-4660 for information. Open daily from 9 a.m. to 5 p.m.; Children's Zoo 9:45 a.m. to 5 p.m.; Farm-in-the-Zoo 9:45 a.m. to 5 p.m.

MILWAUKEE

Milwaukee was founded in 1837 and obtained its present name by 1845. The name of Milwaukee was at one time "Mahnawaukee-Seepe," the gathering place of three rivers known todays as the Milwaukee, Menomonee, and Kinnickinnic. This former settlement has grown to such a great extent that metropolitan Milwaukee has a population of almost 1-1/2 million. Besides being a close gateway to Chicago, it is your departure point for Green Bay and Madison, Wisconsin as well as Minneapolis and Duluth, Minnesota, Fargo and Grand Forks, North Dakota, Winnipeg in the province of Manitoba, Canada, and the Pacific Northwest, as well as Vancouver, in British Columbia, Canada.

To many travelers, Milwaukee has become synonymous with beer—in fact three of the nine largest breweries are located here. You can take tours of their plants and then have an opportunity to sample the product. However, Milwaukee is also a great industrial city with an excellent harbor on Lake Michigan. To obtain more information about Milwaukee, visit the Visitor Information Center at 828 N. Broadway. It is open daily from 8-5. Saturdays, Sundays and holidays it is open at 9:30 in the morning.

MINNEAPOLIS, MINNESOTA

Minneapolis and its twin city of St. Paul, on opposite banks of the Mississippi, are your gateways to the beautiful northern parts of Minnesota and Wisconsin via Superior, Wisconsin and Duluth, Minnesota. By all means visit the Nicollet Mall in Minneapolis, an eight block long pedestrian shopping street. The eleven "skyways," glass-enclosed bridges, lead you across busy streets. It's a joy to walk here—no matter what the weather. You might also want to visit the 57 story skyscraper, the IDS Center, (IDS stands for Investor Diversified Services).

MINNEAPOLIS STATION

The train station in Minneapolis is about 5-6 blocks from the city center. Bus service as well as taxi cabs are available outside the station. You might note that the station is located practically next to the Mississippi River. The actual physical layout of the terminal is quite large. Since the tracks are one level below the main part of the station, elevator/escalator service is available. The personnel at the Amtrak Information/Ticket counter are extremely helpful. If you are traveling west you might have a look at some of the brochures available. Also in this part of the station you will spot the restrooms, telephones and vending machines for both food and books. On the other side, to the left as you are close to exiting from the station, you claim your checked baggage. Rental car companies have direct telephone lines from here to their downtown offices.

ST. LOUIS, MISSOURI

A French fur trader, Pierre Laclede Liquest, founded the city in 1764. It was named in honor of the patron saint of France, Louis IX. The United States obtained this region of New France in 1804 as part of the Louisiana Purchase.

About the middle of the 19th century brewing became an important part of the city. The good supply of grain, plenty of water, the caves along the Mississippi (the cool even temperature was necessary for aging of beer before the days of refrigeration). All of these factors contributed to the growth of the industry. In fact by 1860, St. Louis had about 40 breweries.

Today St. Louis is still an important transportation center. Just north of the city the Missouri River (route of the Lewis and Clark Expedition) joins the mighty Mississippi River. You will find that St. Louis is an easy city to reach.

There are many things to see in St. Louis. The Gateway Arch (which we describe later) gives you an excellent view of the city and its surroundings. Since the Arch is right along the river, you might want to stop by at the Goldenrod Showboat for music and river sightseeing trips. Also take the Riverfront Trolley which enables you to do some sightseeing along the riverfront.

Stop by at the Tourist Information Center near the leg of the Gateway Arch. Also deep in mind that just down Broadway is the Anheuser—Busch brewery, the world's largest. Free guided tours available Monday-Friday between 9:30 a.m. and 3:15 p.m. Call 577-2626 for further information. Remember that St. Louis was also the home of Ulysses S. Grant, the 18th President of the United States of America.

GATEWAY ARCH

The most prominent landmark in St. Louis is the Gateway Arch. In fact, its 630 foot height makes it the nation's tallest monument. (The Washington Monument in comparison is 555 feet high). Each leg of the Arch has a 40 passenger train to carry visitors to the top. These trains are made up of eight five passenger capsules mounted like the baskets of a ferris wheel to permit you to have a smooth and level ride inside the climbing curve of the Arch. About 5,119 tons of steel and 12,127 tons of concrete fill were used in the construction of the Arch.

The Arch, designed by the late and noted architect Eero Saarinen, illustrates the spirit of the pioneer who settled the West after the Louisiana Purchase. It also stands as shining proof of the engineering techniques and materials developed that have brought man to a new frontier—space.

THE OLD COURT HOUSE

Near the foot of the Gateway Arch, at 11 North Fourth Street, you will see the Old Court House, begun in 1839 and completed in 1862. The dome is the first cast-iron dome in the country. The court house was the scene of the Dred Scott trials starting in 1847. Take the opportunity to visit this historic building. Today it houses exhibits which help you learn about St. Louis history. Open daily 9 a.m.—4:30 p.m., except Christmas and New Years day. There is no admission charge. For further information call 622-4465.

KANSAS CITY, MISSOURI

Kansas City is quite an important rail junction for trains traveling north to south between Chicago and Houston and to the southwest from Chicago to Los Angeles and from New York/Washington, D.C. and Los Angeles. The terminal in Kansas City is quite a spacious one and a reminder of the bold and grandiose architecture of yesterday. After you have taken the escalator up from the platforms, you will soon be in the main hall of the station. Take a look at the tremendously high ceiling. A large waiting area is here with several small shops and snack bars. You will also find a number of lockers in this area. Further along you will spot the Amtrak Information/Ticket counter, as well as a large display of departures and arrivals in Kansas City. Across from this counter you will see the Travelers Aid Society Office. Stop in—they even have bus information as well as an assortment of travel information. More lockers are found further along in the station. Restrooms are also on the other side of the Travelers Aid Office.

The train station in Kansas City is not located directly in the downtown area; rather it is about 10-15 blocks away from the hub of the city. Taxis are available outside of the station—the fare to downtown is less than $2. Buses run downtown on a fairly frequent basis between about 6 in the morning until just after 11 in the evening. Bus no. 56 will get you over the bridge by the station and down Main Street for 45¢.

If you are looking for a bus to take you from downtown to the train station, take #56 with "Country Club" written on it. For additional information about bus service, call the Kansas City Area Transportation Authority at 241-0303. Should you have any problems regarding baggage, tickets, reservations or other matters concerning rail travel, just ask at the Amtrak counter. The staff here is very resourceful and helpful.

There is actually quite a lot to see in Kansas City and its surroundings. River Quay is a restored area along the Missouri River. Here you find interesting little stores, boutiques and places to eat. This is where the first building in Kansas City was put up in 1826. For a map of the city and other places to see stop off at the Visitors Information Center at 1221 Baltimore, telephone 221-5242.

The Truman Library and Museum in honor of Harry S. Truman, 33rd President of the United States, is located in Independence, Missouri, just outside of Kansas City. Open daily 9-5, call 795-3830 for more information. Another attraction outside of the city is 'Worlds of Fun' an amusement center open daily 10-10, Saturdays until midnight. The $7.50 admission price include all rides and attractions. For various tours of the city and surroundings call Gray Line at 471-1242.

THE PLAINS

We briefly include North Dakota, South Dakota, Nebraska and Kansas in this grouping. In your discovery of the U.S.A. you will use these states to travel on your transcontinental itinerary. The distances in these states are immense—whether it be traveling across the prairies of Kansas or the wheatfields of North Dakota.

Bismarck is the capital of North Dakota. It is an important point on the Chicago-Seattle route. You might want to stop by at the State Historical Museum as well as view the State Capitol.

As we have pointed out, Cheyenne is your gateway to Rapid City, South Dakota. Some of the sights in this area include the Broken Boot Gold Mine in Deadwood. The Black Hills Passion Play is performed at Spearfish. The Trial of Jack McCall, staged at the Old Towne Hall in Deadwood, re-creates the prosecution of the man who murdered Wild Bill Hickock. The Black Hills 1880 Railroad provides a 32 mile round trip between Hill City and Custer, formerly two mining towns.

Mount Rushmore (5,725 feet) in the Black Hills of South Dakota contains the huge faces of four famous Americans carved into the solid granite. The faces of Presidents Washington, Jefferson, Teddy Roosevelt and Lincoln are awe-inspiring.

Omaha is the largest city in Nebraska. It is located on the banks of the Missouri River. In 1863 the town was the starting point for the westward drive in building a transcontinental railroad. Today it is still an important transportation link between Chicago and Denver/Cheyenne.

ROCKY MOUNTAIN STATES

DENVER, COLORADO

Denver, the capital of Colorado, is your gateway to the beauty of the Rocky Mountains. The 'Mile High City' (its elevation is 5280 feet) has a lot to offer from its many museums, tours of the State Capitol and the U.S. Mint, to its Larimer Square where you can see what Denver was like in the latter part of the 19th century.

SIGHTSEEING IN DENVER

One of the first places you should visit is the Hospitality Center at 225 W. Colfax Ave., where you can get additional information about the city. Telephone 982-1112. You might keep in mind that Denver was first settled in 1858 in the area what is now Larimer Square. And as we are celebrating the Nation's Bicentennial, Colorado is celebrating its Centennial! It became a state in 1876.

The State Capitol, modeled after the U.S. Capitol, is a magnificent building. Guided tours are available almost hourly. From its top you get a great view of the city, the Rocky Mountains and the Great Plains. The gold-leafed dome is a memorial to Colorado's early-day mining industry. The U.S. Mint, at West Colfax and Cherokee Streets, in the vicinity of the modern Civic Center, is the largest depository of gold bullion outside of Fort Knox. Tours are available Monday-Friday. And don't forget to visit a Denver landmark, the Brown Palace Hotel at 17th and Tremont Streets.

LARIMER SQUARE

Larimer Square, at the 1400 block of Larimer Street, is a full city block of interesting shops, restaurants, nightspots and galleries in a mid-Victorian setting. For banjo music you might stop by at "Your Father's Mustache." If you like sweet things you might want to visit "Le Chocolat" in the 1873 built Kettle Building. For Mexican food you might want to try "La Mancha."

DENVER STATION

The Denver Station is a huge place—you will find a coffee shop, souvenir shop, a large waiting area, plenty of lockers and restrooms. The information/reservation counter is on the side opposite from where you entered the station proper from the platform. The station is located not directly in the downtown area. However, bus #40 of Denver Metro Transit waits practically outside the station, to bring you to other parts of the city, including the downtown areas and the Trailways and Greyhound bus terminals. If bus number 40 is not waiting there then you can just walk up one block to 17th street and there you can catch bus #6, 8, 13 or 28 down 17th street to the downtown area and the bus terminals. Here is a note about fares on the city buses. Just as in other cities, you must have the exact change. The fare between 9:30 a.m. and 2:30 p.m. is 25¢ and at other times 35¢. For further information and times call Denver Metro Transit at 744-3111.

Denver, as a rail center, is in an ideal geographical location from which to explore the beauty of Colorado by bus. Resorts such as Vail, Breckenridge or Arapaho/Loveland on the Continental Divide are within easy reach. Colorado Springs and Pike's Peak to the south, as well as Durango, your departure point for the Silverton Line rail trip, can be easily reached by bus. If you want to take a scenic train trip by train to Salt Lake City via Grand Junction, you might try the Rio Grande Zephyr. This train is not part of the Amtrak system. Departures are three times a week Monday, Thursdays and Saturday. You leave Denver at 7:30 a.m. in the morning and arrive in Salt Lake City, Utah by 9:30 p.m. that night. Direct bus connections are available in Salt Lake City for Ogden, where you can catch Amtrak's San Francisco Zephyr to either Oakland/San Francisco or east to Chicago. Cost between Denver and Salt Lake City/Ogden is about $25. For further information and current schedules write to Director, Passenger and Dining Car Service, Room 100, Rio Grande Building, 1531 Stout Street, Denver, Colorado 80202.

CHEYENNE, WYOMING

Not only is Cheyenne the capital of the state of Wyoming, but many claim it is also the capital of the Wild West and what is left of it. Before you explore the town here, do not miss the stagecoach which is on display near the exit to the platform at the train station. This exhibition ought to get you into the right western mood. The stagecoach you will see made its last run between Julesburg, Colorado, and Cheyenne, Wyoming, in December, 1866.

As you walk out of the terminal you will look down Capitol Avenue and see the golden dome of the Wyoming State Capitol. If you can manage to be here during the last week in July, you will witness probably one of the greatest cowboy shows in the world. Even horses are allowed in the downtown area! In fact, if you look closely at the Wyoming car license plates, you will see pictured a rodeo rider and his horse.

For more information about the town, go to the Cheyenne Chamber of Commerce at 122 East 17th Street. When we were here last, we were met by the friendliest Chamber of Commerce representative ever! In the true tradition of the West.

Cheyenne is a major stop on the transcontinental route between Chicago and California. It is an ideal place from which to visit the Black Hills of South Dakota and Mt. Rushmore in which the heads of Presidents Washington, Lincoln, Jefferson, and T. Roosevelt are carved.

After you have re-boarded your train, you will discover that your direction of travel has changed. While you were looking around town, your train crews have changed and the powerful diesel engines which pull the train have been switched to the other end of the train.

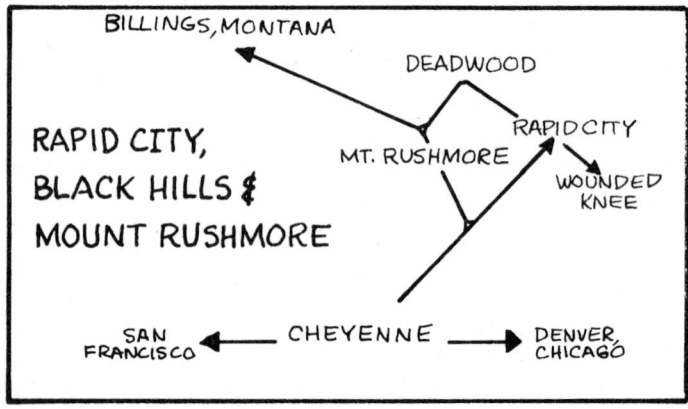

SALT LAKE CITY

On July 24, 1847, Brigham Young surveyed the valley of the Great Salt Lake and proclaimed "This is the place." Salt Lake City is your place to discover this beautiful part of the West. To the north, via Ogden, you can reach Yellowstone National Park and to the east you can discover the scenic Rocky Mountains. To the south are many scenic national parks.

SIGHTSEEING IN SALT LAKE CITY

Before you go anywhere, may we suggest that you visit the Temple Square, the Tabernacle (to listen to the world famous choir), the visitor's center and the museum (with many artifacts from pioneer days). All of these buildings, found right across the street from the terminal, are part of the complex operated by the Mormon Church whose members settled Salt Lake City in the 19th century. You must keep in mind the general public cannot go into the Temple, which looks so beautiful from the outside. However, visitors are welcome, as we were told, to listen to the Tabernacle Choir, which sings in the Tabernacle, a separate building from the Temple but still in the area of the Temple. To hear this famous choir, you can attend choir practice on Thursdays from about 7:30-9:30 in the evening and from about 8:00 a.m. to 9:00 a.m. Sunday mornings. On Sundays at 9:30 a.m. the broadcast of the choir singing is made—visitors are welcome at that time also.

Listening to the choir is not the only thing you can do at the Temple Square and its 210 foot-high Mormon Temple. At the white domed Visitor Center you can learn about the settlers' religion and take free hour long tours from 8-6 daily. Moreover, there is a small museum and the oldest home in Salt Lake City, a log cabin.

The University of Utah, oldest University west of the Missouri River, contains the Utah Museum of Natural History—open daily from 0930-1730. For special events at the university call 581-6773. And for travel information about Utah call 328-5681. For city bus information in Salt Lake City, call 322-0441.

NATIONAL PARKS IN UTAH

As we have pointed out, Salt Lake City is an ideal place to explore this part of the country. There are five national parks in Utah—Zion, Canyonland, Capitol Reef, Archer and Bryce National Park. In the southeast corner of the state, embracing the Colorado River which flows through the Grand Canyon in Arizona, is the Glen Canyon National Recreation Area. And if you ski like we do, you might note that there are a list of ski areas such as Alta, Park City and Snowbird, which can be reached in less than an hour by bus from downtown Salt Lake City.

OGDEN, UTAH

When you are in Ogden, Utah, you are in "Golden Spike Territory." The Golden Spike Monument, commemorating the completion of the transcontinental railroad in 1869, is at nearby Promontory Point.

However, of far greater contemporary importance is the fact that Ogden is your connecting point by bus to nearby Salt Lake City to the south and wild magnificent Yellowstone National Park to the north. The rail station in Ogden is a large one—with lockers, restrooms, a direct telephone line to a rent-a-car company, and a pictorial display of some of the important sights in Ogden. The heart of the town is about four or five blocks away, where you will also find a decent hotel. We do not recommend the hotels around the rail station. Anyway, our little sketch will help you get downtown—just walk down 25th Street past Wall, Lincoln and Grant. At Grant you will find both the Greyhound and Trailways bus terminals, your transportation departure points for Salt Lake City and Yellowstone Park.

Ogden is in part surrounded by mountains—in fact it is said that Ogden lies "beneath Ben Lomond's Peak." This 10,000 foot peak was an important landmark for settlers in the early days. From its top you can see across the Great Salt Lake and other points in Nevada and Utah. One of Ogden's most famous citizens was John Browning. Besides his machine gun invention, he was primarily responsible for introducing the famous Winchester Model 92, known as "the Gun that Won the West." The Ogden Tabernacle is located on 22nd Street and Washington, while the beautiful Municipal Gardens are at 25th and Washington.

THE SOUTHWEST

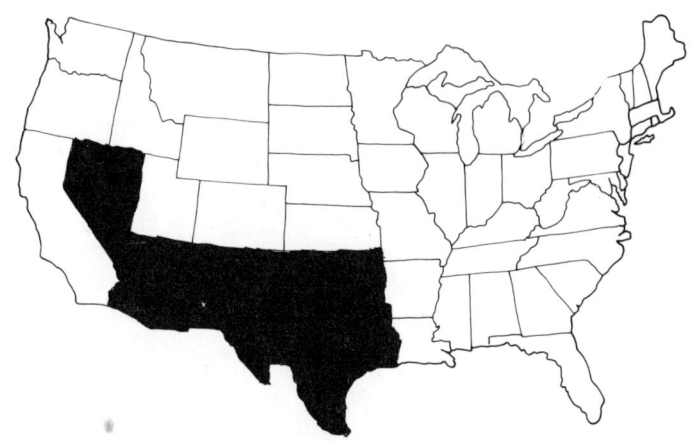

DALLAS, TEXAS

In 1841, John Neely Bryan, a farmer and merchant, gave the city its name. "Big D" as it is known, has grown and grown. Dallas, since it is such an important transportation center, is an excellent place to start your exploration of the Southwest.

One of the best ways to see the city is with the American Sightseeing Buses operated by the Dallas Transit System. Call 827-3400 for further information. You have the choice of a number of tours. The 2-1/2 hour Dallas City Tour leaves daily at 2 p.m. from the main downtown hotels. Cost $4.50. The "Six Flags Over Texas" Tour lasts 6 hours and leaves at 12:30 p.m. between late May and early September. The cost is $4.50 and does not include admission to the amusement park.

Six Flags over Texas, in Arlington between Fort Worth and Dallas, is open daily during the summer from 10 a.m. to 10 p.m. The $7 admission price for adults includes all rides and attractions. And if you are in Dallas in October, do not miss the State Fair of Texas. It has been around since 1886.

HOUSTON, TEXAS

Houston, one of the fastest growing cities in the U.S., is a very important transportation center. Services are available for San Antonio to the west, Dallas to the north, and New Orleans to the east. Keep in mind that Houston is the home of the Johnson Space Center.

Astro World, a popular amusement park in Houston, is open daily during the summer from 10 a.m. to 10 p.m. The admission price of $6.50 includes all rides and all attractions. Nearby is the famous Astrodome Stadium. Guided tours of the stadium are available. Admission is $1.50.

SAN ANTONIO, TEXAS

You will find San Antonio, Texas, a convenient and exciting city to visit. Not only is the city rich in history, but it is also full of life and excitement. The mixing of languages that you will hear as well as the many architectural styles you will see make San Antonio a worthwhile place to stop off in your exploration of the USA. San Antonio is also your gateway city to Laredo, your crossing point into Nuevo Laredo, Mexico and points south such as Monterrey, Mexico City and Merida on the Yucatan Peninsula.

One place you must visit is the Alamo. For relaxation stroll along the scenic River Walk, Paeso del Rio.

The Alamo or Mission San Antonio de Valero was the first of five Spanish colonial missions established in San Antonio in the first part of 18th Century. In 1718, Spanish Viceroy of Mexico authorized Father Antonio de Olivares to establish the mission that was to become internationally famous as the Alamo. The church structure, standing today in downtown San Antonio, was begun about 1755. Less than a century later, in 1836, it established undisputed claim as the "Cradle of Texas Liberty." During 13 days to glory—Feb. 23 to Mar. 6—it became the focal point of one of the most heroic struggles in the annals of mankind. Outnumbered Texans at the

Alamo gallantly challenged a seasoned Mexican army—but in vain. The defenders died to the last man, among them such storied names as William Travis, Davy Crockett and Jim Bowie. You will 'Remember the Alamo.' Open until 5:30 p.m.

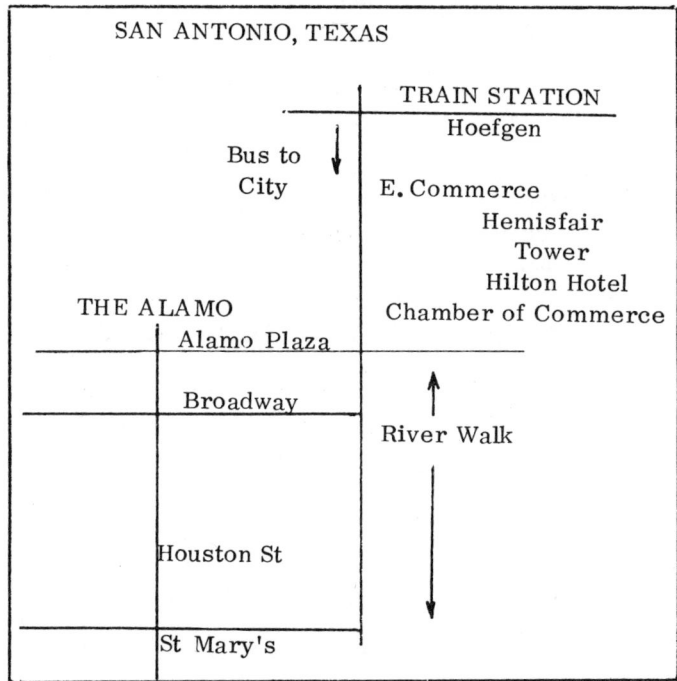

SAN ANTONIO STATION

When you get off at San Antonio you immediately realize you are in western Texas by the architectural style of the station building. Unlike the contemporary Houston Station, another stop on the Sunset Limited route, the San Antonio Station will impress you as a wonderful example of a style popular in the beginning days of railroading in this part of the country. The woodwork is a marvellous piece of craftsmanship. Do not forget to look up at the colorful ceiling; it is magnificent.

So much for the historical perspective of the building. As you walk in from the tracks, you will spot the Amtrak Information/Ticket counter to your left. Restrooms, lockers and a waiting area are also found inside.

156 TO MEXICO

SAN ANTONIO TRANSPORTATION

Getting around by public transportation in San Antonio is easy. The San Antonio Transit System, besides operating on a fairly frequent schedule at reasonable cost, must have some of the friendliest and most helpful bus drivers in the country. Here are just a few things that you might find useful riding around by bus in San Antonio. To get from the train station to the heart of town you can take a bus right across the street from the station at E. Commerce. Cost is 25¢. You must have exact change. This "San Pedro" bus takes you to the corner of E. Houston and Soledad. Here you can catch a number of buses, including those serving Fort Sam Houston. Green signs with bus directions hang at the bus stops in the center of town to help you with finding the right bus.

HOW TO TRAVEL BY TRAIN TO MEXICO CITY

If you want to travel to Mexico City by train from Nuevo Laredo, Mexico (right across from Laredo, Texas) your best bet is to make advance reservations for your seat/sleeping car. The Nuevo Laredo to Mexico City route is quite popular and relatively inexpensive. One way fare to Mexico City is about $11.14 and a roomette for one person (one bed in a small room) is an additional $20.29. The "Aztec Eagle" leaves Nuevo Laredo, Mexico, at 7:10 p.m. and arrives the next afternoon at 8:04 p.m. in Mexico City.

MAKING YOUR MEXICO TRAIN RESERVATIONS

Your Amtrak Inter-American train pulls into Laredo, Texas, in the evening. If you want to continue your rail journey by train to Mexico City or other points in Mexico the next day, you can make the reservations yourself or through your Amtrak ticket office/travel agent for the Mexican portion of your trip. Whatever you do, make your train reservations as much in advance as possible.

The first thing you can do to complete arrangements is write to the National Railways of Mexico, General Agency, P.O. Box 595, Laredo, Texas 78040, Attn: Mr. J. Diaz, General Agent, and state on what day you want to travel and what accommodations you would like. For example you might just want a regular coach seat, a roomette or an upper berth. The phone number in Laredo,

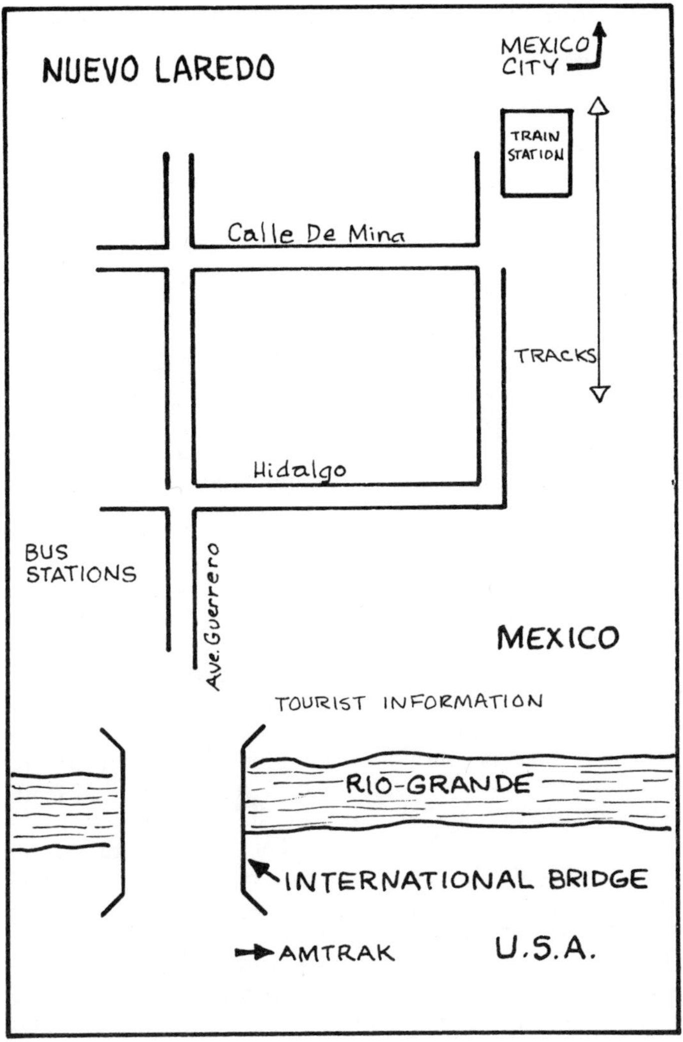
NUEVO LAREDO
MEXICO CITY
TRAIN STATION
Calle De Mina
TRACKS
Hidalgo
BUS STATIONS
Ave. Guerrero
MEXICO
TOURIST INFORMATION
RIO-GRANDE
INTERNATIONAL BRIDGE
AMTRAK
U.S.A.

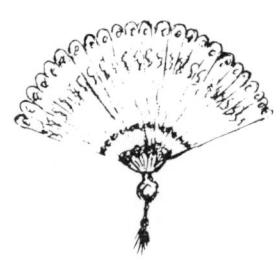

158 LAREDO

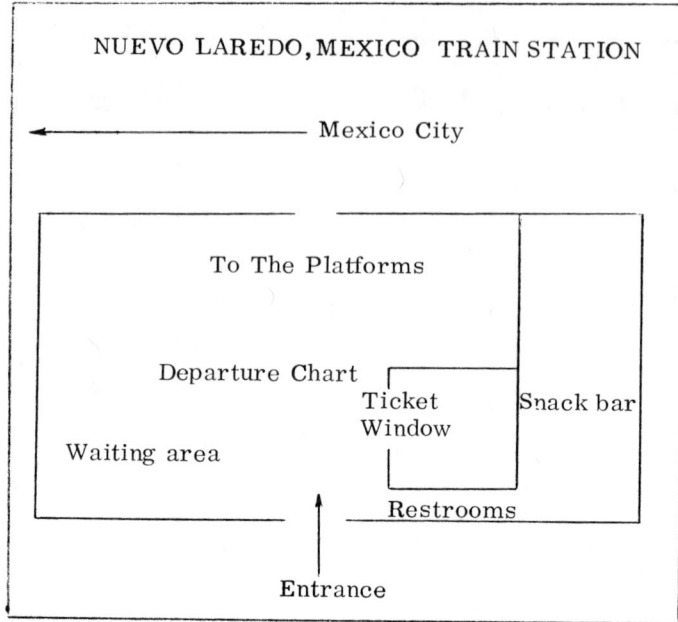

Texas of the National Railways of Mexico office is 723-5152.

You will obtain in the mail a General Information List on Trains 1 and 2 (the numbers of the trains between Laredo and Mexico City), and a confirmation of your transportation/accommodation request. You will then be asked to make out a cashier's check to the National Railways of Mexico and if you requested accommodations, you will make out a separate cashier's check to the Sleeping Car Agency. These checks must be sent at least 8 days prior to your southbound departure from Nuevo Laredo to the National Railways of Mexico address in Laredo, Texas. Your tickets will then be ready for pick up at the ticket window at the train station in Nuevo Laredo on the afternoon of your departure. Our map shows you the relative position of the train station in Nuevo Laredo to the International Bridge.

EL PASO, TEXAS

El Paso is located in the far west corner of Texas and at the center of the southern New Mexico line. At an elevation of 3,700 feet, El Paso is the lowest all weather pass through the Rocky Mountains. With a population of nearly 400,000, this city is an important commercial and transportation center. The city is located on the main San Antonio to Phoenix route. Right across the Rio Grande is the Mexican city of Juarez. The tie with points south of the Rio Grande have extended for over 400 years. In the 1530's Spaniards traveled the El Camino Real—the King's Highway—through the pass on their way from Vera Cruz, Mexico, and the colony of Santa Fe in present-day New Mexico.

The terminal is close to the new Civic Center. This is the location of the El Paso Chamber of Commerce, 544-7880. Stop in to obtain additional information about the city, including a map of the El Paso Walking Tour. The self-guiding two hour tour of interesting sights consists of 33 points. It starts at San Jacinto Plaza, the main square named in memory of the 1836 battle which gave independence to the Republic of Texas. The path between the various points is clearly marked.

EL PASO WALKING TOUR

On the tour you will see such sights as an Aztec calendar, a Confederate monument, a Ponce deLeon plaque as well as a stagecoach marker, among other interesting and historic attractions. At point 6 you will see markers—one for the first railroad bridge across the Rio Grande and one commemorating the coming of the railroads in 1881. That year the Southern Pacific, Santa Fe and the Texas Pacific reached the city. The following year, the Mexican Central came from the South.

When you get to point 27 on the walking tour, take the opportunity to visit La Villita, the El Paso Old Town Shopping Village, at the corner of Oregon and Missouri. As you stand in the archway of the shopping area, you will be at the exact spot where Luz Villa, wife of Mexico's famed General Panch Villa, one had her home. You will like the pleasant surroundings here with its boutiques, gift shops, and restaurants. And if you want to take a break, you might consider stopping off at Gulliver's, upstairs, for some delicious ice cream. For a little snack, drop in at the Queen Anne Bakery, 414 Oregon St., close to the plaza, where you will find public restrooms.

And if you want to visit Mexico, you can reach Juarez by taking a short walk down El Paso Street, near the Paso Del Norte Hotel. If you want to take a bus to the border, you can catch the Red Bus down Stanton Street. Also ask the Chamber of Commerce about the "International Street Car."

ALBUQUERQUE, NEW MEXICO

Albuquerque, named for the Duke of Albuquerque, Viceroy of New Spain, is an important transportation center for exploring not only the beautiful State of New Mexico, but also the entire southwest of the United States. The city was founded back in 1706 and the original settlement, now commonly called 'Old Town', is an assortment of early architectural styles, quaint shops and fine restaurants, many specializing in Mexican cuisine. And if you want to see the integration of traditional Pueblo with contemporary modern building styles, visit the wonderful University of New Mexico, near the center of the city.

One of the first things you might do after your arrival, is call the Albuquerque Chamber of Commerce at 842-0220 to find out about special events and other information. For example, if you are in the city during the latter half of September don't miss the New Mexico State Fair. Every Christmas Eve, the Chamber of Commerce hosts out-of-town guests in member hotels and motels on a tour of the "incomparable" Luminaria Display that has made Albuquerque known as the "City of Christmas Lights."

The University of New Mexico campus houses a great number of interesting exhibits and museums. The Maxwell Museum of Anthropology, features exhibits pertaining to ancient Indian heritage. Open Mon.-Fri. 9 to 4, 10-4 Sat. and 12-5 Sundays. Call 277-4404 for additional information. The Fine Arts Museum is open Tues.-Fri. 11 to 5, Sat. 10-4 and Sundays 1-5. Call 277-4001. For rock and fossil displays, visit the Geology Museum at the University. Open Mon.-Fri. 8 to 5.

SANTA FE

To the north of Albuquerque are the towns of Santa Fe and Taos, while to the south is El Paso, your gateway to Juarez, in Mexico. Bus service to these destinations is fairly frequent. You might also note that the Carlsbad Caverns in southeastern New Mexico, the location of the famous huge caves, can be easily reached from El Paso.

You will find Santa Fe, the capital of New Mexico, a most interesting town to visit. Santa Fe has a lot more to offer than just narrow streets and adobe-type buildings. Our friends, Dr. and Mrs. Scharn of Albuquerque, recommend when you visit Santa Fe during the summer that you do not overlook the great variety of cultural programs available, including the outdoor Opera Theater.

NAVAJO LAND 161

Near the Palace of Governors, the oldest public building in the United States, you will find the Fine Arts Building and the Hall of the Modern Indian—with fine exhibits on contemporary as well as Indian art. For additional information about Santa Fe as well as a free map of this town founded in 1610, stop by at the Chamber of Commerce office near the Santa Fe Plaza.

NAVAJOLAND TOUR

At a time when we are celebrating the events at Lexington, Concord, Philadelphia, Williamsburg and Yorktown in connection with America's Bicentennial, let us not forget those people who lived here before the colonists arrived. One way to experience American Indian life as well as the actual beauty of the Southwest, is to take a tour—a tour on which your guide is a Navajo Indian. The tour we are talking about is operated by the Navajo tribe, with 140,000 members, the largest tribe of American Indians in the United States.

The Navajo Land Tour starts every Sunday from Gallup, New Mexico, between April 1-October 31. Gallup is on the main route between Albuquerque, New Mexico and Flagstaff, Arizona. Gallup, often called the "Indian Capital of the West," is an ideal place to start your exploration of the beauty and splendor of the Southwest and its people. On the tour, you will visit Window Rock, capital of the Navajo Nation; cliff dweller ruins, Monument Valley, Canyon de Chelly, Hopi Indian Villages, Glen Canyon, Hubbell Trading Post, and much more. The six day tour cost $245 per person, with two to a room, or $290 for single occupancy. For more information see your Travel Agent or call Sanders World Travel in Washington, D.C. at (202) 659-2968.

TUCSON

Tucson is an important transportation link on your southern transcontinental trip between Texas and California. Moreover, Nogales, your gateway to Mexico is less than 2 hours away by bus to the south. For information about what to see in Tucson visit the Chamber of Commerce at 420 W. Congress, telephone 624-8111.

This city of almost 300,000, besides being an important transportation center, is famous for its many Dude Ranches. Dude Ranches come in all styles and sizes—your best bet is to see a travel agent and find out the details. Though you might be thinking of a Dude Ranch stay, keep in mind that you usually have to stay a minimum of a week and that most places are closed during the hot summer months.

You can combine a visit to the University of Arizona with a stop at the Arizona State Museum on East 3rd Street. There is much to see about Indian culture here. Hours are Monday-Saturday 10 a.m.-5 p.m. and Sunday afternoons between 2 and 5 p.m. The museum is closed on holidays and there is no admission charge.

Another famous Tucson trademark is 'Old Tucson' (13 miles west of the real Tucson). You can ride a stagecoach, visit museums and even watch gunfights. Admission charge is $2. Call Gray Line for information on tour to the movie-set. And for information on how to get around by public transportation call the Tucson Transit Company at 622-4669.

PHOENIX

Phoenix is the capital of Arizona and is located in the heart of the Valley of the Sun. You are practically guaranteed about 300 days of sunshine a year here! Summers are hot, but the low humidity makes even the high temperatures bearable. For the remainder of the year the weather is perfect. So don't forget your swimsuit and your sunglasses.

The city is an important link between Los Angeles to the west and Tucson and El Paso to the east. Frequent direct bus service is available to Flagstaff, your gateway to the Grand Canyon, and Las Vegas, the city that never sleeps. In fact, if you travel to Las Vegas via Lake Havasu City, you will witness the unbelievable location of the London Bridge, which was assembled here stone for stone from the real one which used to span the Thames River in London, England.

PHOENIX 163

The Amtrak Station is at 4th Ave and Harrison Street, while the bus stations are located just across the street from the new Civic Plaza Symphony Hall, near 5th Avenue and E. Washington Street. To find out about performances at the Symphony Hall, call 246-4754. For information about what to see in Phoenix, visit the Chamber of Commerce at 805 N. Second Street, telephone 254-5521. For information about city-bus transportation, call the Phoenix Transit Corporation at 253-6158.

While you are in the Phoenix area you might want to visit interesting nearby towns such as Tempe, home of Arizona State University. In Tempe at the 'Big Surf' you can surf (honest!) as a result of artificially produced waves in a huge "pool." Scottsdale is a resort famous for its 'Fifth Avenue' shopping street. And Wickenburg has its Gold Rush Days.

Although you might be attracted by the sights around Phoenix, the city itself also contains a number of attractions. For example, the Heard Museum at 22 E. Monte Vista Road contains Indian crafts. Closed on Mondays and during August. Open Tuesday-Saturday 10-5 (Wednesday until 9 p.m.) and on Sunday 1-5. The First National Bank of Arizona at 411 N. Central has a room set aside for exhibits about early Arizona. It is free and is open during banking hours.

GRAY LINE TOURS FROM PHOENIX

In Phoenix you have the opportunity to take 4 hour tours of the city or tours lasting six hours encompassing the attractions around the city and suburbs. A two day-tour which includes the Grand Canyon and Oak Creek Canyon is also offered from Phoenix. Call 258-6011 for further information.

164 HOOVER DAM

PHOENIX/FLAGSTAFF/KINGMAN-LAS VEGAS

Kingman, Arizona, north of Phoenix, is your direct gateway to Las Vegas, Nevada. This is where you will come if you have visited the Grand Canyon (from Flagstaff) or if you have been to the south in Phoenix.

In any case, the bus ride is a very scenic one from Phoenix to Flagstaff and Kingman. First you will be in desolate hilly country, but as you come closer to Las Vegas the distant mountain peaks glistening in the sun becomes more beautiful. You will see the Colorado River.

Soon the twisting road is above the Hoover (Boulder) Dam—the highest dam in the United States. Built between 1931-1935, the dam is high above the Colorado River at Black Canyon. You will enjoy the view you get of the dam as you slowly negotiate the turns in the road and virtually come even with the water level in the dam. You then proceed up the other side where you catch a glimpse of Lake Mead, the 115 mile lake formed by the dam. Before long you will see, out of nowhere, the glittering city of Las Vegas.

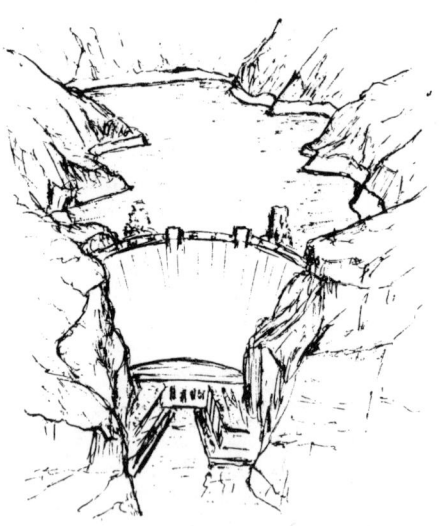

LAS VEGAS

Las Vegas, the gambling and entertainment city, is a marvelous sight as you approach it from the wild and desolate desert. There in front of you is a glittering oasis. The bright lights will absolutely amaze you. The city never seems to sleep. You can get breakfast twenty-four hours a day. Visiting the many gambling places and watching all the people can be a memorable experience. Also, if you are like us, and set yourself a definite limit on how much money you will gamble away (those slot machines are everywhere), you will discover that food and lodging, as well as taking in a show by a top star, can be relatively inexpensive.

Your bus from the south will stop at the Stardust Hotel Greyhound bus terminal, right in the middle of the Strip (the street on which the most famous gambling places/hotels are located). Keep in mind that this little terminal (open 7:45 a.m.-5:45 p.m.) is not the main terminal in Las Vegas. It simply allows you to get off (even if the terminal is already closed) right where the "action" is and to look for a place to stay in the heart of the gambling area. The main bus terminal is in the "other" part of Las Vegas, just a few minutes away from all the lights. If you have a lot of baggage, perhaps it would be a good idea to stay on the bus until you come to the main terminal because lockers are available there. Hotels tend to be somewhat less expensive in this part of town. To get back and forth between the downtown area and the Strip is no problem because bus #6 (a city bus) shuttles back and forth. Cost is 50¢ and the buses usually run every fifteen minutes during the day and evening, and every 30 minutes after 2:00 in the morning. Bus #10 goes to the University of Nevada at Las Vegas.

BARGAINS IN LAS VEGAS

One of the first things made available to you once you have registered at a hotel/motel is a great many coupons. These coupons, designed to entice you to do some gambling, allow you to get free drinks, free continental breakfasts, free "lucky nickels" and so on. We suggest you sit down and sort these coupons and use the ones that interest you. It is a great way to be introduced to all the activities that go on in Las Vegas.

Once you walk into places like the Stardust Hotel (right next to the Strip terminal) you will be almost hypnotized by all the action everywhere. Everybody seems to be gambling. However, in addition to gambling, you can eat very reasonably at many places. Usually somewhere at one end of the gambling hall is a restaurant where a special low-priced breakfast is available, or you can help yourself to a buffet lunch or dinner at a very low price.

166 LAS VEGAS

```
LAS VEGAS & STRIP HOTELS
DOWNTOWN                    │  Fremont St.
BUS STATION                 │
                            │
                            │
                            │  THE
                            │  STRIP ↙
                            │
                            │  SAHARA
          STARDUST          │
       STRIP BUS STATION    │
         Silver Slipper     │
            FRONTIER        │  DESERT INN
                            │  SANDS
                            │  FLAMINGO
         CAESARS            │
         PALACE             │
─────────DUNES──────────────┼──────────────
                            │
────────────────────────────┼──TROPICANA───
          HACIENDA          │
```

Keep in mind that beverages are usually not included in the price of the buffet. Also be alert to the times the buffet is available. For example, at the Silver Slipper for about $1.49 you can have an excellent buffer dinner. If you want to see one of the famous wedding chapels, you will find one next to the parking lot of the Frontier Hotel. This hotel is also a great place to browse around—usually a luncheon buffet is available for about $1.95.

One of the best ways to see what is going on at the Strip is to just visit all the places along the road. That is what we did. From the Stardust terminal you can walk either to the left or right to visit famous hotels like the

Sahara, Stardust, Hilton, Silver Slipper, Frontier, Sands, Flamingo or Caesars Palace and MGM. We suggest that you walk and visit these and other places and then take the city bus back to another section of the Strip. After all, you do not want to spend all your time walking along the street when you can be browsing inside the hotels. The park benches along the Strip serve as your bus stop indicators. Here are a couple of other observations about your stay here. Las Vegas attracts the best in entertainment. Look in the "Las Vegas Panorama" (a newspaper obtainable free) to find out who is entertaining at what hotels. Then make your reservations. A Dinner Show (to give you a rough idea about prices) at many excellent hotels will cost about $11 minimum while for the Late Show the minimum with a drink is about $10. From our observations, dress to these events is a bit more formal than just casual clothes. Another thing we like to do is watch people play Baccarat, the object of which is to come closest to the number 9 with cards. Every large casino has an area designated for this game. You might be interested in noting taxi charges which are about 55¢ for the first 1/5 mile and 10¢ for each additional 1/5 mile. Also, as you are walking along the Strip at night, have a good look at all the lights; they are really fascinating. Caesars Palace with its many fountains must be one of the most magnificent buildings here.

As you can imagine, this city is a popular tourist attraction. Whatever you do, try to plan to visit this city during the week instead of on weekends. It will make it easier to find a place to stay. Instead of exploring the night life of Las Vegas by yourself, you might consider taking a Gray Line Night Club Party (about $17 and 7 hours) or a Deluxe Night Club Party which includes a dinner and show (about $27 and 8 hours). For further details call 384-1234. If you are technically oriented and want to see how the Hoover Dam operates, a four hour tour to the dam is available from about $6.

168 LAS VEGAS

LAS VEGAS DOWNTOWN BUS TERMINAL

The main Greyhound bus station is in the downtown area of Las Vegas (which is about 15 minutes by city bus away from the Strip). You will discover a great number of casinos here which might not be as glamorous as those on the Strip, yet they provide the same attractions—gambling and low priced 24-hour breakfast specials. Also you might note that hotels in this area are generally not quite as expensive as they are on the Strip.

If you just cannot wait to spend your money gambling, you will be happy to know that the Greyhound terminal is practically in the same building as the Plaza Casino. Also keep in mind that bus #6 starts here for the 15 minute trip to the Strip. You will need 50¢ in exact change to board the bus. If you plan to ride back and forth to the Strip, you can get 6 tokens for $2.40 from the driver, thus saving you 60¢. Buses to Phoenix and Los Angeles leave from the Greyhound terminal.

CALIFORNIA

The State of California holds in store a wonderful contrast to the traveler. You have huge Los Angeles, cosmopolitan San Francisco with those great cable cars, Hollywood with its glamour, San Diego with its harbors, parks and flowers, beautiful Yosemite National Park, entertaining Disneyland, the beaches and mountains, the majestic Redwood trees and the serenity of blazing Death Valley and the Mojave Desert.

When Cabrillo came upon this beautiful area of the western United States in 1542, it was the beginning of an exciting history. The state was a province of Mexico for 21 years and in 1846, as a result of the Bear Flag Rebellion, it came closer to becoming a part of the United States. In 1849, gold was discovered at Stutter's Mill near Sacramento (the capital). The growth of the area was so rapid that in 1850 it became a state of the United States. With the discovery of oil, industrial development and of course Hollywood, California grew and grew to such proportions that it is today the most populous state in the country with over 20 million people. A vast change from the lonely Mission Dolores outpost found in San Francisco and built in 1776, when the fever of independence was at a high pitch 3000 miles away on the other side of the continent.

LOS ANGELES

Los Angeles has a population of about 3 million spread all over between the Pacific Ocean and the San Gabriel Mountains. However, getting around this large area is not as difficult as it first seems because bus and tour operators give you service to the major attractions. These include Hollywood, Universal Studios, Disneyland, and Knott's Berry Farm, an area of fine shops and designed

170 LOS ANGELES

ghost towns, close to Disneyland. The Queen Mary, one of the largest passenger liners, is moored in nearby Long Beach. And if your interest is in television, you can tour the NBC studios, Monday-Saturday for $1.75.

If you are like us, you just cannot resist visiting the movie studios to find out all about the stars and movies. The Universal Studios Tour is probably the best known and we recommend it—it will give you a better perspective on how movies are made. The four hour tour costs $4.75 and is given daily during the summer from 9:00 a.m. to 5:00 p.m. and 10:00 a.m. to 3:30 p.m. at other times during the rest of the year. The tour is not given on Thanksgiving, Christmas, and New Year's Day.

SIGHTSEEING IN LOS ANGELES

However, before you plan all your excursions to the outlying area, remember that downtown Los Angeles has been revitalized. There are quite a number of things to see in the Inner City. Besides the "Mexican Street," which we will discuss later, there is the new Arco Plaza at 5th and Flower Streets. The Plaza, with its boutiques and

LOS ANGELES 171

restaurants, is located below a 52 story building. For information call 625-2132.

Just a street away is the Southern California Visitors Council office at 705 West 7th Street, telephone 628-3101. Here you can get the latest information about events. Make certain that you stop by. You can obtain maps of the city here for free. If you plan to do any kind of exploring of the Los Angeles area pick up two extremely helpful brochures. One is "A Guide For Going Places," which is a map of bus routes. The other prepared by the Southern California Rapid Transit District and the Southern California Visitors Council is "20 Self Guided Tours." The excellent brochure gives you step by step instructions about what buses to take to explore the Los Angeles area. It even lists the addresses of some of the movie stars. Both brochures are free.

LOS ANGELES BUS STATION LOCATION

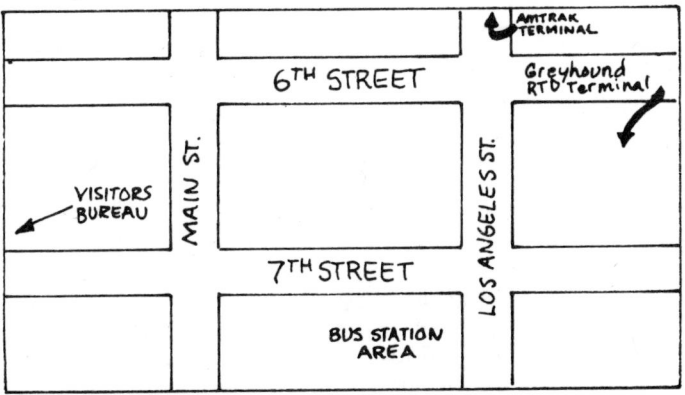

The Greyhound bus terminal is a huge modern place and takes up three floors. On the street level part of the terminal you have a Greyhound Information/Ticket counter as well as an RTD (Rapid Transit District) ticket and information counter. The upper level is for Greyhound departures as well as for the bus to Los Angeles International Airport ($1.25). The lower level is for RTD bus departures.

For your information we suggest you look at two timetables. The Greyhound timetable is at the Greyhound Information counter and in the middle of the hall you will find an RTD arrivals/departures board. Please note the many places you can travel to by local bus at a very small charge.

172 LOS ANGELES

LOS ANGELES STATION

The Los Angeles train station is a huge place. Today the station serves as an important connection point for trains to the south, such as San Diego, north to San Francisco, Portland, Seattle and Vancouver, east to Flagstaff (Grand Canyon), Albuquerque and Chicago, and southeast to Phoenix, Tucson, San Antonio, Houston and New Orleans. In addition, the 'Las Vegas Fun Train,' leaves from here.

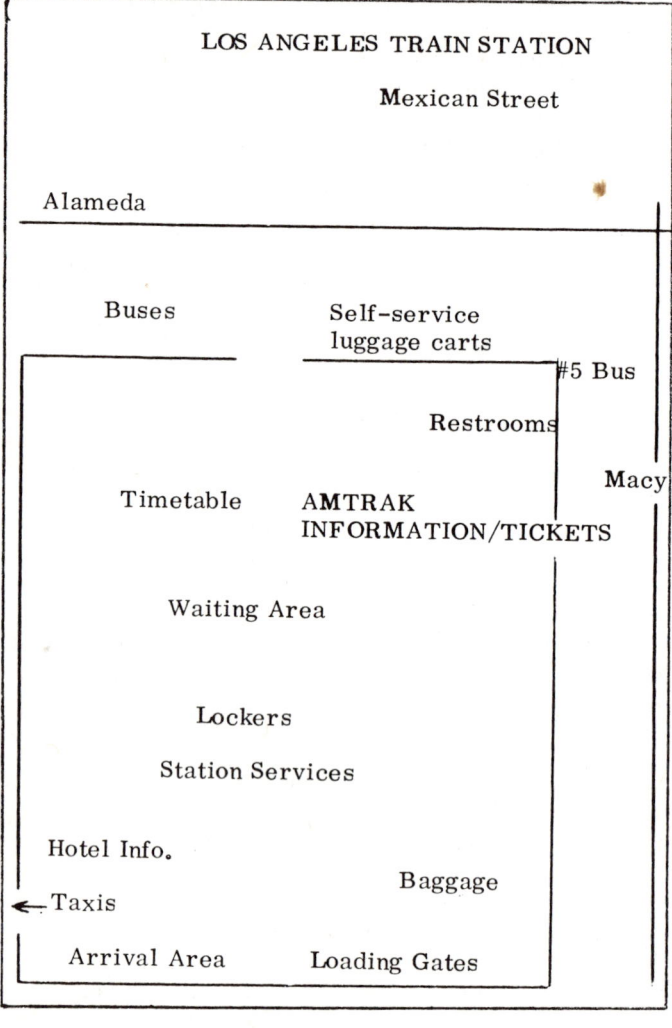

When you have walked from the platform to the main part of the station, you should see to your left in the arrival area taxi stands, a hotel information booth, as well as a courtesy telephone to a car rental company and a hotel. An arrival/departure timetable is also in this part of the station. Should you have questions about train travel or connections, there is a station services office in this area. Here you can pick up city bus timetables (# 5 city bus stop is just to the right about 100 yards as you leave the station) and Amtrak rail timetables. A city map in the office can help you to orient yourself. The personnel here are helpful and they will answer the questions you might have upon your arrival.

Further along you will spot lockers (25¢) and a waiting area. The chairs here are really comfortable and ideal from which to reflect upon your exploration of the USA by rail. Telephones are to the left as you approach the station exit from the platforms, whereas to your right you will see the Amtrak Information/Ticket counter. Further along are the restrooms and additional lockers. As you walk out of the station, you will find the connecting buses which will take you directly to Anaheim (Disneyland-Grand Hotel), Lakewood Shopping Center, Long Beach or Orange. You obtain your ticket for these bus trips from the driver—they are not included in the rail ticket. The cost, for example, to Disneyland is about $2.50 and the trip takes about 40 minutes. If you want to take a city bus, #5 begins its route into the city just to the right. Fare is 30¢. Self service luggage racks are also located near the entrance to the station.

When you are outside of the station, have a good look at the terminal building. Its Spanish style architecture is fascinating. Perhaps what is even more interesting is the tall palm trees which skirt the station. For your information, the fee for parking here on the outside of the station is 25¢ for the first half hour, 35¢ for each additional hour. The maximum rate is $1.75 for each 24 hour period.

The last time we were here we were disappointed not to find a place to eat inside the station. However, we have a suggestion. If you are hungry or have some time before your train departure, visit the little Mexican Street which is just across Alameda from the train station. This lively area will be a marked contrast to the somber atmosphere reigning in the train station.

174 LOS ANGELES

RTD SERVICE

As we have pointed out, the big bus terminal in Los Angeles not only serves Greyhound, but it also caters to the buses of the Los Angeles Rapid Transit District. To keep you from getting confused we will list some of the various local bus lines which serve the Greyhound terminal. They are 33, 34, 36, 37, 51, 53, 55, 58, 60, 120, 122, and 125. Their destinations and departure times are listed on the RTD arrivals/departures board. Thus for example #55 serves Seal Beach, Huntingdon Beach and Newport Beach. Bus #58 goes to Disneyland in Anaheim—cost $2.50 round trip. Also there are departures to the Catalina Terminal for connections to Catalina Island, with #37.

We now include a couple of other facts about the local bus service. You can get many buses close to the Greyhound terminal. For instance #4 and #91 serve the ABC entertainment center, #75 serves the MGM Studio. line 44 serves CBS Television City and #86 serves NBC TV and Disney Studios in Burbank. Number 93 bus serves Universal Studios and you can catch the bus at 7th and Hill, close to the Greyhound terminal. And if you want to take in a baseball game, take #178 directly from the Greyhound terminal to Angels Stadium. Remember that for all RTD buses leaving this terminal, you must buy your tickets before you board the buses.

If you want to visit Beverly Hills, take a southbound Beverly Hills-Santa Monica bus (#4B). At Sunset Blvd. you can take the westbound #76 to UCLA, one of the nine campuses of the University of California. Bus #83 at Westwood and Lindbrook takes you back to Los Angeles via Wilshire Blvd.

If you want to stay closer to downtown, may we alert you to the convenient mini buses which connect City Hall, the Music Center, Arco Plaza, Chinatown, Little Tokyo, Olvera Street and downtown stores, for only 15¢ a ride. They operate Mon.-Sat. 9 a.m. to 4 p.m. For further information about how to get around in Los Angeles, you should visit the Information Office at 1060 S. Broadway for maps and 'how to see Los Angeles by public transit,' or call 747-4455.

A SAMPLE OF MEXICO

Another discovery in "L.A." is across the street from the Los Angeles train Station—the colorful Mexican

Street, Calle Olverra (Olverra Street), the birthplace of Los Angeles. Here you will find a small market place. There are stands from which you can buy items ranging from bracelets to candy. Restaurants are also in plentiful supply here. Rudolfo's, a small and seemingly always crowded place, has a special plate for about $1.50. If you are looking for something a little bit more roomy and formal, then we suggest you stop off at the Lago Pondrina just a few yards further down. Here you can have dinner outside. The Mexican Combination Dinner here which includes tortillas, tamales, enchilada and tacos topped off with Cafe con Leche—all for only about $4.40. The delicious Mexican Carta Blanca beer is extra. Entertainment is inside. In any case, no matter where you stop off, give yourself a chance to relax and just watch the people walk by. That in itself is entertaining. The shopping area also provides you with an excellent last minute place to pick up small gifts.

OTHER ACCOMMODATIONS IN LOS ANGELES

American Youth Hostel—933-4412.
Biola Hotel—536 South Hope Street, (213) 627-9941. From $6/night, $21/week, $84/month.
Evangeline Residence for Women—1005 W. 6th St., (213) 482-4880.
Alexander Hotel—Spring at Fifth Street, (213) 626-7484. Singles from $15 and doubles from $18.

BAKERSFIELD

When you travel north and take the inland route between Los Angeles and San Francisco, up the San Joaquin Valley, you will pass through Bakersfield. About 100 miles north of Los Angeles, Bakersfield is known for its agricultural products and its oil. However, lately the city has received more and more attention as the country and music capital of the West. If you like the music, you might take the opportunity to stop off here and visit places like "Tex's Barrel House" or "The Blackboard" for music entertainment.

DISNEYLAND, CALIFORNIA

Keep in mind that there are two Disney attractions—one in Florida (called Disney World) and the other in California, called Disneyland. We have been to both and find each of them very enjoyable.

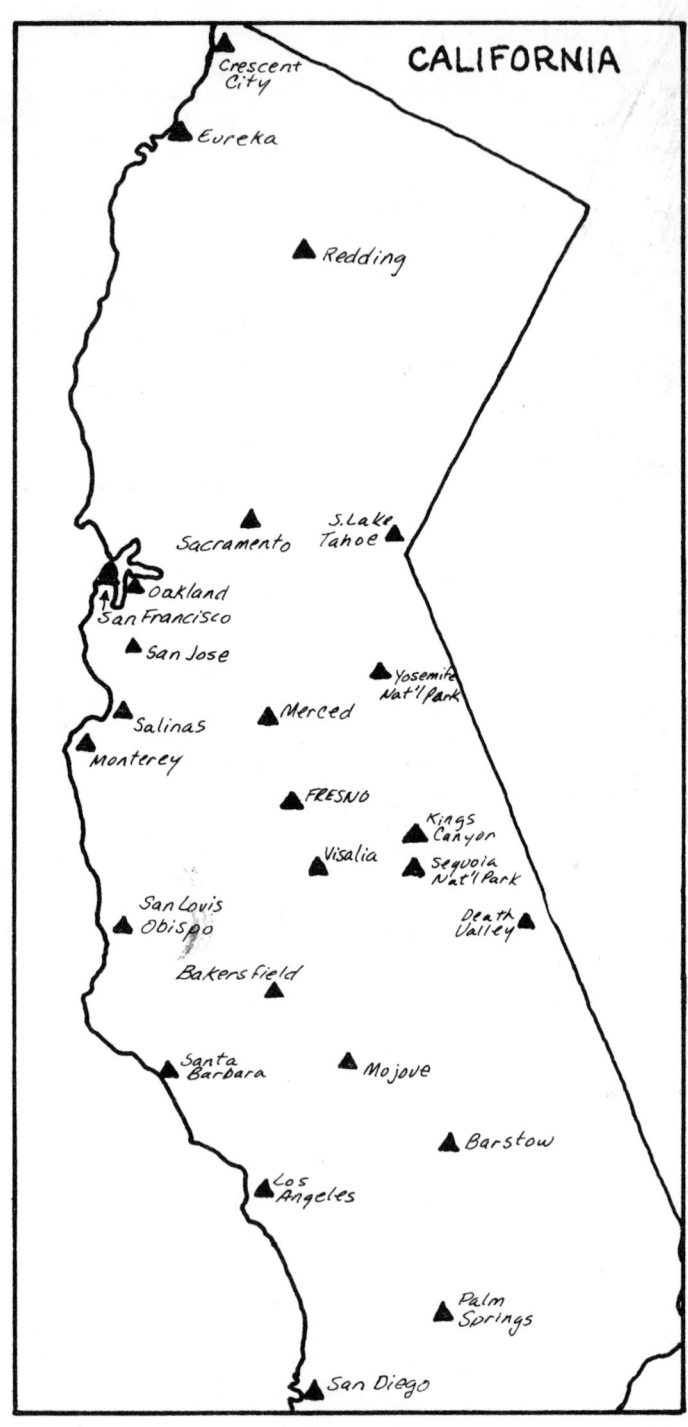

DISNEYLAND

One of the things we want to alert you to is that during parts of the winter months, Disneyland is closed on Mondays and Tuesdays, except for certain holiday periods during that time. For specific hours call (714) 533-4456 or (213) 626-8605, Ext. 101.

Since on your exploration of the U.S.A. you become so aware of the various transportation modes, you will be happy to discover that once you are inside Disneyland, various transportation options are open to you. There is the excellent monorail system, the People-Mover, gondolas, a paddle wheel steamboat, horse-drawn street cars and a railroad.

In our section on Los Angeles, we have told you how you can reach Disneyland by bus. Now let us give you some ideas about prices there. General Admission prices are $4.50. The "Big 11" ticket includes the price of admission & choice of 11 Disneyland attractions. It costs $6.; for the 'Deluxe 15,' which includes the admission and 15 Disneyland attractions, the cost is $7. The Guided Tour costs $7.50 and includes a 2 1/2 hour tour of Disneyland and admission to seven Disneyland attractions. Ideal if you do not have too much time.

Disneyland, located in Anaheim, just south of Los Angeles, has been referred to by many as 'the happiest place on earth'. It certainly is a great place to visit. Remember that for information about bus service to and from the airport call (714) 776-9210 and from downtown Los Angeles to Disneyland call R.T.D. at (213) 747-4455. During the summer Disneyland is open daily from 9 a.m. to 1 a.m.

KNOTT'S BERRY FARM

Knott's Berry Farm, in Buena Park, close to Disneyland is an exciting entertainment park featuring an authentic Ghost Town recreating the gold rush days of the 1840's; a full-scale reproduction of Philadelphia's famous Independence Hall; a lively and colorful Fiesta Village patterned after a Mexican village; the unique John Wayne Theatre which hosts live, big-name entertainment on stage; and the nation's only Gypsy Camp. Twenty-two rides and attractions, two major restaurants, and numerous variety and specialty shops make up the package. Admission is $3 and individual rides range in price from 25¢ to 85¢. A combination ticket which includes admission and 8 rides costs $4.75. For information call (714) 827-1776.

178 SAN DIEGO

To get to either Disneyland or Knott's Berry Farm, take the Fun Bus from the Anaheim area or the Buena Park area. Cost is $1. Call (714) 635-1390 for further information.

SAN DIEGO

San Diego is "where California began." There are so many sights in this beautiful city that we suggest you spend at least a couple of days here. The city is located about 120 miles south of Los Angeles and about a 100 miles away from Disneyland. Also keep in mind that a major gateway to Mexico, Tijuana, is only about an hour to the south via direct bus service from the Amtrak Terminal or the nearby Greyhound station.

SIGHTSEEING IN SAN DIEGO

The first place you should stop at is the Plaza Information booth (234-5191) on Broadway between 3rd and 4th Avenues. It is open daily between 9 in the morning and 7:30 in the evening. And if you plan to visit nearby Mexico, you might call the Mexican Tourist Bureau at 232-6757 for information. For example, in the middle of September, Mexican Independence Day Celebration take place with "El Grito," the shout which led Mexico in rebellion against Spain.

Many of San Diego's attractions can be reached by public transportation. La Jolla (America's Riviera), with its beautiful beach, can be reached from downtown with bus #R. Old Town San Diego, founded in 1769, where many buildings from San Diego's Mexican period before 1846 still stand, can be reached by bus #4, C, 5 or 6. Bus #K takes you to the Cabrillo National Monument, where in 1542 Cabrillo claimed the land for Spain. Visit the Old Point Loma Lighthouse and the Visitor Center (283-5450). Get a spectacular view of the ocean, the city and the mountains. If you are here during the period December—February, you might be able to spot the gray whales as they migrate from the Arctic Ocean to Baja California where they mate and bear their young.

Mission Bay Park, with its beaches, hotels, restaurants, and sporting facilities as well as Sea World (224-3562), can be reached by bus #7. Balboa Park, close to the city center, can be reached by bus #7. Here you find the world famous San Diego Zoo (234-3153) and the

Space Theater and Science Center (238-1233). The University of California at San Diego can be reached by bus #R. For further information, call up the Chamber of Commerce at 232-0124.

The beaches around San Diego are very beautiful. Here are the buses which will take you to the various beaches. Coronado Beach, #9, Imperial Beach #0, Pacific Beach #R, T, J, or C, Ocean Beach #0, La Jolla Beach #0, and Mission Beach #R. And whatever you do, do not miss the sun sinking into the Pacific in the evening. It is a wonderful, colorful spectacle.

Buses in San Diego cost only 25¢ per ride. The two hour harbor excursion cost is $4.00, while the one hour tour is $2. Call 234-4111 for information. The San Diego Zoo costs $2. However, we suggest you get the $3 ticket which includes the $1.25 bus tour. The children's zoo costs 50¢.

180 SAN FRANCISCO

"Y" ACCOMMODATIONS IN SAN DIEGO

Armed Services YMCA—500 West Broadway (corners of Columbia and Broadway), 232-1133. Single $5. "Mainly military, some civilian."

YMCA—1115 8th Ave. (8th Ave. and C St.), 232-7451. Single $4.75, double $4.00, dormitory $1.75. Both men and women. Holds telephone reservations until 6 p.m.

SAN FRANCISCO

One of the first places we suggest you visit is the San Francisco Convention and Visitors Bureau at 1390 Market Street, close to the magnificent Civic Center and Opera House. Telephone (415) 626-5500. Their office, open Monday-Friday, is located in the modern big Grosvenor Plaza, one floor up. In the building you will also find a travel agency, barber shop, beauty salon, restrooms and a place to eat.

SAN FRANCISCO INFORMATION

Airporter Bus ($1.15) from airport to O'Farrell and Taylor Streets.

There is a 6 1/2% sales tax on purchases in the city.

SAN FRANCISCO

Alcatraz tour costs $2.00. Need to book a reservation ahead of time. The number to call is 398-1141. Trip takes 2 hrs.

Fisherman's Wharf has boat excursions, wax museum ($2.00), world of S. F. ($1.25), Ripley's Amazing World, World of Witchcraft, Ghiradelli Square, The Cannery, and sidewalk vendors.

Mannings Cafeteria (Powell & Geary Streets) is good and reasonable.

From Market Street, Bus #5 McAlister goes to Golden Gate Park which has the DeYoung Museum (free), the Museum of Science with Planetarium and Aquarium (50 cents for 18 years and older). Japanese Tea Garden (tea and cookies 35 cents).

Chinatown Wax Museum ($1.50).

For a daily report on what to see and what to do in San Francisco, call 391-2000. For information about buses and cable cars call "673-MUNI". About the BART routes (Bay Area Rapid Transit) and schedule of operation, call 788-BART. And if you are interested in the history of San Francisco, visit the History Room of the Wells Fargo Bank at 420 Montgomery Street. Open 10-3 on banking days. No admission charge. For tickets to special events, you might want to stop by at the San Francisco Ticket Center, 224 Taylor Street. Open Mon.-Sat. 10 to 6. If you need to get your shoes fixed, go to Parkers Shoe Service at 994 Market Street. Open 8:30 a.m. to 5:30 p.m. At 1043 Market is a 'McDonald's.' A self service laundry is located at 730 Bush Street, just off Powell Street. Open Mon.-Sat. 8 to 8 and Sun. 8 to 6. You will recognize Union Square, corner of Geary and Powell Streets, with the palm streets and the many stores, including Macy's. And if you are interested in walking across the San Francisco bridges, keep in mind that pedestrians may walk across the Golden Gate Bridge but not across the San Francisco/Oakland Bay Bridge.

One of the best ways to quickly get an overview of the city as well as visually get acquainted with its magnificent attractions, is to stop by and look at a couple of presentations. One is "ABOVE SAN FRANCISCO", a 46 minute film on the city narrated by Orson Welles at the Theatre Atop Ghirardelli Square, 900 North Point, 673-1124. First show at noon, last one at 9 p.m.; until 11 p.m. Fridays and Saturdays. The other is "SAN FRANCISCO EXPERIENCE." It employs all the latest audio and visual techniques to present this dramatic, 45 minute

182 SAN FRANCISCO

portrait of the city. 333 Jefferson Street, at Fisherman's Wharf, 474-7272; continuous performances begin at 11:15 a.m.; last show is 9 p.m. except Friday and Saturday, last show 11:15 p.m.

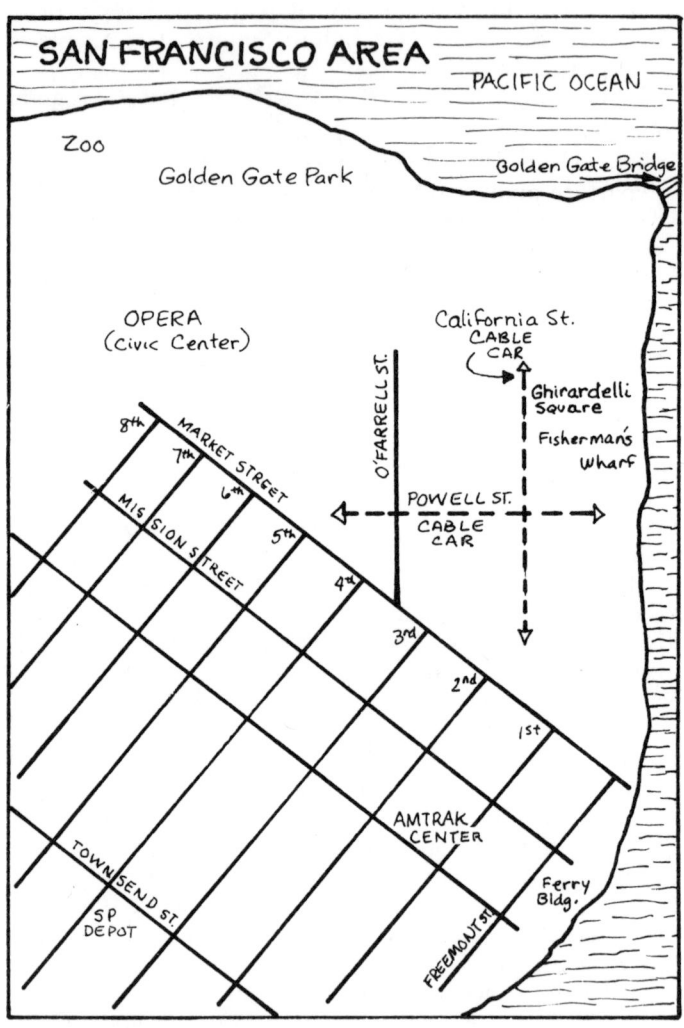

SAN FRANCISCO CABLE CARS

It was just over one hundred and two years ago in August, 1873, that the first of the now famous cable cars became operational in hilly San Francisco. The popularity of these cable cars was so great that by 1900, 600 cars were running on over 110 miles of track. Today you will find only about 39 of the cable cars running on about 10 miles of track over three main routes. The one route is on California over Nob Hill between Market Street and Van Ness Avenue. The other two lines leave from Market and Eddy along Powell and then branch out to Hyde Street Pier via Russian Hill and past Lombard Street ('the crookedest street in the world'). The other line branches off Powell Street toward North Point. Both the Hyde Street Pier and North Point destinations will get you close to the area of Fisherman's Wharf and the harbour tours departure point. Cost per ride is 25 ¢.

And if you are interested in seeing how the cable cars are controlled, stop by at the Cable Car Barn on the corner of Washington and Mason Streets. It is open daily between 8 a.m. and midnight.

SAN FRANCISCO TRANSPORTATION BARGAIN

One bargain you should know about is the Sunday and Holiday Tour Ticket. It only costs 50 cents and is obtainable directly from the conductor on cable cars and buses. This ticket entitles you to an unlimited number of rides on all cable cars and trams/buses operated by MUNI, the municipal railway—the agency that operates the cable cars and trams/buses in San Francisco. Note that this ticket is only good on Sundays or holidays.

The last time we were in San Francisco on a Sunday we used this ticket over and over again to really discover the interesting sights in and around the city. For example, buses 5, 10, 21 and 28 will take you to Golden Gate Park; #18 takes you to the Zoological Gardens; #39 to Telegraph Hill and Coit Tower. Playland at the Beach is served by bus lines 2, 5, 18 and 38. If you cannot take the cable car to Grant Avenue (the start of Chinatown—you'll recognize it by the pagoda), bus #15 and 55 will take you there. Fisherman's Wharf, besides being served by the Powell Street cable car, can also be reached by #15, 19 and 23 buses.

Senior citizens ride free on Sundays. On other days the fare for the elderly is only five cents.

GRAY LINE SIGHTSEEING

Gray Line offers a great number of tours which enable you to see the sights of both the city and the surrounding countryside. Thus you have a choice of "Chinatown By Night," "Oakland, Berkeley, University of California,"

184 SAN FRANCISCO

"Muir Woods, Giant Redwood Trees, Sausalito," (a must if you want to see the Redwood trees), or the "Monterey, Carmel, 17 Mile Drive" tour. For further information and reservations call Gray Line 771-4000.

Y ACCOMMODATIONS

The YMCA Hotel, at 351 Turk Street, telephone (415) 673-2312, is centrally located to many of San Francisco's attractions, including the Powell Street cable cars. Men, women and families can stay here. Singles start at $5.50, doubles at $9. Telephone reservations are accepted. Be sure to ask for the handy pamphlet, "How to get from here to there," it tells you how to get by public transportation to San Francisco attractions. For example, to get to Mission Dolores, founded in 1776, and the sixth of the famous chain of 21 California missions, take "J" street car on Market going west. Get off at 16th Street and walk one block west.

There has been a lot of discussion about San Francisco's weather. The Y personnel here give the following tips. We might add that even in winter it's pleasant here. Temperatures seldom rise above seventy or fall below fifty, and although San Francisco is considered one of the sunniest large cities in America, the summer vacationer should be informed about its unique "built in" air conditioner that exists when the fog is drawn in through the Golden Gate. The traveler's wardrobe should include lightweight wools and a top coat the year around.

AMTRAK TRAVEL CENTER—SAN FRANCISCO

The Amtrak Travel Center in San Francisco is your departure point for rail travel east to Reno, Denver and

Chicago, north to Portland, Seattle and Vancouver, and south to Santa Barbara, Los Angeles (where you have connections east to Phoenix and New Orleans) and San Diego. However, remember that you have to take a bus from the San Francisco Amtrak Travel Center to Oakland (across the Bay). This is an enjoyable and scenic 10-15 minute bus ride which takes you directly to your departing train.

For those of you who have just arrived from the Oakland train station by Amtrak bus, you will be let off at the Natoma Street side of the Amtrak Travel Center. Your bags will be taken off the bus for you. Once you are inside the building, follow the arrows to the main part of the terminal (do not walk downstairs—your Amtrak Information/Ticket counter is on the street level of this huge building). The Amtrak Information/Ticket counter is on your right as you walk in the main hall. Besides giving you train information, the personnel here will try to help you with directions or any other questions you might have about traveling. Here you can also pick up a helpful map of San Francisco. Further along you will find the exit to Mission Street where you will find buses and cabs. You might note that the Trailways office is also here on this level. Upstairs is the location of the AC Transit Company (buses to Berkeley 75¢) and the Gray Line Sightseeing Company. If you are pressed for time you might want to take a city tour. However, if you are like us and cannot wait to get on one of the fabled San Francisco cable cars, keep in mind that the Amtrak Information Center in the city is only about 3 blocks away from California Street, where you can catch the cable car to China Town (Grant Ave.), Nob Hill or transfer to the Beech Hyde cable car line for a magnificent view of San Francisco.

186 PORTLAND

THE NORTHWEST

PORTLAND, OREGON

Portland is the largest city in the State of Oregon. It is an important transportation center, being on the main route from Vancouver/Seattle to San Francisco and Los Angeles. You might first want to stop off at the Portland Chamber of Commerce at 824 S.W. 5th Avenue, telephone 228-9411, for the latest information on what to see. For example, for local history you might want to visit the Oregon Historical Society Center at 1230 S.W. Park Avenue—open Mon. to Sat. 10 a.m. to 4:45 p.m. and Sundays from noon to 4:45 p.m. For Gray Line tours information call 226-6755.

If you have the opportunity, by all means do not miss the beautiful and rugged Oregon coast from Newport to Coos Bay/North Bend to Crescent City, California and the Redwood Tree Area. Coos Bay was the home of super track star Steve Prefontaine who was lost to America so prematurely. Coos Bay and the coastal resorts can be reached by bus from Portland.

SEATTLE, WASHINGTON

Metropolitan Seattle has a population of about 1 1/2 million, a far cry from the few lumbermen who settled

here just over a century ago. Not only has the city become the center for commercial activity in the Pacific Northwest, but it also is an important transportation gateway. Here you are only several hours away from Vancouver, Canada, to the north. To the east there is Spokane, gateway to the Yellowstone National Park, or the Glacier National Park. To the south are scenic Oregon and California.

SEATTLE CENTER

In 1962, Seattle hosted the World's Fair. Today you can visit the Seattle Center where many of the exhibits still stand. Don't miss the view from the 600 foot Space Needle ($1.25 to take the elevator up). To get to the Center we suggest that you take the fast Monorail (25¢) from its downtown terminal at 4th Avenue and Pine Street. It runs Monday—Thursday from 10 a.m. to midnight (until 12:30 a.m. on Friday and Saturday) and from 10 in the morning to 10 in the evening on Sunday. Once you reach the Seattle Center you will see the towering Space Needle to your left.

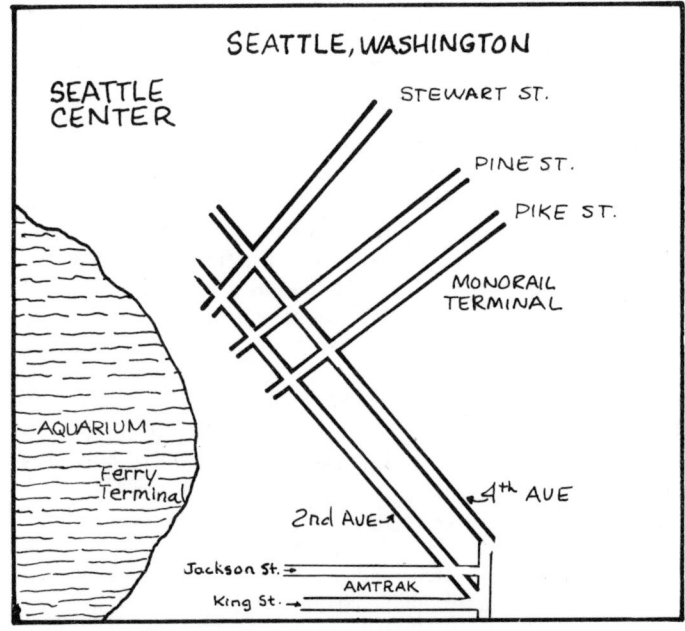

One of the most interesting buildings at the Seattle Center is the Pacific Science Center where you can learn about science as well as perform experiments yourself. It is open Monday—Friday 9 a.m. to 5 p.m. and weekends

188 SEATTLE

and holidays 11 a.m. to 8 p.m.; admission is $2 for adults, $1 for students and fifty cents for senior citizens. For a snack or a meal stop by at the Food Circus Court. The Opera House and the Art Museum Pavilion are also part of the Seattle Center.

OTHER SIGHTS

If you want to learn more about the Indians of the Northwest, we suggest you visit the Burke Memorial Washington State Museum on the University of Washington campus. There is no charge and the museum is closed on Mondays. For a bargain in eating visit the Pioneer Square area where you will find the 'Bread Line.'

SEATTLE STATION

Seattle, Washington, is a very important rail transportation center. From here you have connections north to Vancouver, British Columbia, Canada, south to Portland, San Francisco, Los Angeles and San Diego, and east to Chicago via either the Glacier Park and Minneapolis or Bozeman (Yellowstone Park).

The station in Seattle has a modern interior plus a host of facilities. A good way to orient yourself is to look at the various door designations, as indicated in the big station. Between doors 1 and 2 you will find lockers, around door 4 a train arrivals/departures board and beyond door 5 the Amtrak Information/Ticket counter. Telephones, restrooms and a direct line to a car rental company are also found here. In the back of the hall you will find the baggage deposit office. Further along the wall is the street exit if you want to catch a cab. However, if you want to take a bus to the downtown area, you can take the escalator/stairs up to Jackson Street. Quite a number of city buses take you to the city center from here. You will see the big sign "Buses to City Center Stop Here." Also bus no. 19 takes you down 4th Ave. close to the Trailways and Greyhound Terminals. The YMCA is also located on this street.

SEATTLE-VANCOUVER(via ferry/bus)

Our friend from Vancouver, Martin Lund, suggests that you can take a bus from Seattle to Port Angeles, a 1 1/4 hour ferry ride from Port Angeles to Victoria ($2.50). From Victoria you can take the Pacific Stage Lines bus/ferry trip to Vancouver.

EASTERN CANADA
MONTREAL

Montreal, founded in 1642, now a cosmopolitan city, is one of our all time favorite places anywhere. We suspect that a combination of factors is responsible for this attraction. Probably one of the most practical reasons for liking the city is quite simply because it is easy to reach—whether you are in Toronto, New York City or Washington, D.C. or any other city in the East. Even during our early visits here when "Expo '67" was only a gleam in the planner's eye, we found the city involved in dynamic and purposeful change. "Man and His World" on the island in the St. Lawrence is not the only reminder of what direction Montreal has taken. "Habitat," an example of the bold housing style revolution, the efficient subway system with its magnificently designed stations and the Place Ville Marie, the underground commercial center, which again has made shopping a joy—all are Montreal trademarks. You will like Montreal—a city that looks toward the future. In 1976, the Summer Olympic Games will be held here to focus again attention on this charming city. Back in 1775, over 200 years ago, troops of the American Congress occupied the city.

Because there are two transcontinental railroads in Canada, there are two train stations in Montreal. The Canadian Pacific transcontinental "The Canadian" leaves Montreal's Windsor Station at 11:15 a.m. for its 2880 mile transcontinental trip to Vancouver. Amtrak's "Adirondack" also leaves/arrives at this station.

The Canadian National Railroad operates the 'Super Continental' (departure at 9:25 p.m. or 2125) from Montreal's 'CN Station'. The station is very modern and is in the heart of the huge underground shopping center at Place Ville Marie. The fine Queen Elizabeth Hotel is above the station complex. Amtrak's 'Montrealer' leaves/arrives at the CN Station. Although both the CP and CN have rail service to the Quebec City area, keep in mind the excellent bus service available between Montreal and Quebec City. A day excursion fare is also available. In any case, you have direct subway connections from the CP and the CN rail stations to Montreal's bus station.

The Montreal Bus Station is a modern transportation center. Not only does it serve bus arrivals and departures, but it is also directly served by Montreal's excellent sub-

190 MONTREAL

way, the Metro. Escalators take you directly from the bus station to the Metro platforms. The Metro station serving the bus station is called Berri de Montigny. It is the transfer point to all destinations by subway in Montreal.

The bus station has many facilities. There are a great number of automatic lockers. The baggage deposit office is at the far end of the terminal, in the direction of gate 23. There is an Information Office/Travel Bureau around gate 6. Near gate 9 is a telephone which you can use if you want bus information. Just pick up the receiver (no charge) and ask your question. Across from gate 12 you will find the entrance to the Metro.

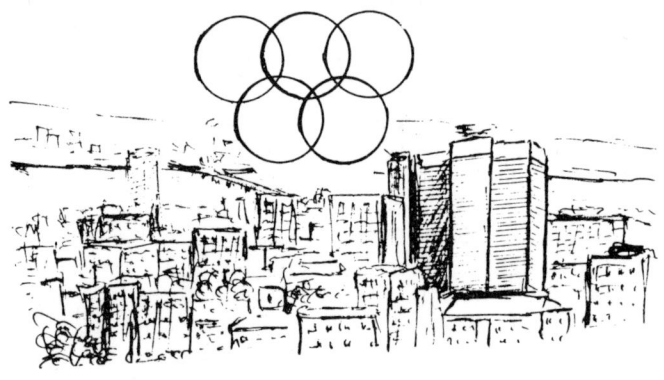

MAN AND HIS WORLD

A good way to get yourself oriented on this island city (yes, Montreal is on a 30 mile long island where the St. Lawrence and Ottawa Rivers meet) is to take the elevator up to the deck of the Canadian Imperial Bank of Commerce Building on Dorchester, right across from the Basilica of Mary Queen of the World in the vicinity of Place Ville Marie and the Queen Elizabeth Hotel. The observation deck is open until 11 in the evening. Cost is 75¢.

We have already mentioned "Man and His World" on the island in the St. Lawrence. Here you will see a variety of exhibits from many countries. The automated train takes you everywhere, thus giving you a great perspective of this area. Remember you can take the Metro from downtown to "Man and His World." After you get through sightseeing here, walk over (just follow the crowds) to La Ronde, the amusement center. There are a lot of things to do here—besides eating and taking rides, we just like to sit down next to the water and watch

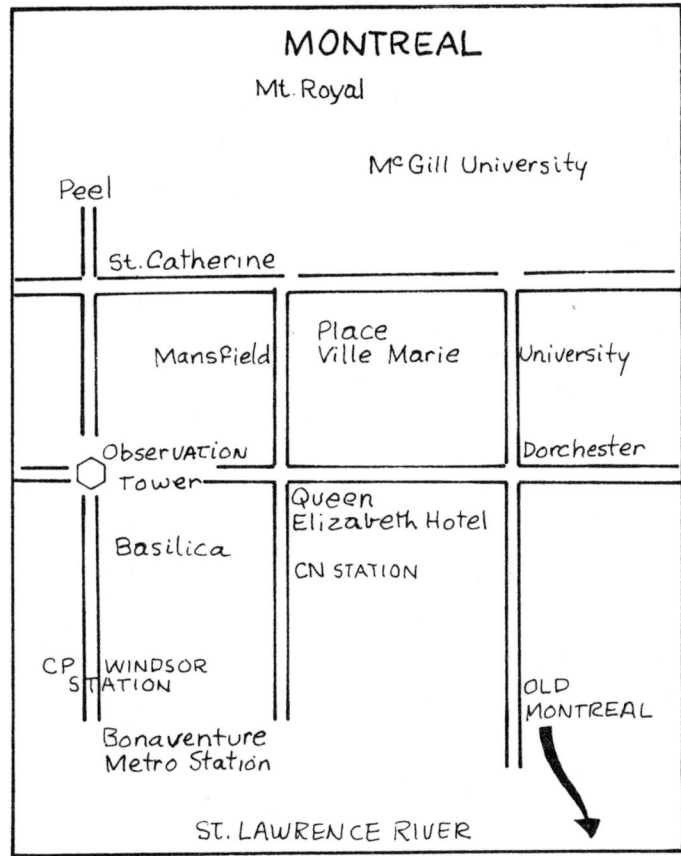

the dancing fountains while we are listening to a concert. (The fountains are synchronized with the musical notes you hear). After your visit to La Ronde (don't miss the French Canadian Village) you will join the crowd trying to get downtown again. Instead of walking back to "Man and His World" you can take a bus (#169) directly from the entrance of La Ronde to the nearest subway station, where you transfer to the Metro. (Make sure you pick up a transfer).

OLD MONTREAL, MOUNT ROYAL, CUISINE

If you found that La Ronde was too much noise or too much action for you, may we suggest you visit Vieux Montreal (Old Montreal). Stroll through this part of the city with its cobblestoned streets and try some of the excellent restaurants here. And if you prefer trees and grass while enjoying a panoramic view of the city, visit Mount Royal Park. Bus #11 from Metro Station Mont Royal goes through the park. A good place to get off is where the horse-drawn carriages are. There you can take walks through the fields or take a mini-train. You not only view the city and the wide river before you, but you can just see the outline of the Green Mountains of neighboring Vermont to the south.

Of course, while you are in Montreal you have to sample the French cuisine. For delicious onion soup (and we mean delicious—it was so good and plentiful we had difficulty finishing our sandwiches) stop by at one of the less formal restaurants you find at street level in the Queen Elizabeth. For a splurge, try the "Restaurant 737" on the 45th floor in the Place Ville Marie complex.

QUEBEC

The bus service between Montreal and Quebec City is excellent. During the day there are departures every hour. Because of the excellent "Autoroute" the approximately 160 mile trip between the two cities takes less than 3 hours, including a rest stop. The road does not follow the St. Lawrence River, but rather cuts across Quebec's picturesque countryside of farms, forests and lakes. However, you cross the mighty St. Lawrence twice—just after you leave Montreal and again prior to reaching Quebec. In both instances you have an excellent view of the river and the city.

The bus station in Quebec is not located directly in the center of the city. However, excellent city bus service is available from the bus station (Gare Centrale) to Chateau Frontenac and the old city. The bus station has facilities both at street level and downstairs. Restrooms, additional lockers, as well as a beauty salon are located downstairs. Call 692-0550 for transit information. Bus #3 will take you to Chateau Frontenac, the focal point in the old part of Quebec. The main Tourist Information Office is at 60 Rue d'Auteuil, telephone 522-4071.

The Chateau Frontenac (a hotel) stands on the site of the former Chateau St. Louis, which was the Residence of the Governors of New France. Place d'Armes, the square in front of the hotel is an excellent place to start your exploration of the old city, founded by Samuel de Champlain. On the square you will find a tourist information office. Pick up your 'Walking Tour' booklet. Near-by is the Battlefields Park where Generals Wolfe and

Montcalm met for control of most of North America. Take the elevator down to the Lower Town, squeezed between the cliff and the mighty St. Lawrence River. And above all, keep in mind as you are looking at the historic attractions that Quebec has that special French atmosphere. Enjoy it. Voila! At no time does this seem to become more apparent than during the Winter Carnival— held three weeks before Lent.

WESTERN CANADA

VANCOUVER

While you are in Vancouver, take the opportunity to obtain more information about the city, British Columbia and the rest of Canada. The Greater Vancouver Visitors and Convention Bureau is at 650 Burrard Street (682-2222). It is open 9-5 Monday-Saturday and on Sundays and holidays from noon to five in the afternoon. Right next door, at 652 Burrard Street is the British Columbia Department of Travel Industry Information Center (681-5177). It is open Monday-Friday 8:30 a.m.-5 p.m. Another place you might want to visit is the Yukon House at 567 Hornby (682-6311). Hours are Monday-Friday 8:30 a.m. to 5 p.m.

If you like swans, ducks, chipmunks, flowers, walks or just a place to relax, then Stanley Park at the end of Georgia Street is a must for you. In fact all visitors to Vancouver should visit this city park, a welcome change from the hustle and bustle of the big city. While you are rambling around, do not miss the view of the harbor from Prospect Point, or the popular gathering place, Lumberman's Arch. There is always something going on here.

GASTOWN

No matter how long you plan to stay in Vancouver, you should definitely make it a point to stop in the evening in Gastown—an exciting new area of good eating places, interesting shops and lively bars.

Two of the important streets in Gastown are Cordova and Water. Let us mention several of the places you pass as you walk down Water Street from Richards. This will give you some idea of the variety of places you can visit. Besides all the pubs and bars, you pass by the Old Spaghetti Factory, Oceanic Cost Plus Imports, the Gastown Wax Museum, the Rail Car Restaurant and Boutique Francoise. Carrall Street is another street that runs into the interesting square at that end of Water Street.

Another place we just have to alert you to is the enchanting little alley across from the Wax Museum. This alley leads you into a magnificent dining area—you have an excellent choice of restaurants here ranging all the way from the Schnitzel Place to fine oriental restaurants. While you are in this general area, note that at 175 W. Cordova St. is the CN-CP Telegram and Cable Office.

EXCURSION TO VICTORIA

An excellent trip to make from Vancouver is the 3-1/2 hour scenic bus/ferry trip to Victoria, capital of British Columbia. The Pacific Stage Lines bus takes you onto the ferry, and you leave the ferry with the same bus once you reach Vancouver Island. As you cross the Gulf of Georgia with its scenic islands, you can enjoy the facilities of a snack bar, restaurant and comfortable lounges. Also from the ferry you can catch a panoramic view of the city as well as the fresh sea breeze.

The fare for the combined bus/ferry trip is $4.25 one way Friday through Monday (and holidays). If you travel on other days you can save yourself one dollar. In Vancouver, buses leave the main Greyhound depot at Cambie and Dunsmuir every hour from 6 in the morning until 9 in the evening. Similarly, buses leave the depot at 710 Douglas Street in Victoria every hour from 6 in the morning until 9 at night. For further information call 683-2421 in Vancouver and 385-4411 in Victoria.

JASPER AND BANFF

Vancouver is your ideal gateway to the picturesque province of Alberta. It is in Alberta that you will find two of Canada's most scenic parks—Jasper and Banff. However, before we discuss more about these two attractions, refer to our map to give you a perspective of the location of these parks. Also note that Kamloops is an important junction for travel to either of the scenic wonders.

JASPER

From our map you will see that Jasper is on the route to Edmonton, Alberta's capital and largest city. In planning your trip through this part of Canada, keep in mind that Edmonton is less than five hours away from Jasper.

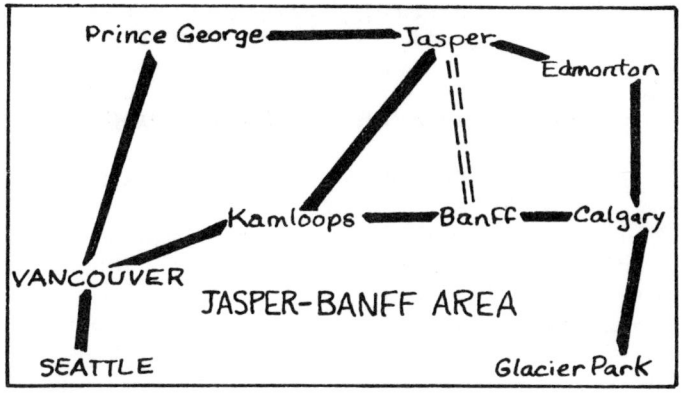

And Calgary, Alberta's second largest city (also your gateway to Banff) is only about 3 1/2 hours directly to the south of Edmonton.

Jasper National Park will give you an opportunity to see some truly wonderful mountain scenery as well as observe a great variety of wildlife. Columbia Icefield, the huge glacier, is one of the outstanding sights in the southern area of the park. Summer tours of the Icefield in a snowmobile cost about $2.50.

BANFF

From Jasper you have several options available. You can take the exceptionally scenic trip by bus between Jasper and Banff via Lake Louise Junction—the cost is $12, and it takes just under five hours. You leave Jasper at 2:30 p.m. and arrive at Lake Louise Jct. at 6:15 p.m., Banff at 7:10 p.m., and the Banff Springs Hotel at 7:20 p.m.

Of course, we have already told you the routing from Jasper to Banff via Edmonton and Calgary. We recommend this routing if you want to visit Calgary for the annual Calgary Stampede—usually held during the first half of July. This event will take you back to the wild days of the Wild West.

NATIONAL PARKS

CARLSBAD CAVERNS NATIONAL PARK

The Carlsbad Caverns in the Carlsbad Caverns Park have some of the world's largest and most spectacular caves. This is one sight you should not fail to see. The Carlsbad Caverns are located about 27 miles southwest of Carlsbad, in the southeastern corner of New Mexico. El Paso, Texas, on your southern transcontinental route, is your gateway by bus to Carlsbad and then on to the Caverns.

Before you discover the beauty of the limestone caves, you should know that the temperature is a constant 56 degrees fahrenheit and that you can explore 3 miles of trails underground. That means that you should take a sweater with you and wear comfortable walking shoes. Also if you should be here in the evening, watch the thousands of bats which leave the caves for the outside.

To get to the Caverns, leave from the modern Greyhound terminal in El Paso for Whites City. From Whites City to Carlsbad Caverns there are bus connections. The special round trip fare between Whites City and Carlsbad Caverns is $2.18. It is possible to return to El Paso by early evening from the Caverns by leaving at El Paso at 7:15 a.m. in the morning. This will give you 3 to 4 hours to explore the caves and then leave the Caverns at 2:43 p.m.

GLACIER NATIONAL PARK

On May 11, 1910, Glacier National Park was established. This scenic park with over 200 lakes and 60 small glaciers is located in the northwest corner of Montana, USA and the extreme southern portion of Alberta, Canada. In fact, Glacier National Park (USA name) and Waterton Lakes National Park (Canada name) is just about the only park which crosses an international border. In fact when it comes to wonderful alpine country and scenery, the Glacier Park stands out most in our minds as an ideal place to visit. Remember that this park and the transportation which is available in the park between the various lodges are usually only in operation from the end of May until the middle of September.

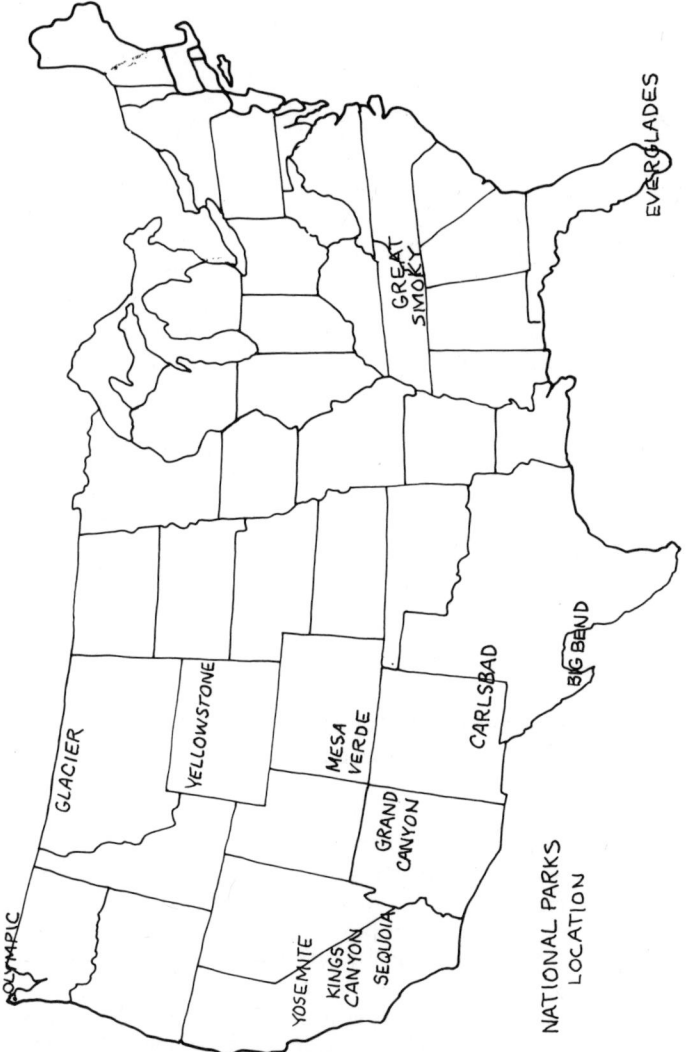

GLACIER PARK ACCOMMODATIONS

There are basically three entrances to the Glacier National Park/Waterton Lakes National Park. On the eastern side of the park is East Glacier. Not far from the small terminal is the spectacular Glacier Park Lodge with its 800 year old Douglas firs. The minimum rate for 2 persons is about $19. Keep in mind that you can get bus transportation from here (at extra cost) to the Prince of Wales Hotel, Many Glacier Hotel (in the real scenic part of the park) and Two Medicine Lake.

198 GRAND CANYON

At the west entrance of the park you will find the Village Inn (minimum $18 for two persons) and further up on Lake McDonald is the Lake McDonald Lodge (starting off at $19 for two persons). Remember that West Glacier is known also as Belton. From the Lake McDonald Lodge there is bus transportation available to Belton (West Glacier) and the Many Glacier Hotel on Swift Current Lake.

The Prince of Wales Hotel (82 rooms) in the Waterton Lakes National Park has a minimum rate for two persons of $19. Keep in mind that you have bus connections to/from Banff here. For instance you arrive at the Prince of Wales Hotel from Banff at 2:45 p.m. There is a departure for Banff at 3:00 p.m.

Besides the above hotels, there are several others in the park. As you can imagine, the demand for rooms at these hotels is very great. If you are traveling independently (2-5 day package tours are also available) you will have to make reservations as soon as your plans are firm. Between May 15—September 15 you can make your reservations by calling the Glacier Park Company at (406) 226-4841. If you are in Montana you can call toll free (800) 332-4114.

FLAGSTAFF, ARIZONA—GRAND CANYON GATEWAY

The Amtrak station in Flagstaff is your gateway to the magnificently beautiful Grand Canyon. As you walk into the train station from the platform, you will spot lockers on your right and the information/ticket office on your left. Here you can also get information on how you can get to the Grand Canyon itself, via a short bus ride. In any case, to help you plan your stay here, we give you the following information. As you walk out of the train station and up the steps to the main street, Santa Fe Street, turn to the left and walk about two blocks and you will be at the Trailways bus station. It is from this terminal that buses to the Grand Canyon leave. Should you require accommodations before you travel to the Grand Canyon, you will find additional hotels/motels in West Flagstaff, about 8 blocks down the street under the railway bridge. This is also the area where the new Greyhound bus terminal is located. Note that buses to the Grand Canyon leave from both the Trailways terminal (closer to the Flagstaff train station but not as close to accommodations) and the Greyhound terminal.

GRAND CANYON 199

When you have completed your 80 mile trip from Flagstaff to the Grand Canyon through the beautiful Kaibab National Forest you will be let off at the Bright Angel Lodge. This lodge is the center of activity here. If you are like us and cannot wait to catch a view of the Grand Canyon, walk through the lodge and you will be on the South Rim of the canyon. The hotel is built practically next to the canyon. In any case, as you walk into the Bright Angel Lodge, to your left you will see the TRANSPORTATION DESK. Here you can find out just about anything you want to know about the Grand Canyon—tours, hotels, sights, mule trips down the canyon and camping facilities. Remember that the Bright Angel Lodge also has accommodations. If you do not want to carry your baggage around (and we suggest you don't), there is a baggage check place on the way to the restrooms on the left side of the lodge as you enter. There is no fixed charge to leave your bags here—just leave a tip when you obtain your deposit receipt.

When you are outside the Bright Angel Lodge looking down and across the mighty sight of the Canyon, remember that you are at an elevation of 6868 feet (2093 meters) and the elevation of the Colorado River below you is 2425 feet (740 meters). This difference in elevation exposes all the various layers of rocks and soil, giving you an excellent study of what has happened to the earth during the past millions of years. Depending on where you are, the Grand Canyon is anywhere from 4-18 miles (7-30 km.) wide. The Colorado River, which is one of the longest rivers in the United States, flows for 105 miles through the Grand Canyon National Park.

The Bright Angel Lodge, your arrival point from Flagstaff, is on the south side of the Canyon, the South Rim. The vegetation you will find here on this side is somewhat similar to what you find in northern Mexico.

There are a great number of ways to explore the Grand Canyon. Probably Major John Powell and his men in the summer of 1869 were the first to explore the entire canyon by boat. Besides taking the rough trip by boat on the wild Colorado River, you have many other options to enjoy the natural beauty of the Grand Canyon. For instance, there is a guided mule trip to the bottom of the canyon and a visit to the Havasapei Indians. You can also enjoy camping, either at the very bottom of the canyon or halfway up, or at the top, and you can watch Indian dances and listen to scheduled lectures by Park Rangers of the National Park Service.

200 SEQUOIA

FLAGSTAFF TOUR DEPARTURES

While you are in the Flagstaff area, you might consider a host of tours available, offered by Gray Line and Nava-Hopi Tours. Here are some of the places you might want to visit—Sunset Crater National Monument, Oak Creek Canyon, Montezuma Castle National Monument or Coal Mine Canyon. For further information call 774-5003 in Flagstaff.

MESA VERDE NATIONAL PARK

A worthwhile trip in the southwestern part of Colorado is to the Mesa Verde National Park. Here you will find large and well-preserved cliff dwellings, the largest of which is the Cliff Palace, with more than 200 rooms. Make sure you pick up the literature available at Mesa Verde National Park from the Park Service. The Archeological Museum is an excellent place to learn about the life style of inhabitants before they left their stone pueblos around the 13th century. Durango is your gateway to the park.

SEQUOIA AND KINGS CANYON NATIONAL PARKS

These two national parks are right next to each other in eastern California in the Sierra Mountains. They are in a vast region of wilderness, mountains, canyons and the giant Sequoia trees.

Your gateway to these parks are Tulare and Visalia, south of Fresno. From these two towns you can catch the Sequoia Motor Coach to Giant Forest Lodge in Sequoia National Park. Lodging and tours of the parks are available here. For more information call toll free (800) 742-2070 from May to mid September or (209) 565-3373.

YELLOWSTONE NATIONAL PARK

Yellowstone National Park is now just over a hundred years old. It was established in 1872 to be "a pleasure ground for the benefit and enjoyment of the people." Well, yearly more than 2 million people visit the 3,472 square miles of National Park. As a result, as you can well imagine, many of the tourist attractions in the park are crowded. There are about 400 miles of roads and

1000 miles of trails for you to discover. Since many people never set foot on these scenic trails, perhaps you can think about hiking on these trails to escape the crowds of people who seem to be everywhere near the major attractions. However, to us the beauty of Yellowstone is the peace and tranquillity you can find off the beaten path. And the variety of wildlife is very great. There are well over 15,000 elk, 1000 moose, 600 bison, 400 black bears and about 150 or so grizzly bears which roam in this general area of Montana, Idaho and Wyoming. Then there are several thousand geysers and hot pools spread throughout the park—the most famous geyser is Old Faithful—not because of its size, but rather because of its dependability. Eruptions average about 65 minutes apart.

You will find that tours can be taken to many of the attractions in the park. However, if there are several of you traveling together, you might find it advantageous to rent a car for it gives you the independence to discover the many remote and magnificent areas of the park. But no matter which way you explore the Yellowstone National Park or Grand Teton National Park (directly to the south) keep your most comfortable walking shoes handy, as well as some warm clothing.

HOW TO REACH YELLOWSTONE NATIONAL PARK

There are quite a number of ways to reach Yellowstone National Park. Because the area of the park is so extensive, have a look at our map to determine which entrance to the park best suits your travel plans. For instance, if you are traveling the route Chicago to Seattle, you will be passing through three towns, Billings, Livingston, and Bozeman, any of which can act as your

202 YELLOWSTONE

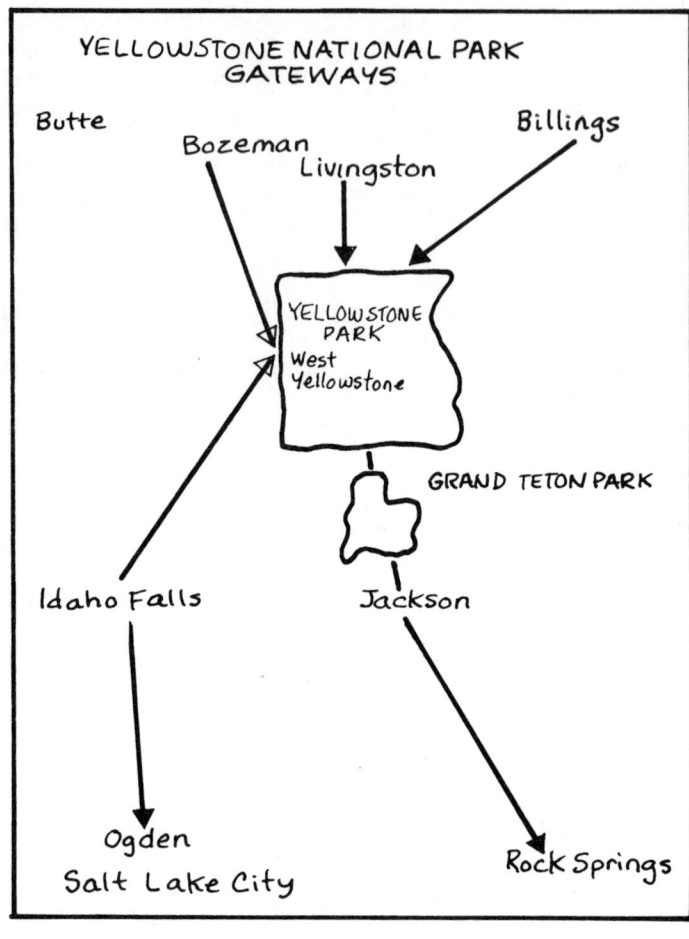

gateway. Schedules through these towns allow you to connect with buses operated by Yellowstone Park Lines and the Yellowstone Park Company. The Billings and Livingston gateways will enable you to reach Mammoth, in the northwestern corner of the park. Here are some departure/arrival times from Billings and Livingston to Mammoth. Keep in mind these bus lines operate only during the summer months.

NORTHEAST ENTRANCE

1:15 p.m.	Lv. Billings	Ar. 10:55 a.m.
6:35 p.m.	Ar. Mammoth	Lv. 7:30 a.m.

NORTH ENTRANCE

| 3:45 p.m. | Lv. Livingston | Ar. 10:55 a.m. |
| 5:10 p.m. | Ar. Mammoth | Lv. 9:30 a.m. |

SOUTH ENTRANCE

Travelers sometimes forget that just to the south of Yellowstone National Park is another wonderful park—the Grand Teton National Park. Here the mountain peaks rise abruptly at times 7000 feet above the surrounding plain. The sight is fantastic.

One of the best ways to reach the Grand Teton National Park and the Yellowstone National Park via the South Entrance is by way of Rock Springs. Rock Springs is on the main Denver-San Francisco route and is your all-important gateway for bus travel to the National Parks. You leave Rock Springs at 8:30 a.m. via the Jackson-Rock Springs Stages and arrive in Jackson at noon. On the way to Jackson you pass through the scenic Snake River Canyon. At Jackson you have connections to Jackson Hole (Grand Teton National Park) and Yellowstone National Park.

WEST ENTRANCE

If the object of your visit is the Old Faithful Geyser and Yellowstone Lake, you might consider coming through the West Entrance. Besides having good connections at Bozeman to West Yellowstone (the entrance to the park), you also have excellent bus connections from Ogden/Salt Lake City, Utah. Here are some times—you leave Bozeman at 3:30 p.m. and arrive at West Yellowstone at 5:50 p.m. For the return trip to Bozeman you leave West Yellowstone at 8:00 a.m. and arrive in Bozeman at 10:35 a.m. where you have connections to the east or to the Pacific Northwest.

If you are coming from the south to West Yellowstone Park you have good connections. You leave the Greyhound terminal in Salt Lake City at 8:15 a.m. (Ogden at 9:10 a.m.) and arrive at West Yellowstone at 5:05 p.m., where at 6:00 p.m. you can leave and arrive at the Old Faithful Geyser Inn, inside the park, at 7:30 p.m. The return trip from the park goes like this—you leave Old Faithful Geyser Inn at 2:35 p.m. and arrive at West Yellowstone at 4:00 p.m. At 6:30 p.m. you can leave West Yellowstone, arriving in Ogden, Utah, at 1:57 a.m. and Salt Lake City at 2:30 a.m. Keep in mind that the Salt

204 YOSEMITE

Lake City/Ogden—West Yellowstone bus service operates only during the last half of May, and in June, July, August, and in the first half of September.

We will now give you some additional departure times from West Yellowstone to Old Faithful for the approximate 75 minute trip. You can leave West Yellowstone at 11 in the morning, or at 3, 6, and 8 p.m. Leaving from Old Faithful to West Yellowstone, you have departures at 7 and 11:30 in the morning and at 6 p.m.

YOSEMITE NATIONAL PARK, CALIFORNIA

Yosemite National Park has become so popular in recent years that parts of the park have been closed to cars. Thus, when you arrive here, you have the option of taking the Yosemite Park buses in the valley or perhaps renting a bicycle. You can also take tram tours ($3.50 for the two hour trip). If you plan to stay longer in these beautiful mountains, you can also participate in hiking tours and riding expeditions lasting several days. However, no matter how short your stay here, do not miss the numerous giant waterfalls in the seven mile long valley.

Merced is your gateway to Yosemite National Park. Buses leave from the Yosemite Transportation Office in Merced for the 2 1/2 hour trip to the beautiful Yosemite Valley. Buses leave Merced for Yosemite Valley at 1:35 and 3:35 in the afternoon and Yosemite Valley for Merced at 8:30 and 11:30 in the monring during the summer months. If Fresno is a more convenient departure point for you, the Yosemite Transportation Company provides 3 1/2 hour bus service between Yosemite Valley and Fresno to the southwest. Buses leave from the Greyhound terminal in Fresno at 4:15 p.m. and from Yosemite Valley at 11:45 in the morning.

CAMPING IN NATIONAL PARKS

A chart of national parks and the activities they offer, the length of the camping season, campground types and fees, availability of swimming, fishing and boating and safety advice are included in an Interior Department publication titled "Camping in the National Park System." Copies may be obtained for 65 cents each from Consumer Information, Pueblo, Colo. 81009

GATEWAYS TO THE USA AND CANADA

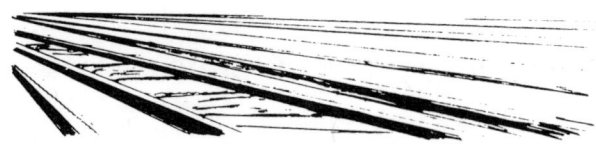

ARRIVING IN NEW YORK BY AIR

Each of our 30 day suggested itineraries starts in New York City because many travelers use the city as the gateway to exploring the U.S.A. If you arrive in New York by air, you will find that there are actually 3 major airports in the New York Metropolitan area. Two of the airports, Newark and La Guardia, cater mainly to domestic arrivals and departures. J.F. Kennedy Airport is the main airport for international arrivals and departures.

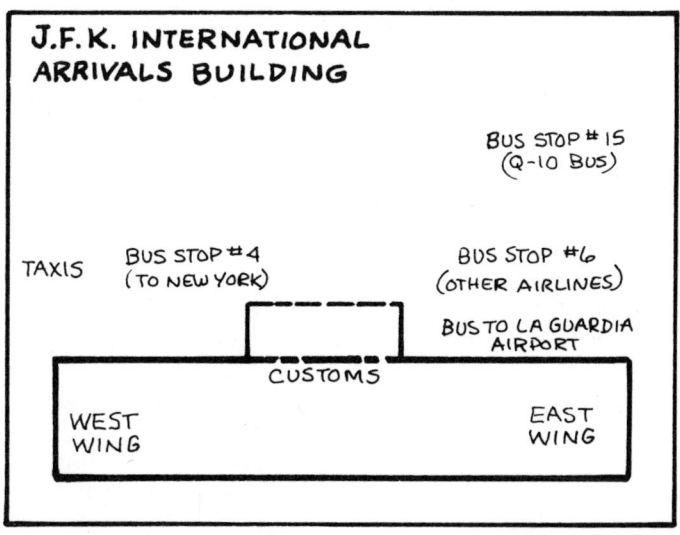

You will find Kennedy Airport a busy place. Many of the international arrivals take place at the big International Arrivals Building. From this building there is direct bus service every 15 minutes to the New York downtown area. Buses are operated by the Carey Transportation Company to the East Side Terminal, at 1st Avenue and 37th Street (near the United Nations Building) and on the East Side of the city. The trip takes about an hour.

206 GATEWAYS

A NOTE TO INTERNATIONAL VISITORS

Since this guide is also used by our friends from abroad, we would like to address ourselves to them for just a moment. New York is such a huge place, a city of contrasts—pleasant and unpleasant, full of entertainment and loneliness, as well as being dotted with wonderful sights and attractions in addition to slums. You will find friendly and helpful people here more often than you will find rude ones, but chances are you will find both. New York does not represent all of the United States and we therefore suggest very strongly that you save your exploration of New York City for the latter part of your visit. After you have seen the rest of the country, you will be in a much better position to put America's largest city in its proper perspective and to appreciate as well as evaluate its good points and some of its disadvantages. So please think seriously of what we have said—visit New York after you have seen other parts of the country. Many visitors to the U.S.A. have used this approach to make their visit to the U.S.A. very successful and memorable.

FROM KENNEDY AIRPORT TO NEW YORK TRAIN STATION

One of the cheapest and convenient ways to travel by public transportation from Kennedy Airport to the train station is to take the Q-10 bus from bus stop #15 across from the International Arrivals Building. You must have 50 cents in exact change (the bus driver does not have the change). Buses leave every 10-15 minutes throughout the day and every 30 minutes between midnight and 6:30 a.m. from the #15 stop. Take the bus to the last stop, get off, and follow the people to the subway station, which is next to the bus stop. You are at the 'Union Turnpike-Kew Gardens' subway stop.

Once you have entered the subway station, go to the ticket window and ask for a 'token' (a special coin) which costs 50 cents. You take the token, put it in the slot at the turnstiles, push and you are close to the platforms. Your platform is one level below—look for the sign 'Manhattan' and 'Downtown.' There are several subway lines which stop here so make certain you get on the 'E' subway. Once you are on the subway you will see a color-coded subway map. To find your location, look at the upper right hand corner of the map in the 'Queens' section and you will find the route of the 'E' train. The train, after a number of other stops, stops at 42nd Street and 8th Avenue in Manhattan, the Port Authority Bus Terminal and then Pennsylvania Station.

IMPORTANT SUGGESTION FOR VISITORS

Since in many cases flights from Europe arrive in New York late in the day, may we suggest that you get a good nights rest before you discover America. To minimize your confusion, take the Airport Bus from just outside International Arrivals Building (stop #4) to downtown New York, the East Side Terminal. Just a few minutes walk from this terminal is the Hotel Tudor, 304 East 42nd Street, New York, N.Y. 10017, telephone 986-8800. Single rooms start at $16 and doubles at $22. You may want to write them a letter with a deposit to reserve a room for your first night in America or call them from the airport as soon as you have arrived.

ARRIVING IN WASHINGTON, D.C. BY AIR

There are three airports which serve the Washington, D.C. area. One is Baltimore-Washington Airport; but since this airport is closer to Baltimore than Washington, D.C., we will briefly discuss the two other airports. International arrivals, as well as some domestic flights, take place in the beautiful Virginia countryside, at Dulles International Airport, named in honor of John Foster Dulles, Secretary of State under President Eisenhower. The best way to reach Washington, D.C. from this airport is with the bus service provided by Greyhound, ($3.75). The bus will let you off at 16th and K Streets, N.W., in downtown Washington, D.C.

National Airport is the airport for domestic arrivals/departures. It is very close to the city on the Potomac River, on the Virginia side.

208 GATEWAYS

ARRIVING IN BOSTON BY AIR

Boston's Logan Airport is one of the busiest airports in the world because of its strategic position in the northeastern part of the U.S.A. as well as its close proximity to Europe. If Boston is your gateway city, you will find that it is very easy to reach the center of Boston by public transportation. Just outside the international arrivals area you will find a bus which will take you to the nearby Airport Subway Station. The same bus also picks up domestic passengers from other airport areas. From the Airport Subway Station you take the subway into the heart of the city. The bus fare is 20¢ and the subway fare is 25¢ to any part of the city. Remember that when you arrive at the Airport Subway Station you must take the "Blue Line Inbound" direction to arrive in the city center. Also you should note that you will find a place to change your money after you have passed through customs at the airport. An information desk as well as restrooms are also located nearby for your convenience.

ARRIVING IN MIAMI BY AIR

Miami International Airport is one of the leading gateways to the U.S.A. International arrivals take place from Europe as well as Central and South America. Of course, Miami Airport is also one of the busiest airports in the country in terms of domestic air traffic. You should note that the airport terminal building is actually a two level structure. International as well as domestic arrivals take place on the lower level. For those visitors who must clear customs, you will find that once you have completed this formality, the international information center will be to your left, inside the terminal building. From this lower level you can also take a limousine for $2 into downtown Miami. We might add that the international information center has information about tourist attractions. The personnel there can provide you with an excellent map of the city with all the bus routes listed. This allows you to plan your trips around the city.

For your trip by city-bus to downtown Miami, you must go up one level. On this upper level you will find many facilities, including restaurants, restrooms and banks (to change your money). Bus number 20 (Miami direction) takes you to downtown for 30 cents. Be alerted to the fact that you must have the exact change to ride on the bus.

ARRIVING IN CHICAGO BY AIR

The big Chicago Airport, O'Hare Airport, is a considerable distance from the center of Chicago. Taxi service as well as limousines can bring you to the downtown area. However, for 75 cents you can use the public transportation system to take you to the center of the city. It may take a little longer, but here is the way it works.

You arrive at the world's busiest airport on the ground level. After you have picked up your bags, just walk to the outside. You will see the bus stop and "O'Harexpress" written on the sign. This no. 40 bus will take you non-stop to the Jefferson Park subway station where you catch the subway to the "Washington" stop. Buses from the airport to the subway station run usually about 15 and 45 minutes past the hour. The trip to the subway station takes about 15 minutes, and the subway trip to downtown takes about 20 minutes.

Once you have boarded the bus at the airport, deposit 75¢ and ask for a transfer. When you have reached the Jefferson Park subway station, walk 50 yards or so along the glass enclosed hall until you reach the entry point for the subway. Show the person your transfer ticket, walk downstairs and board any subway. All subways go to the Washington stop. Once you have reached Washington, walk upstairs. You will be between Washington and Madison Streets. Walk in the direction of Washington Street, cross Washington and continue one more block to Randolph Street.

ARRIVING IN NEW ORLEANS BY AIR

If you have arrived in New Orleans on an international flight, you will find that once you have cleared customs, you will see a hotel/motel reservations map. Passengers from domestic flights will also see the map. Your baggage claim area is just outside the door to your left. Many of the hotels/motels are pictured. To reserve a room, just pick up the telephone receiver, push down on the button to the right of the hotel/motel name and wait about 30 seconds for someone to answer. The map on the wall will give you a chance to get yourself oriented.

Just outside the door you will see the baggage claim area; just to the right is the origination point for the limousine service to downtown New Orleans. The limousine cost is $3 per person while taxi fare is $9 per person. Take the limousine! Remember that arrivals take place at the lower level. If you want a post office, place to eat or departure information, you have to take the escalator upstairs one level. Also upstairs is the Visitor Information booth. Here you can obtain maps, accommodations and tourist information. The main tourist office is at 344 Royal Street, in the French Quarter of New Orleans.

ARRIVING IN LOS ANGELES BY AIR

Los Angeles International Airport is a busy place. It serves as an important gateway to California and the whole West. Once you are outside your arrival terminal, a good way to get yourself oriented is to look up and see the various numbered designations above the terminals. Thus, the area around terminals 2 and 3 is in the vicinity of the international arrivals, and terminals 4-7 handle some of the domestic arrivals. In front of most arrival terminals you will spot little booths where you can buy your bus tickets to the Greyhound/RTD (RTD stands for Rapid Transit District) terminal. From near this terminal you can take #5 city bus service to the colorful Mexican Street. The airport bus which goes to downtown Los Angeles stops off at the Biltmore and Hilton hotels and the Greyhound/RTD terminal. Ask the lady in the booth at the airport for particulars. Cost for the bus downtown is $1.25. Also we call to your attention the fact that direct bus service is available from the airport to Disneyland. As a final note, remember that all buses leave from the traffic island found in front of the terminals at the airport.

ARRIVING IN SAN FRANCISCO BY AIR

Since many travelers start their exploration of the western part of the USA by arriving at San Francisco International Airport, we will briefly tell you a few important points about your arrival. We hope that just before you land you catch a glimpse of the Golden Gate Bridge—it is truly a magnificent sight.

First, you arrival takes place on the lower level. On this level you can take a bus (called "Airporter") to downtown (Taylor and O'Farrell Streets) for $1.15. Buses run about every 15 minutes during peak periods. The bus leaves from either the TWA baggage area or from the Central Terminal. For exact departures you can use one of the white courtesy phones located all over the airport and call 7-0344. There is a second bus available to downtown for 85 cents. This bus leaves from the upper level opposite the TWA ticket counter about every 30 minutes and will take you to the Greyhound Bus Terminal. From the Greyhound Bus Station you can easily catch city buses to the East Bay Bus Terminal (1st and Mission). Here Gray Line Tours has an office. For exact departure times for the bus (line B) from the airport to the Greyhound Terminal use the white courtesy telephone and dial 7-0366.

ARRIVING IN MONTREAL BY AIR

If your gateway city is Montreal, site of the 1976 Olympic Games, you will find the airport in the French speaking part of Canada a very modern one. Domestic arrival and international arrival areas are served directly by bus to the center of the city. The fare is about $2.00. This bus from the airport will take you to the major hotels in the city. The first stop the bus from the airport makes is the Queen Elizabeth Hotel. Since this hotel is close to the Canadian National train station as well as the subway (direct service to the bus station), it is a convenient place to get off, even if you are not staying at this fabulous hotel. To reach the subway station, walk downstairs at the Queen Elizabeth Hotel.

PUBLIC HOLIDAYS IN THE U.S.A.

Here is a listing of some of the major holidays in the U.S.A. New Year's Day, January 1; Lincoln's Birthday, February 12; George Washington's Birthday, 3rd Monday in February; Easter; Memorial Day, last Monday in May; Independence Day, July 4; Labor Day, first Monday in September; Columbus Day, Second Monday in October; Veteran's Day, fourth Monday in October (to be changed back to Nov. 11); Thanksgiving Day, fourth Thursday in November; and Christmas Day, December 25.

PUBLIC HOLIDAYS IN CANADA

Besides holidays such as New Year's Day, and Christmas, we note for you several holidays in Canada. Namely, there is Victoria Day, which in 1976 will fall on May 24. July 1 is Dominion Day. Labour Day is on the first Monday in September, whereas Thanksgiving Day in 1976 will be on October 11. Rememberance Day is on Nov. 11.

212 CHANGING MONEY

WHERE TO CHANGE YOUR MONEY

You will find banks and change offices at the major airports when you arrive in the United States. You will also be able to change your money at major banks in the larger cities. The Deak Company, for example, has a number of change offices in cities across the country. For your information we give you some of their locations in the U.S. and Canada and their telephone numbers.

763 United Nations Plaza
(opposite the United Nations)
New York, New York 10017
Tel: (212) 685-5630

630 Fifth Avenue
(between 50th & 51st Streets)
New York, New York 10020
Tel: (212) 757-6915

International Club Building
1800 K Street, N.W.
Washington, D.C. 20006
Tel: (202) 872-1233

182 Geary Street
San Francisco, California 94108
Tel: (415) 362-3452

San Francisco Hilton Hotel
355 O'Farrell Street
San Francisco, California 94102
Tel: (415) 673-1412

Hilton Hotel Center
677 South Figueroa Street
Los Angeles, California 90017
Tel: (213) 624-4221

10 King Street East
Toronto, Ont., Canada M5W 1G3
Tel: (416) 863-1611

555 Howe Street
Vancouver, B.C., Canada V6C 2P1
Tel: (604) 682-6858

'TRAVEL PHONE USA'

As a visitor to the United States you should be aware of a special telephone number which you can call to get your questions about accommodations, lost passports or any other travel problem answered. You can get answers in French, German, Spanish, Japanese. It does not cost you anything to call this special '800' number.

The cooperative project between Travel Lodge International and the United States Travel Service operates in 48 contiguous states. A foreign visitor needs merely to dial 800 255-3050, except in Kansas where the number is 1-800 332-4350.

COSERV

COSERV community organizations are private, independent groups of volunteer citizens in over 80 cities and towns in the United States that provide assistance to international visitors. Services include information and maps, language aid, escorted sightseeing and opportunities to meet American families. There are several conditions which the international visitor must meet in order to obtain assistance during their visit. You must notify the COSERV organization at least 48 hours in advance for sightseeing and hospitality. You must carry health and accident insurance during travel. Moreover, you must be a short-term visitor in the community and require no financial aid.

We now will provide you with a list of organizations which have indicated their willingness to assist international visitors. Telephone Monday-Friday between 0900 and 1700, except as noted in individual listings. No longer does the international visitor have to feel lost in the big country of the United States. America and Americans welcome our friends from abroad!

Alabama
  HUNTSVILLE—Huntsville-Madison County Council for International Visitors: *205-536-5911 ext. 260*
Arizona
  PHOENIX—World Affairs Council of Phoenix: *602-254-3345*
Arkansas
  LITTLE ROCK—Little Rock Council for International Visitors: *501-375-8164*
California
  LOS ANGELES—International Student Service of Southern California: *213-380-0427*
  RIVERSIDE—International Relations Council of Riverside: *714-787-4113*

SACRAMENTO—People-to-People Council of Greater Sacramento: *916-452-5451*
SAN FRANCISCO—International Hospitality Center: *415-986-1388*

Colorado
BOULDER—Community Hospitality for International Visitors: *303-443-5512*
DENVER—Institute of International Education, Rocky Mountain Office: *303-222-1895*
DENVER—International Hospitality Center of the Colorado Division, UNA, USA-UNESCO: *303-534-1472 (10 a.m. - 4:30 p.m.)*

Connecticut
WESTPORT—International Hospitality Committee of Fairfield County: *203-227-3345*

Delaware
WILMINGTON—Delaware Council for International Visitors: *302-655-3341 ext. 31*

District of Columbia
WASHINGTON—Foreign Student Service Council: *202-232-4979*
WASHINGTON—International Visitors Service Council: *202-347-4554*

Florida
GAINESVILLE—Gainesville Council for International Friendship: *904-376-4687*
MIAMI—Council for International Visitors of Greater Miami: *305-379-4610*

Georgia
ATLANTA—Atlanta Council for International Visitors: *404-577-2248*

Illinois
CHICAGO—Institute of International Education, Midwest Office: *312-236-8232*
CHICAGO—International Visitors Center: *312-332-5875*
FREEPORT—International Fellowship Committee: *815-232-3340*
PARIS—Paris International Fellowship: *217-463-3315 or 217-463-6950*
SPRINGFIELD—Springfield Commission on International Visitors: *217-525-7500*

Indiana
INDIANAPOLIS—Indianapolis Committee for International Visitors of the Indianapolis Council on World Affairs: *317-926-0696; after 2 p.m.: 317-251-1841*

Iowa
DES MOINES—Des Moines Area Council for International Understanding: *515-279-7652*

SIOUX CITY—Mayor's Committee for International Visitors: *712-279-6201*

Kansas
WICHITA—International Visitors Council of the Wichita Area Chamber of Commerce: *316-265-7771*

Kentucky
LOUISVILLE—International Center, University of Louisville: *502-636-4681*

Louisiana
  NEW ORLEANS—Council for International Visitors of Greater New Orleans: *504-866-3906 or 504-525-5353*
Maryland
  BALTIMORE—Baltimore Council for International Visitors: *301-727-1749*
Massachusetts
  BOSTON—Boston Council for International Visitors: *617-742-0460*
  CAMBRIDGE—Harvard University Marshal's Office: *617-495-4726*
  SPRINGFIELD—World Affairs Council of the Connecticut Valley: *413-596-9452 (12:30 - 2:30 p.m.; closed in summer)*
  WORCESTER—International Center of Worcester: *617-752-8414*
Michigan
  ANN ARBOR—International Center, University of Michigan: *313-764-9310*
  DETROIT—International Visitors Council of Metropolitan Detroit: *313-961-9393*
  FLINT—Flint Committee to Welcome International Visitors: *313-238-8136*
  GRAND RAPIDS—World Affairs Council, International Visitors Committee: *616-458-9535*
Minnesota
  MINNEAPOLIS-ST. PAUL—Minnesota International Center: *612-373-3200*
  WORTHINGTON—Worthington-Crailsheim International: *507-376-5644*
Missouri
  KANSAS CITY—Committee for International Visitors and Students of the Chamber of Commerce: *816-221-2424*
  ST. LOUIS—St. Louis Council on World Affairs: *314-361-7333*
Montana
  BOZEMAN—Center for Intercultural Programs, Montana State University: *406-994-3881*
Nebraska
  LINCOLN—Mayor's Committee for International Friendship: *402-471-2256*
  OMAHA—Kiwanis Club of Omaha: *402-342-4140*
New Hampshire
  DURHAM—New Hampshire Council on World Affairs: *603-862-1683*
New Mexico
  ALBUQUERQUE—Albuquerque Committee for International Visitors: *505-265-0265*
  SANTA FE—Santa Fe Council on International Relations: *505-982-4931 (mornings only)*
New York
  ALBANY—Albany International Center: *518-436-9741*
  BUFFALO—Buffalo World Hospitality Association: *716-882-6900*
  NEW YORK CITY—International Center in New York: *212-245-4131*
  ROCHESTER—International Hospitality Service, Rochester Association for the United Nations: *716-232-1080*
  ROCHESTER—Rochester International Friendship Council: *716-546-7290*

SYRACUSE—International Center of Syracuse: *315-471-0252*

Ohio
 CINCINNATI—International Visitors Center: *513-241-7384*
 CLEVELAND—Cleveland Council on World Affairs: *216-781-3730*
 COLUMBUS—Central Ohio Council for International Visitors: *614-885-3241*
 DAYTON—Dayton Council on World Affairs: *513-223-6203*
 TOLEDO—International Institute of Greater Toledo: *419-241-9178*

Oklahoma
 OKLAHOMA CITY—International Visitors Council, Chamber of Commerce: *405-232-6381*

Oregon
 PORTLAND—World Affairs Council of Oregon: *503-229-3049*

Pennsylvania
 PHILADELPHIA—Philadelphia Council for International Visitors: *215-686-1776 ext. 21-261*
 PITTSBURGH—Pittsburgh Council for International Visitors: *412-682-7929*

Rhode Island
 PROVIDENCE—World Affairs Council of Rhode Island: *401-245-5449 or 401-421-8622*

South Carolina
 COLUMBIA—Columbia Council for Internationals: *803-256-1445*

Tennessee
 MEMPHIS—Memphis Council for International Friendship: *901-523-2322*

Texas
 AUSTIN—International Hospitality Committee of Austin: *512-471-1211*
 DALLAS—Dallas Council on World Affairs: *214-521-2171*
 EL PASO—El Paso Council for International Visitors: *915-544-7880*
 HOUSTON—Houston International Service Committee, Institute of International Education, Southern Office: *713-228-7495*

Utah
 SALT LAKE CITY—International Visitors-Utah Council: *801-359-5275*

Virginia
 NORFOLK-VIRGINIA BEACH—Committee for International Visitors: *804-481-0814*
 RICHMOND—Richmond International Council: *804-644-6193*

Washington
 EPHRATA—Ephrata's International Friends: *509-754-4373 (after 5 p.m.)*
 SEATTLE—World Affairs Council of Seattle: *206-682-6985*
 SPOKANE—Spokane International Exchange Council: *509-747-6963*
 YAKIMA—Yakima Valley Council for International Visitors: *509-457-5123*

Wisconsin
 MILWAUKEE—International Institute of Milwaukee County: *414-933-0521*

USARAIL PASS INFORMATION FOR VISITORS FROM ABROAD

WHAT IS A USARAIL PASS?

The USARAIL PASS is a red, white and blue colored card for unlimited travel anywhere on the Amtrak U.S. rail passenger system network of over 24,000 miles (38,600 kilometers).

WHO CAN USE THE USARAIL PASS?

The pass can be used by visitors to the United States entering the U.S.A. on tourist, student, or business visas. Citizens of the U.S. (and its territories), Mexico and Canada cannot use the USARAIL PASS.

HOW MUCH DOES A USARAIL PASS COST?

The pass can be bought for various periods. The cost varies according to the validity period of the pass. Costs are in U.S. dollars.

14 Days — $150
21 Days — $200
30 Days — $250

IS THE USARAIL PASS A GOOD BUY?

The answer to that question depends on the amount of traveling you do. However, if you consider that a round trip ticket between New York and Los Angeles costs more than $300, the USARAIL PASS is a real bargain. Moreover, you do not have to have to pay for seat reservations when you travel with your pass.

WHERE CAN I OBTAIN A USARAIL PASS?

Amtrak has appointed many travel agents outside of North America to sell its tickets. Thus you can obtain your USARAIL PASS at travel agents in your country.

WHAT RESTRICTIONS ARE THERE?

The USARAIL PASS is not transferable. It is good for travel in coaches (second class) only and not on premium trains. The Metroliner between New York City and Washington, D.C. is a premium train. However, by paying the difference between the regular fare and the special fare applicable on the Metroliner (the difference is about $8), the USARAIL PASS holder can travel on these super-fast trains. Remember that the pass is not applicable for meals and not for sleeping accommodations. Sleeping accommodations can be obtained at extra charge.

HOW DO I USE THE USARAIL PASS?

You buy your pass before you arrive in the U.S.A. On the first day you want to travel in the United States, go to the nearest Amtrak terminal (such as Pennsylvania Station in New York) with your pass and passport. The Amtrak ticket agent will then validate your pass with date, and this will be your first day of travel. Tell the ticket agent where you want to travel, and if seats are available (remember that seats have to be reserved on most trains), you will receive a ticket to your next destination. And if you have planned a part of your itinerary, you can also make reservations and obtain tickets for those segments of your trip. The suggested itineraries we have included in this book can help you plan an itinerary to meet your individual needs.

In any case, with your ticket, your USARAIL PASS and your passport, you can then board your train. Relax and enjoy the beauty of America.

USARAIL PASS 219
FOR VISITORS FROM ABROAD
SUMMARY OF AVAILABILITY AND CONDITIONS

USARAIL Pass Availability

1. Can *only be purchased overseas* by *foreign nationals* entering the U.S. on a student, business or tourist visa.
2. Citizens of Mexico, Canada and U.S. possessions *excluded* from Pass use.
3. Available only through *overseas Amtrak-appointed agents.*
4. USARAIL Pass *Card-Passport and ticket coupon* are all needed to secure passage aboard trains. *Any one item missing* will result in payment of the full applicable fare over the entire segment being traveled.

USARAIL Pass Conditions:

1. **Pass card alone not valid** aboard trains.
2. **Pass validity** is effective on the day the first segment is used.
3. Passenger **has to present card** at Amtrak ticket office prior to every journey to obtain his tickets.
4. Coach (2nd) class reservations (free of charge) available when picking up tickets.
5. Any segment may be upgraded by paying fare differential from a basic coach (2nd) class fare to the desired first class (or Metroliner) service. Reservations (free of charge) can **then** be made for the upgraded service.
6. Use of pass must begin within 90 days of date of issue. Travel on the ticket must be completed by midnight on the last day of validity.
7. This pass can only be purchased through an overseas Amtrak-appointed travel agent.

INFORMATION FOR VISITORS FROM FRANCE

Disponibilité de la carte USARAIL

1. *Elle ne peut être achetée qu'à l'étranger,* par *des étrangers* venant aux Etats-Unis avec un visa d'étudiant, d'affaires ou de tourisme.
2. Les personnes de nationalité mexicaine ou canadienne, ou des territoires appartenant aux Etats-Unis, *n'ont pas le droit* d'utiliser la carte.
3. Elle est vendue uniquement par les *agents Amtrak accrédités à l'étranger.*
4. *La carte USARAIL, le passeport et le coupon du billet* sont tous nécessaires pour avoir le droit de monter dans le train. *Toute pièce manquante* entraînera le paiement du billet au tarif normal correspondant au parcours faisant l'objet du voyage.

La carte USARAIL pour mieux profiter des Etats-Unis... Plus facilement

Vous avec le choix entre 14 ... 21 ... ou 30 jours, pour 150 ... 200 ... ou 250 dollars respectivement.

Conditions d'utilisation de la carte USARAIL

1. *La carte seule n'est pas valable* à bord des trains.
2. La validité de la carte commence le jour de la première utilisation sur un parcours.
3. Le voyageur *doit présenter sa carte* à un guichet Amtrak de vente des billets pour s'y faire délivrer des billets.
4. Les réservations en classe Coach (2ème classe) sont possibles au moment de la délivrance des billets.
5. Tout parcours peut donner lieu à reclassement moyennant le paiement de la différence entre le tarif de base coach (2ème classe) et le tarif première classe (ou Metroliner). Les réservations (gratuites) peuvent *alors* être faites pour la nouvelle classe.
6. L'utilisation de la carte doit commencer moins de 90 jours après sa délivrance. Le voyage avec le billet doit être terminé à minuit le dernier jour de validité.
7. Cette carte ne peut être achetée qu'à un agent de voyages Amtrak accrédité.

CONSULTEZ VOTRE AGENT DE VOYAGES

INFORMATION FOR VISITORS FROM GERMANY

Erwerb des USARAIL-Passes

1. Verkauf nur in übersee, and Ausländer, die in die USA mit Studenten-, Geschäfts- oder Besuchervisum einreisen.
2. Mexikanische, kanadische und U.S.-Staatsangehörige sind von der Benutzung des Passes ausgeschlossen.
3. Der Pass ist nur über von AMTRAK lizenzierte, überseeische Vertretungen erhältlich.
4. USARAIL-*Passkarte, Reisepass* und *Fahrscheincoupon* sind alle drei zur Zugbenutzung erforderlich. *Das Fehlen eines der oben angeführten Dokumente* zieht eine Nachzahlung in Höhe des vollen, für den befahrenen Streckenabschnitt gültigen Fahrpreises nach sich.

Mit dem USARAIL-Pass haben Sie mehr von Amerika... und dazu noch auf viel bequemere Weise...

Sie haben die Wahl zwischen 14, 21 und 30 Tagen Reisedauer. Zum Preis von jeweils $150, $200 oder $250.

USARAIL PASS 221

Bedingungen für den Gebrauch des USARAIL-Passes:

1. Die *Passkarte allein* berechtigt nicht zur Benutzung der Züge.
2. Die Gültigkeit der Passkarte beginnt an dem Tag, an dem der erste Abschnitt benutzt wird.
3. *Nach Vorlage der Karte* bei einer AMTRAK-Kartenverkaufsstelle erhält der Reisende den Fahrschein.
4. Coach- (zweite Klasse-) Buchungen werden (gratis) bei Abholung des Fahrscheins vorgenommen.
5. Die Benutzung einer höheren Beförderungsklasse ist grundsätzlich auf jedem Streckenabschnitt durch Aufzahlung der Differenz zwischen dem Grundtarif für die zweite Klasse und der gewünschten ersten Klasse (oder Metroliner) möglich. *Danach* kann dann die Buchung (gratis) für die höhere Beförderungsklasse vorgenommen werden.
6. Die Benutzung der Passkarte muss innerhalb von 90 Tagen nach dem Ausstellungs-Datum erfolgen. Die Reise mit diesem Fahrschein muss vor Mitternacht des letzten Gültigkeitstages beendet werden.
7. Dieser Pass kann nur über ein von AMTRAK lizenziertes Reisebüro bezogen werden.

KONSULTIEREN SIE IHREN REISEVERTRETER

INFORMATION FOR VISITORS FROM SOUTH AMERICA

Disponibilidad del USARAIL Pass

1. *Sólo puede comprarse este pase en ultramar y su uso se limita a los extranjeros* que visiten EE.UU. con visa de estudiante, o en viaje de negocios o de turismo.
2. *No está disponible* para residentes del Canadá, México y posesiones de EE.UU.
3. Se obtiene sólo en *las agencias autorizadas de AMTRAK en ultramar.*
4. Para viajar en los trenes son necesarios *la tarjeta* de USARAIL PASS, *el talonario de cupones y el pasaporte.* De faltar alguna de estas tres cosas, el viajero pagará la tarifa completa que sea aplicable en cuanto a la etapa del viaje que lleve a cabo sin cumplir con dichos requisitos.

USARAIL Pass: para disfrutar más y tener mayor comodidad al visitar EE.UU.

Válido por períodos de 14, 21 ó 30 días, según convenga. A US$ 150, US$ 200 y US$ 250, respectivamente.

Reglamentos sobre empleo del USARAIL Pass:

1. Para viajar en el tren *no basta la tarjeta del pase solamente.*
2. Validez es efectiva el día de viaje del primer segmento.
3. El viajero *deberá presentar la tarjeta* en la ventanilla de billetes de AMTRAK, antes de cada viaje a fin de obtener los billetes de pasaje.

222 ITINERARIES

4. Las reservaciones de clase económica o de turista (coach) pueden hacerse (sin cargo) al recoger los billetes de pasaje.
5. En cualquiera de las etapas del viaje el pasajero podrá solicitar el cambio a primera clase (o Metroliner) pagando la diferencia entre la tarifa básica de clase económica o de turismo (coach) y la de primera. *Entonces* es posible hacer reservaciones (sin cargo) para los servicios que se deseen en esa clase más alta.
6. Uso del USARAIL Pass deberá comenzar dentro de los 90 días de la fecha de emisión. Viajes deberán ser completados hasta la medianoche del último día de validez.
7. Este pase sólo puede comprarse por intermedio de un agente de viajes en el exterior autorizado por AMTRAK.

CONSULTE A SU AGENTE DE VIAJES

SUGGESTED RAIL ITINERARIES FOR ALL USARAIL PASS TRAVELERS

On the following pages you will find 14, 21, and 30 day suggested itineraries to help you plan your own trip throughout the U.S.A. The itineraries are complete with departure and arrival times. Keep in mind that all times are subject to change.

Here are some other comments. Beside each segment of your trip you will find a number—it keeps track of the day of travel. Thus, the 'Day 3' next to the Washington, D.C.-Chicago segment of our 14-day suggested itinerary infers that you spent the previous two days traveling between New York and Washington, D.C. (perhaps stopping off at Philadelphia) and sightseeing. You will also spot "(18; 866/1394)" on this first line of your 'Day 3.' The 18 represents the approximate hours it takes you to travel between Washington and Chicago, while the '866' represents the distance in miles between the cities. the '1394' represents the number of kilometers between Washington and Chicago.

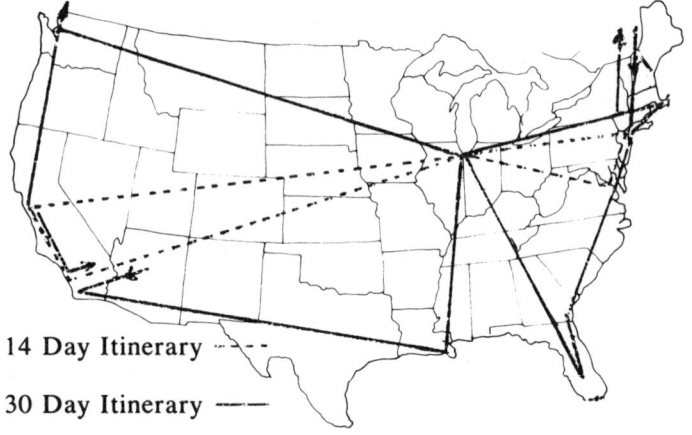

14 Day Itinerary - - -

30 Day Itinerary ———

ITINERARIES 223

On the next line you will see '1545-1035, day 4.' The 1545 represents the departure time from Washington, D.C. To avoid confusion, we have used a 24 hour clock system in listing times. The system is quite simple—0100 is 1 a.m., 1100 is 11 a.m., 1300 is 1 p.m., 1600 is 4 p.m. and 2300 is 11 p.m., etc. Thus 1545 represents 3:45 p.m. Your arrival time in Chicago is 1035, 10:35 a.m. next morning, 'day 4' of our suggested itinerary. The train you travel on is the 'Broadway Limited.'

14-DAY ITINERARY

New York-Washington, D.C.-Chicago-Grand Canyon-Los Angeles-San Francisco-New York

Day 1: New York-Washington, D.C. (4; 224/361)
Leave 0700-Arrive 1059, day 1. "The Montrealer"

Day 3: Washington, D.C.-Chicago (18; 866/1394)
1545-1035, day 4. "The Broadway Limited"

Day 4: Chicago-Flagstaff (Grand Canyon); (29; 1681/2706)
1830-2150, day 5. "The Southwest Limited"

Day 5: Flagstaff-Los Angeles (11; 542/873)
2150-0905, day 6.

Day 7: Los Angeles-San Francisco (10; 467/752)
1000-2035, day 7. "The Coast Starlight"

Day 10: San Francisco-Chicago (50; 2413/3885)
1025-1335, day 12. "The San Francisco Zephyr"

Day 12: Chicago-New York (18; 904/1455)
1530-1117, day 13. "Broadway Limited"

21-DAY ITINERARY

New York-Washington, D.C.-Miami-Chicago-San Francisco-Los Angeles-Grand Canyon-New York

Day 1: New York-Washington, D.C. (4; 224/361)
Leave 0700-Arrive 1059, day 1. "The Montrealer"

Day 3: Washington-Miami (22; 1164/1874)
2010-1805, day 4. "The Silver Meteor"

Day 6: Miami-Chicago (38; 1601/2578)
1645-0700, day 8. "The Floridian"

224 ITINERARIES

Day 9: Chicago-San Francisco (50; 2413/3885)
1600-1555, day 11. "The San Francisco Zephyr"

Day 13: San Francisco-Los Angeles (10; 467/752)
0820-1855, day 13. "The Coast Starlight"

Day 16: Los Angeles-Flagstaff (11; 542/873)
2000-0705, day 17. "The Southwest Limited"

Day 18: Flagstaff-Chicago (29; 1681/2706)
0705-1405, day 19. "The Southwest Limited"

Day 19: Chicago-New York (18; 904/1455)
1530-1117, day 20. "The Broadway Limited"

30-DAY ITINERARY

New York-Washington, D.C.-Miami-Chicago-Seattle-Vancouver-San Francisco-Grand Canyon-Los Angeles-New Orleans-Montreal-Boston-New York

Day 1: New York-Washington, D.C. (4; 224/361)
Leave 0700-Arrive 1059, day 1. "The Montrealer"

Day 3: Washington-Miami (22; 1164/1874)
2010-1805, day 4. "The Silver Meteor"

Day 6: Miami-Chicago (38; 1601/2578)
1645-0700, day 8. "The Floridian"

Day 9: Chicago-Seattle (48; 2288/3684)
1430-1205, day 11. "The Empire Builder"

Day 11: Seattle-Vancouver, Canada (5; 156/251)
1815-2300, day 11. "The Pacific International"

Day 13: Vancouver-Seattle; Seattle-San Francisco (25; 1059/1705)
0650-1120; 1150-0855, day 14. "The Coast Starlight"

Day 16: San Francisco-Los Angeles; Los Angeles-Flagstaff (21; 1009/1625)
0820-1855; 2000-0705, day 17. "The Coast Starlight"/"The Southwest Limited"

Day 17: Flagstaff-Los Angeles (11; 542/873)
2150-0905, day 18. "The Southwest Limited"

Day 21: Los Angeles-New Orleans (44; 2035/3276)
2100-1900, day 23. "The Sunset Limited"
Note: The Sunset Limited departs Los Angeles on Sunday, Tuesday and Friday only. It does not operate daily.

Day 25: New Orleans-Chicago (17; 923/1486)
1630-1035, day 26. "The Panama Limited"

Day 26: Chicago-Boston/Montreal (24; 1038/ 1730)
1415-1540, day 27. "The Lakeshore Limited"

Note: This new Chicago-Boston train allows you to stop off at Buffalo (Niagara Falls) and make connections in Albany-Rensselaer (in New York State) for Montreal, Canada, on "The Adirondack." The Adirondack leaves Albany-Rensslaer at 1305 and arrives in Montreal at 1945.

Day 29: Boston-New York (5; 232/374)
1345-1843, day 29. "The Senator" or:
Montreal-New York (12; 446/718)
1810-0635, day 30. "The Montrealer"

AMTRAK CITY TICKET OFFICES

Besides your Amtrak Travel Agent and the station ticket offices, you can also visit conveniently located Amtrak City Ticket Offices in the following cities:

387 King St.
Charleston, S.C. 29403

Pentagon Ticket Office
Arlington, Va.

80 East Jackson Blvd.
Chicago, Ill. 60604

U.S. Capitol, Room S-101
Washington, D.C.

315 N. Julia St.
Jacksonville, Fl. 32202

1721 K St., N.W.
Washington, D.C.

1604-A Washington Ave.
Miami Beach, Fl. 33139

12 West 51st St.
New York, N.Y. 10020

7 Penn Center Plaza
Philadelphia, Pa.

Transbay Terminal
425 Mission St.
San Francisco, CA. 94105

Nassif Bldg.—Room 3216
7th and D Streets, S.W.
Washington, D.C.

TOURS

Amtrak offers you a host of tours which you can take to discover the U.S.A. by train. We have included a brief discussion of a couple of popular tour arrangements, as well as a list of many of the tours which are offered. For all the information and particulars, see your Amtrak Travel Agent.

WEEK OF WHEELS IN FLORIDA

One of the most popular travel bargains that Amtrak offers is the 'Week of Wheels' (WOW) program. It enables you to have use of a car in Florida for a week if three full round-trips to Florida are purchased from the Northeast or the Midwest. It's ideal for a family (2 half fares are equal to one full fare). Besides that, Amtrak's Family Plan can be utilized. For example, if a family of three leaves from New York, the head of the household would pay the regular round-trip fare of $144, the spouse would pay $108, and a child between 12-21 would also be charged $108. The total of $360 for the family of 3 represents a saving of $72 over the regular fare; besides that, the family gets use of a car for a week. For all the details about conditions, periods of applicability, and auto pick-up/drop-off points see your Amtrak Travel Agent.

RAIL AND DRIVE U.S.A. TOUR

The "Rail 'n Drive U.S.A." tour allows an Amtrak vacationer to pick up an Avis car and stay at a selection of 300 Holiday Inns in or near 114 Amtrak destination cities. The price is the same for four persons as for one. Prices range from a minimum of $126 ($15.75 each per day for a party of four) for two hotel nights and three days' unlimited use of a Gremlin car to $260 ($10.84 each per day) for six hotel nights and seven days' use of the car. Keep in mind that all prices are subject to change. Here are some typical ways Amtrak suggests you could use the Rail 'n Drive plan:

Take Amtrak's Southwest Limited or Coast Starlight to Los Angeles to pick up the Avis car for visits to Disneyland, Knott's Berry Farm and other Southern California attractions, staying at any of more than a dozen Holiday Inns thereabout. (In California and Florida you can return the Avis car to another city in the state with free drop-off).

TOURS 227

Visit Yellowstone Park via Amtrak's North Coast Hiawatha, picking up your car and using the Holiday Inn at Bozeman, Mont.

Take one of Amtrak's new Turboliners or another train to St. Louis, have your pick of eight Holiday Inns there, drive your Avis car to Six Flags Over Mid-America, see a bit of the Ozarks.

Ride one of Amtrak's Empire Service trains to Rochester, N.Y., to tour the Finger Lakes wine country and see the Corning Glass Museum.

Amtrak ticket and travel agents, besides booking train reservations, will make the Rail 'n Drive arrangements with the tour operator who will reserve the Avis car and the first night's Holiday Inn stay. Succeeding confirmations for each subsequent stay may be made at any Holiday Inn using the free Holidex Reservations system. Before departure, a traveler will receive, besides his rail tickets, a packet including car rental voucher, lodging vouchers for each night purchased, plus an instruction booklet including locations of Avis offices and Holiday Inns. The Rail 'n Drive plan will provide larger cars, if requested, for a supplement. Amtrak passengers not requiring a car, may book cooperating Holiday Inns through the tour for $23.50 per room per night.

California
    Bonanza Americana
    California Rail/Drive
    Disneyland
    Disneyland Area Fantasy Holiday
    Golden Whistle Stop
    Grand Circle Americana
    Hearst Castle Tour
    Mountain of Fun, Los Angeles
    San Diego
    San Francisco
    San Francisco Holiday
    San Francisco and The High Sierra
    Silver Whistle Stop
    Southern California Sunburst
    The Golden State
    Two City Bonanza, Disneyland/San Diego
    Western Americana

228 TOURS

Canada
- Autumn Color Rail-Cruise Tours
- Canadian Rockies and U.S. East Coast
- Evangeline Americana
- Grand Circle Americana
- Majestic Americana
- Montreal Weekender
- Quebec City and Montreal
- The Great Northwest (from Chicago)
- The Great Northwest (from San Francisco)
- Timberline Americana
- Trans-Canada Americana

Caribbean
- Caribbean Calypso Cruise Tours
- S.S. Rotterdam
- The Caribbean Rail/Ship Cruise

Circle Tours
- Autumn Color Rail-Cruise Tours
- Bonanza Americana
- Canadian Rockies and U.S. East Coast
- Caribbean Calypso Cruise Tours
- Circle America
- Grand Circle Americana
- Western Americana

City Packages
- Atlanta
- Boston
- Chicago
- Cincinnati
- Colonies of Liberty, Bicentennial Cities
- Dallas-Ft. Worth
- Daytona Beach
- Disneyland Area Fantasy Holiday
- Hearst Castle Tour — San Simeon
- Holy Year Domestic Pilgrimage (Washington, D.C.)
- Kansas City
- Las Vegas
- Los Angeles
- Miami Beach
- Montreal
- New Orleans

New York
New York Adventures
Orlando
Philadelphia
Poinciana
Portland
Quebec City
Reno and The High Sierra
Richmond
St. Louis
San Diego
San Francisco
San Francisco Holiday
San Francisco and The High Sierra
Seattle
Theatre Weekend — JFK Center (Washington)
Vancouver
Victoria
Washington, D.C.
Yankee Heritage Combo (Boston and New England)

Cruises

Caribbean Calypso Cruise Tours
Schooner Sail Cruise
Steamboat Delta Queen
S.S. Rotterdam
S.S. Statendam
The Caribbean Rail/Ship Cruise

Disneyland

Bonanza Americana
Disneyland
Disneyland Area Fantasy Holiday
Golden Whistle Stop
Grand Circle Americana
Silver Whistle Stop
Southern California Sunburst
The Golden State
Two City Bonanza, Disneyland/San Diego
Western Americana

Florida

Caribbean Calypso Cruise Tours
Daytona Beach

230 TOURS

Florida Rail 'n Drive
Florida Tradewinds
Florida Triangle
Lake Buena Vista Family Holidays
Miami Beach
Poinciana
Roamin' Holiday
Seabreeze Americana
The Caribbean Rail/Ship Cruise
The Family Fling
The Gadabout
The Magic Kingdom
The Wanderer
Walt Disney World
Week of Wheels

Group Tours

Bicentennial Adventures
Boston
Daytona Beach/St. Augustine/Cape Canaveral
Jamestown-Williamsburg and Monticello
New York
New York Theater Tour
Ponce Inlet/Daytona Beach-Deep Sea Fishing
Port Canaveral/Cocoa Beach
Walt Disney World/Sea World
Walt Disney World/Sea World/Deep Sea Fishing
Washington, D.C.

Mexico

Fiesta Americana
Mexico/Yucatan Rail Cruise Tours

Motorhomes

Roamin' Holiday

National Parks

Banff
Bonanza Americana
Bryce Canyon
Canadian Rockies and U.S. East Coast
Canyon De Chelly

TOURS 231

Circle America
Crater Lake National Park and The Oregon Coast
Glacier Park
Glacier Park Tour
Golden Whistle Stop
Grand Circle Americana
Grand Canyon
Grand Teton
Jasper
Majestic Americana
Mesa Verde
Mt. Rainier
Navajolands Americana
Navajo Nation Scenic Tour
North Cascades
North Cascades and Mt. Rainier National Parks
The Golden State
The Grand Canyon (from Chicago)
The Grand Canyon (from San Francisco)
The Great Southwest Adventure (from Chicago)
The Great Southwest Adventure (from San Francisco)
Timberline Americana
Trans-Canada Americana
Waterton Lakes
Western Americana
Western National Parks
Yellowstone Park
Yellowstone Park Tour
Yosemite Park
Zion Park

New England
Yankee Holidays

Northwest
Canadian Rockies and U.S. East Coast
Crater Lake National Park and The Oregon Coast
Glacier Park Tour
Grand Circle Americana
Lewis and Clark Western Adventure Tour
Majestic Americana
North Cascades and Mt. Rainier National Parks
Pacific Northwest International
The Great Northwest (from Chicago)
The Great Northwest (from San Francisco)

232 TOURS

Timberline Americana
Trans-Canada Americana
Visit Portland
Yellowstone Park Tour

Southwest

Bonanza Americana
Circle America
Gateway to Fun, Dallas/Ft. Worth
Las Vegas Whirlwind
Navajolands Americana
Navajo Nation Scenic Tour
The Grand Canyon (from Chicago)
The Grand Canyon (from San Francisco)
The Great Southwest Adventure (from Chicago)
The Great Southwest Adventure (from San Francisco)
Western Americana

Visit U.S.A.

The Eastbounder
The Easterner
The Midwesterner
The Westbounder
The Westerner

Walt Disney World

Caribbean Calypso Cruise Tours
Florida Tradewinds
Florida Triangle
Lake Buena Vista Family Holidays
Poinciana
Seabreeze Americana
The Caribbean Rail/Ship Cruise
The Family Fling
The Gadabout
The Magic Kingdom
The Wanderer

West

Bonanza Americana
Golden Whistle Stop
Las Vegas Whirlwind
Navajolands Americana
Navajo Nation Scenic Tour
Reno and The High Sierra
Rocky Mountain Odyssey
San Francisco and The High Sierra
Silver Whistle Stop
The Golden State
Western Americana
Western National Parks

RAIL-BUS TRAVEL

Since there are certain destinations that cannot be reached by rail, Amtrak and Greyhound have a through ticketing arrangement which allows you to reach your destination on the following Greyhound routes. The cities shown in bold face are Amtrak stops. Thus, for example, you can make use of the convenient through ticketing arrangement if you have arrived in Tampa by Amtrak but want to travel to Ft. Myers. The segment Tampa-Ft. Myers would be completed via Greyhound.

Albuquerque-Amarillo-Oklahoma City-Tulsa; **Bakersfield-Los Angeles; Boston**-Portland-Bangor; **Cleveland**-Akron-**Columbus-Cincinnati, OH; Columbus, WI.**-Madison, WI; **Detroit-Toledo-Lima; Minneapolis**-Des Moines-**Kansas City; New Orleans**-Biloxi-Gulfport-Mobile-Pensacola-Tallahassee-**Jacksonville; Ogden**-Pocatello-Idaho Falls-West Yellowstone; **Tampa**-Sarasota-Ft. Myers.

AMTRAK TRAVEL CENTERS

Besides your Amtrak Travel Agent, one of the best places to obtain literature and information about rail tours and other special rail programs is from an Amtrak Travel Center. There are four main ones—one in Canada and three in the United States.

Amtrak Travel Center
P.O. Box 3000
Bellmore, N.Y. 11710

Amtrak Travel Center
P.O. Box 4733
Chicago, IL. 60680

Amtrak Travel Center
P.O. Box 9000
Van Nuys, CA. 91406

Amtrak Travel Center
P.O. 749
Montreal, P.Q., Canada

STATION INDEX

The following list includes not only the towns and cities served by Amtrak (well over 450), but also those served by non-Amtrak inter-city railroads such as the Southern Railway, Georgia Railroad, Rock Island Line and the Denver & Rio Grande Western. Keep in mind that the list is subject to change as Amtrak expands its nation-wide network (for example the route Washington, D.C. to Denver in May 1976), and as the non-Amtrak railroads drop various services.

AKRON, CO
ALBANY-RENSSELAER, N.Y.
ALBION, MI
ALBUQUERQUE, NM
ALEXANDRIA, VA
ALHAMBRA, CA
ALPINE, TX
ALTAVISTA, VA
ALTON, IL
ALTOONA, PA
AMSTERDAM, NY
ANN ARBOR, MI
ANNISTON, AL
ARDMORE, OK
ARDMORE, PA
ARKANSAS CITY, KS
ASHLAND, KY
ATLANTA, GA
AUBURN, WA
AUGUSTA, GA
AURORA, IL
AUSTIN, TX
BAKERSFIELD, CA
BALTIMORE, MD
BARSTOW, CA
BATESVILLE, MS
BATTLE CREEK, MI
BEAUMONT, TX
BECKLEY, WV
BEDFORD, VA
BELLINGHAM, WA
BELLOWS FALLS, VT
BELTON, MT
BENSON, AZ
BERLIN, CT
BERWYN, PA
BILLINGS, MT
BIRMINGHAM, AL
BISMARCK, ND
BLACKSTONE, VA
BLAINE, WA
BLOOMINGTON, IL
BLOOMINGTON, IN
BLUEFIELD, WV
BLUE ISLAND, IL
BOND, CO
BOSTON, MA
BOWLING GREEN, KY
BOZEMAN, MT
BRATTLEBORO, VT
BRECKENRIDGE, MN
BRENHAM, TX
BRIDGEPORT, CT
BROOKHAVEN, MS
BROWNING, MT
BRUNSWICK, MD
BRYN MAWR, PA
BUFFALO, NY
BUREAU, IL
BURLINGTON, IA
BURLINGTON, ON
BURLINGTON, VT
BUTTE, MT
CAIRO, IL
CAMBRIDGE, MN.
CAMDEN, SC
CANTON, MS
CANTON, OH
CAPITAL BELTWAY STATION, MD

INDEX

CARBONDALE, IL
CARLIN, NV
CARLINVILLE, IL
CARROLLTON, MO
CATLETTSBURG, KY
CENTRALIA, IL
CENTRALIA, WA
CHAMPAIGN-URBANA, II
CHARLESTON, SC
CHARLESTON, WV
CHARLOTTE, NC
CHARLOTTESVILLE, VA
CHELSEA, MI
CHEYENNE, WY
CHICAGO, IL
CHILLICOTHE, IL
CHRISTIANSBURG, VA
CINCINNATI, OH
CLEARWATER, FL
CLEBURNE, TX
CLEMSON, SC
CLEVELAND, OH
CLIFTON FORGE, VA
COATESVILLE, PA
COLONIE-
   SCHENECTADY, NY
COLUMBIA, SC
COLUMBUS, OH
COLUMBUS, WI
CONCORD, NC
CRESTLINE, OH
CRESTON, IA
CROTON-HARMON, NY
CULPEPER, VA
CUMBERLAND, MD
DALLAS, TX
DANVILLE, VA
DAVIS, CA
DAYTON, OH
DECATUR, AL
DEERFIELD BEACH, FL
DEER LODGE, MT
DELAND, FL
DEL MAR, CA
DELRAY BEACH, FL
DEL RIO, TX
DEMING, NM
DENVER, CO
DETROIT, MI
DETROIT LAKES, MN
DEVILS LAKE, ND
DICKINSON, ND
DODGE CITY, KS
DOTHAN, AL
DOWNINGTOWN, PA
DUBUQUE, IA
DULUTH, MN
DUNSMUIR, CA
DURAND, MI
DURANT, MS
DYERSBURG, TN
EAST AUBURN, WA
EAST DUBUQUE, IL
EAST GLACIER, MT
EAST LANSING, MI
EAST OLYMPIA, WA
EDMONDS, WA
EFFINGHAM, IL
ELIZABETHTOWN, PA
ELKHART, IN
ELKO, NV
ELLENSBURG, WA
ELMHURST, IL
EL PASO, TX
ELYRIA, OH
EMPORIA, KS
ENFIELD, CT
ENGLEWOOD, IL
EPHRATA, WA
ERIE, PA
ESSEX JCT., VT
EUGENE, OR
EUTAW, AL
EVANSTON, WY
EVERETT, WA
FARGO, ND
FARMVILLE, VA
FAYETTEVILLE, NC
FENWICK, ON
FLAGSTAFF, AZ
FLINT, MI
FLORENCE, SC
FORSYTH, MT
FORT EDWARD, NY
FORT ERIE, ON
FORT LAUDERDALE, FL

236 INDEX

FORT MADISON, IA
FORT MORGAN, CO
FORT TICONDEROGA, NY
FORT WAYNE, IN
FORT WORTH, TX
FRAMINGHAM, MA
FREDERICKSBURG, VA
FREEPORT, IL
FRESNO, CA
FULLERTON, CA
FULTON, KY
GAINSEVILLE, GA
GAINESVILLE, TX
GAITHERSBURG, MD
GALENA, IL
GALESBURG, IL
GALLUP, NM
GARDEN CITY, KS
GARY, IN
GASTONIA, NC
GENESEO, IL
GLASGOW, MT
GLENDALE, CA
GLENDIVE, MT
GLENVIEW, IL
GLENWOOD SPRINGS, CO
GRANBY, CO
GRAND FORKS, ND
GRAND JUNCTION, CO
GREELEY, CO
GREEN RIVER, UT
GREEN RIVER, WY
GREENSBORO, NC
GREENSBURG, PA
GREENVILLE, SC
GRENADA, MS
GUTHRIE, OK
HAMILTON, ON
HAMLET, NC
HAMMOND, LA
HANCOCK, WV/MD
HANFORD, CA
HARPERS FERRY, WV
HARRISBURG, PA
HARTFORD, CT
HASTINGS, NE
HATTIESBURG, MS
HAVRE, MT
HAZELHURST, MS
HELENA, MT
HELPER, UT
HENDERSONVILLE, NC
HENRY, IL
HIGHLAND, NY
HIGH POINT, NC
HINTON, WV
HOLDREGE, NE
HOLLYWOOD, FL
HOMEWOOD, IL
HOUSTON, TX
HUDSON, NY
HUNTINGDON, PA
HUNTINGTON, WV
HUTCHINSON, KS
INDIANAPOLIS, IN
INDIO, CA
JACKSON, MI
JACKSON, MS
JACKSONVILLE, FL
JAMESTOWN, ND
JEFFERSON, CITY, MO
JOHNSTOWN, PA
JOLIET, IL
KALAMAZOO, MI
KANKAKEE, IL
KANSAS CITY, MO
KELSO-LONGVIEW, WA
KENOVA, WV
KEWANEE, IL
KINGMAN, AZ
KINGSTON, NY
KINGSTON, RI
KIRKWOOD, MO
KISSIMMEE, FL
KLAMATH FALLS, OR
LA CROSSE, WI
LAFAYETTE, IN
LAFAYETTE, LA
LA GRANGE ROAD, IL
LA JUNTA, CO
LAKE CHARLES, LA
LAKELAND, FL
LAMAR, CO
LAMY, NM
LANCASTER, PA
LANSING, MI

INDEX 237

LAPEER, MI
LA PLATA, MO
LARAMIE, WY
LAREDO, TX
LA SALLE-PERU, IL
LAS VEGAS, NM
LATROBE, PA
LAUREL, MS
LAWRENCE, KS
LEWISTOWN, PA
LEXINGTON, NC
LIBBY, MT
LIMA, OH
LINCOLN, IL
LINCOLN, NE
LITTLE ROCK, AR
LIVINGSTON, AL
LIVINGSTON, MT
LOGANSPORT, IN
LONGVIEW, TX
LORDSBURG, NM
LOS ANGELES, CA
LOUISVILLE, KY
LYNCHBURG, VA
MACOMB, IL
MADISON, WI
MALTA, MT
MALVERN, PA
MANASSAS, VA
MANDAN, ND
MARCELINE, MO
MARION, IN
MARSHALL, TX
MARTINEZ, CA
MARTINSBURG, WV
MATTOON, IL
McCOMB, MS
McCOOK, NE
McGREGOR, TX
MECHANICVILLE, NY
MEMPHIS, TN
MENDOTA, IL
MERCED, CA
MERIDEN, CT
MERIDIAN, MS
MERION, PA
METROPARK, NJ

METUCHEN, NJ
MIAMI, FL
MIDDLETOWN, PA
MILES CITY, MT
MILWAUKEE, WI
MINNEAPOLIS, MN
MINOT, ND
MISSOULA, MT
MONMOUTH, IL
MONROE, VA
MONTGOMERY, AL
MONTPELIER JCT., VT
MONTREAL, PQ
MONTREAL WEST, PQ
MORRIS, IL
MORRIS, MN
MOUNT JOY, PA
MOUNT PLEASANT, IA
MOUNT VERNON-
  BURLINGTON, WA
MUNCIE, IN
MYSTIC, CT
NARBERTH, PA
NARROWS, VA
NASHVILLE, TN
NEEDLES, CA
NEWARK, NJ
NEW BRITAIN, CT
NEW BRUNSWICK, NJ
NEW HAVEN, CT
NEW IBERIA, LA
NEW LONDON, CT
NEW ORLEANS, LA
NEWPORT, AR
NEWPORT NEWS, VA
NEWTON, KS
NEW WESTMINSTER, BC
NEW YORK, NY
NILES, MI
NORFOLK, VA
NORMAN, OK
NORTHAMPTON, MA
NORTH
  PHILADELPHIA, PA
NOTTOWAY COUNTY
  STATION, VA (CREWE)
OAKLAND, CA

238 INDEX

OAKVILLE, ON
OCALA, FL
OCEANSIDE, CA
OGDEN, UT
OKLAHOMA CITY, OK
OLD SAYBROOK, CT
OLYMPIA, WA
OMAHA, NE
ORANGE, VA
ORLAND, CA
ORLANDO, FL
OSCEOLA, IA
OTTAWA, IL
OTTUMWA, IA
OVERBROOK, PA
OXNARD, CA
PALO ALTO, CA
PAOLI, PA
PARADISE, MT
PARKESBURG, PA
PASADENA, CA
PASCO, WA
PAULS VALLEY, OK
PEORIA, IL
PERRY, OK
PERU, IN
PETERSBURG, VA
PHILADELPHIA, PA
PHOENIX, AZ
PITTSBURGH, PA
PITTSFIELD, MA
PLANO, IL
PLATTSBURGH, NY
POINCIANA, FL
POMONA, CA
PONCA CITY, OK
PONTIAC, IL
POPLARBLUFF, MO
POPLARVILLE, MS
PORTAGE, WI
PORT HURON, MI
PORTLAND, OR
POUGHKEEPSIE, NY
PRICE, UT
PRINCE, WV
PRINCETON, IL
PRINCETON JUNCTION, NJ
PROVIDENCE, RI
PROVO, UT
PURCELL, OK
PURVIS, MS
QUANTICO, VA
QUINCY, IL
RACINE, WI
RALEIGH, NC
RANTOUL, IL
RATON, NM
RAWLINS, WY
REDDING, CA
RED WING, MN
REIDSVILLE, NC
RENO, NV
RHINECLIFF, NY
RICHMOND, IN
RICHMOND, VA
RIFLE, CO
RIVERBANK, CA
ROANOKE, VA
ROCHESTER, NY
ROCK ISLAND, IL
ROCK SPRINGS, WY
ROCKFORD, IL
ROCKVILLE, MD
ROCKY MOUNT, NC
ROME, NY
ROUSES POINT, NY
ROUTE 128, MA
RUGBY, ND
RYE, NY
SACREMENTO, CA
ST. ALBANS, VT
ST. CLOUD, MN
ST. LOUIS, MO
ST. PAUL, MN
ST. PETERSBURG, FL
SALEM, OR
SALINAS, CA
SALISBURY, NC
SALT LAKE CITY, UT
SAN ANTONIO, TX
SAN BERNARDINO, CA
SAN CLEMENTE, CA
SANDERSON, TX
SAN DIEGO, CA
SANDPOINT, ID

SANDSTONE, MN
SANFORD, FL
SAN FRANCISCO, CA
SAN JOSE, CA
SAN JUAN
  CAPISTRANO, CA
SAN LUIS OBISPO, CA
SAN MARCOS, TX
SANTA ANA, CA
SANTA BARBARA, CA
SARATOGA SPRINGS, NY
SAVANNAH, GA
SCHRIEVER, LA
SEATTLE, WA
SEBRING, FL
SEDALIA, MO
SHEFFIELD, IL
SHELBY, MT
SILVER SPRING, MD
SLIDELL, LA
SMITHVILLE, ON
SOUTH BEND, IN
SOUTHERN PINES, NC
SPARKS, NV
SPARTANBURG, SC
SPOKANE, WA
SPRINGFIELD, IL
SPRINGFIELD, MA
STAMFORD, CT
STANLEY, ND
STAPLES, MN
STAUNTON, VA
STOCKTON, CA
STREATOR, IL
STURTEVANT, WI
SUPERIOR, WI
SUFFOLK, VA
SYRACUSE, NY
TACOMA, WA
TAMPA, FL
TEMPLE, TX
TERRE HAUTE, IN
TEXARKANA, AR
THALMANN, GA
THOMASVILLE, GA
THOMASVILLE, NC
THOMPSON, UT
THOMPSONVILLE, CT
TOCCOA, GA
TOLEDO, OH
TOMAH, WI
TOPEKA, KS
TORONTO, ON
TRENTON, NJ
TRINIDAD, CO
TRI-STATE STATION, KY
TRUCKEE, CA
TRYON, NC
TUCSON, AZ
TUSCALOOSA, AL
TYRONE, PA
UNION, SC
UTICA, NY
VALDOSTA, GA
VALLEY CITY, ND
VANCOUVER, BC
VANCOUVER, WA
WACO, TX
WALDO, FL
WALLINGFORD, CT
WALNUT RIDGE, AR
WARREN, IL
WARRENSBURG, MO
WASHINGTON, DC
WATERBURY, VT
WATERVLIET, NY
WAYCROSS, GA
WAYNE, PA
WELCH, WV
WELLAND, ON
WENATCHEE, WA
WESTERLY, RI
WEST PALM BEACH, FL
WESTPORT, NY
WHITEFISH, MT
WHITEHALL, NY
WHITE RIVER JCT., VT
WHITE SULPHUR
  SPRINGS, WV
WHITFORD, PA
WICHITA, KS
WILDWOOD, FL
WILLIAMSBURG, VA
WILLIAMSON, WV

240 RESERVATIONS

WILLISTON, ND
WILLMAR, MN
WILMINGTON, DE
WILSON, NC
WINDSOR, CT
WINDSOR, ON
WINDSOR LOCKS, CT
WINONA, MN
WINONA, MS
WINSLOW, AZ
WINTER HAVEN, FL
WINTER PARK, FL
WISCONSIN DELLS, WI
WOLF POINT, MT
WORCESTER, MA
YAKIMA, WA
YEMASSEE, SC
YPSILANTI, MI
YUMA, AZ

RESERVATION AND INFORMATION TELEPHONE NUMBERS

The telephone numbers which we have listed below for cities and states in the United States are for information and reservations. Locate the city or state from which you are calling and use the telephone number which appears opposite it. For Canadian telephone number consult the local telephone director. Keep in mind that these numbers are available from any location in the states listed below. Also please remember all 800-numbers are toll-free long distance numbers. In many areas a dialing prefix is required for long distance calls. For example, in Orlando, Florida, to obtain Amtrak reservation and information one must dial 1-800-342-2520. If you receive a busy signal or Amtrak does not answer please consult the local telephone directory or local telephone information operator for the proper way to place a long-distance call.

Alabama 800-874-2800

Arizona 800-421-8320

Arkansas 800-874-2775

California

(except Los Angeles)
  800-648-3850

(Los Angeles only) 624-0171

Colorado 800-421-8320

Connecticut 800-523-5720

Delaware 800-523-5700

District of Columbia . 800-523-5720

Florida
(except Jacksonville)
800-342-2520
(Jacksonville only) 731-1600

Georgia 800-874-2800

Idaho 800-421-8320

Illinois
(except Chicago) ..800-972-9147
(Chicago only) 786-1333

Indiana 800-621-0353

Iowa 800-621-0353

Kansas 800-421-8320

Kentucky 800-874-2775

Louisiana 800-874-2800

Maine 800-523-5731

Maryland 800-523-5700

Massachusetts 800-523-5720

Michigan
(except Area Code 906)
800-621-0353
(Area Code 906 only)
800-621-0317

Minnesota 800-621-0317

Mississippi 800-874-2800

Missouri 800-621-0317

Montana 800-421-8320

Nebraska 800-421-8320

242 RESERVATIONS

Nevada 800-421-8320

New Hampshire 800-523-5720

New Jersey 800-523-5700

New Mexico 800-421-8320

New York
  New York boroughs of Bronx, Brooklyn, Manhattan, Queens, and Staten Island only) 736-4545
  (except Area Code 716)
    800-523-5700

  (Area Code 716 only)
    800-523-5720

North Carolina 800-874-2800

North Dakota 800-421-8320

Ohio 800-621-0317

Oklahoma 800-421-8320

Oregon 800-421-8320

Pennsylvania
  (except Philadelphia)
    800-562-5380
  (Philadelphia only) 824-1600

Rhode Island 800-523-5720

South Carolina 800-874-2800

South Dakota 800-421-8320

Tennessee 800-874-2800

FREEDOM TRAIN 243

Texas 800-421-8320

Utah 800-421-8320

Vermont 800-523-5720

Virginia 800-523-5720

Washington 800-421-8320

West Virginia 800-523-5720

Wisconsin 800-621-0353

Wyoming 800-421-8320

FREEDOM TRAIN SCHEDULE

The 'Freedom Train,' a special train which contains articles of America's past, is visiting a number of cities as part of the country's Bicentennial celebration. We have included the train's schedule as compiled by the Bicentennial Administration. Keep in mind that the schedule is subject to change. The first set of bold-faced figures is the project number while the last is an indication of how many days the train is scheduled to stop in a particular city.

001776 - 032   11/03/75 - 11/06/75
FREEDOM TRAIN DISPLAY DAYS
PORTLAND, OR **CD:** 03

001776 - 033   11/08/75 - 11/09/75
FREEDOM TRAIN DISPLAY DAYS
EUGENE, OR **CD:** 04

001776 - 034   11/12/75 - 11/13/75
FREEDOM TRAIN DISPLAY DAYS
RENO, NV **CD:** 01

001776 - 035   11/16/75 - 11/19/75
FREEDOM TRAIN DISPLAY DAYS
SACRAMENTO, CA **CD:** 03

001776 - 036   11/21/75 - 12/02/75
FREEDOM TRAIN DISPLAY DAYS
SAN FRANCISCO, CA **CD:** 05

001776 - 037   12/04/75 - 12/06/75
FREEDOM TRAIN DISPLAY DAYS
FRESNO, CA **CD:** 16

001776 - 038   12/08/75 - 01/09/76
FREEDOM TRAIN DISPLAY DAYS
LOS ANGELES, CA **CD:** 22

001776 - 039   01/11/76 - 01/15/76
FREEDOM TRAIN DISPLAY DAYS
SAN DIEGO, CA **CD:** 40

001776 - 040   01/18/76 - 01/21/76
FREEDOM TRAIN DISPLAY DAYS
PHOENIX, AZ **CD:** 04

001776 - 041   01/24/76 - 01/26/76
FREEDOM TRAIN DISPLAY DAYS
ALBUQUERQUE, NM **CD:** 01

001776 - 042   01/30/76 - 01/31/76
FREEDOM TRAIN DISPLAY DAYS
LUBBOCK, TX **CD:** 19

001776 - 043   02/03/76 - 02/06/76
FREEDOM TRAIN DISPLAY DAYS
AUSTIN, TX **CD:** 10

001776 - 044   02/08/76 - 02/13/76
FREEDOM TRAIN DISPLAY DAYS
HOUSTON, TX **CD:** 07

001776 - 045   02/15/76 - 02/22/76
FREEDOM TRAIN DISPLAY DAYS
DALLAS, TX **CD:** 05

001776 - 046   02/24/76 - 02/26/76
FREEDOM TRAIN DISPLAY DAYS
OKLAHOMA CITY, OK **CD:** 04

001776 - 047   02/28/76 - 03/01/76
FREEDOM TRAIN DISPLAY DAYS
TULSA, OK **CD:** 01

001776 - 048   03/05/76 - 03/06/76
FREEDOM TRAIN DISPLAY DAYS
WICHITA, KS **CD:** 01

001776 - 049   03/08/76 - 03/12/76
FREEDOM TRAIN DISPLAY DAYS
KANSAS CITY, KS **CD:** 03

244 FREEDOM TRAIN

001776 - 050   03/14/76 - 03/19/76
FREEDOM TRAIN DISPLAY DAYS
ST LOUIS, MO **CD:** 01

001776 - 051   03/22/76 - 03/24/76
FREEDOM TRAIN DISPLAY DAYS
LITTLE ROCK, AR **CD:** 02

001776 - 052   03/26/76 - 03/29/76
FREEDOM TRAIN DISPLAY DAYS
MEMPHIS, TN **CD:** 08

001776 - 053   03/31/76 - 04/03/76
FREEDOM TRAIN DISPLAY DAYS
JACKSON, LA **CD:** 06

001776 - 054   04/08/76 - 04/12/76
FREEDOM TRAIN DISPLAY DAYS
NEW ORLEANS, LA **CD:** 01

001776 - 055   04/15/76 - 04/20/76
FREEDOM TRAIN DISPLAY DAYS
BIRMINGHAM, AL **CD:** 06

001776 - 056   04/22/76 - 04/25/76
FREEDOM TRAIN DISPLAY DAYS
NASHVILLE, TN **CD:** 05

001776 - 057   04/28/76 - 05/05/76
FREEDOM TRAIN DISPLAY DAYS
ATLANTA, GA **CD:** 04

001776 - 058   05/10/76 - 05/12/76
FREEDOM TRAIN DISPLAY DAYS
JACKSONVILLE, FL **CD:** 03

001776 - 059   05/14/76 - 05/18/76
FREEDOM TRAIN DISPLAY DAYS
ORLANDO, FL **CD:** 09

001776 - 060   05/20/76 - 05/23/76
FREEDOM TRAIN DISPLAY DAYS
TAMPA, FL **CD:** 07

001776 - 061   05/26/76 - 06/01/76
FREEDOM TRAIN DISPLAY DAYS
MIAMI, FL **CD:** 14

001776 - 062   06/11/76 - 06/12/76
FREEDOM TRAIN DISPLAY DAYS
SAVANNAH, GA **CD:** 01

001776 - 063   06/14/76 - 06/17/76
FREEDOM TRAIN DISPLAY DAYS
CHARLESTON, SC **CD:** 01

001776 - 064   06/22/76 - 06/25/76
FREEDOM TRAIN DISPLAY DAYS
CHARLOTTE, NC **CD:** 09

001776 - 065   06/27/76 - 07/05/76
FREEDOM TRAIN DISPLAY DAYS
RALEIGH, NC **CD:** 04

001776 - 066   07/08/76 - 07/10/76
FREEDOM TRAIN DISPLAY DAYS
ROANOKE, VA **CD:** 06

001776 - 067   07/11/76 - 07/14/76
FREEDOM TRAIN DISPLAY DAYS
CHARLESTON, WV **CD:** 03

001776 - 068   07/17/76 - 07/25/76
FREEDOM TRAIN DISPLAY DAYS
RICHMOND, VA **CD:** 03

001776 - 069   07/27/76 - 08/01/76
FREEDOM TRAIN DISPLAY DAYS
NORFOLK, VA **CD:** 02

001776 - 070   08/04/76 - 08/13/76
FREEDOM TRAIN DISPLAY DAYS
WASHINGTON, DC

001776 - 071   08/15/76 - 08/26/76
FREEDOM TRAIN DISPLAY DAYS
BALTIMORE, MD **CD:** 03

001776 - 072   08/28/76 - 09/07/76
FREEDOM TRAIN DISPLAY DAYS
WILMINGTON, DE **CD:** 01

001776 - 073   09/09/76 - 09/22/76
FREEDOM TRAIN DISPLAY DAYS
PHILADELPHIA, PA **CD:** 04

001776 - 074   09/24/76 - 10/12/76
FREEDOM TRAIN DISPLAY DAYS
TRENTON, NJ **CD:** 04

001776 - 075   10/16/76 - 11/14/76
FREEDOM TRAIN DISPLAY DAYS
NEW YORK, NY **CD:** 18

001776 - 076   11/17/76 - 11/28/76
FREEDOM TRAIN DISPLAY DAYS
HARTFORD, CT **CD:** 01

001776 - 077   11/30/76 - 12/05/76
FREEDOM TRAIN DISPLAY DAYS
PROVIDENCE, RI **CD:** 02

GRAY LINE

Wherever you go, be sure to "see it like it is" with one of Gray Line's many sightseeing tours of great cities, National Parks historic sites. Each is personally, professionally conducted in modern, climate controlled buses. Phone the Gray Line offices listed below in advance of your planned sightseeing tour. You will be given complete information on tour departure times, pick up points, etc.

GRAY LINE 245

UNITED STATES

Albuquerque, N.M.	243-5501
Asheville, N.C.	252-8450
Aspen, Colorado	925-1234
Atlanta, Ga.	524-6086
Atlantic City, N.J.	344-2211
Boston, Mass.	427-8650
Brownsville, Texas	542-8962
Buffalo, N.Y.	853-3377
Charleston, S.C.	722-4444
Chicago, Ill.	329-1444
Colorado Springs, Colo.	633-1747
Corpus Christi, Tex.	884-8482
Denver, Colo.	825-8201
Detroit, Mich.	224-1555
Durango, Colorado	247-2733
El Paso, Tex.	533-4976
Estes Park, Colorado	586-3301
Flagstaff, Ariz.	774-5003
Fort Lauderdale, Fla.	587-8080
Fort Worth, Tex.	265-4879
Gatlinburg, Tenn.	436-4182
Harlingen, Tex.	423-4710
Hartford, Conn.	525-1624
Hot Springs, Ark.	623-2527
Houston, Tex.	223-9113
Indianapolis, Ind.	635-8515
Knoxville, Tenn.	522-7911
Lake Tahoe, Nevada	588-6688
Lancaster, Pa.	397-8186
Las Vegas, Nev.	384-1234
Little Rock, Ark.	376-2535
Los Angeles, Calif.	481-2121
McAllen, Tex.	682-3401
Memphis, Tenn.	526-3548
Minneapolis, Minn.	827-4071
Mobile, Ala.	432-7711
Monterey-Carmel, Calif.	373-4989
Nantucket, Mass.	288-0174
Nashville, Tenn.	244-7330
New London, Conn.	443-1831
New Orleans, La.	524-0271
New York, N.Y.	765-1600
Orlando, Fla.	422-0744
Palm Springs, Calif.	325-4414
Philadelphia, Pa.	569-3666
Phoenix-Scottsdale, Ariz.	258-6011
Port Angeles, Wash.	825-4140
Portland, Me.	774-7871
Portland, Ore.	226-6755
Rapid City, S.D. (Black Hills)	342-4461
Reno, Nevada	329-1147
Sacramento, Calif.	444-2877
St. Louis, Mo.	241-1224
St. Petersburg, Fla.	896-2655
Salt Lake City, Utah	521-7060
San Antonio, Tex.	227-5371
San Francisco, Calif.	771-4000
Santa Fe, N.M.	983-9161
Seattle, Wash.	682-1234
Spokane, Wash.	624-4116
Springfield, Mass.	781-2900
Tampa, Fla.	229-5708
Tucson, Ariz.	622-8811
Tulsa, Okla.	627-9797
Washington, D.C.	347-0600

CANADA

Banff, Alberta	762-2241
Calgary, Alberta	266-5658
Edmonton, Alberta	423-2765
Gaspe, Canada	775-4500
Halifax, N.S.	454-9321
Montreal, Que.	937-2871
Niagara Falls, Ont.	354-4524
Ottawa, Ont.	741-6440
Prince Rupert, B.C.	624-6236
Quebec, Canada	688-9630
Toronto, Ont.	362-2681
Vancouver, B.C.	681-6381
Victoria, B.C.	385-4417
Winnipeg, Man.	586-4777

Many Gray Line affiliates do not operate year round. For complete information, check with the appropriate Gray Line office

ROUTE DESCRIPTIONS

In this section of your travel guide we include Amtrak's descriptions of some of the popular rail routes. These descriptions will make your trip more enjoyable and interesting.

THE BROADWAY LIMITED
NEW YORK/WASHINGTON, D.C.-CHICAGO

NEW YORK, N.Y. (Population 7,771,730) is the world's financial center, United Nations headquarters and business, entertainment and publishing capital of the U.S. The city employs more people (170,000) and spends more money ($3 billion plus annually) than any other city, state or most foreign countries. One of its five boroughs (Brooklyn) has more residents than any other U.S. city except Chicago and Los Angeles. New York was discovered by accident in 1609 when Henry Hudson failed in his mission to find a new route to China for the Dutch. Henry must have become attached to the New York area, for it is said that he returned every 20 years to play ninepins.

NEWARK, N.J. (Population 382,417) is the largest city in New Jersey and is one of the world's greatest manufacturing centers and a home of Anheuser Busch, world's largest brewery.

TRENTON, N.J. (Population 102,211) is the capital of New Jersey and was named Trent's Town in 1714 by a not-so-humble Scottish immigrant, William Trent. General Washington crossed the ice-clogged Delaware River on Christmas Eve, 1776, to attack the Hessian garrison near Trenton. Today, the city's slogan is "Trenton makes — the world takes," and over 400 industries support its claim. New Jersey State Fair, one of the nation's largest, is held in Trenton in late September.

PHILADELPHIA, PA. (Population 1,927,863) is served by the Broadway Limited through North Philadelphia Station, and is one of the most innovative of U.S. cities. It was the first city to have an art museum, circulating library, fire department, fire insurance company, hospital, theatre and zoo. Other "firsts" include: railroad track in 1809; business college, Wharton School of Commerce and Finance, in 1881; and baseball game, a 9-inning, no-hitter on July 28, 1875. The city also originated pepperpot soup, cinnamon buns, ice cream and the ice cream soda. In colonial days, "Hokey-Pokey" men, ancestors of today's "Good Humor" men, peddled ice cream on Philadelphia's cobbled streets. The city's Rodin Museum has the largest collection of Rodin sculptures outside of France. On Mondays, admission is free to Philadelphia's art galleries and other points of interest.

Three minutes after leaving North Philadelphia Station, on your left (going west) can be seen the Philadelphia zoo. You will go west for the next twenty miles through the "Main-Line" suburbs.

PAOLI, PA. (Population 2,500) took its name from a local tavern. The tavern had been named for Pasquale di Paoli, known and admired during the American Revolution as the leader of the Corsican revolt in the mid-18th century.

LANCASTER, PA. (Population 57,693) is situated in one of the most fertile agricultural regions in the U.S. Many farms are tilled by members of the Amish community, a religious sect whose style of living has not changed in 300 years. The Amish originated the customs of Santa Claus, the Christmas tree and the Easter Bunny. Woolworth's first store was opened in Lancaster in 1879. All merchandise was 5¢.

WASHINGTON, D.C. PASSENGERS

WASHINGTON, D.C. (Population 746,169, alt. to 310 ft.) The nation's Founding Fathers decided early on a "Federal City" and the States of Maryland and Virginia each agreed to donate land on both sides of the Potomac River. Thus the original District of Columbia was a ten-mile square with the Potomac meandering diagonally through it. After considerable Congressional argument (seven years to be exact) it was decided the east bank, or Maryland side of the river, was best for the Federal City. Probably because Maryland agreed to contribute $120,000 to the project while Virginia would give only $72,000. In 1790, George Washington himself selected the exact site and enlisted the talents of Pierre L'Enfant to design the new city. Actually, the site Washington selected was a mosquito-infested marsh, and the fact that L'Enfant could envision a city of broad avenues, marble monuments, spacious circles and sweeping vistas is a testament to his talent. Or to his foolhardiness. In his lifetime he was variously praised and damned. "That crazy Frenchman" is one of the milder epithets to survive. Truth to tell, a hundred years passed before Washington began to resemble a real city. Nobody wanted to live there and the streets remained deeply rutted dirt roads that after every rain turned into impassable bogs. In 1846, Congress, with a sigh, returned to Virginia that part of the District of Columbia on the west bank of the Potomac — Arlington and Alexandria. It would never be needed. But after the smoke of the Civil War settled in 1865, a sense of civic pride began to grip the nation's capital. Modern sewer lines were laid, streets and sidewalks were paved, parks were laid out and hundreds of trees were planted. Today Washington is a cosmopolitan metropolis with a clean, unhurried air. And to this restful atmosphere come the problems of the world. Pierre L'Enfant should be pleased.

CAPITAL BELTWAY, MD. — Modern suburban station with convenient auto access to Maryland suburbs.

BALTIMORE, MD. (Population 895,222, alt. to 491 ft.) is the great economic heart of Maryland. It has a fine harbor for oceangoing vessels, and a thriving industrial complex. During the War of 1812, the British attacked Fort McHenry and, as the battle raged, Francis Scott Key was inspired to write "The Star-Spangled Banner." Baltimore is the home of the world-famous Johns Hopkins Medical Center.

One-half hour after leaving Baltimore, we cross the **SUSQUEHANNA RIVER** where it joins **CHESAPEAKE BAY**. From this point on to Harrisburg, scenic views of the river may be seen. We will pass through **COLUMBIA, PA.** (population 12,075) which, for a brief period, was capital of the United States.

HARRISBURG, PA. (Population 65,828), capital of Pennsylvania, was named for John Harris who operated a ferry on the Susquehanna River in the 1700s. In 1785, the Executive Council of Pennsylvania changed the name to Louisburg in honor of the French King. The townspeople ignored the change and "Harrisburg" it has remained. At Harrisburg, the Washington section of the Broadway Limited joins the train from New York.

Ten minutes west of Harrisburg, our route crosses the **SUSQUEHANNA RIVER** on the Rockville Stone Arch Bridge. We then follow the Susquehanna and the **JUNIATA RIVER.**

ALTOONA, PA. (Population 62,385) means "uncertain" in Cherokee. The city was founded in 1849 by the Pennsylvania Railroad as its base of operations for building the first railroad over the Alleghenies. Altoona had the country's first steel railroad rails in 1864, and the first steel passenger coach in 1902.

Ten minutes west of Altoona, we will round the Horseshoe Curve as the train gains altitude to cross the Allegheny Mountains. Look on the left side of the train, going west (right side, going east), for a panorama of the train. The three lakes below the train are reservoirs for the city of Altoona.

JOHNSTOWN, PA. (Population 42,065) has been the victim of three major floods. The second, in 1889, was one of this country's worst peacetime disasters, killing 2,205 people. Today, Johnstown is the location of one of Bethlehem Steel Corporation's mills.

Although **PITTSBURGH, PA.** (Population 512,789) is best known as the greatest iron and steel producer in the world, the city has 6,000 different products. Pittsburgh had the country's first commercial high school in 1868, moving picture theatre in 1905, and black news correspondent, J. A. Rogers, in 1935. The city also experienced the first armored car holdup on March 11, 1927.

Just after leaving Pittsburgh (going west), we cross the **ALLEGHENY RIVER** about one-half mile upstream from where it joins the **OHIO RIVER.** For the next 25 miles we will follow the Ohio River (on the left) to Beaver Falls, where we pass cataracts of the **BEAVER RIVER.**

CANTON, OHIO (Population 108,872) was so named because its first residents, poor students of geography, thought that their city was the global opposite of Canton, China. Canton is an industrial city, manufacturing 1,500 products as diverse as anchovy pizzas and the Hoover vacuum cleaner. National Football Hall of Fame is located in Canton.

CRESTLINE, OHIO (Population 5,890) is so named because it is at the divide between the Ohio River and Lake Erie drainage. Crestline started as a railroad junction and remains a rail center today.

The residents of **LIMA, OHIO** (Population 53,373) named their town in honor of Lima, Peru because of a bark in the Peruvian city which treated swamp fever. Baltimore and Ohio Railroad put Lima on the map. Steam locomotives were perfected in Lima. During World War I, the city developed the Liberty Truck. Lima is one of three U.S. cities to own its own observatory.

FORT WAYNE, IND. (Population 175,083) houses the nation's largest Lincoln library. John Chapman, better known as Johnny Appleseed, is buried in a park on Parnell Avenue. The filling station pump was invented in Fort Wayne, and the city still leads in its production. Fort Wayne is the birthplace of night baseball. On October 23, 1910, residents watched the first woman to make a public airplane flight, B. S. Scott.

In 1905, U.S. Steel Company selected land for their future steel-producing center. The site was named for the company's president, E. H. Gary. Today, besides steel, **GARY, IND.** (Population 175,415) produces most of the building limestone in the country and is first in the cultivation of popcorn and peppermint. Gary is internationally known for its innovative school system. Community church schools originated in Gary.

Algonquin Indians named **CHICAGO, ILL.** (Population 3,369,359) for the "wild onions" that grew on the site. The city's first permanent cabin was built in 1779 by Jean Baptiste Point du Sable, a black explorer and fur trader. Many of Chicago's traditional images are inaccurate: the "windy city" is actually the 19th windiest in the country and, although it is the second largest U.S. city, 19% of Chicago is park or playground. Chicago had the country's first skyscraper, 11 stories high, and many of its buildings were designed by Louis Sullivan and Frank Lloyd Wright.

250 MERCHANTS

THE MERCHANTS LIMITED
BOSTON-WASHINGTON, D.C.

WASHINGTON, D.C. (Population 746,169, alt. to 310 ft.) The nation's Founding Fathers decided early on a "Federal City" and the States of Maryland and Virginia each agreed to donate land on both sides of the Potomac River. Thus the

BALTIMORE, MD. (Population 895,222, alt. to 491 ft.) Baltimore is the great economic heart of Maryland. It has a fine harbor for oceangoing vessels, and a thriving industrial complex. During the War of 1812, the British attacked Fort McHenry and, as the battle raged, Francis Scott Key was inspired to write "The Star-Spangled Banner." Baltimore is the home of world-famous Johns Hopkins Medical Center.

One-half hour after leaving Baltimore (going north), we will cross the **SUSQUEHANNA RIVER** where it joins **CHESAPEAKE BAY.**

WILMINGTON, DEL. (Population 79,978, alt. 134 ft.) Although the city was first settled by the Swedes, the English eventually took over. Wilmington fell under the governorship of William Penn, which accounts for the Quaker character of the city to this day. Here is the home of E.I. du Pont de Nemours and all the attendant chemical companies and their laboratories which are the world's largest.

PHILADELPHIA, PA. (Population 1,927,863) is one of the most innovative of U.S. cities. It was the first city to have an art museum, circulating library, fire department, fire insurance company, hospital, theatre and zoo.

TRENTON, N.J. (Population 102,211) was named Trent's Town in 1714 by a not-so-humble Scottish immigrant, William Trent. General Washington crossed the ice-clogged Delaware River on Christmas Eve, 1776, to attack the Hessian garrison near Trenton. Today, the city's slogan is "Trenton makes — the world takes," and over 400 industries support its claim. New Jersey State Fair, one of the nation's largest, is held in Trenton in late September.

PRINCETON, N.J. (Population 11,981, alt. 213 ft.) Primarily a college town, its most famous school, Princeton University, was founded by royal charter in 1746, although it didn't move to its present site until ten years later. (Some of the tallest towers on the campus can be seen from the train — on your left, going north.) Princeton served for a time as the capital of New Jersey, and the official governor's mansion is still there. Besides Princeton University there are numerous other colleges including the Institute for Advanced Study, where Albert Einstein worked and studied.

NEWARK, N.J. (Population 382,417) is one of the world's greatest manufacturing centers and a home of Anheuser Busch, world's largest brewery.

NEW YORK, N.Y. (Population 7,798,757, alt. to 430 ft.) In 1653 the population of the thriving Dutch colony of New Amsterdam was a burgeoning 800.

MERCHANTS 251

RYE, N.Y. (Population 14,225) An affluent and popular suburban community of New York City. Playland Amusement Park and Rye Beach are major summer attractions.

STAMFORD, CONN. (Population 107,907, alt. 34 ft.) On the shore of Long Island Sound, Stamford keeps its old New England charm. Many New York City commuters live there. Its excellent shipping facilities have also encouraged the growth of more than 250 industries.

BRIDGEPORT, CONN. (Population 155,359, alt. 12 ft.) Bridgeport was so named because of a drawbridge that was built over the Pequonnock River. Today it boasts more than 400 firms and the University of Bridgeport. Once the home of P. T. Barnum, self-proclaimed "Greatest Showman on Earth," it was also the birthplace of his greatest attraction, "General" Tom Thumb. At 28 inches tall, Tom Thumb was possibly the world's most celebrated midget.

NEW HAVEN, CONN. (Population 133,543, alt. 33 ft.) Originally laid out by the Puritans in 1639, New Haven was designed in nine equal squares. Today, of course, the city sprawls far beyond those boundaries. Yale University, founded in 1701 by Elihu Yale, occupies most of the original nine squares, and is one of the nation's most distinguished universities. Other colleges in New Haven include Albertus Magnus College and Southern Connecticut State College. Although New Haven is primarily a college town, it boasts many important manufacturing establishments: Olin Mathieson Chemical Corp., Sargent Lock Co., and Gilbert Toys, to name only a few.

OLD SAYBROOK, CONN. (Population 8,344, alt. 10 ft.) Saybrook Parish was first settled by the Dutch in 1623, and 12 years later the English arrived. Yale University originated here and moved to New Haven when its campus was completed in 1716. It also has the dubious distinction of giving birth to the world's first submarine used for war purposes. In 1776, David Bushnell built the *American Turtle,* and it operated briefly during the Revolution.

NEW LONDON, CONN. (Population 29,234, alt. 27 ft.) New London was founded in 1646 by a group of Puritan families under the leadership of John Winthrop the younger. During the Revolution it became a principal rendezvous for privateers and so was attacked by Benedict Arnold's Tory force in 1781 and burned to the ground. The city was rebuilt and in 1784 the whaling industry began in New London. It reached its peak early in the nineteenth century when 75 whaling vessels called New London their home port. Today the city is still an important port, for even larger oceangoing vessels can navigate the 3-mile stretch of the Thames from Long Island Sound. Connecticut College has a large campus in the city and New London is the seat of the U.S. Coast Guard Academy. The nation's most important submarine base is also here.

MYSTIC, CONN. (Population 2,536, alt. 9 ft.) A complete colonial seaport has been re-created at the Mystic Seaport Museum.

252 MERCHANTS

WESTERLY, R.I. (Population 17,146, alt. 35 ft.) Fifth in the colony to be founded, Westerly was incorporated in 1669. During the War of 1812, Oliver Hazard Perry built gunboats here for the government.

KINGSTON, R.I. (Population 5,601, alt. 250 ft.) A quiet village, Kingston is the seat of the University of Rhode Island. Founded about 1700, many of its houses date from pre-Revolutionary days.

Kingston is the detraining point for Newport, R.I. Between Kingston and Providence, we will pass along the shore of **NARRAGANSETT BAY.**

PROVIDENCE, R.I. (Population 176,920, alt. 80 ft.) Providence was named by Roger Williams who founded the city in 1636. He'd been banished from Massachusetts for his religious views and named it "for God's merciful providence unto me in my distress." Being a natural harbor at the head of navigation on Narragansett Bay, Providence early became a shipping and ship-building town. A thriving East India and China trade developed after the Revolutionary War. Today, Providence is still one of the most important distributing ports on the Atlantic seaboard for oil, coal and lumber. Industry has thrived in Providence, the principal one being textile manufacturing—primarily woolen and worsteds. The city is also one of the largest jewelry manufacturing centers in the world. There are many schools and colleges, including Brown University and the famous Rhode Island School of Design. You will pass the Gorman Silver Plant (on your left, going north) entering Providence.

BOSTON, MASS. (Population 628,215, alt. 34 ft.) John Winthrop, the elder, led early colonists to the site of Boston in 1630. Within two years it was named the capital of the Massachusetts Bay Colony and, because of its excellent port facilities at the mouths of the Charles and Mystic Rivers, the city thrived. Its importance as a port was not lost on either the British or the early revolutionaries, which probably explains why the Revolutionary War actually started in and around Boston. First there was the "Boston Massacre" (six people died), then the "Boston Tea Party" (no taxation without representation), and finally Paul Revere's famed midnight ride to alert the Minutemen, and the war was on. After the war, Boston boomed and over the years has assimilated ethnic groups from everywhere. But the feeling for rugged individuality remains. The streets in modern Boston were once cow paths, and the result is a bewildering maze. None of these planned city grid systems for Bostonians. The greater Boston area actually encompasses nearly three-and-a-half million people, but Bostonians refer to their city as "The Hub" (of the world). Towering skyscrapers stand next to revolutionary landmarks. Subway trains burrow under cobblestone streets that were paved with ballast from early sailing ships. (Waste not, want not.) The first free public school opened in Boston and, across the river in Cambridge, America's first university — Harvard.

THE MONTREALER

WASHINGTON, D.C.—MONTREAL

The "Montrealer" takes the same route as the "Merchants Limited" for part of its trip. In New Haven, the Montrealer, on its way to Montreal via Meriden, Hartford, Springfield, Vermont and Quebec points. The first stop, northbound, after New Haven, is Meriden.

MERIDEN, CONN. (Population 55,073, alt. 150 ft.), where Samuel Yale created the first pewterware in 1794, is one of the country's "silver cities." Here, in 1847, the Rogers brothers invented a process for depositing silver on other metals by electricity. Settled in 1661 and incorporated shortly after the end of the Civil War, Meriden, just 16 miles northeast of New Haven, is a truck-farming region whose green slopes are scenically dramatized by the 1,000-ft.-high Hanging Hills, adjacent to Merimere Reservoir.

BERLIN, CONN. (Population 13,948, alt. 64 ft.), eleven miles south of Hartford, is where the "Yankee Peddler" was born, fashioned by the Patterson brothers around 1740, who peddled their tinware around the countryside.

HARTFORD, CONN. (Population 155,868, alt. 100 ft.) is home of 38 insurance companies with combined assets of more than $12 billion. Mark Twain lived here. Hartford started as a Dutch fort and trading post in 1633, and was settled two years later by a band of colonists from Massachusetts Bay. It was the scene of the historic Charter Oak incident in 1687. Joseph Wadsworth hid the city's charter (which gave local sovereignty to the colonists) in a hollow oak tree to avoid turning it over to Edmund Andros, Governor of New York and newly appointed Governor General of the Dominion of New England. During the Revolution, Hartford was an important military supply depot and the Connecticut artillery from Hartford played an important role in the Civil War. Among the artifacts on display in the Connecticut Historical Society Museum are Mark Twain's bicycle, Nathan Hale's diary and Israel Putnam's sword. And the nearby State Capitol Building Museum contains Lafayette's camp bed and the figurehead of Admiral Farragut's flagship, the Hartford. The *Hartford Courant,* America's oldest newspaper founded in 1764, lists George Washington as a former subscriber.

From Hartford we travel through the scenic Connecticut River Valley as far as White River Junction, a distance of approximately 150 miles.

SPRINGFIELD, MASS. (Population 174,463, alt. 101 ft.) is where basketball was invented by Dr. James A. Naismith in 1891, using a bottomed-out peach basket, probably nailed to the side of a barn. The Naismith Memorial Basketball Hall of Fame on the Springfield College campus includes memorabilia from the earliest days of the game including uniforms, equipment and some of the first rule books written. Springfield, however, is not limited to the basketball courts; a horseless carriage manufactured here won the country's first automobile race in Chicago in 1895. The city, founded in 1636 as a trading post, was completely destroyed in 1675 during what history records as King Philip's War. One hundred and ten years later, Shay's Rebellion took place here. In 1794, the United States opened an armory in the city. Merriam-Webster Dictionaries come from Springfield. Here, too, is Westover Air Force Base, a Strategic Air Command installation.

Approximately eight miles north of Springfield is Holyoke, Mass. (Population 52,689, alt. 115 ft.), an old New England manufacturing center whose site was selected along the **CONNECTICUT RIVER** to take advantage of power from this river. Nine miles north of Holyoke is Northampton, Mass. (Population 27,726, alt. 125 ft.), home of Smith College. Amherst, location of Amherst College and the University of Massachusetts, is nearby. For many miles, our train passes through some of the finest stands of deciduous forests in New England, of which sugar maple and white birch are particularly significant.

BRATTLEBORO, VT. (Population 12,070, alt. 281 ft.), known to every serious skier in the Northeast, is surrounded by the lush Green Mountains and is the center for Stratton, Maple Valley, Mount Snow and Haystack ski areas. The Brattleboro Outing Club Ski Jump is one of the finest in the East; three national championship competitions have taken place here. The city, which is just 8 miles north of the Massachusetts border, was settled in 1724 by a garrison from Fort Drummer. Although Northeasterners tend to think of Brattleboro only as a ski resort, it has a business side as well, manufacturing pipe organs, cotton goods, wooden products and granite tombstones.

BELLOWS FALLS, VT. (Population 3,831, alt. 298 ft.), on the **CONNECTICUT RIVER,** is a historic railroad town with Steamtown, U.S.A. (on the northern edge of the city) housing one of the largest collections of steam locomotives from the United States and Canada. The green and proper New England city stretches up and over the surrounding hills with the view from the top preempted by the residential community and industry relegated to the lowlands. The middle ground belongs to the businessmen. Industries include wood products, plastics, paper and hydroelectric power from the Connecticut River which, incidentally, was discovered first by the Indians who left their creative carvings in the river rocks.

At Windsor, Vt., about 20 minutes before arriving at White River Junction, Mount Ascutney is located on the left, while on the right is a long covered bridge across the **CONNECTICUT RIVER.** After leaving Bellows Falls, and until passing through Windsor, our train will be in New Hampshire, the Granite State.

MONTREALER 255

WHITE RIVER JUNCTION, VT. (Population 2,546, alt. 320 ft.) For several miles into White River Junction our train has been following the **WHITE RIVER**. At White River Junction the White River joins the **CONNECTICUT RIVER**. White River Junction is located close to Lebanon, N. H., a small manufacturing city, and Hanover, N. H., the home of Dartmouth College. Dartmouth, one of the Ivy League colleges, was founded in 1769 to "spread education to the Indians." Dartmouth is known for its annual Winter Carnival. Concord, the capital of New Hampshire, and Rutland, Vermont, are easily reached from White River Junction.

MONTPELIER JUNCTION, VT. (Population 9,102, alt. 484 ft.) Nearby Montpelier is the capital of Vermont, and the magnificent State Capitol is built of Barre granite, in Doric style. Admiral George Dewey, hero of Manila Bay, was born here on the banks of the Winooski River. And, like most areas in Vermont, Montpelier taps its trees for the precious maple that has made Vermont world famous. Vermont College is located here. Nearby Barre is famous for its granite quarries.

WATERBURY, VT. (Population 4,303, alt. 480 ft.), on the **WINOOSKI RIVER** in north central Vermont and 10 miles northwest of Montpelier Junction, produces dairy and maple products. This is a woodworking center, also the site of granite quarries and talc mines. Waterbury is the gateway to Stowe, Bolton Valley and other ski resorts.

ESSEX JUNCTION, VT. (BURLINGTON) (Population 38,266, alt. 112 ft.) Ethan Allen lived here and is buried on the hillside. Nearby Burlington, Vermont's largest city, is located on Lake Champlain and is a summer and winter resort and seat of the University of Vermont and Trinity College. The city, chartered by the Province of New Hampshire in 1763, played a major role as a military base and center for naval activity during America's War of 1812. Today, Burlington is an important industrial and retail center, manufacturing textiles, marble, lumber and wooden products.

ST. ALBANS, VT. (Population 7,983, alt. 383 ft.) is a syrup center, producing 250,000 gallons of the famed maple syrup annually. St. Albans had its moment in history during the Civil War when a small band of Confederate soldiers, entering from the Canadian side, raided the town, looting the local banks and causing one fatality. The city is one of the best fishing areas in the Lake Champlain region, and is also noted for turkeys and dairy products.

East Alburgh, Vt. (Population 75, alt. 125 ft.) Here our train leaves the United States and crosses a portion of **LAKE CHAMPLAIN.**

Between **ST. LAMBERT, QUE.** (Population 18,590, alt. 74 ft.) and Montreal, our train crosses the **ST. LAWRENCE RIVER** on Victoria Bridge, longest railroad bridge in Canada. (The south side of this bridge has routes around both ends of the locks so that ships passing through the St. Lawrence Seaway will not delay trains.)

256 MONTREALER

MONTREAL, QUE. (Population 1,320,232, alt. 200 ft.) Jacques Cartier was the first white man of record to reach Montreal in 1535 when it was still a quiet Hochelaga Indian town. In 1642, Sieur de Maisonneuve founded the first permanent settlement and called it "Ville-Marie de Montreal." But the resident Iroquoians and the white man couldn't coexist and the settlement was abandoned in 1663, turned over to the Seminary of St. Sulpice. It soon became a fur trading center and the starting point for expeditions into the interior. When neighboring Quebec City fell to English colonists in 1760, all Canadian lands were ceded to Great Britain with the 1763 Treaty of Paris at the close of the French and Indian War. Montreal is actually two islands on the north side of the **ST. LAWRENCE RIVER,** and named for Mount Royal, in the city center. In addition to being Canada's largest city and gateway to the Laurentian Mountain resort areas, Montreal is the main business and banking center and the country's main port of entry. Principal exports are timber, grain, flour, cattle, butter, cheese and furs. The city manufactures textiles, machinery, shoes, rubber, paints, electrical goods and lumber. It is the home of world-famous McGill and Montreal Universities, and Ste. Marie and Loyola Colleges.

Amtrak's trains use Central Station in Montreal, which is connected to Place Ville Marie, a fabulous collection of shops and restaurants located below a skyscraper.

PROVINCES AND CAPITALS IN CANADA

Newfoundland, St. John's
Prince Edward Island, Charlottetown
Nova Scotia, Halifax
New Brunswick, Fredericton
Quebec, Quebec
Ontario, Toronto
Manitoba, Winnipeg
Saskatchewan, Regina
Alberta, Edmonton
British Columbia, Victoria
Yukon Territory, Whitehorse
Northwest Territories, Yellowknife

FLORIDA TRAINS 257

THE CHAMPION-THE SILVER STAR-THE SILVER METEOR
NEW YORK-MIAMI/ST. PETERSBURG

NEW YORK, N.Y. (Population 7,895,563, alt. to 430 ft.) The nation's largest city, New York is also the leading center for business, entertainment, fashion, publishing and printing. Most people think of New York as Manhattan, but there are actually four other boroughs. These are Brooklyn, Queens, Bronx, and Richmond (Staten Island). All boroughs except Richmond are connected by a vast underground rapid transit system on which the visitor can take a 236-mile ride for 50¢. The great port is the busiest in the world and ships of all countries handle 40% of America's trade. The harbor has the largest single-span suspension bridge in the world, the Verrazano-Narrows Bridge. New York has many educational institutions including the City University of New York and its branches, Columbia University, Cooper Union, Fordham University, Juilliard School of Music and New York University. Among its many tourist attractions New York lists the Statue of Liberty, reached by boat from the Battery; Central Park; Lincoln Center, which includes the Metropolitan Opera House and Philharmonic Hall; the Empire State Building Observatory; and Rockefeller Center, St. Patrick's Cathedral, and Metropolitan Museum of Art. The United Nations complex on the East River is easily reached from the center of town. Theaters, movie houses, shops and restaurants offer a breathtaking variety of entertainment, gifts and meals.

NEWARK, N.J. (Population 381,930, alt. to 225 ft.) Although it is considered part of the greater New York metropolitan area, Newark is a great city in itself and one of the nation's major seaports and manufacturing centers. Beautiful Branch Brook Park has many recreational facilities including boating and fishing, and cherry trees that burst into glorious bloom in April.

TRENTON, N.J. (Population 104,638, alt. 42 ft.) is the capital of New Jersey and rich in colonial history. It was here, on the day after Christmas in 1776, that Washington crossed the Delaware to surprise and defeat the Hessians. The city has many monuments, historical buildings and museums.

PHILADELPHIA, PA. (Population 1,950,098, alt. 45 ft.) The nation's fourth largest city combines past and present in an unusual blend of modern glass and steel skyscrapers, and narrow, cobblestoned streets with venerable houses. Here, in Independence Hall, the Declaration of Independence and the Constitution were signed, and the Liberty Bell is on view. One may roam the same streets Benjamin Franklin walked, or visit some of the finest museums and art galleries in the world, such as the Academy of Arts and Sciences, Historical Society of Pennsylvania, Franklin Institute, Philadelphia Museum of Art, and many others.

WILMINGTON, DEL. (Population 80,386, alt. 134 ft.) Although the city was first settled by the Swedes, the English took control of the colony and it was governed by William Penn. Its Quaker character is evident to this day. Home of E. I. du Pont de Nemours, and the location of the world's largest chemical companies and their laboratories. Horseracing at Delaware Park late May to late July.

BALTIMORE, MD. (Population 905,759, alt. to 491 ft.) is the great economic heart of Maryland. It has a fine harbor for oceangoing vessels, and is a thriving industrial complex. Here at Fort McHenry during the War of 1812 the British attacked and "The Star-Spangled Banner" was written during the battle by Francis Scott Key. Home of the world-famous Johns Hopkins Medical Center. Many fine museums and galleries.

CAPITAL BELTWAY, MD. — Modern suburban station with convenient auto access to Maryland suburbs.

WASHINGTON, D.C. (Population 756,510, alt. to 310 ft.) The nation's capital is a cosmopolitan metropolis with a clean, unhurried air; a city of broad avenues, majestic monuments, spacious circles and sweeping vistas. Its chief attractions are, of course, the White House and the congressional buildings on Capitol Hill where the nation's Federal laws are made. This complex of buildings is situated in a lovely 131-acre park. Other points of interest include the famous Lincoln, Washington and Jefferson Memorials and the Tomb of the Unknown Soldier in Arlington National Cemetery across the Potomac. Ford's Theater where President Lincoln was shot has been renovated and restored to its original state. The city abounds in museums, the most famous of which is probably the Smithsonian Institution, the "nation's attic," which contains thousands of items and relics illustrating the country's history, progress and achievements.

After emerging from the tunnel (which goes underneath the Capitol) upon leaving Washington, you may see the Capitol, Washington Monument, and Jefferson Memorial on the right side.

ALEXANDRIA, VA. (Population 110,938, alt. to 50 ft.) This charming suburb across the Potomac River from Washington is really a city in its own right. Once it boasted such distinguished residents as George Washington and Robert E. Lee. A walking tour of old Alexandria is a delightful experience that provides both excellent sightseeing and interesting shopping in a genuine colonial atmosphere. North of Alexandria, you cross the Potomac River and pass by the Pentagon. Twenty minutes south of Alexandria, you will again see the Potomac.

QUANTICO, VA. (Population 1,000, alt. 35 ft.) One of the largest Marine Corps posts, and site of the Marine Corps Development and Education Command, Quantico is the home of the Marine Corps Museum, which traces the history of the Marine Corps from its origin in 1775 to the present. The Museum displays weapons, uniforms, accouterments and dioramas depicting various engagements in which the Marines participated. Quantico is on the Potomac River, 35 miles south of Washington, D.C.

FREDERICKSBURG, VA. (Population 14,308, alt. 40 to 69 ft.) is possibly the most historic city of its size in the country. It was officially founded in 1727, although settlers had built a fort here in 1676. Fredericksburg was the last home of George Washington's mother and the home of his only sister (Betty Washington Lewis) whose mansion, Kenmore, is a beautiful example of 18th century Georgian manor house and gardens. George Washington was initiated as a Mason in 1752 at the Masonic Lodge, which survives and is open to the public, as is the first law office of James Monroe, and other fascinating colonial structures. Crucial Civil War battles fought in and around the city are commemorated in the Fredericksburg and Spotsylvania National Military Park.

RICHMOND, VA. (Population 249,430, alt. 312 ft.) Capital of Virginia and one of the most important industrial and intellectual centers of the South. Richmond, capital of the Confederacy, is so rich in history that it would take several days to cover even the highlights: Lee House, John Marshall House, Museum of the Confederacy, the Edgar Allan Poe Museum, University of Richmond and Union Theological Seminary. The Virginia Convention met at St. John's Church in 1775. It was here that Patrick Henry made his famous speech, "Give me liberty or give me death."

PETERSBURG, VA. (Population 36,103, alt. 100 ft.) Although Petersburg is a bustling tobacco and manufacturing center, its place in history was won during the long siege of Richmond by General Grant. The Petersburg National Battlefield includes many miles of the original earthworks constructed by both armies during the months of bitter trench warfare.

From Petersburg to Savannah, Amtrak's Florida trains use two different routes. Check your timetable to determine which route your train will follow. If your train operates via Charleston, resume reading at entry for "Rocky Mount, N.C."

RALEIGH, N.C. (Population 121,577, alt. 352 ft.) Named in honor of Sir Walter Raleigh, this state capital was founded in 1792 and planned to become the "Unalterable seat of government" for North Carolina by a state convention in 1788. Andrew Johnson, 17th President, was born in Raleigh. His modest birthplace is now on the North Carolina State University's Raleigh campus. An educational and cultural center, Raleigh has several colleges and universities, noted Museums of Art and Natural History. The Nuclear Reactor Building, first facility of its kind to be devoted exclusively to development of the atom for peaceful purposes, and the first to be open without restriction to the public, is decidedly worth visiting.

SOUTHERN PINES, N.C. (Population 5,937, alt. 550 ft.) Favored by a dry, bracing climate, Southern Pines is a famous, year-round resort. It is noted for the many fine homes and estates among the beautiful, long-leaf pines. Southern Pines is a mecca for golfers—there are fifteen renowned courses—and several important tournaments are played here annually. Horseback riding, hunting, sailing and tennis are other popular sports. Southern Pines' attractive natural surroundings are further enhanced by the 403-acre Weymouth Woods (Sandhills Nature Preserve) which is one mile southeast of town.

HAMLET, N.C. (Population 7,000, alt. to 300 ft.) is that special kind of American community known as a "railroad town." It is complete with a railroad yard and all the impressive equipment needed to keep the trains on the right track. Hamlet also has diversified industry, including furniture factories and a weaving mill.

CAMDEN, S.C. (Population 8,532, alt. 222 ft.) was settled by Irish Quakers in 1750 and named Pine Tree Hill. The name was changed in 1768 in honor of Lord Camden, friend of the colonies. Fourteen revolutionary battles were fought within a radius of 30 miles and "Historic Camden," an authentic restoration of the original town, is now being developed. Contemporary Camden is a popular center for horse shows, steeplechases and flat races. There are 200 miles of bridle paths and country roads, plus three racetracks and a polo field. The Carolina Cup Steeplechase is run here every year on the Springdale course, considered one of the finest steeplechase plants in the country.

COLUMBIA, S.C. (Population 113,542, alt. 260 ft.) was decreed the state capital in 1786. The University of South Carolina opened here in 1805 and now has a 56-acre campus in Columbia. When General Sherman entered Columbia in 1865, the city was almost entirely destroyed by fire. Today, rebuilt, Columbia has a handsome State House, impressive churches and a notable Museum of Art and Science.

ROCKY MOUNT, N.C. (Population 34,284, alt. 121 ft.) Settled in 1818, this Southern industrial center is a major market for leaf tobacco. Cotton, corn and peanuts are grown here.

WILSON, N.C. (Population 29,347, alt. 145 ft.) Lays claim to being the largest bright-leaf tobacco market in the country. Between mid-August and November, auctioneers sell thousands of pounds of tobacco per hour.

FAYETTEVILLE, N.C. (Population 53,510, alt. 135 ft.) At the head of navigation on the Cape Fear River, Fayetteville is North Carolina's farthest inland port. Its First Presbyterian Church, erected in 1816, is considered one of the finest examples of the classic colonial style of architecture in the South. Fort Bragg and its famed 82nd Airborne Division also make their homes here.

FLORENCE, S.C. (Population 25,997, alt. 137 ft.) became an important rail junction around the middle of the last century. Each spring a Beauty Trail of flowers and gardens is clearly marked. The famous Air and Missile Museum a few miles

FLORIDA TRAINS 261

outside of the city has a fine display of planes, missiles and helicopters.

CHARLESTON, S.C. (Population 66,945, alt. 13 ft.) One of the oldest and most picturesque cities in America. Situated on a splendid harbor, it has lovely walks and drives lined with palmettos, from which can be seen busy waterfront traffic composed of all kinds of vessels from steamers to sailboats. The city is especially noted for quaint older homes with walled gardens entered through iron gates. Plantation gardens in the surrounding countryside are world famous, and offshore is a lovely group of sea island resorts.

YEMASSEE, S.C. (Population 750, alt. 10 ft.) Joe Frazier, former heavyweight boxing champion, makes his home at Bruton Plantation nearby, and South Carolina's Sea Islands are but a scant 40 miles away. During the Civil War, General Sherman burned the town, and the area is rich in history and lore going back to the time of the American Revolution.

SAVANNAH, GA. (Population 118,349, alt. 43 ft.) The first settlement in Georgia was established here in 1773 by General James Edward Oglethorpe and his group of English settlers. Since then, a succession of Portuguese, Spanish, German, Scottish and other immigrants has added flavor and atmosphere to the life of the city. Savannah has preserved its older buildings. The old Commercial Center at Factors Walk has also been preserved. The streets are laid out on a spacious scale, and a cobblestoned riverfront with tree-shaded squares makes this a truly beautiful Southern metropolis. Besides its many fine museums, galleries, libraries and shops, Savannah is blessed by Savannah Beach on nearby historic Tybee Island, a delightful resort with a pleasantly mild climate.

THALMANN, GA. (Population 3,558, alt. 50 ft.) is just 20 minutes from Georgia's largest coastal resort area, the lovely and historic islands of St. Simons, Jekyll and Sea Island. Fort Frederica on St. Simons Island, built in 1736, is the largest fortress constructed by the British on this continent.

JACKSONVILLE, FLA. (Population 528,865, alt. sea level to 140 ft.) refers to itself as the "bold New City of the South," and with good reason. Although it is surrounded by historical and recreational attractions, it is hardly a typical Florida resort. Its strong points are industry and business, and many national firms have their regional offices here. In addition to its cosmopolitan character, there is evident much of the culture and hospitality of the deep South. And there is much to see and do: a variety of entertainment and outdoor sports, theaters, parks, a zoo, art galleries, lovely beaches and sunny skies. And the gamefishing is among the best in the world. The 'Gator Bowl football game is played here in January.

FLORIDA TRAINS

From Jacksonville, Amtrak's Florida trains offer two routes for Miami passengers; the eastern one via Orlando and the western via Wildwood. Check your timetable to determine which route your train will follow.

DE LAND, FLA. (Population 11,641, alt. 27 ft.) This small city is situated in a region of many lakes. Huge oaks line the streets, and many are hung with moss creating a picturesque effect. De Land is the home of Stetson University where the L. L. Rice Planetarium offers periodic showings November through March. Closest Amtrak point to Daytona Beach.

SANFORD, FLA. (Population 17,393, alt. 30 ft.) The first permanent settlement was established here in 1836, when Federal troops were stationed on the banks of Lake Monroe to protect settlers from Indian attacks. Industry is modern, diversified and relatively free of pollutants. Fishing in Lake Monroe is superb.

WINTER PARK, FLA. (Population 21,895, alt. 100 ft.) An ideal subtropical climate, elegant shopping areas, and many cultural facilities have earned this picturesque community the title of "City of Gracious Living." Its unique waterways connect a chain of lakes which provide excellent freshwater fishing. The Ben White Raceway is the winter home of fine trotters and pacers. And the fabulous Walt Disney World is a mere 20 minutes away.

ORLANDO, FLA. (Population 99,006, alt. 111 ft.) Situated in the heart of the lake country, Orlando offers many opportunities for recreation and sport. The city's Sunshine Park features an auditorium, tennis, shuffleboard, lawn bowling, croquet and horseshoes. The Sanford-Orlando Kennel Club holds dog races every night of the 120-day winter season. The annual $150,000 Citrus Open Golf Tournament also takes place here. The Minnesota Twins hold spring training at Tinker Field. Walt Disney World is only 15 miles from Orlando.

POINCIANA, FLA. (Population 250, alt. 62 ft.) This new Amtrak stop places Florida-bound passengers right in the center of central Florida attractions. It is the closest, most convenient gateway to Walt Disney World—just 13 miles from the train. Circus World is 12 miles away. Cypress Gardens and Sea World are 20 miles from the new station. Poinciana and vicinity has a number of excellent motels. They offer fine family accommodations and serve as a handy, nearby base for visits to Walt Disney World and other attractions. Rental cars are available at the station.

LAKELAND, FLA. (Population 41,550, alt. 227 ft.), as its name implies, has 13 lovely lakes within the city limits. The annual Orange Cup Regatta, held around February 1, has resulted in many world speed records. Florida Southern College houses the largest architectural collection in the world by the late Frank Lloyd Wright. The new $9 million auditorium has established Lakeland as a convention center.

FLORIDA TRAINS 263

TAMPA, FLA. (Population 277,767, alt. to 72 ft.) There is a lively Latin section called Ybor City here which is one of Tampa's greatest attractions. The leading cigar factories of the United States are here, and plants manufacture everything from wire and cable to citrus and beer. Tampa has year-round swimming at superb beaches, greyhound racing from September through early January, jai alai, spring training with the Cincinnati Reds, the University of Tampa, museums and an amusement park.

CLEARWATER, FLA. (Population 52,074, alt. 29 ft.) Primarily a year-round resort city, Clearwater overlooks the Gulf of Mexico and boasts a beautiful, broad, white sand beach. The International Snipe Regatta, held every March, has gained worldwide fame. The harbor has a large sailing fleet including charter fishing boats.

ST. PETERSBURG, FLA. (Population 216,232, alt. to 45 ft.) Once known as the "last resort" of senior citizens, St. Petersburg began a vigorous campaign to change its image. The town fathers emphasized St. Petersburg's constant activities, educational opportunities, sports and fishing. Now there is a thriving industrial belt on the city's outskirts, and new arrivals include many young people attracted to St. Petersburg's beautiful beaches, palm-lined shore drive and one-mile-long Waterfront Park. The N.Y. Mets and St. Louis Cardinals train here. There is excellent golf, horseback riding, greyhound racing (late December through March), and thoroughbred racing (mid-January through mid-March).

WALDO, FLA. (Population 840, alt. 170 ft.) The site of Waldo has been occupied since 1830, when a plantation was established there, but the town did not incorporate itself until 1907. Outdoor life focuses on the Waldo Canal which leads to Lake Alto, where the favored sports are water skiing and boat races. Closest Amtrak point to Gainesville.

OCALA, FLA. (Population 22,583, alt. 104 ft.) Moss-draped oaks and stately Southern mansions line many streets of this industrial and resort city, well known among horse breeders for its excellent thoroughbred stables and farms. Nearby is famed Silver Springs where crystal-clear waters can be viewed from glass-bottom boats, live deer abound and reptiles are de-fanged for spectators. A museum pictures early Americana and "Six-Gun Territory" offers an amusement park atmosphere. Ocala National Park has 360,000 acres of swimming, boating, fishing and camping.

WILDWOOD, FLA. (Population 2,500, alt. 170 ft.) is a popular town with fishermen since it is in the midst of many lakes that provide fine piscatorial sport. The lakes have such interesting names as Lake Panascosskee, Lake Miona and Lake Okahumpka. The Dade Memorial Battlefield is a prominent Wildwood landmark.

264 FLORIDA TRAINS

WINTER HAVEN, FLA. (Population 16,136, alt. 180 ft.) Sixteen of this city's 100 lakes are connected by canals to form a 30-mile waterway stocked with fish and steeped in aquatic pleasures. The Boston Red Sox train here every spring. Winter Haven is the home of famed Florida Cypress Gardens, one of the state's most outstanding attractions. Pathways lead through incredibly colored gardens along which stroll models in "Southern belle" gowns. Electric boats cruise along canals and each day is highlighted by exciting water ski exhibitions in a 1,000-seat, all-weather stadium. Cypress Gardens has been the scene of countless Hollywood films.

SEBRING, FLA. (Population 7,223, alt. 160 ft.) The annual International Grand Prix Sports Car 12-Hour Endurance Race is held here in mid-March. (Make hotel reservations early.) Nearby is Highlands Hammock State Park, 3,800 acres of jungle, exotic vegetation and mirror pools. Roads and trails are well marked. Exhibits and guided tours.

WEST PALM BEACH, FLA. (Population 57,375, alt. 18 ft.) The Atlanta Braves do their spring training here. Lucky residents and vacationers can spend the entire year enjoying the balmy weather and complete resort facilities. Nearby is not-to-be-missed Lion Country Safari game preserve—a five-mile drive in a simulated African veldt past live lions, elephants, giraffes, etc. (Keep your windows closed; no convertibles allowed. Cars can be rented at the entrance.) Here also you can take a boat ride through a lagoon replete with hippopotamuses, camels, monkeys and other animals. Open daily. The new Municipal Auditorium features everything from ice shows to circuses. Also see the Henry Flagler Museum, and the Science Museum and Planetarium featuring daily programs.

DELRAY BEACH, FLA. (Population 19,336, alt. 19 ft.) offers one of Florida's finest stretches of ocean beach, plus golf, tennis, boating, deep-sea fishing and other water sports. The annual "Delray Affair," a showcase for a great many local artists, is held the first weekend after Easter. The Delray Beach Playhouse is open November through April. Nearby Laka Ida is a water-skiing center.

DEERFIELD BEACH, FLA. (Population 17,130, alt. 15 ft.) Primarily an agricultural center for the lush citrus and vegetable farms in the vicinity, Deerfield Beach is situated on the Atlantic Ocean, 38 miles north of Miami.

FORT LAUDERDALE, FLA. (Population 139,590, alt. to 7 ft.) An elegant city of islands interlaced by rivers, inlets, bays, man-made canals and waterways. Many sun lovers come here in November and stay until May or June. Easter time brings thousands of college students to cavort on the 6 miles of unbroken beach. The Yankees spring-train here. Things to do and see: Ocean World — alligator wrestling, trained porpoise and sea lion acts; Pirates World — amusement center with rides and entertainment for the young; Jungle Queen — 3-hour sightseeing cruise around the city's waterways. Horseracing at Pompano Park (harness) and

Gulf Stream (flat). Fine restaurants and night spots. Interesting shops and boutiques. Tennis, golf, deep-sea fishing and water sports abound.

HOLLYWOOD, FLA. (Population 106,873, alt. to 7 ft.) In the heart of Florida's Gold Coast, midway between Miami and Fort Lauderdale, this seaside resort was initially hacked from a palmetto jungle in 1921. Often called Florida's "golfingest" city because it has 17 courses. Nearby are the trotters, greyhound racing and jai alai. Excellent deep-sea fishing. Philharmonic Orchestra plays at the Beach Theater Under the Stars.

MIAMI, FLA. (Population 334,859, alt. to 20 ft.) The name Miami derives from a Calusa Indian word meaning "big water." Miami today is enormously big in just about everything that spells vacation fun and entertainment. It also offers a myriad of sports activities. For a great many people it is the vacation capital of America and the world. It has everything from glittering shows featuring the most famous entertainers to poolside bars and sauna baths for the morning after. Suggested things to see and do: Miami Wax Museum; Vizcaya, a fabulous Italian-style palazzo furnished with European treasures; Miami Seaquarium, home of television's "Flipper" and much exciting aquatic activity; Monkey Jungle, 22 miles south, where the monkeys run wild and spectators are in cages; Parrot Jungle, 11 miles south; and the miles of luxury hotels fronting on the ocean in Miami Beach, just across Biscayne Bay. Horseracing at Hialeah, Tropical and Gulfstream. The annual Orange Bowl Festival takes place here mid-December to mid-January, highlighted by the Orange Bowl Football Classic. During the peak winter season, reservations should be made well in advance. Spring, summer and fall offer excellent values.

THE FLORIDIAN
CHICAGO-MIAMI/ST. PETERSBURG

CHICAGO, ILL. (Population 3,369,359, alt. 607 ft.) The Algonquin Indians named Chicago for the "wild onions" that grew on the site. The city's first permanent cabin was built in 1779 by Jean Baptiste Point du Sable, a black explorer and fur trader. Many of Chicago's traditional images are inaccurate: the "windy city" is actually the 19th windiest in the country and, although it is the second largest U.S. city, 19% of Chicago is park or playground. Chicago had the country's first skyscraper, 11 stories high, and many of the buildings were designed by Louis Sullivan and Frank Lloyd Wright. The nation's center of industrial distribution and transportation, Chicago has a buying income 24% above national average.

266 FLORIDIAN

LOGANSPORT, IND. (Population 19,120, alt. 599 ft.) Located where the Eel River meets the Wabash River, Logansport's growth was spurred by the arrival of the Wabash and Erie Canal in 1853. Logansport is noted for its unique Carving Exhibits, works that were skillfully carved in granite, gumwood, limestone, plate glass and plywood. Included is a 7-foot reproduction of da Vinci's "Last Supper" in granite.

South of Logansport you cross the Wabash River, celebrated in the popular song, "On the Banks of the Wabash."

INDIANAPOLIS, IND (Population 742,613, alt. 708 ft.) Capital and largest city of the Hoosier State, Indianapolis became the capital in 1825. Located in the middle of the state, the city is surrounded by coalfields and large areas rich in corn, wheat and building stone. It is also an important rail, banking, and industrial center. Noted educational institutions in the city include Butler University, Indiana Central University, and the Medical and Dental Colleges of Indiana University. Indianapolis has outstanding public buildings, among them are the impressive Indiana World War Memorial in a spacious plaza; the Indianapolis Museum of Art with a fine collection of international art; the State Capitol built of Indian limestone (you can see it from the train); the Benjamin Harrison Memorial Home—a national shrine—and the Home of James Whitcomb Riley. The famous Indianapolis Motor Speedway, five miles from town, is world-renowned for the 500-mile race held every Memorial Day. A museum on the Speedway grounds features racing car exhibits.

Just north of Louisville we cross the "Beautiful Ohio" River which forms the northern boundary of Kentucky, separating it from the states of Ohio and Indiana.

LOUISVILLE, KY. (Population 361,472, alt. 380 to 540 ft.) Its theme song is "My Old Kentucky Home," its great festival is the ten-day jubilee preceding the celebrated Kentucky Derby. Churchill Downs, the famed track on which the Derby is run, has a museum with Derby Day memorabilia. But Louisville is much more than the home of thoroughbreds and mint juleps. First settled in 1779, it is the largest city in Kentucky, with a long tradition of cultural activities and many industries. Among its prominent museums is the J. B. Speed Art Museum, first art museum in Kentucky and among the finest in the South, with an exceptional collection of old masters, modern paintings and American Indian artifacts. Near Eastern and Biblical antiquities are exhibited at the Nichols Museum and the Eisenberg Museum. Railroad buffs will enjoy the Kentucky Railroad Museum which has displays of locomotives, engines and elegant private cars from the early days of the railroads. An old-fashioned stern-wheeler, the Belle of Louisville, is docked on the Ohio River and a 3-hour cruise is available from Memorial Day to October 1. Louisville is one of the biggest tobacco-manufacturing cities in the world and has large distilleries—some 25% of all the liquor distilled in the country is produced here. The University of Louisville, founded in 1798, is the oldest municipal university in the U.S. And there is a firm that manufactures major league baseball bats (the "Louisville Slugger") and gives guided tours of the plant. The attached museum features displays of bats used by famous big-leaguers.

Sixty miles south of Louisville, the train passes Mammoth Cave National Park. Two picturesque rivers run through this scenic forest park of 51,000 acres. Mammoth Cave, one of the country's great natural wonders, has about 150 miles of caverns on five levels and is famed for its spectacular gypsum crystals and "Frozen Niagara," cascades of stalactites and stalagmites.

BOWLING GREEN, KY. (Population 36,253, alt. 500 ft.) On high land overlooking the Barren River, Bowling Green is the site of Western Kentucky University which occupies a hill called College Heights—once used as a fort in the Civil War. The university has some 20,000 volumes in a library of Kentucky history and a museum with Moundbuilder and Indian lore, pioneer relics, and a collection of dolls and antiques. Two miles away from Bowling Green is Lost River Cave, rumored to have been a hideout of the infamous James brothers. Lost River vanishes into the earth a few miles south of town.

The train now passes through the picturesque Kentucky bluegrass region, with its white fences (white, to keep the spirited thoroughbreds from running into them) and many farms that raise the splendid horses that are Kentucky's pride —the saddlebreds, and the standardbreds, the latter used in harness racing.

NASHVILLE, TENN. (Population 447,877, alt. 498 ft.) Founded on Christmas Day, 1779, Nashville became the state capital in 1843. During the Civil War, the city was held by the Confederate Army, until the Federal forces defeated the Confederates in a decisive battle in 1864. Nashville, called "The Athens of the South" has an exceptionally wide selection of cultural and entertainment facilities. These range from the Parthenon—the world's only full-size reproduction of the Parthenon in Athens, Greece—to the famous Grand Old Opry House, the mecca of country music fans and where the famous broadcasts originated. The Country Music Hall of Fame and Museum is devoted to the history of our native music and the composers and entertainers who contributed to its development. Nashville is also a noted educational center with 13 universities and colleges, including Vanderbilt University, Belmont College, Fisk University and Tennessee State University. The State Capitol is an outstanding example of Greek Revival architecture. The Hermitage, home of President Andrew Jackson, is a beautiful mansion located near Nashville. The home and its lovely garden is maintained as it was when President Jackson and his wife lived there. Nashville produces diversified industrial items and is surrounded by a rich farming area which you will see from the train.

DECATUR, ALA. (Population 38,044, alt. 573 ft.) This city was named for Stephen Decatur, the heroic naval officer of the War of 1812. Wheeler Lake, one of the Tennessee Valley Authority reservoirs, gives Decatur a waterfront that is both industrial and recreational. Wheeler Refuge, a 41,000-acre wildlife preserve, adjoins Decatur. Thousands of waterfowl spend the winter here.

BIRMINGHAM, ALA. (Population 300,910, alt. 565 to 900 ft.) The vast deposits of iron ore, coal and limestone in the Birmingham vicinity were first used by the Confederate Army which made armaments here. Today, Birmingham is the South's greatest steel and iron manufacturing center. It has the largest steel furnaces south of Pittsburgh—two are in the city and eighteen are nearby. Birmingham covers some 15 miles along the rolling Jones Valley which is overlooked by the Red and Shades Mountains. The Vulcan Statue—a 60-ton figure of the god of fire made of Birmingham-produced iron—is the second largest statue in the U.S. It is atop Red Mountain and can be seen from the train.

MONTGOMERY, ALA. (Population 133,386, alt. 191 ft.) The capital of Alabama, Montgomery is called the "Cradle of the Confederacy" because the Articles of Secession were signed here in 1861 and here Jefferson Davis took his oath of office. The handsome Colonial-style Capitol, which dates from 1851, was the Capitol of the Confederacy at the start of the Civil War. Today's Montgomery is an agricultural and livestock center and, due to the development of hydro-electric power, an important manufacturing city. Oddly enough, one of the products made possible by this modern source of power is the manufacture of Victorian furniture.

DOTHAN, ALA. (Population 36,733, alt. 355 ft.) In the 1880's, Dothan was a tough sawmill settlement whose first mayor, it is alleged, resigned after only 24 hours. Today the city is calmer and more colorful. Every spring along Dothan's dogwood-azalea trail the flowers are beautifully in bloom. Peanut growing is an important part of the economy and, each October, there is a week-long National Peanut Festival. Other industries include the manufacture of cigarettes, peanut oil, hosiery and tricycles.

THOMASVILLE, GA. (Population 18,155, alt. 290 ft.) "The city of roses among the pines," Thomasville is noted for its natural beauty and is a favorite winter health resort. The environs of Thomasville boast a number of fine old plantations and estates of historic and architectural interest. There is excellent hunting and fishing in the countryside.

VALDOSTA, GA. (Population 32,303, alt. 220 ft.) Approaching and leaving Valdosta you will see its beautiful setting in south-central Georgia's scenic lake region. Bright-leaf tobacco is grown in this area and the city is a leading market and tobacco auction center. It also has the world's largest inland naval stores market and is the home of Valdosta State College.

WAYCROSS, GA. (Population 18,996, alt. 135 ft.) A railroad and commercial center, Waycross produces items as varied as honey, naval stores, tobacco and furs. South of Waycross is Okefenokee Swamp Park with its multitude of animals, birds and plant life in their natural habitat.

FLORIDIAN 269

JACKSONVILLE, FLA. (Population 528,865, alt. sea level to 140 ft.) refers to itself as the "bold New City of the South," and with good reason. Although it is surrounded by historical and recreational attractions, it is hardly a typical Florida resort. Its strong points are industry and business, and many national firms have their regional offices here. In addition to its cosmopolitan character, there is evident much of the culture and hospitality of the deep South. And there is much to see and do: a variety of entertainment and outdoor sports, theaters, parks, a zoo, art galleries, lovely beaches and sunny skies. And the gamefishing is among the best in the world. The 'Gator Bowl football game is played here in January.

> *From Jacksonville, Amtrak's Florida trains offer two routes: one via Orlando to Tampa-St. Petersburg, and one to Miami via Wildwood. Check your timetable to determine which route your train will follow.*

THE PANAMA LIMITED
CHICAGO-NEW ORLEANS

CHICAGO, ILL. (Population 3,369,359) was named by the Algonquin Indians for the "wild onions" that grew on the site. The city's first permanent cabin was built in 1779 by Jean Baptiste Point du Sable, a black explorer and fur trader. From that start, Chicago grew vigorously and built prodigiously. It had the first skyscraper, eleven stories high, and many of its milestone buildings were designed by the innovative architects Louis Sullivan and Frank Lloyd Wright. Chicago's architectural originality is still apparent in its dramatic new buildings.

While Chicago is called the country's "Second City," it is second to none in tourist interest. Among its many visitor attractions are the Chicago Art Institute, which has impressive French Impressionist and Oriental collections; Shedd Aquarium, first and largest of its kind; Adler Planetarium; and Lincoln Park and Brookfield Zoos. The Museum of Science and Industry is a showcase for space technology, electronics and industry, while the Field Museum of Natural History focuses on advances in anthropology, botany, zoology and geology.

Chicago has forty universities and colleges including University of Chicago, Illinois Institute of Technology, Roosevelt University, University of Illinois, Loyola University, De Paul University and Northwestern University.

Visitors should also know that the term "Windy City" is inaccurate. Actually, Chicago is only the 19th windiest city in the country.

HOLLYWOOD, ILL. (Population 13,371) A suburb of Chicago, Homewood is a convenient suburban station for The Panama Limited, serving the communities of this area.

KANKAKEE, ILL. (Population 30,529) On the banks of the **KANKAKEE RIVER,** the city was formerly a part of Bourbonnais, one of the earliest French settlements in Illinois. Kankakee has numerous old stone buildings and long stretches of stone fences built by pioneers and French Canadians with stones quarried from the riverbed. Close to Kankakee are some of the world's biggest gladiolus fields with a daily harvest of some 150,000 flowers from July to Autumn.

RANTOUL, ILL. (Population 25,377) Named for an officer of the Illinois Central Gulf Railroad, Rantoul is home of the Chanute Air Force Base. The Chanute training center has a yearly graduating class of 28,000 technicians. The Chanute Display Center is open to the public.

CHAMPAIGN, ILL. (Population 55,976); **URBANA, ILL.** (Population 32,624) The main campus of the University of Illinois is divided between these twin cities. The campus has an impressive collection of academic buildings and structures devoted to the arts, including the Krannert Art Museum and the Krannert Center for the Performing Arts, a $21 million complex designed by Max Abramovitz, architect of Lincoln Center in New York. The University of Illinois experimental farm—1,688 acres—adjoins the campus.

MATTOON, ILL. (Population 19,616) Mattoon is surrounded by a rich farming area which grows hybrid Indian corn, wheat, soybeans and broomcorn, which is used in broom manufacture. Industrial products of the city include heavy machinery, precision springs and clothing. Mattoon was named for an officer of the Illinois Central Gulf Railroad.

EFFINGHAM, ILL. (Population 9,360) Effingham was settled by Germans who emigrated to this country after the German Revolution of 1848. The surrounding region is rich farmland, much of it used for dairying. South of Effingham, our train crosses the **LITTLE WABASH RIVER.**

CENTRALIA, ILL. (Population 13,904) Originally settled by Germans, Centralia was named for the Illinois Central Gulf Railroad. Cordwood was used as locomotive fuel until 1855, when the shops at Centralia were the first to successfully use local coal. In 1868 the "Thunderbolt Express," the first refrigerated fruit train, originated in Centralia.

CARBONDALE, ILL. (Population 22,582) Southern Illinois University is in Carbondale, which is also noted for its recreational facilities. The 43,000-acre Crab Orchard National Wildlife Refuge is nearby. It has the state's largest man-made lake. In the center of southern Illinois coal fields, Carbondale is close to oil-producing areas, limestone quarries and forests.

CAIRO, ILL. (Population 6,159) Once a booming riverboat town, Cairo was so named because its site resembles that of Cairo, Egypt. The junction of the **OHIO** and **MISSISSIPPI RIVERS** here separates Illinois, Kentucky and Missouri. As our train glides over the high bridge, you can see far up the Ohio River and south toward the confluence of the Ohio and Mississippi. Just south of the bridge you will see Kentucky (the state you are now in), the southern tip of Illinois, and Missouri—across the river. Cairo is actually farther south than Richmond, Virginia.

FULTON, KY. (Population 3,265) This city, separated by the Kentucky-Tennessee state line, was named in honor of the inventor of the steamboat, Robert Fulton.

DYERSBURG, TENN. (Population 12,499) The main trading center of the cotton-growing bottomlands. South of Dyersburg our train crosses the **FORKED DEER RIVER,** the **HATCHIE RIVER** and the **LOOSAHATCHIE.** To the west are **REELFOOT LAKE** and **OPEN LAKE,** created by the New Madrid earthquake of 1811.

MEMPHIS, TENN. (Population 515,000) The site of Tennessee's largest city was first visited by de Soto in 1541. The French established a fort here in 1739, but the present city was not founded until 1819, with Andrew Jackson one of the founding fathers. The city resembled a brawling river boomtown in its early years, due to the heavy traffic of the great riverboats. Decades later, Beale Street became legendary as the place where W. C. Handy composed his immortal "Beale Street Blues," "Memphis Blues" and "St. Louis Blues." Modern Memphis is a prominent educational and medical center with a number of colleges, universities and 26 hospitals. The city is one of the world's largest cotton markets, and it is estimated that over one-third of the U.S. cotton crop is bought or sold in Memphis every year. The colorful Cotton Carnival is held in Memphis each May.

BATESVILLE, MISS. (Population 3,284) Before reaching Batesville, our train crosses the **COLDWATER** and **TALLAHATCHIE RIVERS.** Batesville is the transportation center for the North Delta cotton area.

GRENADA, MISS. (Population 8,000) Grenada was formed by the merger of two towns, Pittsburg and Tulahoma, in 1836. It is surrounded by a cotton-growing and beef-raising region. The river our train crosses here is the **YALOBUSHA.**

WINONA, MISS. (Population 4,282) An agricultural trading center. Between Winona and Canton, The Panama Limited follows the **BIG BLACK RIVER** for many miles. This is deep in cotton country.

DURANT, MILL. (Population 2,617) A farming center for the rich bottomlands of the **BIG BLACK RIVER.** A large cotton products plant is located in Durant.

CANTON, MISS. (Population 9,707) Canton was originally a town on the Natchez Trace, an early wilderness road. The Trace followed an Indian trail and was used by flatboat men returning from trips downriver. Canton also prospered from cotton, and many fine old homes display this wealth.

272 PANAMA

JACKSON, MISS. (Population 155,000) Originally a trading post, Jackson was a stopping-off place for followers of the old Natchez Trace to the Southwest. In 1821 it was chosen as the site of the state capital and named for Andrew Jackson. The dome of the new capital building may be seen from the east side of the train. Built on a bluff overlooking the **PEARL RIVER**, Jackson—largest city of Mississippi—is a spacious, uncrowded metropolis.

HAZLEHURST, MISS. (Population 3,400) A county seat, Hazlehurst is a shipping center for fruits and vegetables.

BROOKHAVEN, MISS. (Population 9,885) The first creamery in Mississippi was established here in 1907.

McCOMB, MISS. (Population 12,020) Founded by Colonel McComb, president of the New Orleans, Jackson & Northern Railroad (now a part of the Illinois Central Gulf Railroad).

HAMMOND, LA. (Population 12,000) Called the "Strawberry Capital of America," Hammond ships some 850 carloads of strawberries a year throughout the country. The Agri-Dustrial Futurama, held every April, features industrial and agricultural exhibits from the world over.

NEW ORLEANS, LA. (Population 650,000) One of the oldest cities in the country, New Orleans was founded in 1718 by Sieur de Bienville, the French governor, and named for the Duke of Orleans. In 1803 the city was acquired by the U.S. as part of the Louisiana Purchase.

Today New Orleans is a picturesque combination of old-world charm and modern progress. Famed for its spectacular Mardi Gras, the romantic French Quarter, classic jazz, lively Bourbon Street nightclubs, the lovely Garden District and super restaurants serving Creole cuisine, New Orleans is a fascinating place to visit. The flavor of old New Orleans can be captured in the Bayou Tour—a forty-mile excursion on the *Mark Twain*, a replica of an oldtime sternwheeler.

THE SUNSET LIMITED
LOS ANGELES-NEW ORLEANS

NEW ORLEANS, LA.
Creole country, land of the Mardi Gras, birthplace of Dixieland jazz, a parcel of Old World in the New, with the famous French Quarter one of the nation's leading tourist attractions. Founded by Sieur de Bienville, the French governor, in 1718 and named after the Duke of Orleans, New Orleans joined the United States in 1803 as part of the Louisiana Purchase, known around the country as "Jefferson's Folly." It's difficult to think of New Orleans commercially, but the city is, nevertheless, one of the largest ports and distribution centers in the United States, an important marketing area for cotton, oil, salt, sulphur, natural gas, agriculture and forest products. The New Orleans "tourist season" starts with the classic Sugar Bowl college football championship game on New Year's Day, and is followed by Mardi Gras, a 2-week carnival in late March or early April. Modern New Orleans, a city of wide thoroughfares, is lined with tall buildings, surrounded by magnificent mansions. The Vieux Carre, famous French Quarter, covers about 70 city blocks—a melange of quaint, narrow streets lined with wrought-iron-balconied houses. Rue Royal is still the main street with fashionable antique and boutique shops, restaurants and cafes. The French Quarter includes Beauregard Square, where slaves once danced; the Cabildo, which was the old Governor's Palace; Casa Hove, one of the oldest buildings in New Orleans; the New Orleans Jazz Museum; and Jackson Square, where artists congregate just as they do behind Sacre Coeur in Paris. One of the country's best bargains in sightseeing is a scenic ride on the St. Charles streetcar line, which passes through some of the city's most lovely residential areas. New Orleans streetcars, built in 1923-24, are the last conventional cars operating in regular service in the United States and Canada, and have been immaculately maintained over the years. Ten miles west of New Orleans, our train crosses the mighty **MISSISSIPPI** via the Huey P. Long Bridge. Including approaches, the bridge is 4.4 miles long and extends 3,524 feet across the river.

After crossing the bridge you will see native flora so characteristic of this bayou and lowland area, including bald cypress trees, water hyacinths and Spanish moss. Des Allemands, 33 miles west of New Orleans, is a quaint old settlement founded in colonial days. The community is situated on the banks of Des Allemands Bayou, whose waters empty into Barataria Bay, an inlet of the Gulf of Mexico, onetime haunt of Jean Lafitte and his pirate crew.

NEW IBERIA, LA. (Population 30,147, alt. 21 ft.) is known locally as the "sugar bowl." Sugar mills dot the skyline around Lafourche where, from your train window, you will catch glimpses through the magnolia trees of the planters' homes, all built to face the bayous, which were the only highways before the advent of the railroad. Further west, your train passes the Chacahoula Swamp just beyond Schriever. This area, abounding with fur-bearing animals, is a popular resort for trappers. Just before reaching New Iberia, the railroad follows the high south bank of Bayou Teche through thick canefields and small woodlands. Bayou Teche is the locale for much Teche country literature, including Longfellow's "Evangeline." Approximately ten miles south of New Iberia is Avery Island, site of Edward Avery McIlhenny's famous bird sanctuary and home of the famous Tabasco Sauce factory.

Between **LAFAYETTE** (Population 40,400, alt. 39 ft.) and **LAKE CHARLES, LA.** (Population 63,392, alt. 16 ft.), your train passes through a succession of rice fields, and you will see many mills at Crowley. You are approaching oil country and in the distance you can see the derricks of the Welsh oil field. McNeese State College is located in Lake Charles. West of the city, your train crosses the **CALCASIEU RIVER,** once a popular outpost for smugglers when the region between here and the Sabine River was neutral land, belonging neither to Mexico nor the United States. Derricks of the Vinton Oil Field are visible about a mile from Sulphur. Your train then crosses the **SABINE RIVER** at Orange and you are now in Texas, the "Lone Star State." Orange is located on a deepwater port connected with the Gulf of Mexico by the Sabine-Neches Waterway. Pirate Jean Lafitte haunted nearby swamps and bayous.

BEAUMONT, TEX. (Population 115,716, alt. 22 ft.) is where the first of the Texas wells was to gush with happy news: OIL! Spindletop Monument now marks the site of the Lucas Gusher. Your train crosses the **NECHES RIVER** to enter Beaumont, seat of Jefferson County. Situated on a deepwater channel, Beaumont is a shipping center supplying materials to major cities in the north, east and west. There is also a major ship and barge building industry here, and Beaumont, together with the surrounding communities, forms the largest concentration of oil refineries in the country. The Babe Zaharias Golf Tournament is held here annually. Your route from Beaumont to Houston passes through some of the country's most important oil fields. At Dayton, the derricks of the North Dayton oil fields may be seen from your train. And further west, you can see the Esperson oil fields to the south.

HOUSTON, TEX. (Population 1,800,000, alt. 47 ft.), fastest growing metropolitan center in the United States, is best known now for NASA's Manned Spacecraft Center at Clear Lake. It's difficult to remember that the city's first claim to fame was cotton. Named for Sam Houston, hero of the Battle of San Jacinto in which Texas won its independence from Mexico, Houston became the state's first capital city. Much of Houston's pre-space-age growth can be attributed to the building of the Houston Ship Channel, turning the city that is situated 50 miles inland from the coast into a major seaport. And just to add to the city's wealth, the Gulf

Coast heaped oil upon the landowners. But don't think that the ranchers have been replaced. Mechanization has invaded the prairie but Houston retains a touch of the Wild West in spirit and character. Although the cowboy is very much alive and well and still living in Houston, he's become cultured. The city has eight institutions of higher learning, is a medical, teaching, research and treatment center, and a music center featuring symphony, opera, jazz, ballet. And Houston is home of the famous Astrodome and Astroworld.

Between Houston and San Antonio, your train passes through Sugarland where a sugarcane factory may be seen from the train. Plainly visible from your train window, too, are the derricks of the De Walt oil field at Columbus. The **COLORADO RIVER** curves about the city like a horseshoe and flows under your train just east of the town.

SAN ANTONIO, TEX. (Population 650,188, alt. 661 ft.) is where you will remember the Alamo! The Spanish Conquistadores were the first to come to San Antonio, followed by the Mexicans. It's one of the prettiest American cities, with adobe houses and modern skyscrapers creating curious contrast. This is where Teddy Roosevelt's Rough Riders were assembled. And it's where Davy Crockett and Jim Bowie died. The Paseo del Rio (River Walk) is still the place where couples stroll hand in hand; it's a tree-lined river promenade, alive with tropical foliage, lined with shops, restaurants and night spots. As your train leaves San Antonio, you will pass through the villages of Lacoste, Noonan and Dunlay to Hondo, where the old Comanche Indian villages were once located. Further west, the Sunset Limited crosses the **NUECES RIVER** where pecans grow along the banks.

DEL RIO, TEX. (Population 20,928, alt. 964 ft.) might well be called the "water works" of America's second largest state. More than 70 million gallons of water flow daily from San Felipe Springs. The water is for irrigation as well as domestic use. Del Rio is one of the world's largest shipping points for wool and mohair. This is the home of the original blue jeans. Laughlin Air Force Base is just a few miles away.

Fourteen miles west of Del Rio, your train crosses **DEVIL'S RIVER,** one of the clearest streams in the world. Below the bridge you can see **AMISTAD (FRIENDSHIP) DAM,** a joint project of the United States and Mexico which has harnessed over 5 million acre-feet of water. As your train proceeds west from Del Rio, the scenery will change. The climate is drier. There are few trees, and sagebrush and similar cactus-like flora dot the countryside. This is sheep and goat grazing land. About 50 miles west of Del Rio, the Sunset Limited crosses the **PECOS RIVER** over the 1,390-ft. Pecos River High Bridge, 321 feet above the water, which flows through a deep canyon below.

Fifteen miles west of the Pecos River High Bridge our train passes through Langtry, a small trading and shipping community, famous as headquarters for "Judge" Roy Bean. "Judge" Bean dispensed liquor and supplies and acted as the "Law west of the Pecos" during the frontier days when no legitimate law courts existed in this area. He changed the name of the settlement from Vinegarroon to Langtry in honor of the actress Lillie Langtry, and had high expectations that she would visit the place. Some years later, on her way east, she stopped over to inspect her namesake; meanwhile, the autocratic old judge had died.

SANDERSON, (Population 1,229, alt. 1,397 ft.) is a shipping center for wool and mohair, and has both an oil and gas refinery and an agriculture industry. Sanderson is in goat country, but even the sheep roam free. In the region southwest of Sanderson and south of Alpine, the **RIO GRANDE** flows south to Big Bend country which once harbored outlaws who smuggled cattle across the river. The Apache Lipans lived here. One of the most remarkable plants to grow in this area is the Resurrection Plant, which, when dry, rolls itself into a ball and, when wet, stretches out into a mass of fernlike fronds. Many of these plants are sold as curiosity souvenirs. The trompillo, a common weed in this area with violet flowers and a small, black marble-like berry, is used by the Mexicans for curdling milk for cheese. Flourishing here, too, is the peyote, a small, low, radish-shaped cactus whose greenish berry—called "white whiskey"—was chewed by the Indians for its mildly intoxicating effect.

ALPINE, TEX. (Population 5,811, alt. 4,484 ft.) is home to the Highland Hereford. As we approach the cow town, we can see the Del Norte Mountains and the Glass Mountains at a distance. Sul Ross State University is in the city with the Museum of Big Bend on the campus. Alpine was born as a result of the building of the Southern Pacific Railroad. Texas Rangers were sent to protect the railroad builders from the Indians who were not happy about the coming of the Iron Horse. A hill, just a mile northeast of Alpine Station, was the scene of an Apache Indian raid in which a caravan of 40 freight wagons was surrounded. One man, slipping away to the army post at Presidio 100 miles off, succeeded in sending forces to the rescue. Alpine is Amtrak's gateway to Big Bend National Park, 75 miles south.

Thirteen miles west is Paisano Pass (alt. 5,074 ft.), highest point on the route of Amtrak's Sunset Limited. To the north is Toronto Mountain (5,350 ft.) and to the south is the summit of Paisano Peak (5,750 ft.). Yuccas, abundant flora in this area, extend far to the west. Before reaching El Paso, our train passes through some interesting mountain country. 4½ miles west of Marfa, you can see the McDonald Observatory on the right. It's the second largest in the country. About 15 miles west of Sierra Blanca, the train drops down into a small valley which, in prehistoric times, was the bed of a lake. Continuing westward, the Sunset Limited passes Fort Hancock and the ruins of the fort, a former frontier post which guarded the mail near the banks of the Rio Grande. The bluffs on the Mexican side of the river are beautifully marked by weathered crystalline strata.

As you approach El Paso, the south end of Hueco Mountain is visible from the train. At Clint, where the tracks parallel fields of alfalfa, a large irrigation ditch runs along the train route for several miles.

Time changes from Central to Mountain time just east of El Paso, so set your watch back one hour, going west ... ahead one hour, going east.

EL PASO, TEX. (Population 317,462, alt. 3,719 ft.) is a principal gateway to old Mexico and adjacent to its sister city Ciudad Juarez, Mexico. El Paso means "passage." The city is truly bilingual with signs, sounds and street names in Spanish and English. El Paso's endless summer makes it a popular winter resort. It's the scene of the Sun Carnival during the last week of the year, culminating in the annual New Year's Day Sun Bowl football game, the Sun Carnival basketball game and, of course, the crowning of the Sun Carnival Queen. Ft. Bliss, the U.S. Army Air Defense Center, is at the northeast edge of the city and missile firings may be viewed by visitors. The Ft. Bliss Museum contains U.S. Cavalry and early infantry exhibits, showing how the West was won, or at least how the routes to the West were surveyed. Excellent views of the city may be had from the Aerial Tramway, a 5,622-ft. ride to the top of Mount Franklin's Rangers Peak. El Paso is home of the University of Texas, and is Amtrak's gateway to Carlsbad Caverns National Park. Just outside of El Paso, our train crosses the **RIO GRANDE,** entering New Mexico. Three miles west of El Paso, you will be able to see "The Christ of the Rockies," a statue of Christ on the Cross on the 4,756-ft. Sierra de Cristo Rey mountain peak. The Cross, standing on a 9-ft. base, is 33½ ft. wide, supporting a 27-ft.-high statue of Christ. It is the largest monument of its kind in America and commemorates the 19th centennial of the Redemption.

Seven miles west of El Paso is Anapra, junction point where Southern Pacific's former South Line diverged from our route to skirt the Mexican border, passing through the settlements of Hachita, Rodeo, Bernardino and Douglas. Travelers will also remember passing through the cattle-country town of Columbus, noted in history as the scene of a 1916 raid by the Mexican outlaw Pancho Villa, who used a hill west of the depot as an emplacement for his machine guns. This line, formerly a portion of the El Paso and Southwestern Railroad, rejoined our line at Mescal, nine miles west of Benson. Only the Benson Jct.-Douglas portion of the South Line remains in freight service today.

DEMING, N. MEX. (Population 6,764, alt. 4,330 ft.) is rock country where agate, jasper and carnelian attract the serious miners. This is the rich cattle and farming area of the Mimbres Valley. Cotton, feed grain and livestock are the principal products. Thirty-two miles west of Deming, our train crosses the Continental Divide separating the Atlantic and Pacific watersheds at an elevation of 4,587½ ft. This is the lowest railroad crossing of the Continental Divide in the United States.

LORDSBURG, N. MEX. (Population 3,429 ft., alt. 4,249 ft.) is a railroad crew change and mining town in Hidalgo County where green patches of farmland vie with copper and silver mines for their share of territory. To the south you can see the Pyramid Mountains, rich with silver, copper and gold deposits. Seventy miles north at Morenci are extensive Phelps Dodge copper mines.

As your train crosses the border into Arizona, it becomes obvious that we've entered wild country; even the mountain peaks have a more rugged quality. On the crest of Chiricahua Mountains near San Simon, you may see a remarkable rock formation, called "Cochise Head" because of its unmistakable likeness for the fierce Apache chief. Continuing on, six miles west of Willcox we pass the dry bed of an ancient lake famous for mirages under the right atmospheric conditions. Frequently, passengers get the feeling that the train is rolling along near a body of water.

TUCSON, ARIZ. (Population 236,877, alt. 2,386 ft.) is one of America's favorite health spas. The reason is summed up in sunshine... lots of it, all the year round. Tucson, surrounded by mountains, has grown with the tourist in mind, offering facilities including modern hotels, dude ranches, mountains, lodges and camping grounds. The largest industry is Howard Hughes; his aircraft company is the city's major employer. Tucson, on the banks of the **SANTA CRUZ RIVER,** is one of the West's oldest Spanish settlements. It was founded in 1692 by a Jesuit priest, and it retains its Spanish character even as it grows modern. In 1776, Mexicans sought refuge in the Indian village protected by adobe walls. Back in 1880 when the Apaches were still on the warpath here, the old Pueblo's 2,000 inhabitants greeted the track builders as they reached Tucson with a 38-gun salute and a cavalry band playing a medley of patriotic songs. As the construction crews continued east from Tucson, they were protected by military escort. The University of Arizona is in Tucson and the Cleveland Indians have their winter training here. Papago Indian Reservation is nearby. Tucson Mountain Park, covering more than 30,000 acres of natural desert growth, is a state game preserve.

Between Tucson and Phoenix, just seven miles west of Red Rock, your train passes Picacho Peak, a large butte to the south rising abruptly from the desert floor. Beginning here and continuing west for five miles, one of the finest natural cactus gardens in Arizona, the Picacho Peak Sahuaro Forest, extends along the south side of the track. And seven miles further west, a stone monument just south of the railroad tracks marks the scene of the only battle fought in Arizona between Union and Confederate forces during the Civil War.

PHOENIX, ARIZ. (Population 505,666, alt. 1,084 ft.) Fertile fields in a desert land—an oasis—as much a sign of immortality as the bird after whom it is named. It was the prehistoric Indians who first settled in Phoenix and brought their ingenious irrigation methods with them. The Hohokam Indians were farmers and "artists" who etched canals into the arid earth and brought life to the desert sands. They came. They flourished. They disappeared, like the symbolic Egyptian phoenix which consumes itself every 500 years and then rises from its own ashes. The first white settlers arrived in 1860, attracted by the Indian canals, and a civilization was reborn just as Egyptian myth predicted.

Phoenix is Arizona's capital city, near the Roosevelt Dam which has made the fields greener—ripe for olives, citrus fruits and dates. When Arizona became the 48th state in 1912, the State Capitol was erected out of native stones. The State's Museum housed in the Capitol Building contains exhibits of prehistoric Indian cultures, modern Indian crafts and historical documents. Frank Lloyd Wright left his strongest imprint here; you'll see it in the uninhibited architecture around the city. Taliesin West, housing Wright's architectural school and office, is open to the public. The healthy climate makes this a popular winter resort. The Phoenix Thunderbird PGA Open Golf Tournament is held here in February. Sixteen miles west of Phoenix, our train crosses the **AGUA FRIA RIVER** before passing the town of Litchfield, where a U.S. Naval Air Facility is located. Here, a considerable area of desert land has been reclaimed by irrigation. Between Phoenix and Yuma, our train passes through the agricultural communities of Litchfield, Buckeye and Wellton.

YUMA, ARIZ. (Population 28,005, alt. 147 ft.) is named for the Yuma Indians who inhabited the area before the white man's arrival. The sand dunes west of Yuma are probably the most photographed in the world; Hollywood shoots desert scenes here. The dunes may be seen from your train after we cross the **COLORADO RIVER.** Francisco Garces, who founded two missions in Yuma, was massacred along with the colonists during the last Indian uprising in 1781. His statue stands in the gardens of the Catholic Indian Mission, erected on the site of the massacre. The Fort Yuma Indian Reservation is on the west bank of the Colorado River. To the north, at the edge of the river, is the Old Territorial Prison of frontier days. The All-American Canal near Yuma irrigates much of California's Imperial and Coachella Valleys. Today, the city is a popular winter resort with fishing and boating on the Colorado River, which serves as the border between Arizona and California.

The time changes from Mountain to Pacific time here, so set your watch back one hour, going west ... ahead one hour, going east.

Sixty-six miles west of Yuma is Niland. To the north, extending from Yuma to Niland, are the Chocolate Mountains. Leaving Niland, the Sunset Limited speeds west past the Salton Sea (alt. 231 ft. below sea level), the lowest point on your trip between New Orleans and Los Angeles. Twenty-nine miles west of Niland is a valley which, in prehistoric times, was the bed of a vast inland sea whose waters rose up the sides of Mt. San Jacinto to the south. At Mecca our train enters the Coachella Valley, irrigated by artesian wells which tap water flowing from the San Jacinto Mountains two miles above the level of the valley.

INDIO, CALIF. (Population 14,361, alt. 22 ft. below sea level) is date land, and is located in the Coachella Valley. The National Date Festival takes place here in mid-February, featuring camel races and horse shows. This is the Amtrak Station for nearby Palm Springs. Leaving Indio your train climbs from the desert almost to the summit of San Gorgonio Pass, gateway to Southern California. Along with Mt. San Jacinto (10,805 ft.) to the south and Mt. San Antonio (10,080 ft.) to the west, these are the highest peaks in Southern California. From Banning we move on into cherry country, and in spring, when the blossoms bloom, thousands travel to Beaumont to see them. From Beaumont the grade descends through San Timoteo Canyon. Cherries give way to oranges at Redland until finally, at Bloomington, your train enters an area of vast vineyards bordered on the north by a huge steel plant. To the south of Guasti are the San Gabriel Mountains.

POMONA, CALIF. (Population 87,384, alt. 855 ft.), named after the Roman Goddess of Fruit, gets its fame from the Los Angeles County Fair held here mid-September to early October. More than a million visitors come to Pomona each year for the festivities. Oranges and lemons are Pomona's principal products. Arabian horses are raised and trained at the Kellogg Campus of California State Polytechnic College, where Arabian Horse Shows are held throughout the year. At Padua Hills Theatre, Mexican actors perform traditional Californian and Mexican plays. Mount Baldy, a winter skiing and recreational area, is located 15 miles north of here.

ALHAMBRA, CALIF. (Population 62,125, alt. 455 ft.), incorporated in 1903, is part of the big, sprawling megalopolis of Los Angeles. Alhambra is a gateway to Pasadena and the San Gabriel Valley. At San Gabriel, north of our track, is San Gabriel mission, founded in 1771.

LOS ANGELES, CALIF. (Population 2,816,061, alt. 297 ft.) is not a city in the conventional sense. Los Angeles is Hollywood, Beverly Hills, Burbank, Culver City, Glendale, Inglewood, Pasadena, Santa Monica and Malibu. It was founded in 1781 by Felipe de Neve as the "Village of our Lady, Queen of the Angels" and was the last town to surrender to the United States in 1847. Los Angeles is movieland and, although the great Hollywood days may be over, still more than two-thirds of the world's motion pictures are produced here. Los Angeles's earliest growth was largely due to the citrus industry which today is in evidence mostly in private back yards. It is now an oil refinery center and the city has attracted both light and heavy industry. Great views of the city may be seen from on top of the Civic Center.

THE SOUTHWEST LIMITED
CHICAGO-LOS ANGELES

Algonquin Indians named **CHICAGO, ILL.** (Population 3,369,359, alt. 590 ft.) for the "wild onions" that grew on the site. The city's first permanent cabin was built in 1779 by Jean Baptiste Point du Sable, a black explorer and fur trader. Many of Chicago's traditional images are inaccurate: the "windy city" is actually the 19th windiest in the country and, although it is the second largest U.S. city, 19% of Chicago is park or playground. Chicago had the country's first skyscraper, 11 stories high. Many buildings were designed by Louis Sullivan and Frank Lloyd Wright. The nation's center of industrial distribution and transportation, Chicago has a buying income 24% above national average.

JOLIET, ILL. (Population 78,817, alt. 541 ft.) is a growing community located in the Des Plaines River Valley, 39 miles southwest of Chicago. The city was first known as "Stone City" because a large number of its buildings were made of limestone. Later it was named for Louis Joliet, famous French-Canadian explorer who visited the area in 1673. Today Joliet has 337 manufacturing industries producing more than 1,800 different items. St. Francis College and Lewis College are located in Joliet.

STREATOR, ILL. (Population 15,600, alt. 625 ft.), named for early industrialist Dr. Streator, is the glass container capital of the world.

East of Chillicothe the **ILLINOIS RIVER** is crossed.

Eastern pioneers came to **GALESBURG, ILL.** (Population 36,290, alt. 781 ft.) to establish a community centering around a college for the training of ministers. The town was named for its leader, G. W. Gale. In 1858 Knox College was scene of one of the Lincoln-Douglas debates. Birthplace of Carl Sandburg, poet and biographer of Lincoln, Galesburg was once selected by noted editor and author Edward Bok as one of the four ideal American cities.

West of Galesburg the **MISSISSIPPI RIVER,** boundary between Illinois and Iowa, is crossed. The Mississippi is crossed on a 24-span steel bridge, 3,347 feet long. The bridge has the longest and heaviest swing span ever built and is double-decked to accommodate both vehicle and rail traffic.

FT. MADISON, IOWA (Population 13,996, alt. 524 ft.), first outpost west of the Mississippi River, was built in 1808. It was twice taken by Indians and in 1813 was burned by defending soldiers when they were forced to abandon it. Today Ft. Madison is a thriving community known for its Tri-State Rodeo held in late summer and featuring top contestants and well-known personalities.

282 SOUTHWEST

KANSAS CITY, MO. (Population 507,087, alt. 804 ft.) was named for the Kansas Indians (also called Kaw), a Sioux tribe that originally lived at the junction of the Missouri and Kansas Rivers. The name means "South Wind People." Kansas City, once the beginning point on the Santa Fe Trail, owed its own beginnings to fur trade and steamboat transportation on the Missouri River. Today Lewis and Clark Point and the Kersey Coates Parkway offer a panoramic view of the area which was the principal crossing of the Big Missouri River for pioneers starting west.

Culturally, Kansas City has much to offer. Linda Hall Library of Science and Technology is second only to Harvard in the scope of its reference materials; William Rockhill Nelson Gallery of Art is outstanding in the Chinese field; and Kansas City Museum offers exhibits on regional history, anthropology, natural history and North American Indian cultures. Harry S. Truman Library and his home, once known as the "Summer White House," are located in nearby Independence, Mo. Other historical sites include Loose Memorial Park, site of the Battle of Westport (first major Civil War engagement); Old Independence Courthouse, oldest courthouse west of the Mississippi; and a Kansas City jail which held Frank James in 1859.

Excelsior Springs, Missouri, famous mineral spa, is a thirty-five minute drive from Kansas City. Often called the "city of beautiful homes," Kansas City is home to fifteen colleges including University of Missouri at Kansas City, Kansas City Art Institute, Rockhurst College and University of Kansas Medical Center.

EMPORIA, KAN. (Population 23,327, alt. 1,138 ft.) is a cattle, manufacturing, trade and transportation center. Emporia, from the Latin meaning "a place to trade," was named after a historic market center on the African coast of the Mediterranean Sea. Home of William Allen White, editor of the "Emporia Gazette" and famous for editorials such as "What's the Matter With Kansas?". Kansas State Teachers College of Emporia and College of Emporia are both here.

NEWTON, KAN. (Population 15,439, alt. 1,439 ft.) was settled by Mennonites from southern Russia and named after Newton, Massachusetts. In 1893 Bethel College, first Mennonite college in the U.S., was founded. Points of interest in Newton include Bethel College Art Gallery; Mennonite Monument; Harvey County Park; and Warkentin House, restored home of Bernard Warkentin, pioneer and Mennonite leader.

HUTCHINSON, KAN. (Population 36,885, alt. 1,530 ft.), fifth largest city in the state, was named for C.C. Hutchinson, Baptist preacher and Indian agent. Truly the heart of the wheat belt, Hutchinson is located in the largest wheat-producing county in Kansas, the state which leads the U.S. in number of bushels harvested. Salt mining and refining is a second important industry.

A cowboy statue standing on Boot Hill symbolized **DODGE CITY, KANSAS's** (Population 14,127, alt. 2,479 ft.) infamous past. From 1875-1887 Dodge City was the world's largest cattle market and the "wickedest little city in America."

Wyatt Earp, Bat Masterson, "Doc" Holliday and H. B. "Ham" Bell were among those who tried to "clean 'er up."

Formerly old Fort Dodge, the site was selected by General Grenville Dodge as a protection point for the Santa Fe Trail. Today Dodge City carefully preserves traces of its notorious past. Front Street (visible from the train—right side going west) has been reproduced as it was in 1872, the height of its vice and violence. Long Branch Gambling Room features the original gambling devices; old Fort Dodge jail has been grimly standing since 1864, and visitors can actually order a glass of Sarsaparilla in the Long Branch Saloon. Boot Hill overlooks the city; its Hangman's Tree exacted justice on at least three horse thieves. Dodge City even re-enacts a gun fight each evening at 8 o'clock. Home of St. Mary of the Plains College.

Set your watches at Dodge City for the time change between Central and Mountain Times. One hour backward, going west; one hour forward, going east.

GARDEN CITY, KAN. (Population 14,790, alt. 2,830 ft.) has a lot to brag about. It is the world's largest known gas field; largest irrigation area in the Midwest with unlimited supply of underground water; home of the largest Kansas zoo, buffalo herd in the Midwest and grain elevator in the world.

LAMAR, COLO. (Population 7,797, alt. 3,603 ft.) is retail trade and wholesale headquarters for tri-state area of southeastern Colorado, western Kansas and the Oklahoma panhandle. Besides its strategic geographic location, Lamar enjoys sunshine over 95% of the year.

Madonna of the Trail may be seen from the train. It is one of twelve DAR monuments marking National Old Trails. "Big Timbers," twenty miles of cottonwood trees along the Arkansas River north and west of Lamar, was once a refuge for Indians of the Plains, Cheyennes, Comanches, Arapahoes, Kiowas, and other tribes. Bent's New Fort, most famous trading post in Colorado, was located ten miles west of Lamar. Home of Lamar Community College and the Sand and Sage Roundup.

LA JUNTA, COLO. (Population 7,938, alt. 4,045 ft.), meaning "where the trail divides," is the center of a fertile farm section producing onions, melons, sugar beets, potatoes, alfalfa, hay and many other crops under large irrigation systems. Eight miles east of La Junta are the remains of Bent's Old Fort, fur trading post, Indian rendezvous and way station on the Santa Fe Trail. From 1833 to 1849 Bent's Old Fort was the chief point of contact between white men and the South Plains Indians. Kit Carson was once employed at the fort. Home of Otero Junior College and the famous Koshare Indian dancers.

RATON PASS, at 7,588 feet, is the highest point on our route. Located on the Colorado-New Mexico state line, this pass has been famous in the history of the West from the early days of the explorers and covered wagon caravans. The Colorado-New Mexico state line is crossed only a few feet before entering the one-half-mile-long tunnel built at the top of the pass.

284 SOUTHWEST

RATON, N.M. (Population 6,692, alt. 6,666 ft.), located at the base of Sangre de Cristo Mountains, is gateway to Cimarron Valley, Taos Indian pueblo, Taos Ski Valley, Red River Ski Area, Philmont Scout Ranch and Capulin National Monument. A summer chairlift to the top of Raton Pass offers a fantastic view of the surrounding countryside. Home of Kaleidoscope Players, national touring theatre company.

LAS VEGAS, N.M. (Population 13,835, alt. 6,392 ft.) is a stock-raising, fruit-growing and dairying town. A scenic highway from Gallinas Canyon to El Porvenir passes historic Montezuma Hotel, now a seminary, and other points in this recreational area of Santa Fe National Forest. Hermit's Peak, 10,500 ft., is 18 miles away with numerous guest ranches. Home of the New Mexico Highlands University and scene of Teddy Roosevelt Rough Rider's Association Reunion.

Passengers change at **LAMY, N.M.** *(Population 195, alt. 6,457 ft.) for Santa Fe, capital of New Mexico and oldest city of Southwest.*

ALBUQUERQUE, N.M. (Population 243,751, alt. 5,196 ft.), named for the Duke of Albuquerque, Viceroy of New Spain from 1702-17, is the oldest metropolitan city west of the Mississippi. At an elevation of 5,314 ft., it is also the highest metropolitan city. The original townsite of 1706 known as "Old Town" continues to hold its traditional fiestas and religious ceremonies. The Old Town Church of San Felipe de Neri has been offering Mass every Sunday since 1706.

Albuquerque has been aptly called "gateway city to the land of enchantment." It is located in the fertile Rio Grande valley; east and west are great mesas and towering mountains. To the east the Sandias rise 10,678 ft. at the crest. Sandia means watermelon. Every evening at sundown the mountains turn a breathtaking watermelon pink. To the north and south of Albuquerque are more mountains and northwest of the city are five extinct volcano cones.

Albuquerque is New Mexico's largest commercial center. It is a young city—the median age of its residents is 23. Sun shines virtually every day of the year and temperatures range from 46.4 to 91.2 degrees.

Albuquerque is home to the University of Albuquerque and the University of New Mexico, which is known for its outstanding exhibits of ancient Southwest Indian heritage. Albuquerque has its own symphony orchestra, and the Santa Fe Opera, with its lovely outdoor setting, is only an hour's drive away. The city hosts the New Mexico Arts and Crafts Fair, one of the largest gatherings of Southwest artists, and the New Mexico State Fair.

More than half the population of **GALLUP, N.M.** (Population 13,779, alt. 6,506 ft.) are American Indians of the Navajo, Zuni and Hopi tribes. Historically, the city has been an Indian trading center; today it continues to be the primary trade center for 1,580 square miles in northwest New Mexico and northeast Arizona.

Zuni Pueblo, only surviving pueblo of the Zuni Indians, is 38 miles south. In early December the Zuni hold their most famous ceremony, the Shalako.

SOUTHWEST 285

Mesa Verde National Park, 165 miles north, is site of the finest cliff dwellings in the U.S. Canyon de Chelly National monument was also home to the cliff dwellers; they left their paintings, many still visible, as a record. "Basket Makers" have left traces here from 2,000 B.C. Considered one of the seven wonders of the Navajo world, Canyon de Chelly was scene in 1863 of the last stand of the Navajo against Kit Carson and his troops.

To the northeast is Chaco Canyon National Monument, among the largest pueblos in the Southwest and most extensive surface ruins in the U.S. Nature has chiseled magnificent mesas in Monument Valley, part of the great Colorado plateau and home to many tribes for centuries.

WINSLOW, ARIZ. (Population 8,066, alt. 4,850 ft.) is known as "The Meteor City" because of Meteor Mountains 23 miles west of the city. Directly north is Navajo country and several Hopi Indian villages continuously inhabited for more than 1,000 years. About 40 miles south, in the country made famous by Zane Grey, is the largest stand of Ponderosa Pine in the nation. Painted Desert is 52 miles northeast.

In 1876, F. F. McMillan stripped a tall pine tree, tied an American flag to it and gave the town of **FLAGSTAFF, ARIZ.** (Population 26,117, alt. 6,092 ft.) its name. Today Flagstaff is noted for commercial, lumbering, cattle and tourist interests. During the Southwest Indian Pow Wow, 4th-of-July weekend, the city hosts 20 tribal nations.

Lowell Observatory, one of the foremost astronomical observatories in the country, is located on a mountain one mile west. Planet Pluto was discovered there in 1930.

Oak Creek Canyon, considered one of Arizona's most beautiful canyons, inspired Zane Grey's "Call of the Canyon." Arizona Snow Bowl, 15 miles northwest in the San Francisco Peaks, offers a breathtaking view of five states and the Grand Canyon. Museum of Northern Arizona and Pioneers Historical Museum are located in Flagstaff. Antelope, elk, buffalo and other animals roam free in Buffalo Park. This 217-acre forest can be toured via stagecoach or car. Home of Northern Arizona University.

Motorcoach connections at Flagstaff for Grand Canyon National Park.

KINGMAN, ARIZ. (Population 7,312, alt. 3,335 ft.) is shipping, shopping and recreation center for a large area of northwest Arizona. Scene of year-round boating, water-skiing, swimming and fishing. Gateway to Hoover Dam.

Set your watch at Kingman for the change between Mountain and Pacific zones. One hour backward, going west; one hour forward, going east.

NEEDLES, CAL. (Population 4,051, alt. 484 ft.), one of the oldest towns on the Mojave Desert, was named for a series of pinnacles which rise abruptly out of the surrounding landscape. A supply center for miners, ranchers, hunters and fishermen, the city is located close to Havasu National Wildlife Refuge and Mitchell Caverns, state reserve.

East of Needles, the **COLORADO RIVER** *is crossed.*

286 SOUTHWEST

BARSTOW, CAL. (Population 17,442, alt. 2,105 ft.) was named in 1886 for William Barstow Strong, president of Santa Fe Railroad. The town took his middle name because of Strong City, Kansas.

This is "high desert" country where evaporation exceeds precipitation; the sun shines virtually all the time and mountains glow with mineral stains. Once Barstow was a desert junction for overland wagon trains and an outfitting station for Death Valley expeditions. Nearby Calico, a booming "silver city" from 1881-1896, was restored in 1950. Lil's Saloon houses an interesting collection of "Gunslingers of the Old West" by Lea Franklin McCarty.

SAN BERNARDINO, CAL. (Population 104,251, alt. 1,046 ft.) was discovered by missionaries in 1810 on the feast of San Bernardino de Siena. Located amid deserts, valleys and mountains, the city enjoys a vast citrus industry. National Orange Show, held since 1915, marks the completion of the winter citrus crop harvest with rodeos, fiestas and sports events. Rim o' the World Highway, a 45-mile scenic mountain road, leads to Big Bear Lake, Snow Summit, Rung Springs, Lake Arrowhead, and Blue Jay and Sky Forests. The highway, varying in altitude from 4,000-7,000 ft., offers a superb view particularly from Lakeview Point. Blue Ridge and Holiday Hill ski areas are 20 miles north of San Bernardino. Home of California State College at San Bernardino.

In 1875 Solomon Gates won a free lot when he named the city of **POMONA, CAL.** (Population 87,384, alt. 860 ft.) after the Roman Goddess of Fruit. The name was appropriate; today oranges and lemons are still among the city's primary products. Since 1922 Pomona has hosted the Los Angeles County Fair, boasting the largest buildings and attendance (over one million) of any fair in the U.S. Also of interest are the Arabian Horse Shows held on Kellogg Campus of the California State Polytechnic College, and Padua Hills Theatre, where Mexican actors and singers perform in traditional Californian and Mexican plays. Fifteen miles north is the Mount Baldy ski area. California State Polytechnic College and Mt. San Antonia College are located in Pomona. The Claremont Colleges are located in nearby Claremont.

PASADENA, CAL. (Population 113,327, alt. 700 to 1,200 ft.), from a Chippewa Indian word meaning "crown of the valley," is a noted winter resort and one of southern California's most attractive communities. It is famous for the Pasadena Rose Tournament held New Year's Day and Pasadena Playhouse College of Theatre Arts, often called the "back door" to Hollywood. Other attractions include the noted Huntington Library and Art Gallery, Carnegie Solar Observatory on nearby Mount Wilson, and Santa Anita Race Track. Area colleges include Pasadena City College, California Institute of Technology, Pasadena College and Fuller Theological Seminary.

LOS ANGELES, CAL. (Population 2,816,061, alt. 316 ft.) is a most unusual city. Not the kind of city which can be explored on foot, LA is a sprawling umbrella for many intermingled communities, each with its own identity and attractions. Founded as the "City of the Angels" in 1781.

THE NORTH COAST HIAWATHA
CHICAGO-SEATTLE

Algonquin Indians named **CHICAGO, ILL.** (Population 3,369,359, alt. 595 ft.) for the "wild onions" that grew on the site. The city's first permanent cabin was built in 1779 by Jean Baptiste Point du Sable, a black explorer and fur trader. Many of Chicago's traditional images are inaccurate: the "windy city" is actually the 19th windiest in the country and although it is the second largest U.S. city, 19% of Chicago is park or playground.

GLENVIEW, ILL. (Population 24,880, alt. 639 ft.) is a growing community conveniently located seventeen miles north of Chicago's "Loop."

MILWAUKEE, WISC. (Population 717,372, alt. 588 ft.) "Milwaukee" is derived from the Indian word "Millioke," meaning "good lands." The name fits this family-oriented city noted for its parks, parades, picturesque lake front and progressive school system. Principal products are auto bodies and parts, machinery, farm implements, meat packing, leather, and, of course, malt liquors.

Milwaukee is located in the heart of Wisconsin's dairyland and is a most convenient gateway to hundreds of picturesque lakes noted for fishing and water sports.

The city itself has many places of interest including its new Center for the Performing Arts and the War Memorial Center, a striking lakefront building which houses the Milwaukee Art Center. Three glass domes in the Mitchell Park Horticultural Conservatory duplicate climate and plant life found throughout the world.

Milwaukeeans celebrate almost every occasion with a parade. The biggest and best is held on the 4th of July, climaxing four days of celebration with a parade of wild animals and reconstructed circus wagons from Circus World Museum in Baraboo, Wisconsin.

Temperatures in the Milwaukee area average 20.6 degrees in January and 68.7 degrees in July.

Bus connections are available from **COLUMBUS, WISC.** (Population 3,789, alt. 850 ft.) to Madison.

MADISON (Population 172,007, alt. 863 ft.) is a fitting setting for both **WISCONSIN's** capital and its state university. Besides being located in the center of one of the richest dairy regions in the country, the city is built on an isthmus formed by Lakes Mendota and Monona. Two equally lovely lakes, Waubesa and Kegonsa are directly southeast of Madison. Quite understandably, its location makes Madison a prime summer resort area. Madison mixes industry with its scenic beauty; the city is home to over 200 industries.

Wisconsin State Historical Museum and Henry Villas Park Zoo are located in Madison. An interesting feature of the zoo is its free camel rides.

PORTAGE, WISC. (Population 7,821, alt. 817 ft.) is located between the Fox and Wisconsin rivers. Goods were once hauled from one river to another, providing the name for the city. Later a canal was dug eliminating the need for a "portage," but the name stuck.

Today Portage is business center for a wealthy farming area. Swan Lake and Silver Lake are noted for fishing and water sports. Cascade Mountain ski area is four miles southwest of Portage.

The name **WISCONSIN DELLS** (Population 2,105, alt. 899 ft.) refers to a village and also to a dramatic stretch of the scenic Wisconsin River which has become one of the United States' most popular tourist spots.

For fifteen miles, the river has gorged extraordinary shapes in the cliffs that tower above it. At some places, the channel has been cut to a depth of 150 feet. The awesome Upper and Lower Dells may be explored by water on several different boat trips or by foot on trails along the river shore and crests of the cliffs. During the summer months, Army "ducks" and a miniature steam railroad are also in operation.

The Dells also sponsors water shows and Winnebago Indian ceremonies and dances. Nearby Lost Canyon offers horse-drawn cart tours of 80-foot sandstone formations.

TOMAH (Population 5,647, alt. 962 ft.) is gateway to **WISCONSIN's** cranberry country. Lake Tomah offers swimming, boating, fishing, camping and picnicking. Tomah is close to Wildcat Mountain State Park, 2,911 acres of foothills and lookout towers which provide a panoramic view of the countryside.

LA CROSSE (Population 51,153, alt. 653 ft.) is located in the heart of **WISCONSIN's** lush resort land. A picturesque community, La Crosse preserves many unique local customs and celebrations.

From La Crosse to Little Falls, the MISSISSIPPI RIVER parallels our route. The "Father of Waters" flows from Lake Itasca in Northern Minnesota for 2,350 miles into the Gulf of Mexico. With the Missouri River, its principal tributary, the Mississippi drains an area of over one million square miles, one-eighth of North America and two-fifths of the United States.

WINONA, MINN. (Population 26,438, alt. 664 ft.) is set on the west bank of the Mississippi River at a point where the river is unusually wide and scenic. Home of Winona State College and Wilkie Steamboat Museum, which has an interesting collection of converted river steamers. Watch for "Sugar Loaf," a truncated monolith of limestone atop a bluff that rises 500 feet above the city. Bus connections to the Mayo Clinic.

RED WING, MINN. (Population 10,441, alt. 712 ft.) is a quiet river town in the Mississippi Valley. Formerly a Dakota Indian village, the town was named for Chief Whoopadooto, "Scarlet Wing." Red Wing's principal products are clay pipe, boots and shoes. At this point, the Mississippi widens into 34-mile-long Lake Pepin.

HIAWATHA 289

ST. PAUL (Population 309,828, alt. 723 ft.), **MINNESOTA's** capital and second largest city, was dedicated to St. Paul in 1841; prior to that time it was known as "Pig's Eye" in honor of its first resident, Pierre "Pig's Eye" Parrant. Its capitol building, designed by Cass Gilbert, has the largest unsupported marble dome in the world, and is similar to St. Peter's in Rome. The dome may be seen from the train; going west it is on the left side.

Today St. Paul is a manufacturing, printing, wholesale and transportation center.

St. Paul's annual "Winter Carnival" is billed as the Mardi Gras of the North and its Minnesota State Fair as the nation's largest. Como Park Zoo and Conservatory, Arts and Science Center, and the Minnesota Historical Society's Museums are well worth seeing. Local colleges include Hamline University, Concordia, Macalester, St. Catherine and St. Thomas Colleges.

In the Minneapolis-St. Paul area, temperatures range from an average of 12.4 degrees in January to 72.3 degrees in July

MINNEAPOLIS, MINN. (Population 434,400, alt. 818 ft.) began as a mill town in 1856 and grew into one of the largest grain centers in the world. "Minneapolis" is a combination of the Sioux word (minne) for water and the Greek word (polis) meaning city. This lovely "water city" encircles 11 lakes and 152 parks, an acre of park for every 80 residents. Home of Minnehaha Falls, immortalized as the "laughing waters" of Longfellow's "Hiawatha," Minneapolis is a center of both summer and winter sports.

Visitors to Minneapolis will enjoy the Minneapolis Institute of Arts, one of the foremost galleries in the country with outstanding collections of El Greco, Van Gogh, Rembrandt, Gauguin and Matisse; and the Walker Art Center, showcase for current trends in art. Other attractions include the noted Minnesota Orchestra and the Tyrone Guthrie Theatre. Unversity of Minnesota and Augsburg College are located here.

Just west of Minneapolis is LAKE MINNETONKA. A lovely, clear lake, Minnetonka is ten by two-and-a-half miles and drains into the Mississippi River.

Many of the United States' finest buildings have been built with granite from **ST. CLOUD, MINN.** (Population 39,691, alt. 1,027 ft.) quarries. The city has a pretty, non-industrial appearance. Minnesota State Teachers College is located here. Benton County fairgrounds may be seen from the train.

STAPLES (Population 2,657, alt. 1,277 ft.) claims to be the exact center of the state of **MINNESOTA.** It is the center of a good farming district; its creameries and cheese factories annually yield large returns.

DETROIT LAKES (Population 5,797, alt. 1,364 ft.) is capital of the **MINNESOTA** park region with its 500 adjacent lakes and numerous resorts catering to thousands of U.S. and Canadian summer visitors.

To the north of Detroit Lakes are numerous small lakes which are the source of most of this country's WILD RICE.

290 HIAWATHA

CHIPPEWA INDIANS still harvest wild rice in the precise, primitive method of their ancestors.

First, Indians paddle into the swamp, two to a canoe. One rows, the other threshes the rice heads into the boat with two sticks. On shore the rice is heated in large kettles over open fires to loosen the hulls and enhance the flavor. Then it is poured into wide, bark baskets, tossed and shaken until hulls, stalks and foreign substances have blown away. The rice is then placed in a cement or wooden vat, and a man or boy with mocassins on his feet "jigs" it, with a peculiar tramping step, to loosen all shells from the grain. Again the rice is tossed, then bagged and marketed.

Just east of Fargo, the RED RIVER of the NORTH crosses our route. Its source is the confluence of the Bois de Sioux and Otter Tail Rivers and its outlet, Lake Winnipeg in Canada. Although the river is actually 545 miles long, it meanders to such an extent that its mouth is only 270 miles from its source, measured directly.

FARGO (Population 53,365, alt. 900 ft.), largest city in **NORTH DAKOTA,** was named for William G. Fargo of the Wells-Fargo Express Company. Located in the famed Red River Valley where the waters of a glacier stood 200 feet deep 100 centuries ago, Fargo is an important livestock center and distribution point serving one-half million people.

JAMESTOWN, N.D. (Population 15,385, alt. 1,410 ft.) is the center of an extensive agricultural area. Home of Jamestown College. The James River is crossed here.

BISMARCK (Population 34,703, alt. 1,673 ft.), capital of **NORTH DAKOTA,** was named for Prince Bismarck, German Chancellor. Garrison Dam is sixty miles to the north.

West of Bismarck our route crosses the MISSOURI RIVER. The "Big Muddy," with its source at the confluence of the Jefferson, Madison and Gallatin rivers in western Montana, carves its way through seven large states on its way to the Mississippi River. The Missouri drains a basin of 529,350 square miles on its 2,714-mile journey.

MANDAN, N.D. (Population 11,093, alt. 1,648 ft.) is located on the western shore of the Missouri where it is joined by the Heart River. The town was named for the Mandan Indians; some of their old lodges have been reconstructed in Pioneer Park near Bismarck and Fort Lincoln State Park. Sioux, Gros, Ventres, Aukara and Crow reservations are also located within a few miles of Mandan.

From Mandan, Sacajawea, a sixteen-year-old Indian girl, guided Lewis and Clark to the mouth of the Columbia River. Fort Abraham Lincoln, just below Mandan, was headquarters for the famous 7th Cavalry and the starting point of the Custer expedition.

Set your watch at Mandan for the time change between Central and Mountain zones. (Going west, one hour backwards.)

The HEART RIVER parallels our route from Dickinson to Mandan. It rises in southwest North Dakota and flows northeast and east for 180 miles into the Missouri at Mandan.

West of Mandan our route crosses KNIFE RIVER. Its source is the Killdeer Mountains in North Dakota. The Knife flows east for 165 miles to the Missouri River near Stanton.

DICKINSON (Population 12,405, alt. 2,412 ft.) is an important livestock and grain center in the **NORTH DAKOTA** prairie region.

WILLISTON BASIN, where oil was first discovered in April, 1951, extends west from Dickinson to Central Montana, covering part of South Dakota and Canada. Derricks and producing wells are on both sides of the train.

Sir George Gore, Irish nobleman, hunted buffalo in the **GLENDIVE, MONT.** (Population 6,305, alt. 2,076 ft.) area in 1855. The city was later named in honor of Gore whose Irish estate was "Glendive."

Today Glendive is the center of Montana's portion of the Williston oil basin. The area surrounding Glendive contains 332 producing wells. Oil derricks may be seen from the train.

The YELLOWSTONE RIVER parallels our route from Glendive to Livingston. Few rivers have the power, variety of scenery and tourist appeal of the Yellowstone. From its source in the Absaroka Range, Wyoming, the river travels 671 miles into the Missouri River, irrigating more than 200,000 acres.

POWDER RIVER crosses our route west of Glendive. Named because the black sand along its banks resembles gunpowder, the Powder River rises in the southern foothills of the Bighorn Mountains and flows 486 miles into the Yellowstone River. The river was described during World War I as "the longest river in the world an inch deep, a mile wide and flung uphill." Part of the slogan of the famous 91st Division of World War I was "Powder River — let er buck!"

The **MILES CITY** (Population 9,023, alt. 2,363 ft.) area's livestock ranches raise more than one-fourth the cattle and sheep in **MONTANA**. It is also an important producer of sugar beets and wheat. Fort Keogh is across the Tongue River from Miles City. Signal Butte, a high knob to the south, was once used by officers from Fort Keogh for signaling messages by heliograph to Black Hills, 175 miles away. Spotted Eagle Recreation Area, southwest of the city, is a picnic, swimming and boating area. Range Riders Museum contains interesting antiques, artifacts, archeological and geological specimens.

Just west of Miles City our route crosses the TONGUE RIVER. One of the Yellowstone River's most important tributaries, the Tongue River rises in northeastern Wyoming and joins the Yellowstone northwest of Miles City.

FORSYTH, MONT. (Population 1,873, alt. 2,528 ft.) is a thriving town in the Yellowstone Valley, named for General J. W. Forsyth, one of this country's more militant pioneers.

292 HIAWATHA

West of Forsyth, our route crosses the BIGHORN RIVER. Custer Battlefield is south and west of the Bighorn.

POMPEY'S PILLAR, 200 feet of stark, jutting rock, is visible from the train, on your right traveling west. Captain William Clark climbed Pompey's Pillar in 1806 and autographed its surface. Named after the only son of Sacajawea, it is the only remaining physical evidence of the Lewis and Clark expedition.

BILLINGS, MONT. (Population 61,581, alt. 3,122 ft.) was named for Frederick Billings, a former President of the Northern Pacific Railroad. Industrially the area is noted for its oil and sugar refineries and livestock yards. Home of East Montana College and Rocky Mountain College. Scenic Chief Black Otter Trail transverses the edge of Rimrocks, five hundred feet above the Yellowstone River. Places which preserve the Western spirit include Gallery '85, Yellowstone Art Center, and Yellowstone Historical Museum. Seasonal events of interest are Midland Empire Fair and Rodeo and Billings Horse Show.

West of Billings we cross the STILLWATER RIVER.

BEARTOOTH MOUNTAINS, northeast spur of the Absaroka Range, are located between Stillwater River and Clark Fork of the Yellowstone River. Part of the range is in southern Montana, part in northwestern Wyoming. Granite Peak (12,850 ft.) is the highest point in Montana. Beartooth Range includes parts of Custer and Shoshone National Forests.

CRAZY MOUNTAINS, a range of the Rockies in central Montana, extends thirty miles south toward the Yellowstone River. Its highest point, Crazy Peak, is 11,214 feet.

The ABSAROKA RANGE of the Rockies forms the eastern boundary of Yellowstone National Park. It runs 150 miles into Northwest Wyoming from the extreme southern corner of Montana, roughly between the Yellowstone River and the Bighorn Basin. Frances Peak, the highest point, is 13,140 feet.

LIVINGSTON, MONT. (Population 6,883, alt. 4,500 ft.) is located at the head of Paradise Valley through which flows the Yellowstone River and around which rise the Absaroka and Gallatin Ranges of the Rockies. Livingston's main occupations are farming, timber processing and travertine production. The area is also known for trout fishing, big game hunting and its numerous dude ranches. It is a most scenic drive from Livingston to Gardiner, north entrance to Yellowstone National Park.

YELLOWSTONE NATIONAL PARK, located mainly in northwestern Wyoming, is the oldest and largest national park in the United States. It was discovered in 1807 by John Colter, a member of the Lewis and Clark expedition.

Today over 500,000 tourists visit Yellowstone each year. They are as much in awe of its out-of-this-world landscape as the local Sioux, Algonquin and Shoshone Indians once were when they believed the area to be the haunt of powerful spirits.

HIAWATHA 293

At Muir, Montana, BOZEMAN TUNNEL cuts through BOZEMAN PASS, over which the Indian girl, Sacajawea, guided Captain Clark in July, 1806. The original tunnel was completed January 20, 1884, and the present one in July, 1945. For some distance here through Gallatin National Forest, the railroad follows the original wagon trail of Captain John M. Bozeman.

GALLATIN MOUNTAIN, a range of the Rockies in northwestern Wyoming and southwest Montana, rises south of Bozeman and extends 45 miles south between Gallatin and Yellowstone Rivers into the northwest corner of Yellowstone National Park. Major peaks are: Mt. Holmes (10,300 ft.); Mt. Blackmore (10,196 ft.); and the highest point, Electric Peak (11,155 ft.).

BOZEMAN, MONT. (Population 18,670, alt. 4,761 ft.) is located in the rich Gallatin Valley with Bridger Mountains on the north and Gallatin National Forest to the south. The town was settled by Captain John M. Bozeman in 1864. He was killed in 1867 by Blackfoot Indians, 14½ miles east of Livingston.

Today Bozeman is a livestock center and grain and alfalfa producer. Bridger Bowl Ski Area is 16 miles northeast. Home of Montana State College.

Rocky Canyon opens into the fertile GALLATIN VALLEY at Bozeman. The valley was named for Thomas Jefferson's Secretary of the Treasury, Albert Gallatin, who, as our ambassador to England in 1826, asserted our claims to the Pacific Northwest.

BUTTE, MONT. (Population 23,368, alt. 5,485 ft.) was named for Butte Hills, "the richest hill on earth." Here copper, zinc, manganese, lead, silver and gold worth several billion dollars have been extracted. Butte produces more copper than any other district in the world. Montana School of Mines is located at Butte.

West of Butte our route crosses the CLARK FORK RIVER. Its source is near Butte on the Continental Divide. The river flows to Pend Oreille Lake, then as the Pend Oreille River to the Columbia River — a journey of 499 miles.

Bus connection at Butte for HELENA.

DEER LODGE, MONT. (Population 4,081, alt. 4,519 ft.) Mt. Powell, overlooking the city of Deer Lodge, soars 10,300 ft. above Deer Lodge National Forest and is the most prominent peak seen from the train. A hot spring, a conical mound resembling an Indian mound in winter, and the prevalence of deer nearby, suggested the name Deer Lodge.

MISSOULA, MONT. (Population 29,497, alt. 3,208 ft.) derives its name from the Salish Indian word meaning "Land of Sparkling Water." The city is located in the Bitter Root Valley, first locality west of the Mississippi where fruit is raised in large commercial quantities. Site of University of Montana.

FLATHEAD RIVER parallels our route from Missoula to Paradise. The river's source is southeast British Columbia.

PARADISE (Population 500, alt. 2,487 ft.), **MONTANA's** name is a polite modification of "Pair o' Dice," the name of a roadhouse once located nearby.

Set your watch at Paradise for the time change between Mountain and Pacific zones. (One hour backward, going west.)

At Paradise, the CLARK FORK RIVER follows our route almost as far west as Sandpoint.

SANDPOINT, IDA. (Population 4,144, alt. 2,092 ft.) is a lumbering center located at the point where Pend Oreille River empties into Lake Pend Oreille. Both bodies of water were named for an Indian Tribe given to wearing pendant ornaments in their ears. Sandpoint is the site of Kullyspell House, first fur trading post in the Northwest.

SPOKANE, WASH. (Population 170,516, alt. 1,922 ft.), from the Indian meaning "Children of the Sun," began as a saw mill powered by Spokane Falls. Railroading was responsible for much of the city's early growth; even today, it is the largest rail center west of Omaha. The Spokane area's diverse natural resources include: grain, apples and other fruits, timber, minerals, and power from Grand Coulee Dam, 95 miles northwest. The city is encircled by a scenic 128-mile loop drive; its business district is divided from the Northside residential area by the Spokane River. The river produces a series of waterfalls of rare beauty which may be seen from the train. Spokane is the home of Whitworth College and Gonzaga University.

EPHRATA, WASH. (Population 6,548, alt. 1,276 ft.) is headquarters for the Columbia River District of the U.S. Bureau of Reclamation. The objective of the Columbia Basin project is to reclaim over one million acres of semiarid land and convert it into 12,000 to 15,000 fertile farm units averaging 65 to 85 acres each. The Ephrata area has excellent hunting and fishing.

WENATCHEE, WASH. (Population 16,726, alt. 648 ft.) Set amid orchards and flower gardens, Wenatchee is known as the "Apple Capital of the World." Over 15% of the nation's apple crop, as well as other fruits, are grown in this vicinity. The Washington State Apple Blossom Festival is celebrated here every spring. There are many scenic and recreational attractions in and around Wenatchee, including the Ohme Gardens with regional shrubs and flowers, the Rocky Reach Dam whose Information Center has an interesting Columbia River Indian Exhibit, and the Mission Ridge Ski Area.

Between Wenatchee and Everett the North Coast Hiawatha passes through the Cascade Tunnel, longest in the Western Hemisphere. This engineering marvel pierces the rugged Cascade Mountain Range for almost eight miles.

EVERETT, WASH. (Population 40,304, alt. 39 ft.) A picturesque port on Puget Sound, Everett faces the snow-capped Olympic Range. To the east soar the Cascades with the towering peaks of Mt. Baker and Mt. Rainier. Chief industries are lumber, paper and pulp, fed by the vast adjacent forests.

From Everett, the Amtrak line extends north to Vancouver, British Columbia.

EDMONDS, WASH. (Population 8,016, alt. 9 ft.) A suburb of Seattle, Edmonds overlooks Puget Sound and is backed by the Cascade Range. Seventeen miles north of downtown Seattle, Edmonds is Amtrak's suburban station for this area. This convenient station location saves miles of city driving for Amtrak passengers to and from North Seattle and surrounding communities. A ferry connects Edmonds and Olympic National Park.

One of the most important import-export cities in the nation, **SEATTLE, WASH.** (Population 530,831, alt. 13 ft.) is the gateway to Alaska and the nearest American port to the Orient. The city is built on nine hills, with a fresh-water lake on one side and salt-water Puget Sound on the other, and mountains on three sides. Seattle is both a popular vacation area and an important industrial area. It is an aircraft and lumber center and a fishing port. Seattle was pioneered by five families who named the town for Sealth, an Indian Chief who befriended them. Its settlement owed much to the "Mercer Girls," who were recruited as wives for the predominantly male settlers.

Seattle has much to offer besides scenic beauty. Seattle Center, a 74-acre legacy from the 1962 Century 21 Exposition (better known as Seattle World's Fair), houses an opera house, arena, playhouse, two exhibit halls, coliseum, the well-known Space Needle and the Pacific Science Center. Other places of interest include: Seattle Art Museum; Fyre Art Museum; Henry Art Gallery; Burke Memorial Museum, and the Museum of History and Industry. Seattle Symphony Orchestra is highly regarded as is the Seattle Opera and the Seattle Repertory.

In August, a Seafair is held climaxed by hydroplane racing on Lake Washington. Seattle is home to the University of Washington, Seattle University, and Seattle Pacific College.

Amtrak connections at Seattle to and from . . .

PORTLAND, ORE. (Population 380,620, alt. 30 ft.), third largest Pacific Coast port, is located inland, 98 nautical miles from the sea, on both sides of the Willamette River near its junction with the Columbia River. Portland is noted for its gorgeous scenery: Columbia River Gorge; Mount Hood; waterfalls; forests; ski slopes; and an outstanding public park system. Washington Park is the home of the International Rose Festival Garden and outdoor summer theater. It is adjacent to the Portland Zoo and the Oregon Museum of Science and Industry. The International Rose Festival Garden is the principal test garden for the American Rose Society and has earned Portland the title, "Rose City." Lloyd Center boasts of being one of the world's largest shopping centers, and Hoyt Arboretum is the largest forest inside a U.S. city limits. Area colleges and universities include: Portland State University; University of Portland; Lewis & Clark College; Reed College; Maryhurst College; and Concordia College. Portland averages 38.4 degrees in January and 67.2 degrees in July.

THE SAN FRANCISCO ZEPHYR
CHICAGO-SAN FRANCISCO

Algonquin Indians named **CHICAGO, ILL.** (Population 3,369,359, alt. 590 ft.) for the "wild onions" that grew on the site. The city's first permanent cabin was built in 1779 by Jean Baptiste Point du Sable, a black explorer and fur trader. Many of Chicago's traditional images are inaccurate:

In the 1830's **AURORA, ILL.** (Population 74,182, alt. 662 ft.) was an important stagecoach transfer point. Today it is a diversified manufacturing community noted for its beautiful homes. Built in 1857, its interesting Historical Museum building houses a famous astronomical clock, mastodon bones and local historical items. Aurora claims two firsts: the first city to light itself with electricity (1881), and development of the first rail car with an observation dome (1945). Home of Aurora College.

GALESBURG, ILL. (Population 36,290, alt. 781 ft.) is an important manufacturing and distributing city with a colorful history. During the Civil War, Galesburg was one of the key stations on the Underground Railroad. The famous 1858 Lincoln-Douglas debates took place here. Galesburg is the birthplace of Carl Sandburg and home of Knox College.

MONMOUTH, ILL. (Population 11,022, alt. 775 ft.) was named in commemoration of the Revolutionary War battle of Monmouth, New Jersey. Today the city is located in a region noted for beef cattle feeding. Monmouth holds a three-day Prime Beef Festival each September. One of the world's largest pottery manufacturers is located here. Home of Monmouth College and birthplace of Wyatt Earp.

At Burlington, the **MISSISSIPPI RIVER** whose Indian name means "River of the Meadows," crosses our route and forms the boundary between Illinois and Iowa. The "Father of Waters" flows from Lake Itasca in Northern Minnesota for 2,350 miles into the Gulf of Mexico. With the Missouri River, its principal tributary, the Mississippi drains an area of over one million square miles, one-eighth of North America and two-fifths of the United States.

BURLINGTON, IOWA (Population 32,366, alt. 503 ft.) was originally known as "Flint Hills" because local Indians regarded the area as neutral ground where various tribes could quarry flint and make weapons and other implements. It was renamed Burlington in 1834 by settlers from Burlington, Vermont. Burlington served as capital of the Wisconsin Territory in 1837 and capital of the Iowa Territory from 1838-1841. Today Burlington is the center for a rich agricultural district and manufacturer of items as diverse as concrete blocks and potato chips. There are 80 parks covering more than 350 acres in Burlington. Snake Alley, billed as the "crookedest street in the world," makes five sharp turns within one block. Burlington Jazz Festival & Steamboat Carnival is a community-wide riverfront celebration held in early June.

MT. PLEASANT (Population 7,007, alt. 720 ft.) is one of the oldest towns in **IOWA**. Home of Iowa Wesleyan College, one of the oldest colleges west of the Mississippi River, and the Harlan-Lincoln Museum. Mt. Pleasant is the setting each September for the Midwest Old Settlers and Threshers Reunion. This five-day event draws crowds of 200,000 or more from all over the country.

OTTUMWA, IOWA (Population 29,610, alt. 649 ft.) was born in the land rush. Settlers staked out the town's site on both sides of the Des Moines River. One of Iowa's largest parks, Lacey-Keosauqua State Park, is located in Ottumwa. Ely's Ford, famous Mormon Crossing, is located in the park. Each Labor Day the Antique Airplane Association holds a "Fly-in" in Ottumwa.

The **DES MOINES RIVER** crosses our route at Ottumwa. The Des Moines flows for 535 miles from Lake Shetek in southwest Minnesota into the Mississippi River. Above Humboldt, Iowa, the river is known as West Fork.

OSCEOLA, IOWA (Population 3,124, alt. 1,139 ft.) was settled by pioneers from Indiana and Ohio who named the town for a Seminole Chief. Nine Eagles State Park is a 1,080-acre park with a 56-acre, crystal-clear lake. Thirty-two miles northwest of Osceola is the original delicious apple tree discovered in 1872 and parent of eight million trees.

CRESTON, IOWA (Population 8,234, alt. 1,291 ft.) is in the heart of Iowa's bluegrass country. The city is a trading mart for surrounding farmlands. Green Valley State Park has 988 acres of rolling hills and a 390-acre artificial lake.

East of Omaha the **MISSOURI RIVER** crosses our route. Called "Mini-Souri" by local Indians, the Missouri forms the boundary between Iowa and Nebraska. The "Big Muddy," with its source at the confluence of the Jefferson, Madison and Gallatin rivers in western Montana, carves its way through seven large states on its way to the Mississippi River. The Missouri drains a basin of 529,350 square miles on its 2,714-mile journey.

OMAHA, NEB. (Population 346,929, alt. 1,040 ft.) was named for Indians who lived in the area until a treaty was signed with the Federal Government on June 24, 1854. Omaha, "Crossroads of the Nation," played an important part in this country's westward expansion. It was the winter headquarters for the Mormons in 1846-1847. During the '49ers gold rush, it was an important trading post. Today Omaha is a midwest education leader, biggest livestock market and meat packing center in the world, and buys and sells a large portion of the grain produced in America. Omaha has 70 parks, 3,000 acres connected by 125 miles of boulevards. Omaha has a resident symphony, the city's Joslyn Art Museum houses collections from the Middle Ages to the present in a magnificent marble building, and Henry Doorly Zoo is home to many rare and endangered animals. Educational institutes located in Omaha include Creighton University, University of Nebraska at Omaha and its medical school, and the College of St. Mary. Omaha is host to the NCAA

College Baseball World Series and the World's Championship Rodeo. Boy's Town, a 1,500-acre community of 1,000 boys governed by a boy mayor and his six commissioners, is located 10 miles west of Omaha.

West of Omaha, the **PLATTE RIVER** crosses our route. Its source is the confluence of the North Platte and South Platte rivers. Together they flow 310 miles into the Missouri River. This river played an important part in the early history of the West. It formed a natural route for pioneers who followed the river as far as Casper in Wyoming. The Pony Express route joined the Platte near Hastings, Nebraska, and then at Chimney Rock the route crossed to Cheyenne, Wyoming. It was in operation only eighteen months until the telegraph was completed (1860-1861). During those eighteen months, mail was carried from St. Joseph to San Francisco in seven to eight days as compared to three weeks by stage. This was accomplished by relays of men and horses traveling day and night, averaging 250 miles daily.

LINCOLN, capital of **NEBRASKA** (Population 149,518, alt. 1,169 ft.), is a major grain market, railroad and insurance center, and farm equipment distributor. The capitol building is one of this country's most outstanding examples of modern architecture, and houses the only unicameral legislature in the United States. Lincoln's twenty-eight park system includes Antelope Park, with lovely sunken gardens and municipal zoo, and Pioneer Park, home to herds of buffalo, elk, deer and wildfowl. As a young lawyer, William Jennings Bryan went to Congress from Lincoln. Fairview, his family home for fifteen years, has been restored and opened to the public. Places of interest also include the Nebraska State Historical Society Museum, with displays on Indian history and life as well as pioneer exhibits; Walter J. Charnley firearms collection; and Sheldon Memorial Art Gallery. University of Nebraska State Museum houses one of the best collections of modern and fossil elephants in the world, including the world's largest mammoth. Nebraska Wesleyan University, Union College and the University of Nebraska are located in Lincoln.

HASTINGS, NEB. (Population 23,580, alt. 1,928 ft.) is a manufacturing city—producer of farm machinery, irrigating equipment and air conditioners. Hastings Museum includes an extensive natural history collection. Home of Hastings College. Willa Cather Pioneer Memorial and Museum is thirty-eight miles south of Hastings.

HOLDREGE, NEB. (Population 9,389, alt. 2,335 ft.) was born with the coming of the railroad in 1883 and named for Burlington General Manager George W. Holdrege. The town's fortunes fluctuated widely until irrigation stabilized crop production and made Holdrege the retail trade center of a large and productive wheat farming and cattle feeding area.

McCOOK, NEB. (Population 8,285, alt. 2,508 ft.) was founded in 1882 as a rail division point and named for General Alexander McDowell McCook, one of the "fighting McCooks" of Civil War fame. Today McCook is a trading center in the midst of a reclamation, irrigation and oil-producing area.

Set your watch at McCook for the time change between Central and Mountain Zones. Going west, one hour backward; going east, one hour forward.

AKRON, COLO. (Population 1,685, alt. 4,660 ft.) takes its name from the Greek, meaning "high." Located 110 miles northeast of Denver, Akron boasts 307 days of sunshine annually. It ranks among the top producing wheat counties in the state. Eastern Colorado Roundup is held each year in August.

A military post was established at the site of **FT MORGAN, COLO.** (Population 7,594, alt. 4,338 ft.) on the South Platte River in 1864 as protection for travelers. This post later became a stop on the Overland Stage route between the Missouri River and Denver. Portions of the old trail are still visible in the western part of Morgan County. Today Ft. Morgan, known as the "City of Light," is trading capital of an area that produces beet sugar, sheep fattened on beet pulp, grains, beans and dairy products.

Just north of our route at Ft. Morgan flows the **SOUTH PLATTE RIVER.** The South Platte rises in South Park in central Colorado, carving its way through the Front Range in Platte Canyon, passing through Denver, and through the irrigated land near Greeley, Colorado. From Greeley, it flows northeast into the North Platte River.

As Denver is approached from the east, the rail traveler is treated to a marvelous 200-mile panoramic view of the towering Rockies with the Continental Divide running along their crest. Since crossing the Missouri, the Great Plains have been sloping upward to the foothills of the Rockies.

Mountain men criss-crossed Colorado trapping beaver in the 1830's. Their trading posts and an occasional ranch were the only settlements in the Denver area until the 1850's. It was not until the Russell party found gold in paying quantities in Cherry Creek in 1857 that the gold rush was on and **DENVER** (Population 514,678, alt. 5,280 ft.) was born. With "Pike's Peak or Bust" painted on their wagons, 100,000 emigrants had crossed the plains to Denver by the end of 1859. The fabulous Leadville silver strike was made in 1875. When gold was discovered in even more fantastic amounts at Cripple Creek in 1890, Denver was the center of one of the richest mining regions in the world. Today Denver is a great manufacturing, distributing and transportation center which combines a cosmopolitan atmosphere with the friendly spontaneity for which the West is known. Its central location is ideal for one-day tours of Colorado's many magnificent scenic and historic sites. There are 40 ski areas near Denver, the nearest less than 25 miles from the city. Denver is known for its excellent symphony orchestra, theater group, several fine museums, outstanding recreational facilities, unique park system and some of the finest restaurants in the country. Area schools include Regis College, Loretto Heights College, Temple Buell College,

University of Colorado Medical School, University of Colorado Denver Center, Metropolitan State College and University of Denver.

GREELEY, COLO. (Population 38,902, alt. 4,652 ft.) was an outgrowth of Union Colony, a cooperative community of New Yorkers conceived by and named for Horace Greeley and founded in 1870 by his agriculture editor, Nathan C. Meeker. Temperance was the colony's first rule. When a would-be businessman set up a sod hut saloon on the edge of town one Sunday, the congregation moved to confer with the proprietor. A fire mysteriously started and the saloon was destroyed. Today Greeley is a rich agricultural area and producer of items as diverse as office desks and fishing rods. Home of Colorado State College.

CHEYENNE (Population 40,914, alt. 6,060 ft.), capital of **WYOMING,** was named for a tribe of plains Indians who, with the Arapahos and Sioux, once inhabited this area. Cheyenne's chief attractions in 1867 were quick money and cheap liquor. Described as "Hell on Wheels," the town was home to professional gunmen, soldiers, promoters, trainmen, gamblers, and confidence men. It was the scene of vigilante law and wars between cattlemen and sheepmen. Today Cheyenne remains a headquarters for sheep and cattle interests. Its former spirit is revived annually during Cheyenne Frontier Days, held the last week in July, and one of our largest rodeos. Cheyenne is located near Snowy Range, a beautiful section of fishing streams and lakes.

Leaving Cheyenne, the train ascends Sherman Hill and reaches an elevation of 8,013 feet above sea level—the highest point on Amtrak's route.

LARAMIE, WYO. (Population 23,143, alt. 7,151 ft.) was named for the legendary French-Canadian trapper, Jacques La Ramie, who worked in what became southwest Wyoming in approximately 1820 and was killed by Indians somewhere along the river that bears his name. Laramie is a town with a colorful past. Jack McCall was arrested in Laramie on August 30, 1876 for shooting Wild Bill Hickock in the back of the head in a Deadwood, South Dakota saloon. One year later, Jesse James was lodged in the Laramie jail as a suspect in a nearby stagecoach holdup. Humorist Bill Nye, famous lecturer and writer, published the Laramie "Boomerang." A Laramie hardware store where Nye used to sit and spin yarns was the site of his "Den of the Forty Liars." Laramie is located near Snowy Range, one of the West's most beautiful recreation areas. Sherman Mountains between Laramie and Cheyenne are unusually rocky ridges eroded into distinct and grotesque shapes.

RAWLINS, WYO. (Population 7,855, alt. 6,758 ft.) is a farming and ranching area. "Rawlins Red" pigment from local paint mines was used for the Brooklyn Bridge, 2,000 miles away. In 1878, vigilantes hung one train robber and sent warning notes to 24 other desperadoes; 24 tickets were sold the next morning at the Rawlins railroad depot.

Our route crosses the **NORTH PLATTE RIVER** 21 miles east

of Rawlins and passes north of the Medicine Bow National Forest, national range for thousands of deer, elk and antelope, with choice hunting in the fall and trout fishing in season. We will cross the Continental Divide twice; once in Rawlins and again 22 miles west of Creston.

The streets of **ROCK SPRINGS, WYO.** (Population 11,657, alt. 6,261 ft.) make intricate bends and turns because houses were built anywhere that suited the builder's taste. Underlying this sheep raising area are some of the greatest bituminous coal reserves west of the Mississippi River.

GREEN RIVER, WYO. (Population 4,196, alt. 6,100 ft.) is the home of Sweetwater County Museum and is located near Flaming Gorge National Recreation Area.

The Green River is bordered by sandstone cliffs; the most prominent one, Castle Rock, rises 1,000 feet above the river. Mormons cut a pass at Tollgate Rock and charged a toll of those who passed. Brigham Young is said to have delivered a sermon from Pulpit Rock. Wildflowers are numerous along the rivers, especially red Indian Paintbrush, the state flower.

The Green River played an important role in the exploration of the West. Early trappers met annually at the Green River Rendezvous where it is joined by Sandy Creek. John Wesley Powell traveled down the Green River by boat starting here in 1869 and again in 1871.

EVANSTON, WYO. (Population 4,462, alt. 6,745 ft.) is a trading center, tourist stopping point and cattle and sheep raising area. Fort Bridger State Museum, 36 miles east, is located in a restored fort named for Jim Bridger, scout and explorer. An annual rodeo is held Labor Day weekend.

OGDEN, UTAH (Population 69,478, alt. 4,300 ft.) was called "Ogden's Hole" and named for Peter Skene Ogden, one of the mountain men who came looking for beaver in 1825. Mormons arrived at Salt Lake in 1847 and established a Mormon town there. Brigham Young chose this area because of its isolation and excellent soil. An annual celebration, held throughout the week of July 24, is highlighted by Ogden Pioneer Days Rodeo, parades and "All Faces West," an outdoor drama which tells the story of the Mormon migration to Utah. Snow Basin, 18 miles from Ogden on the east slope of Mount Ogden, offers winter and summer recreation. Salt Lake City is 35 miles south.

Set your watch leaving Ogden for the time change between Mountain and Pacific Zones. Going west, one hour backward; going east, one hour forward.

Sixteen miles west of Ogden, Amtrak "goes to sea by rail" for 32 miles as our train crosses **GREAT SALT LAKE.** Great Salt Lake is all that is left of the prehistoric Lake Bonneville which once filled the whole basin. Its evaporation left an exceptionally high concentration of salts and minerals—between 15-28% in the present lake. The Great Salt Lake has an average width of 30 miles and length of 75 miles but is only 10-30 feet deep.

From the Great Salt Lake to Sparks, the **HUMBOLDT RIVER** parallels our route. The Humboldt was named after

Baron Alexander von Humboldt, explorer and scientist. It rises in Humboldt Wells in the Ruby Mountains and flows 300 miles before disappearing into Humboldt Sink. A historically important river, the Humboldt marked part of the "California Trail" from Salt Lake City to central California.

ELKO, NEV. (Population 7,621, alt. 5,160 ft.), from an Indian word meaning "white woman," is the chief trade and service center for a county as large as New Jersey, Connecticut and Rhode Island combined. Its main industries are raising beef cattle, sheep raising and mining. Headquarters for Humboldt National Forest. Ruby Lakes Area, 60 miles southeast, is a migratory waterfowl refuge, outstanding in this semi-desert country. North of Elko are a wide range of outdoor recreation areas accessible on foot or horseback.

CARLIN, NEV. (Population 1,313, alt. 4,850 ft.) is located near Carlin Canyon, scene of large gold mining operations. Hot springs and small geysers are located nearby.

SPARKS, NEV. (Population 23,922, alt. 4,407 ft.) is located near Toiyabe National Forest. It lies along the rugged Monitor, Toquima, Toiyabe and Shoshone Ranges, eastern slopes of the Sierras and Charleston Mountains.

PYRAMID LAKE, a U.S. bird refuge, is 30 miles northeast of Reno.

RENO, NEV. (Population 72,863, alt. 4,490 ft.), "the biggest little city in the world," was named for Civil War General Jesse L. Reno. The city grew up in the wake of discovery of Comstock silver and still has the look and feel of a frontier town. Its Old West image extends to the casinos which made Reno a tourist center since gambling was legalized in 1931. Casinos are open round the clock. Often they are doorless with a warm air screen partition and carpeting extending outdoors into the streets.

Reno's climate is known for wide ranges in temperatures within short periods of time; hot and dry days with cool evenings. Reno is located on the western edge of Truckee Meadows on a semiarid plateau, bordered on the west by the forested Sierra Nevada range. Truckee River runs through the middle of the city on its way from Lake Tahoe to Pyramid Lake. Tourism, based on gambling and nightclub entertainment, and the city's proximity to Lake Tahoe and Virginia City are the most important factors in Reno's economy. Home of University of Nevada, Reno, and scene of winter sports at 16 major resorts in the Ski Reno complex.

Between Reno and Sacramento our train crosses the spectacularly scenic Sierra Nevada Range and passes through many famous Mother Lode settlements, including Dutch Flat and Gold Run.

SACRAMENTO, CAL. (Population 254,413, alt. 30 ft.) occupies the site at which John A. Sutter, Swiss ex-army officer, built his self-sustaining ranchero in 1839. He ruled his Indian subjects in kingly fashion until January 24, 1848, when gold was discovered by James Marshall while building a sawmill for Sutter. This was the beginning of the gold rush and Sutter's ruin. A gold-maddened mob invaded his land; his men deserted, stole his stock, his provisions, tools and wagons and destroyed his grain. Sutter moved to Pennsylvania in 1875 and died a poor man in 1880, after vainly beseeching Congress for the return of his property. Today Sacramento is the capital of California and center of an immense fertile agricultural district. Most of the U.S.'s sweet prunes are grown here. Home of Sacramento State College. Sutter's Fort, first outpost of white civilization in the interior of California, has been restored and houses relics of pioneer and gold rush days.

West of Sacramento, the **SACRAMENTO RIVER** crosses our route. The Sacramento and its tributary, the San Joaquin River, are the two principal rivers that flow the length of the California valley, 450 miles long and, on the average, 50 miles wide.

OAKLAND, CAL. (Population 361,561, alt. 25 ft.) extends along the mainland side of San Francisco Bay opposite the Golden Gate. The city varies in altitude from sea level to 1,500 feet and is connected with San Francisco by the San Francisco-Oakland Bay Bridge. Oakland is one of the most important manufacturing centers of the West Coast with some 1,500 factories. It is also a rapidly developing port and shipbuilding point and a leading electrical, chemical, fabric, and glass producing center. Adjoining Oakland are five regional parks offering trails as well as picnicking, fishing and swimming. Points of interest include Lakeside Park Garden Center, a gardening library surrounded by Japanese, dahlia, and chrysanthemum gardens; Morcom Amphitheater of Roses, eight acres of 400 varieties of roses blooming all year round; and Skyline Bowl, which follows the rim of Oakland's low hills through parks and private estates —one of the most beautiful drives in the country. Oakland is the home of California College of Arts and Crafts, College of Holy Name and Mills College.

At Amtrak's 16th Street Station, passengers make trainside transfer to connecting motorcoach for scenic trek across Bay Bridge to ...

SAN FRANSICSO, CAL. (Population 715,674, alt. 0—938 ft.) is one of the most scenic and cosmopolitan cities in the U.S. It is also an important industrial city and a great port. San Francisco rests on a series of hills at the end of a narrow peninsula bordered on one side by the Pacific Ocean and on the other by the San Francisco Bay, one of the largest land-linked harbors in the world. Connecting that bay with the ocean is the Golden Gate, a strait about one mile wide, bordered by high rocky shores. San Francisco's altitude varies from sea level to 938 feet. Cable cars originated on San Francisco's steep streets and are preserved. At night, the view is majestic from practically any point, particularly Twin Peaks.

The first permanent white settlement was made in 1776, but there were less than 100 inhabitants until 1848 when the gold rush soared the population to 10,000.

ACCOMMODATIONS

In this chapter of your guide to exploring the USA and Canada by train, we include a listing of a number of hotels. The hotels we have listed are by states—from Arizona to Wyoming and in Canada from British Columbia.

We first list the city, name of the hotel and the reservations number, including the area code. In case you want to make reservations by letter, we have provided you with the hotel address, minimum room rates for single rooms (S) and double rooms (D). The list does not include all the hotels we have included in this guide. For example, under 'District of Columbia' we have listed two hotels. When you turn to the Washington, D.C. section of your guide, you will note we have included a great number of other hotels.

ARIZONA

PHOENIX—The Adams Hotel (602) 257-1525, Central and Adams, Phoenix, AZ. 85001. S-25; D-32; Higher rates in winter;
TUCSON—Aztec Inn (602) 795-0330, 102 N. Alvernon Way, Tucson, AZ. 85711. S-26; D-28; Higher rates in winter; call for pick-up;
TUCSON—Howard Johnson's (800) 654-2000; 1025 E. Benson, Tucson, AZ. 85725. S-19; D-24;
TUCSON—Ramada Inn (602) 624-8341, 434 N. Freeway, Tucson, AZ. 85705. S-13; D-16; call for pick-up.

ARKANSAS

LITTLE ROCK—Sam Peck Motor Inn (501) 367-1304, 625 Capitol Avenue, Little Rock, AR. 72201; S-12; D-16;

CALIFORNIA

ANAHEIM—Marco Polo Motel (714) 635-3630, 1604 So. Harbor Blvd., Anaheim, CA. 92802, S-12, D-14; Higher rates in summer. "opposite Disneyland Main Gate."
LOS ANGELES—Mayflower Hotel (213) 624-1331, 535 South Grand Avenue, Los Angeles, CA. 90017, S-18; D-23;
MONTEREY—Hotel San Carlos (408) 375-2662, Franklin and Calle Principal, Monterey, CA. 93940, S-18; D-23;

OAKLAND—Lake Merritt Hotel (415) 832-2300, 1800 Madison Street, Oakland, CA. 94612, S-18; D-22;

PASADENA—Pasadena Hilton (213) 577-1000, 150 So. Los Robles, Pasadena, CA. 91101, S-29; D-36;

SAN DIEGO—El Cortez Hotel (714) 232-0161, 7th and Ash Streets, San Diego, CA. 92101; S-18; D-23;

SAN DIEGO—Master Hosts Inn (714) 298-0511, 950 Hotel Circle, San Diego, CA. 92108; S-18; D-23; Golf, Tennis, Fun Fiesta Package Plans available;
SAN DIEGO—Pickwick Hotel (714) 234-0141, 132 West Broadway, San Diego, CA. 92101; S-11; D-13;

SAN DIEGO—Sheraton Half Moon Inn (714) 224-3411, 2303 Shelter Island Drive, San Diego, CA. 92106; S-26; D-32.
SAN FRANCISCO— Handlery Motor Inn (415) 986-2526, 260 O'Farrell Street, San Francisco, CA. 94102, S-28; D-34;
SAN FRANCISCO—Hilton (415) 771-1400, 333 O'Farrell Street, San Francisco, CA. 94102, S-33; D-44.
SAN FRANCISCO—Shaw Hotel (415) 626-5200; Toll free in California (800) 622-0812, outside of California (800) 227-4248; 1112 Market Street (corner of 7th Street), San Francisco, CA. 94102; S-15; D-17;

SAN FRANCISCO—Sir Francis Drake (415) 392-7755, Powell and Sutter Streets, San Francisco, CA. 94101. S-27; D-34;

SAN FRANCISCO—Hotel Stewart (415) 781-7800, 351 Geary Street, San Francisco, CA. 94102. S-18; D-22;

306 HOTELS

COLORADO

DENVER—Hotel Colburn (303) 623-6261, 980 Grant St., Denver, CO. 80203; S-14; D-16;

CONNECTICUT

HARTFORD—Hilton (203) 249-5611, 10 Ford Street, Hartford, CT. 06101, S-23; D-34;

DISTRICT OF COLUMBIA

WASHINGTON, D.C.—The Pick Lee House (202) 347-4800, 1100 15th St., N.W., Washington, D.C. 20005; S-21; D-27;
WASHINGTON, D.C.—Sheraton Park Hotel (202) 265-2000; 2660 Woodley Ave., N.W., Washington, D.C. 20001, S-29; D-38.

FLORIDA

MIAMI—Columbus Hotel (305) 373-4411, 312 N.E. First St., Miami, FL. 33101. May-Nov.: S-14; D-16; Dec.-April: S-17; D-22;

MIAMI—Howard Johnsons (305) 235-8362; 1100 Biscayne Blvd., Miami, FL. 33132; S-21; D-24;

MIAMI—Leamington Hotel (305) 373-7783, 307 N.E. First Street, Miami, FL. 33132. April-Dec. 14:S- 8; D-10; Dec. 15-March: S-$10; D-$13;

RIVIERA BEACH (PALM BEACH AREA)—Hilton, (305) 848-5502, 3800 North Ocean Drive, Riviera Beach, FL. 33404. May 1-Dec. 14: S-18; D-21; Dec. 15-Apr. 30: S-30; D-36;

GEORGIA

AUGUSTA—Ramada Inn (404) 722-4344, 1365 Gordon Hwy., Augusta, GA. 30900. S-15; D-21; Courtesy car available;
MACON—Hilton (912) 746-1461, 180 First Street, Macon, GA. 31202. S-20; D-26;

ILLINOIS

CHAMPAIGN—Century Twentyone (800) 323-1776 (out of state) and (800) 942-8888 in Illinois, 302 East John Street, Champaign, IL. 61820. S-18; D-24;

CHICAGO—The Midland Hotel (312) 332-1200, 172 West Adams Street, Chicago, IL. 60603. S-18; D-22;

CHICAGO—Pick Congress Hotel (312) 427-3800, 520 South Michigan Ave., Chicago, IL. 60605. S-24; D-34;

CHICAGO—YMCA Hotel (312) 922-3183, 826 So. Wabash Ave., Chicago, IL. 60605. S-5.80; D-10.50; "Rooms available to men, women and families."

INDIANA

SOUTH BEND—Albert Pike Motor Inn (219) 232-3941, 213 W. Washington Street, South Bend, IN. 46601, S-19; D-25;
TERRE HAUTE—Albert Pick Motel (812) 299-1181, 4800 Dixie Bee Hwy., Terre Haute, IN. 47802, S-12.50; D-15.50; Courtesy car available;

IOWA

DES MOINES—Hotel Fort Des Moines (515) 243-1161, 10th & Walnut, Des Moines, Iowa 50309, S-19; D-24;

DES MOINES—Ramada Inn #2 Downtown (515) 282-5251, 929 3rd Street, Des Moines, Iowa, 50309, S-20; D-26; Courtesy car available.

KANSAS

SALINA—Hilton Inn (913) 827-0461, 5th and Iron, Salina, KS. 67401, S-13; D-18;

LOUISIANA

NEW ORLEANS—Hotel LaSalle (504) 523-5831, 1113 Canal Street, New Orleans, LA. 70112, S-15; D-17.50; 10 blocks from Terminal; 'Clairborne Bus';

MARYLAND

BALTIMORE—Sheraton Baltimore Inn (301) 675-6800; 400 N. Broadway, Baltimore, MD. 21231, S-23; D-30;

MASSACHUSETTS

BOSTON—Hotel Avery (617)482-8000, 24 Avery Street, Boston, MA. 02112, S-13; D-17.

MICHIGAN

DETROIT—Howard Johnson; (313) 965-1050; Washington Blvd. at Michigan Ave., Detroit, Mich. 48226, S-26; D-34;

MINNESOTA

MINNEAPOLIS—Hotel Dyckman (612) 332-7244 Ext. 55, 27 S. 6th St., Minneapolis, MN. 55402; S-10; D-14;

MINNEAPOLIS—Radisson Hotel (612) 332-2181, 45 South Seventh Street, Minneapolis, MN. 55402; S-19; D-23.50;
MINNEAPOLIS—Sheraton Ritz Hotel (612) 336-5711, 315 Nicollet Mall, Minneapolis, MN. 55401, S-26; D-34; located on Nicollet Mall.
ST. PAUL—Hilton (612) 222-7711, Kellogg Blvd., St. Paul, MN. 55101, S-26; D-34;

MISSOURI

KANSAS CITY—Continental Hotel (816) 421-6040, Baltimore at Eleventh Stree, Kansas City, MO. 64105, S-14; D-19;
ST. LOUIS—Mayfair (314) 231-7500, 806 St. Charles, St. Louis, MO. 63101, S-16; D-18;

MONTANA

BILLINGS—Northern Hotel (406) 245-5121, Broadway at First Avenue North, Billings, Montana. 59101, S-15; D-19; free limousine;
BUTTE—Finlin Hotel (406) 723-5461, Broadway and Wyoming, Butte, Montana 59701, S-15; D-17;

NEW JERSEY

BORDENTOWN—Howard Johnson; (609) 298-5000, Routes 130 # 206, Bordentown, N.J. 08505, S-14; D-21;

NEW MEXICO

ALBUQUERQUE—Hotel Plaza (505) 243-4421, 125 2nd St., N.W., Albuquerque, N.M. 87103, S-14; D-18; Courtesy van;
SANTA FE— Hilton Inn, 100 Sandoval Street, Santa Fe, N.M. 87501, June-Sept. S-26; D-34; Oct.-May S-21; D-26;

NEW YORK

BUFFALO—Hotel Lafayette (716) 852-5470, Lafayette Square, Buffalo, N.Y. 14205, S-12; D-16.
NEW YORK—Hotel Empire (212) 265-7400, Broadway at 63rd Street, New York, N.Y. 10023, S-16.50; D-20.50.
NEW YORK—Hotel Piccadilly (212) 246-6600, 227 West 45th Street, New York, N.Y. 10036, S-16.50; D-22;

ROCHESTER—Hilton Inn on the Campus, (716) 436-0520, 175 Jefferson Road, Rochester, N.Y. 14623, S-19; D-25.

NORTH CAROLINA

WINSTON-SALEM—Hilton Inn (919) 723-7911, 420 High Street, Winston-Salem, N.C. 27101, S-18; D-23; limousine service available;

NORTH DAKOTA

FARGO—Powers Motor Hotel (701) 232-2517, 400 Broadway, Fargo, N.D. 58102, S-5; D-7;

OHIO

CLEVELAND—Sheraton Cleveland (216) 861-8000, 24 Public Square, Cleveland, Ohio 44101, S-22; D-29;

310 HOTELS

OKLAHOMA

OKLAHOMA CITY—Tivoli Inn Motor Hotel (405) 232-1551, 202 W. Sheridan, Oklahoma City, OK 73102, S-15; D-18;

OREGON

PORTLAND—Heathman Park Haviland (503) 228-5262, Ext. 238, S.W. Broadway and Park, Portland, OR. 97205, S-13; D-16;

PENNSYLVANIA

GETTYSBURG—Travelodge (717) 334-6235, 10 East Lincoln Ave., Gettysburg, PA. 17325, S-16; D-18; higher rates June-Aug.
HARRISBURG—Nationwide Inn (717) 233-1611, Front and Paxton Streets, Harrisburg, PA. 17104, S-19; D-25; 5 blocks from terminal;
PITTSBURGH—Hilton (412) 391-4600, Gateway Center, Pittsburgh, PA. 15222; for S-26; D-32; 10 blocks from terminal.
SCRANTON—Hilton Inn (717) 343-2481, 225 Washington Ave., Scranton, PA. 18503, S-21; D-27;

STROUDSBURG—Hilton Inn (717) 421-2200, 700 Main Street, Stroudsburg, PA. 18360, S-17; D-25;

TENNESSEE

CHATTANOOGA—Choo Choo Hilton Inn (615) 266-6484, Terminal Station, Chattanooga, TN. 37402, S-18; D-24.
CHATTANOOGA—Read House (615) 266-4121, West Ninth Street, Chattanooga, TN. 37402, S-13.50; D-18; courtesy limousine;
NASHVILLE—Albert Pick Motel (615) 242-5424, 320 Murfreesboro Rd., Nashville, TN. 37210; S-16; D-21; Courtesy car;

TEXAS

EL PASO—Hotel Paso del Norte-(915) 533-2421 San Antonio & El Paso Streets, El Paso, TX 79901 S-$15; D-$18;

HOTELS 311

HOUSTON—Sheraton Houston (Toll Free call.), 777 Polk Ave., Houston, TX. 77002, S-29; D-36;

LAREDO—Plaza Hotel (512) 723-4311, 904 Hidalgo, Laredo, TX. 78040, S-11; D-14;

SAN ANTONIO—Hilton (512) 222-2481, 200 South Alamo Street, San Antonio, TX.78206, S-23; D-33.

UTAH

SALT LAKE CITY—Hotel Miles (801) 363-4571, 110 West 3rd So., Salt Lake City, UT. 84101, S-8; D-11;

SALT LAKE CITY—Temple Square Hotel (801) 355-2961, 75 West South Temple, Salt Lake City, UT. 84101, S-11; D-14;

VIRGINIA

RICHMOND—Jefferson Hotel (804) 643-3411, Main and Jefferson Streets, Richmond, VA. 23220, S-13; D-18.

WASHINGTON STATE

SEATTLE—Roosevelt (206) 624-1400, 1531 Seventh Avenue, Seattle, WA. 98101, S-15; D-19;

YAKIMA—Cosmopolitan (509) 452-8533, 4th & E. Yakima Ave., Yakima, WA. 98901, S-15; D-18;

WISCONSIN

MILWAUKEE—Hotel Wisconsin-(414)271-4900, 720 North Third St., Milwaukee, WI. 53203, S-$12; D-$15;

WYOMING

CHEYENNE-Downtowner Motor Inn-(307)634-1331, 1719 Central Ave., Cheyenne, WY. 82001, S-$14; D-$17; 4 blocks from terminal, "Reservations are required from May 1st-Sept. 30"

BRITISH COLUMBIA

VICTORIA—Strathcona Hotel (604) 383-7137, 919 Douglas Street, Victoria, B.C. V8W 2C2, S-16.50; D-19.50;

YMCA/YWCA ACCOMMODATIONS IN THE U.S.A.

In this chapter we have included many of the YMCA/YWCA accommodations you will find throughout the country. "Y" accommodations in most cases are in new, modern buildings such as in Miami or Hartford. Prices are reasonable and the Y is usually located centrally to many of the city's attractions. In our description we have stated if the Y will only admit men only or women only or both. We have included the address, telephone number, including the area code, the price of a single room (doubles, when available, are usually a great deal lower in price).

The Y accommodations are listed by state. However, in certain cities, such as San Francisco, San Diego, Miami, Philadelphia, New York City and Washington, D.C., we have included the Y accommodations in the description of the particular city. In any case, always try to call ahead to make your reservations as soon as your plans are firm. And by all means try to arrive in a city by afternoon. This will give you the best chance of obtaining a room. For additional addresses just look under YMCA or YWCA in the telephone book.

CONNECTICUT

BRIDGEPORT—YMCA of Greater Bridgeport; Men and Women; 651 State Street, Bridgeport, CT. 06604; (203)334-5551; Single $8.08;

HARTFORD—Central Branch YMCA; Men and Women; 160 Jewell St., Hartford, CT. 06103; (203)522-4183; Single $8.98;

NEW HAVEN—New Haven Family YMCA; Men and Women; 52 Howe Street, New Haven, CT. 06511; (203)865-3161; Single $9.

DELAWARE

WILMINGTON—Central Branch YMCA; Men only; 501 W. 11th St., Wilmington, Del. 19801; (302)571-6900; Single $6;

FLORIDA

WEST PALM BEACH—Central YWCA; Women only; 901 South Olive Ave.; West Palm Beach, FL. 33401; (305)833-2439; Single $6;

GEORGIA

ATLANTA—East Central Branch YMCA; Men only; 22 Butler St., N.E., Atlanta, GA. 30303; (404)659-8085; Single $5.50;

AUGUSTA—YMCA of Augusta; Men only; 945 Broad Street, Augusta, GA. 30902; (912)722-4801; Single $3.50;

ILLINOIS

PEORIA—Peoria Family YMCA; Men and Women; 714 Hamilton Blvd., Peoria, Ill. 61603; (309)673-8591; Single $7.86;

ROCKFORD—Rockford YMCA; Men only; 200 Y Blvd., Rockford, Ill. 61101; (805)965-0546; Single $24/week;

ROCKFORD—Rockford YWCA; Women only; 220 S. Madison St., Rockford, Ill. 61101; (815)968-9681; Room-$4;

LOUISIANA

NEW ORLEANS—New Orleans YMCA; Men and Women; 936 St. Charles Street, New Orleans, LA. 70130; (504)524-1574; Single $5;

MAINE

PORTLAND—YWCA; Women only—87 Spring Street, Portland, Maine, 04111; (207)772-1906; Single $7.35;

MARYLAND

BALTIMORE—Center City YMCA; Men only; 24 W. Franklin St., Baltimore, Md., 21201; (301)539-7350; Single $8.

HAGERSTOWN—YMCA; Men only; 147 N. Potomac St., Hagerstown, Md.; (301)739-3990; Single $5.

MASSACHUSETTS

BOSTON—Greater Boston YMCA, Men only; 316 Huntington Avenue, Boston, MA. 02115; (617)536-7800; Single $8.

BOSTON—Berkeley Residence Club, Women only; 40 Berkeley Residence Club, Boston, MA., 02116; (617)482-8850; Single $8.

CAMBRIDGE—Cambridge YMCA, Men only; 820 Massachusetts Avenue, Cambridge, MA. 02139; (617)876-3860; Single $7.

CAMBRIDGE—Cambridge YWCA, Women only; 7 Temple Street, Cambridge, MA. 02139; (617)491-6050; Single $7. Subway. Cambridge Sights—Howard, MIT, Longfellow's Home, Harvard Square, Charles River.

SPRINGFIELD—Springfield YMCA; Men and Women; 275 Chestnut St., Springfield, MA. 01104; (413)781-5600; Single $9.50;

SPRINGFIELD—Springfield YWCA; Women only; 26 Howard St., Springfield, MA. 01105; (413)732-3122; Single $6. 12 blocks, Bus direction "Dickinson." SPRINGFIELD SIGHTS—Basketball Hall of Fame, Civic Center, Bay State Shopping Center, Armory Museum and Tanglewood, where music is played in summer.

MICHIGAN

DETROIT—Downtown YMCA; Men only; 2020 Witherell, Detroit, Mich. 48226; (313)962-6126; Single $7.

DETROIT—Northern Branch YWCA; Women only; 13130 Woodward, Highland Park, Mich. 48203; (313)868-3939; Single $10;

DETROIT—Downtown Branch YWCA; Women only; 2230 Witherell Ave., Detroit, Mich. 48201; (313)961-9220; Single $9

PORT HURON—Blue Water YMCA; Men only; 700 Fort Street, Port Huron, Mich. 48060; (313)984-1566; Single $7;

MINNESOTA

DULUTH—Duluth YWCA; Women only; 202 West Second Street, Duluth, MN. 55802; (218)722-7425; Single $8.15;

MINNEAPOLIS—Downtown YMCA; Men and Women; 30 S. 9th Street, Minneapolis, MN. 55402; (612)332-2431; Single $7;

MISSOURI

ST. LOUIS—Phyllis Wheatly Branch; Women only; 2709 Locust Blvd., St. Louis, Mo. 63103, (314)533-9400; Single $6;

NEBRASKA

OMAHA—Downtown YMCA; Men and Women; 430 So. 20th St., Omaha, Nebr. 68102; (402)341-1600; Single $6.50;

NEW YORK

BUFFALO—Downtown Branch of Buffalo and Erie County—Men only; 45 W. Mohawk St., Buffalo, N.Y. 14202; (716)853-9350; Single $7.

BUFFALO—YWCA of Buffalo and Erie County—Women only; 245 North St., Buffalo, N.Y. 14201;

316 YMCA/YWCA

(716)884-4761; Single $6.

NIAGARA FALLS—Niagara Falls Family YMCA—Men and Women; 1317 Portage Road, Niagara Falls, N.Y. 14301; (716)285-8491;

ROCHESTER—Central Branch YMCA—Men only; 100 Gibbs St., Rochester, N.Y. 14601; (716)325-2880; Single $8.75.

ROCHESTER—YWCA of Rochester and Monroe County—Women only; 175 North Clinton Avenue, Rochester, N.Y. 14604; (716)546-5820; Single $8.

SYRACUSE—YMCA of Syracuse and Onondaga County—Men only; 340 Montgomery Street, Syracuse, N.Y. 13202; (315)474-6851; Single $7.

SYRACUSE—YWCA of Syracuse—Women only; 339 E. Onondaga St., Syracuse, N.Y. 13202; (315)422-9167; Single $6.25.

NORTH CAROLINA

DURHAM—Durham YMCA; Women only; 515 West Chapel Hill Street, Durham, N.C. 27701; (919)688-4396; Single $6;

NORTH DAKOTA

FARGO—YWCA; Women only; 15 South 7th St., Fargo, N.D. 58102; (701)232-2546; Single $5.20;

OHIO

CLEVELAND—Central YMCA; Men only; 2200 Prospect Ave., Cleveland, Ohio 44022; (216)696-2200; Single $5.75;

COLUMBUS—Central YMCA Branch; Men only; 40 W. Long Street, Columbus, Ohio, 43215; (614)224-1131; Single $5.85;

DAYTON—YMCA; Men only; 117 W. Monument Ave., Dayton, Ohio 45402; (513)223-5201; Single $7;

DAYTON—YWCA; Women only; 141 W. 3rd Street, Dayton, Ohio 45402; (513)461-5550; Single $5.50;

RHODE ISLAND

PAWTUCKET—Pawtucket YMCA—Men only; 20 Summer St., Pawtucket, R.I. 02860; (401)722-4900; Single $7.50 per night/$20 per week.

TENNESSEE

CHATTANOOGA—YWCA; Women only; 300 E. 8th Street, Chattanooga, TN. 37403; (615)267-5493; Single $13;

MEMPHIS—Memphis YWCA; Women only; 200 Monroe Avenue, Memphis, TN. 38103; (901)527-9486; Single $4.20;

VERMONT

BURLINGTON—Greater Burlington YMCA—Men only; 266 College Street, Burlington, VY. 05401; (802)862-2970; Single $6.

VIRGINIA

LYNCHBURG—Central YWCA; Women only; 626 Church Street, Lynchburg, VA. 24504; (804)847-7751; Single $5.50;

NORFOLK—Norfolk Central YMCA; Men and Women; 312 W. Bute St., Norfolk, VA. 23510; (804)622-6328; Single $8.50;

RICHMOND—Central Branch YMCA; Men only; 2 W. Franklin Street, Richmond, VA. 23220; (804)649-0791; Single $6.75;

WEST VIRGINIA

CHARLESTON—Charleston YWCA; Women only; 1114 Quarrier, Charleston, WV. 25301; (304)346-0597;

WHEELING—Wheeling YMCA; Men only; 32 20th Street, Wheeling, WV. 26003; (304)233-3560; Single $5.15;

USA RAIL ITINERARY

Day	From	To
1		
2		
3		
4		
5		
6		
7		
8		
9		
10		
11		
12		
13		
14		
15		
16		
17		
18		
19		
20		
21		
22		
23		
24		
25		
26		
27		
28		
29		
30		

WE NEED YOUR HELP

Many travelers have found this guide an excellent idea and a helpful aid in exploring the U.S.A. and Canada. The suggestions in this book have come not only from American and Canadian travelers, but also from visitors from abroad. To provide you, the traveler, the best possible travel guide, we need your suggestions. If you find during your travels by bus, information that would be helpful to other travelers, let us know about your discoveries. Try to make your comments short, objective and quotable. If we use your information in the book, we will provide you a free copy of the next edition of this guide. We need your help to constantly improve this book. Please send your information to:

Dr. Robert Baxter
Transportation Consultant
P.O. Box 3255
Alexandria, Va. 22302

RAIL-EUROPE books available or in preparation —

Baxter's EURAILPASS TRAVEL GUIDE @ $6.95

Baxter's AMTRAK PICTURE BOOK @ $14.95

Baxter's BRITRAIL PASS TRAVEL GUIDE @ $3.95

Baxter's USARAIL PASS GUIDE @ $6.95

BICENTENNIAL IMAGES @ $14.95

Baxter's BICENTENNIAL EAST @ $8.95

Copies of the above books can be obtained at major bookstores or directly from the publisher by mailing the above amounts, plus 50 cents for postage and handling per book, to Rail-Europe, P.O. Box 3255, Alexandria, Va. 22302.

HAVE A NICE TRIP!